# the Top 10 of everything

# the Top 10 of everything

## Russell Ash

BB Bounty
BOOKS

# Contents

Produced for Hamlyn by
Palazzo Editions Ltd
15 Gay Street, Bath, BA1 2PH

Publishing director: Colin Webb
Art director: Bernard Higton
Project editor: Sonya Newland
Picture researcher: Melinda Revesz

First published in Great Britain in 2007 by
Hamlyn, a division of
Octopus Publishing Group Ltd

This edition published in 2008 by
Bounty Books, a division of
Octopus Publishing Group Ltd
2–4 Heron Quays, London E14 4JP

ISBN: 978-0-753717-59-2

A CIP catalogue record for this book is
available from the British Library

Printed and bound in China

# The Top 10 of 'Top 10 of Everything'

## 1. LISTMANIA

We are constantly bombarded with lists. The press and TV programmes present rankings based on market research and polls, lists of the best places to live, top schools, the greatest films, the bestselling books, the worst crime rates and so on. Ranked lists have become a way of managing what might otherwise be a daunting mass of facts and figures, putting our world into a perspective that we can readily grasp. *Top 10 of Everything* provides a unique collection of lists in a diverse array of categories that are, I hope, informative, educational and entertaining.

## 2. WHY 10?

Firstly, it's a manageable number – most of us can remember 10 telephone numbers, but not, say, 100. We have 10 fingers and 10 toes, historic lists such as the 10 Commandments and modern lists of bestsellers, whether records or books, are traditionally 10s, while the decimal system is a feature of many areas of daily life. There is a magic roundedness about 10 that just doesn't apply to any other number.

## 3. BEST AND WORST, FIRST AND LAST

The book makes no claim to offering the '10 Best of Everything'. Not only is that not its title, but nor is it its intention. *Top 10 of Everything* is a book of definitive, strictly quantifiable Top 10 lists – not anyone's favourites. The only 'bests' are those that are measurably bestsellers, while 'worsts' such as disasters or worst serial killers are similarly ranked by cost or the number of victims. Some lists represent the first or latest achievers in categories, from the fastest cars to the winners of major awards, high achievers in numerous world sports to the last 10 holders of the record as world's tallest building.

## 4. GROUND RULES

Countries are independent countries, not dependencies or overseas territories. All the lists are all-time and global unless a specific year or territory is stated. Film lists are based on cumulative global earnings, irrespective of production or marketing budgets and, as is standard in the industry, inflation is not taken into account – which inevitably means that recent releases feature more prominently.

## 5. OLD AND NEW, RICHER OR POORER

*Top 10 of Everything* contains hundreds of Top 10s – old favourites brought up to date with the latest facts and figures, lists that change radically from year to year – such as the most-watched films and bestselling albums – and a range of entirely new lists, such as those that focus on the emerging powers of China and India. Along with these are curiosities, from the most obese countries to the fattest US presidents, the oldest and the tallest people, the most popular first names and most watched films across the decades, or the countries with the most people in prison. In such lists as, for example, the highest prices paid for works of art and the countries drinking the most Champagne, we can see that the rich are getting richer (even certain deceased celebrities keep on earning, proving that in the world of the dead rich it is possible to be worth more dead than alive), while some reveal the other side of the wealth divide. These lists are enhanced with a variety of features covering everything from the 100th anniversaries of the marathon race and the Scouts to the 50th anniversary of NASA.

## 6. WHO SAYS SO?

My sources encompass international organizations, commercial companies and research bodies, specialized publications and, especially, a network of individuals around the world who have shared their knowledge of everything from snakes and skyscrapers to ships and spiders. As ever, I gladly acknowledge their invaluable contribution (see page 255 for a full list of credits), as well as those who have been involved with the book at all stages of its development on this and the previous 18 annual editions.

## 7. A QUESTION OF DEFINITION

While sporting lists, for example, are definitive in that an individual or team either won or lost or broke a record, many

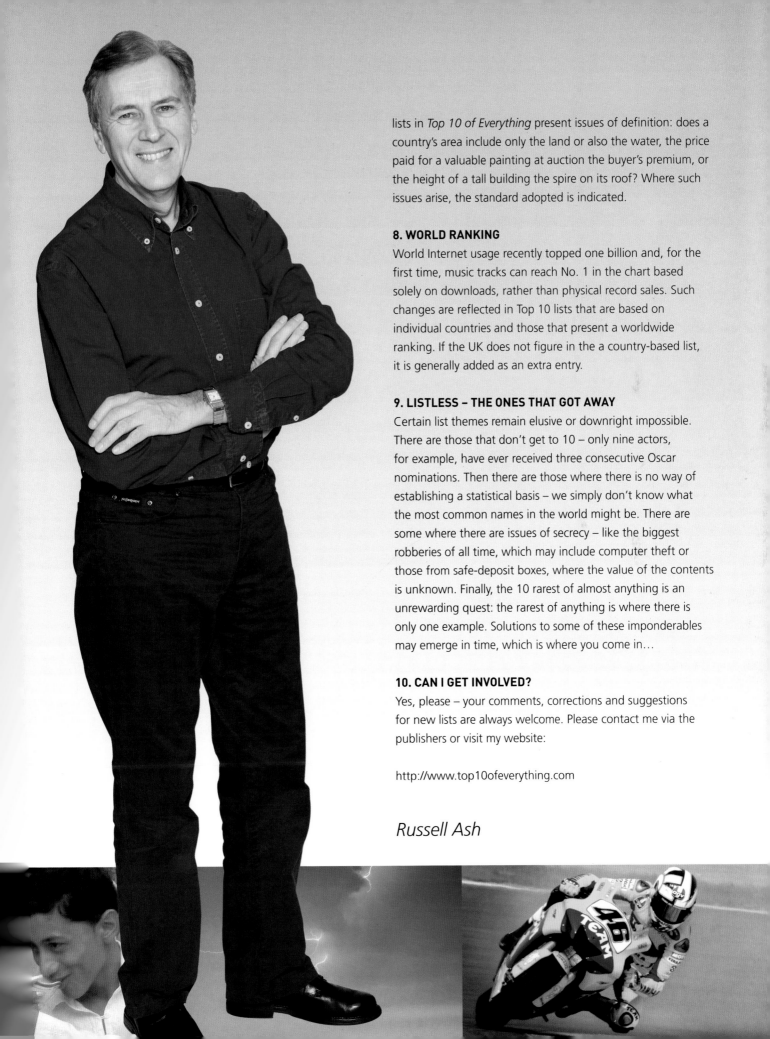

lists in *Top 10 of Everything* present issues of definition: does a country's area include only the land or also the water, the price paid for a valuable painting at auction the buyer's premium, or the height of a tall building the spire on its roof? Where such issues arise, the standard adopted is indicated.

### 8. WORLD RANKING

World Internet usage recently topped one billion and, for the first time, music tracks can reach No. 1 in the chart based solely on downloads, rather than physical record sales. Such changes are reflected in Top 10 lists that are based on individual countries and those that present a worldwide ranking. If the UK does not figure in the a country-based list, it is generally added as an extra entry.

### 9. LISTLESS – THE ONES THAT GOT AWAY

Certain list themes remain elusive or downright impossible. There are those that don't get to 10 – only nine actors, for example, have ever received three consecutive Oscar nominations. Then there are those where there is no way of establishing a statistical basis – we simply don't know what the most common names in the world might be. There are some where there are issues of secrecy – like the biggest robberies of all time, which may include computer theft or those from safe-deposit boxes, where the value of the contents is unknown. Finally, the 10 rarest of almost anything is an unrewarding quest: the rarest of anything is where there is only one example. Solutions to some of these imponderables may emerge in time, which is where you come in…

### 10. CAN I GET INVOLVED?

Yes, please – your comments, corrections and suggestions for new lists are always welcome. Please contact me via the publishers or visit my website:

http://www.top10ofeverything.com

*Russell Ash*

# 1

# THE UNIVERSE
# & THE EARTH

# The Universe

## TOP 10 **ASTEROIDS DUE TO COME CLOSEST TO EARTH**

| | NAME/DESIGNATION | DUE DATE* | DISTANCE KM | MILES |
|---|---|---|---|---|
| 1 | Aphosis | 13 Apr 2029 | 34,677 | 21,547 |
| 2 | 2005 YU55 | 8 Nov 2011 | 159,322 | 98,998 |
| 3 | 2000 WO107 | 2 Dec 2169 | 242,797 | 150,867 |
| 4 | 2000 WN5 | 26 Jun 2028 | 249,828 | 155,235 |
| 5 | 1998 OX4 | 22 Jan 2148 | 299,794 | 186,283 |
| 6 | 1999 AN10 | 7 Aug 2027 | 388,954 | 241,684 |
| 7 | 1998 MZ | 26 Nov 2116 | 411,394 | 255,628 |
| 8 | 1997 XF11 | 28 Oct 2136 | 413,189 | 256,743 |
| 9 | 2003 QC10 | 24 Sep 2066 | 508,034 | 315,677 |
| 10 | 2001 GQ2 | 27 Apr 2100 | 508,632 | 316,049 |

\* Closest point to Earth

It is believed that there are up to 2,000 'Near-Earth Objects' (mostly asteroids and comets) over 1 km (0.6 miles) in diameter, and many thousands of smaller ones, that approach Earth's orbit and could potentially impact with our planet. The PHAs (Potentially Hazardous Asteroids) listed here are predicted to make the closest approaches. It is widely accepted that an asteroid impact with Earth some 65 million years ago was responsible for the extinction of the dinosaurs. However, although coming closest, the chance of Aphosis impacting with Earth or the Moon is put at 0.017 per cent. Among recent visitors, asteroid 2004 XP14 approached to within 432,487 km (268,734 miles) on 3 July 2006, and we lived to tell the tale.

### Canyon Diablo, Arizona
*The fragments that have been recovered from the Meteor, or Barringer Crater and adjacent Canyon Diablo, from which the meteorite takes its name, represent a fraction of the total. Much of it vaporized before impact, but it may have weighed up to 300,000 tonnes.*

## TOP 10 **LARGEST METEORITES EVER FOUND**

| | LOCATION | ESTIMATED WEIGHT (TONNES) |
|---|---|---|
| 1 | Hoba West, Grootfontein, Namibia | >60.0 |
| 2 | Ahnighito ('The Tent'), Cape York, West Greenland | 57.3 |
| 3 | Campo del Cielo, Argentina | 41.4 |
| 4 | Canyon Diablo*, Arizona, USA | 30.0 |
| 5 | Sikhote-Alin, Russia | 27.0 |
| 6 | Chupaderos, Mexico | 24.2 |
| 7 | Bacuberito, Mexico | 22.0 |
| 8 | Armanty, Western Mongolia | 20.0 |
| 9 | Mundrabilla#, Western Australia | 17.0 |
| 10 | Mbosi, Tanzania | 16.0 |

\* Formed Meteor Crater; fragmented – total in public collections about 11.5 tonnes
\# In two parts

Meteorites have been known since early times: fragments of meteorite have been found mounted in a necklace in an Egyptian pyramid and in ancient Native American burial sites. The Hoba meteorite, the largest in the world, was found on a farm in 1920. A 2.73 x 2.43 m (9 x 8 ft) slab, it consists of 82 per cent iron and 16 per cent nickel. 'The Tent', now known by its original Inuit name, Ahnighito, was long used as a source of metals for harpoons and other tools. Along with two other large fragments, it was discovered in 1894, taken to the USA in 1897 by the American Arctic explorer Admiral Robert Peary, and is now in the Hayden Planetarium at the New York Museum of Natural History. It is the largest meteorite in the world on exhibition.

## TOP 10 **GALAXIES NEAREST TO EARTH**

| | GALAXY | DISCOVERED | DIAMETER (1,000 LIGHT YEARS) | APPROXIMATE DISTANCE (1,000 LIGHT YEARS) |
|---|---|---|---|---|
| 1 | Sagittarius Dwarf | 1994 | 10 | 82 |
| 2 | Large Magellanic Cloud | Prehist. | 30 | 160 |
| 3 | Small Magellanic Cloud | Prehist. | 16 | 190 |
| 4 | = Draco Dwarf | 1954 | 3 | 205 |
| | = Ursa Minor Dwarf | 1954 | 2 | 205 |
| 6 | Sculptor Dwarf | 1937 | 3 | 254 |
| 7 | Sextans Dwarf | 1990 | 4 | 258 |
| 8 | Carina Dwarf | 1977 | 2 | 330 |
| 9 | Fornax Dwarf | 1938 | 6 | 450 |
| 10 | Leo II | 1950 | 3 | 660 |

Source: Peter Bond, Royal Astronomical Society

These, and other galaxies, are members of the so-called 'Local Group', although with such vast distances 'local' is clearly a relative term. As our Solar System and Earth are at the outer edge of the Milky Way, this is excluded. Over the next 100 million years, the Sagittarius Dwarf Elliptical Galaxy, our nearest neighbouring galaxy, will be progressively absorbed into the Milky Way.

*By and large*
*In astronomical terms, at a distance of 160,000 light years, the Large Magellanic Cloud is considered one of our nearest neighbours.*

## TOP 10 **BRIGHTEST STARS***

| | STAR | CONSTELLATION | DISTANCE# | APPARENT MAGNITUDE |
|---|---|---|---|---|
| 1 | Sirius | Canis Major | 8.61 | −1.44 |
| 2 | Canopus | Carina | 312.73 | −0.62 |
| 3 | Arcturus | Boötes | 36.39 | −0.05† |
| 4 | Alpha Centauri A | Centaurus | 4.40 | −0.01 |
| 5 | Vega | Lyra | 25.31 | +0.03 |
| 6 | Capella | Auriga | 42.21 | +0.08 |
| 7 | Rigel | Orion | 772.91 | +0.18 |
| 8 | Procyon | Canis Minor | 11.42 | +0.40 |
| 9 | Achernar | Eridanus | 143.81 | +0.45 |
| 10 | Beta Centauri | Centaurus | 525.22 | +0.61 |

* Excluding the Sun
# From Earth in light years
† Variable

This Top 10 is based on apparent visual magnitude as viewed from Earth – the lower the number, the brighter the star, since by convention 1 was considered a star of first magnitude and 6 the faintest visible to the naked eye. On this scale, the Sun would be −26.73 and the full Moon −12.6.

## TOP 10 **COMETS COMING CLOSEST TO EARTH**

| | COMET | DATE* | DISTANCE KM | DISTANCE MILES |
|---|---|---|---|---|
| 1 | Comet of 1491 | 20 Feb 1491 | 1,406,220 | 873,784 |
| 2 | Lexell | 1 Jul 1770 | 2,258,928 | 1,403,633 |
| 3 | Tempel-Tuttle | 26 Oct 1366 | 3,425,791 | 2,128,688 |
| 4 | IRAS-Araki-Alcock | 11 May 1983 | 4,682,413 | 2,909,516 |
| 5 | Halley | 10 Apr 1837 | 4,996,569 | 3,104,724 |
| 6 | Biela | 9 Dec 1805 | 5,475,282 | 3,402,182 |
| 7 | Grischow | 8 Feb 1743 | 5,834,317 | 3,625,276 |
| 8 | Pons-Winnecke | 26 Jun 1927 | 5,894,156 | 3,662,458 |
| 9 | Comet of 1014 | 24 Feb 1014 | 6,088,633 | 3,783,301 |
| 10 | La Hire | 20 Apr 1702 | 6,537,427 | 4,062,168 |

* Of closest approach to Earth

# Space Exploration

*Eyes to the skies*
*Sited at the summit of Mauna Kea, Hawaii, the twin Keck telescopes combine to form the most powerful on Earth.*

## TOP 10 **LARGEST REFLECTING TELESCOPES**

| TELESCOPE NAME / YEAR BUILT / LOCATION | APERTURE M | FT |
|---|---|---|
| **1** Large Binocular Telescope (2007) Mt Graham, Arizona, USA | 11.8 | 38.7 |
| **2** Southern African Large Telescope (2005) Sutherland, South Africa | 11.0 | 36.1 |
| **3** Gran Telescopio Canarias (2005) La Palma, Canary Islands, Spain | 10.4 | 34.1 |
| **4** = Keck I Telescope* (1993) Mauna Kea, Hawaii, USA | 9.8 | 32.2 |
| = Keck II Telescope* (1996) Mauna Kea, Hawaii, USA | 9.8 | 32.2 |
| **6** Hobby-Eberly Telescope (1997) Mt Fowlkes, Texas, USA | 9.2 | 30.2 |
| **7** Subaru Telescope (1999) Mauna Kea, Hawaii, USA | 8.3 | 27.2 |
| **8** = Antu Telescope# (1998) Cerro Paranal, Chile | 8.2 | 26.9 |
| = Kueyen Telescope# (1999) Cerro Paranal, Chile | 8.2 | 26.9 |
| = Melipal Telescope# (2000) Cerro Paranal, Chile | 8.2 | 26.9 |
| = Yepun Telescope# (2001) Cerro Paranal, Chile | 8.2 | 26.9 |

\* Twin
\# Combine to form VLT (Very Large Telescope)

## TOP 10 **MOST FREQUENTLY SEEN COMETS**

| | COMET | YEARS BETWEEN APPEARANCES |
|---|---|---|
| **1** | Encke 1 | 3.29 |
| **2** | NEAT (Near Earth Asteroid Tracking) 22 | 4.20 |
| **3** | Helfenzrieder 1 | 4.35 |
| **4** | Catalina 3 | 4.42 |
| **5** | LINEAR (Lincoln Near-Earth Asteroid Research) 30 | 4.85 |
| **6** | LINEAR 46 | 4.86 |
| **7** | = Grigg-Skjellerup 1 | 4.98 |
| | = NEAT 10 | 4.98 |
| **9** | LONEOS (Lowell Observatory Near-Earth-Object Search 6) | 5.01 |
| **10** | Blanpain 1 | 5.10 |

Source: NASA, Planetary Data System Small Bodies Node

The comets in the Top 10 and several others return with regularity (although with some variations), while others may not be seen again for many thousands, or even millions, of years. Encke's Comet, Earth's most frequent visitor, was named after German astronomer Johann Franz Encke (1791–1865), who calculated the period of its elliptical orbit – the second after that of Halley's Comet.

## THE 10 **FIRST ARTIFICIAL SATELLITES**

| | SATELLITE | COUNTRY | LAUNCH DATE |
|---|---|---|---|
| **1** | Sputnik 1 | USSR | 4 Oct 1957 |
| **2** | Sputnik 2 | USSR | 3 Nov 1957 |
| **3** | Explorer 1 | USA | 1 Feb 1958 |
| **4** | Vanguard 1 | USA | 17 Mar 1958 |
| **5** | Explorer 3 | USA | 26 Mar 1958 |
| **6** | Sputnik 3 | USSR | 15 May 1958 |
| **7** | Explorer 4 | USA | 26 Jul 1958 |
| **8** | SCORE | USA | 18 Dec 1958 |
| **9** | Vanguard 2 | USA | 17 Feb 1959 |
| **10** | Discoverer 1 | USA | 28 Feb 1959 |

Geostationary artificial satellites for use as radio relay stations were first proposed by the British science-fiction writer Arthur C. Clarke in the October 1945 issue of *Wireless World*, but it was 12 years before his fantasy became reality with the launch of the Soviet *Sputnik 1*, the first artificial satellite to enter Earth orbit.

## THE 10 FIRST BODIES TO HAVE BEEN VISITED BY SPACECRAFT

| | BODY | SPACECRAFT / COUNTRY | DATE |
|---|---|---|---|
| 1 | Moon | Luna 1, USSR | 2 Jan 1959 |
| 2 | Venus | Venera 1, USSR | 19 May 1961 |
| 3 | Sun | Pioneer 5, USA | 10 Aug 1961 |
| 4 | Mars | Mariner 4, USA | 14 Jul 1965 |
| 5 | Jupiter | Pioneer 10, USA | 3 Dec 1973 |
| 6 | Mercury | Mariner 10, USA | 29 Mar 1974 |
| 7 | Saturn | Pioneer 11, USA | 1 Sep 1979 |
| 8 | Comet Giacobini-Zinner | International Sun-Earth Explorer 3 (International Cometary Explorer), Europe/USA | 11 Sep 1985 |
| 9 | Uranus | Voyager 2, USA | 30 Jan 1986 |
| 10 | Halley's Comet | Vega 1, USSR | 6 Mar 1986 |

Only the first spacecraft successfully to approach or land on each body is included. Several of the bodies listed have been visited on subsequent occasions. Other bodies also visited since the first 10 include Neptune (by *Voyager 2*, USA, 1989) and asteroids Gaspra (*Galileo*, USA/Europe, 1991) and Hyakutake (*NEAR*, USA, 1996).

*Venus revisited*
*Following the Soviet* Venera *probes, NASA's* Pioneer Venus *orbiters spent almost 14 years (1978–92) sending data from the planet.*

## THE 10 FIRST PLANETARY MOONS TO BE DISCOVERED

| | MOON | PLANET | DISCOVERER | YEAR |
|---|---|---|---|---|
| 1 | Moon | Earth | – | Ancient |
| 2 | Io | Jupiter | Galileo Galilei (Italian) | 1610 |
| 3 | Europa | Jupiter | Galileo Galilei | 1610 |
| 4 | Ganymede | Jupiter | Galileo Galilei | 1610 |
| 5 | Callisto | Jupiter | Galileo Galilei | 1610 |
| 6 | Titan | Saturn | Christian Huygens (Dutch) | 1655 |
| 7 | Iapetus | Saturn | Giovanni Cassini (Italian/French) | 1671 |
| 8 | Rhea | Saturn | Giovanni Cassini | 1672 |
| 9 | Tethys | Saturn | Giovanni Cassini | 1684 |
| 10 | Dione | Saturn | Giovanni Cassini | 1684 |

While Earth's Moon has been observed since ancient times, it was not until the development of the telescope that Italian astronomer Galileo Galilei (1564–1642) was able to discover (on 7 January 1610) the first moons of another planet. These, which are Jupiter's four largest, were named by German astronomer Simon Marius and are known as the Galileans. After the discoveries appearing in this list, no further moons were found until 1787, when German-born British astronomer William Herschel discovered Oberon and Titania, the largest of the 27 satellites of Uranus, followed in 1789 by Enceladus and Mimas, two further moons of Saturn.

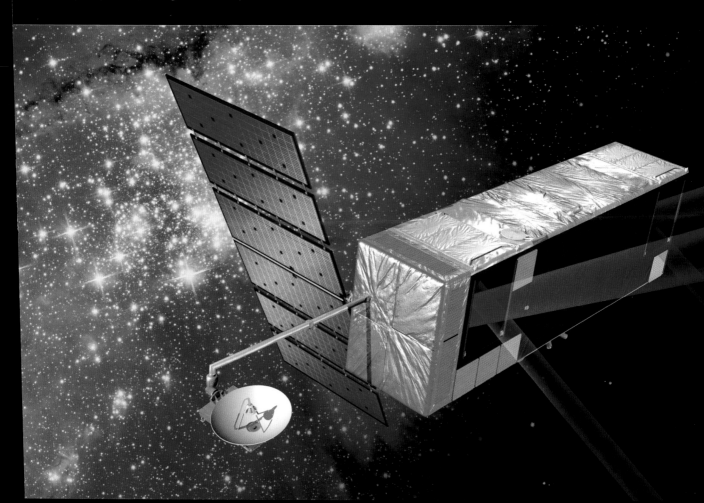

# Human Spaceflight

## THE 10 **FIRST MOONWALKERS**

| | ASTRONAUT* | SPACECRAFT | TOTAL EVA# HR:MIN | MISSION DATES |
|---|---|---|---|---|
| **1** | Neil Armstrong | Apollo 11 | 2:32 | 16–24 Jul 1969 |
| **2** | Edwin 'Buzz' Aldrin | Apollo 11 | 2:15 | 16–24 Jul 1969 |
| **3** | Charles Conrad Jr. | Apollo 12 | 7:45 | 14–24 Nov 1969 |
| **4** | Alan Bean | Apollo 12 | 7:45 | 14–24 Nov 1969 |
| **5** | Alan Shepard | Apollo 14 | 9:23 | 31 Jan–9 Feb 1971 |
| **6** | Edgar Mitchell | Apollo 14 | 9:23 | 31 Jan–9 Feb 1971 |
| **7** | David Scott | Apollo 15 | 19:08 | 26 Jul–7 Aug 1971 |
| **8** | James Irwin | Apollo 15 | 18:35 | 26 Jul–7 Aug 1971 |
| **9** | John Young | Apollo 16 | 20:14 | 16–27 Apr 1972 |
| **10** | Charles Duke Jr. | Apollo 16 | 20:14 | 16–27 Apr 1972 |

\* All USA – the only country to have sent men to the Moon
\# Extra-Vehicular Activity – time spent out of the lunar module on the Moon's surface

### Second man on the Moon
*The now-iconic image of Buzz Aldrin on the surface of the Moon during the first lunar landing, 21 July 1969.*

## THE 10 **FIRST COUNTRIES TO HAVE ASTRONAUTS OR COSMONAUTS IN ORBIT**

| | COUNTRY | ASTRONAUT/COSMONAUT | DATE* |
|---|---|---|---|
| **1** | USSR | Yuri Gagarin | 12 Apr 1961 |
| **2** | USA | John Glenn | 20 Feb 1962 |
| **3** | Czechoslovakia | Vladimir Remek | 2 Mar 1978 |
| **4** | Poland | Miroslaw Hermaszewski | 27 Jun 1978 |
| **5** | East Germany | Sigmund Jahn | 26 Aug 1978 |
| **6** | Bulgaria | Georgi Ivanov | 10 Apr 1979 |
| **7** | Hungary | Bertalan Farkas | 26 May 1980 |
| **8** | Vietnam | Pham Tuan | 23 Jul 1980 |
| **9** | Cuba | Arnaldo T. Mendez | 18 Sep 1980 |
| **10** | Mongolia | Jugderdemidiyn Gurragcha | 22 Mar 1981 |

\* Of first orbit of a national of that country

During the first 20 years of space travel, representatives of just 10 nations entered space. All missions by non-Soviet or non-Russian and non-US citizens were as guests of one of these countries until 2003, when China conducted its first mission. Western media – but not China – have dubbed the latter's space travellers as 'taikonauts'.

## TOP 10 **YOUNGEST ASTRONAUTS AND COSMONAUTS**\*

| ASTRONAUT/COSMONAUT# | FIRST FLIGHT | YEARS | AGE MONTHS | DAYS |
|---|---|---|---|---|
| **1** Gherman Titov | 6 Aug 1961 | 25 | 10 | 25 |
| **2** Valentina Tereshkova | 16 Jun 1963 | 26 | 3 | 10 |
| **3** Boris B. Yegoro | 15 Oct 1964 | 26 | 10 | 19 |
| **4** Yuri Gagarin | 12 Apr 1961 | 27 | 1 | 3 |
| **5** Helen Sharman (UK) | 18 May 1991 | 27 | 11 | 19 |
| **6** Mark Shuttleworth (South Africa) | 25 Apr 2002 | 28 | 7 | 7 |
| **7** Dumitru Prunariu (Romania) | 14 May 1981 | 28 | 7 | 24 |
| **8** Valery Bykovsky | 14 Jun 1963 | 28 | 10 | 19 |
| **9** Salman Abdel Aziz Al-Saud (Saudi Arabia) | 17 Jun 1985 | 28 | 11 | 20 |
| **10** Vladimir Remek (Czechoslovakia) | 2 Mar 1978 | 29 | 5 | 6 |

\* To 31 March 2007
\# Soviet unless otherwise indicated

## TOP 10 **OLDEST ASTRONAUTS AND COSMONAUTS**\*

| ASTRONAUT/COSMONAUT# | LAST FLIGHT | YEARS | AGE MONTHS | DAYS |
|---|---|---|---|---|
| **1** John Glenn | 6 Nov 1998 | 77 | 3 | 19 |
| **2** Mike Melvill | 29 Sep 2004 | 63 | 9 | 29 |
| **3** F. Story Musgrave | 7 Dec 1996 | 61 | 3 | 19 |
| **4** Dennis Tito | 6 May 2001 | 60 | 8 | 21 |
| **5** Gregory Olsen | 1 Oct 2005 | 60 | 5 | 11 |
| **6** Vance D. Brand | 11 Dec 1990 | 59 | 7 | 2 |
| **7** Jean-Loup Chrétien (France) | 6 Oct 1997 | 59 | 1 | 7 |
| **8** Valey Ryumin (Russia) | 12 Jun 1998 | 58 | 9 | 27 |
| **9** Karl G. Henize | 6 Aug 1985 | 58 | 9 | 20 |
| **10** Roger K. Crouch | 17 Jul 1997 | 56 | 10 | 5 |

\* Including payload specialists, space tourists, etc.; to 31 March 2007
\# US unless otherwise indicated

John Glenn, who in 1962 had been the first American astronaut to orbit Earth, re-entered space on 29 October 1998 aboard the Space Shuttle flight STS-95 *Discovery*, at the age of 77, becoming the oldest astronaut of all time by a considerable margin, and with the longest gap between missions. American businessman Dennis Tito's 2001 flight was as the first 'space tourist'. At 53, American astronaut Shannon Lucid holds the record as the oldest woman in space.

## 50 YEARS OF NASA

Up to 1958, the US space programme was largely conducted as a military operation, principally by the Air Force and Navy, but on 29 July of that year President Eisenhower signed the so-called 'Space Act', enabling the formation of NASA, the National Aeronautics and Space Administration, with the civilian exploration of space its principal objective. NASA came into existence on 1 October 1958. The Soviet Union had launched its *Sputnik* satellite the previous year, and the race to put a human in orbit was gaining momentum. That goal was achieved within three years of NASA's founding, with the *Mercury* programme. It was followed by the *Gemini* (two-man capsules) and the *Apollo* missions that resulted in the first Moon landing in 1969, a year ahead of the target set by President Kennedy. In addition to its unmanned programme, NASA has been responsible for over 115 Space Shuttle flights and has a pivotal role in the construction of the International Space Station.

**NASA patches**
*Official NASA mission patches date from that of Gemini 5 (1965). Each includes a unique graphic device along with the designation of the mission and names of the crew members.*

# Elements

## TOP 10 **MOST COMMON ELEMENTS IN THE EARTH'S CRUST**

| ELEMENT | PARTS PER MILLION* |
|---|---|
| 1 Oxygen | 461,000 |
| 2 Silicon | 282,000 |
| 3 Aluminium | 82,300 |
| 4 Iron | 56,300 |
| 5 Calcium | 41,500 |
| 6 Sodium | 23,600 |
| 7 Magnesium | 23,300 |
| 8 Potassium | 20,900 |
| 9 Titanium | 5,650 |
| 10 Hydrogen | 1,400 |

* mg per kg; based on average percentages of elements in igneous rock

Source: *CRC Handbook of Chemistry and Physics* (77th ed.)

## TOP 10 **MOST COMMON ELEMENTS IN THE UNIVERSE**

| ELEMENT | PARTS PER MILLION* |
|---|---|
| 1 Hydrogen | 750,000 |
| 2 Helium | 230,000 |
| 3 Oxygen | 10,000 |
| 4 Carbon | 5,000 |
| 5 Neon | 1,300 |
| 6 Iron | 1,100 |
| 7 Nitrogen | 1,000 |
| 8 Silicon | 700 |
| 9 Magnesium | 600 |
| 10 Sulphur | 500 |

* mg per kg

## TOP 10 **MOST COMMON ELEMENTS IN THE OCEANS**

| ELEMENT | AMOUNT (MG PER LITRE) |
|---|---|
| 1 Oxygen* | 857,000 |
| 2 Hydrogen* | 107,800 |
| 3 Chlorine | 19,870 |
| 4 Sodium | 11,050 |
| 5 Magnesium | 1,326 |
| 6 Sulphur | 928 |
| 7 Calcium | 422 |
| 8 Potassium | 416 |
| 9 Bromine | 67 |
| 10 Carbon | 28 |

* Combined as water

## TOP 10 **MOST VALUABLE TRADED METALLIC ELEMENTS***

| ELEMENT | PRICE ($ PER KG) |
|---|---|
| 1 Rhodium | 176,825 |
| 2 Platinum | 36,506 |
| 3 Gold | 20,463 |
| 4 Ruthenium | 20,174 |
| 5 Iridium | 12,699 |
| 6 Osmium | 12,217 |
| 7 Palladium | 10,738 |
| 8 Rhenium | 5,500 |
| 9 Germanium | 980 |
| 10 Indium | 750 |

* Based on 10–100 kg quantities of minimum 99.9 per cent purity; excluding radioactive elements, isotopes and rare earth elements traded in minute quantities

Source: Lipmann Walton, London Metal Bulletin, W. C. Heraeus GmbH & Co KG and www.thebulliondesk.com

## TOP 10 **METALLIC ELEMENTS WITH THE GREATEST RESERVES**

| ELEMENT | MINIMUM ESTIMATED GLOBAL RESERVES (TONNES) |
|---|---|
| 1 Iron | 100,000,000,000 |
| 2 Magnesium | 20,000,000,000 |
| 3 Potassium | 10,000,000,000 |
| 4 Aluminium | 6,000,000,000 |
| 5 Manganese | 3,000,000,000 |
| 6 = Chromium | 1,000,000,000 |
| = Zirconium | 1,000,000,000 |
| 8 Titanium | 600,000,000 |
| 9 Barium | 400,000,000 |
| 10 Copper | 300,000,000 |

This list includes accessible reserves of commercially mined metallic elements but excludes calcium and sodium, which exist in such huge quantities that their reserves are considered 'unlimited' and unquantifiable. In contrast, there are relatively small estimates of certain precious metals – gold, for example, is put at 15,000 tonnes. A further 500 kg of gold may be present in a cubic kilometre of seawater, but no economic method of extracting it has yet been devised.

### Davy's Discoveries

By using the newly invented electric battery, British chemist Sir Humphry Davy (1778–1829) first isolated no fewer than six elements – potassium and sodium in 1807, and calcium, magnesium, strontium and barium in 1808. He also proved chlorine to be an element in 1810. He went on to invent the Davy safety lamp.

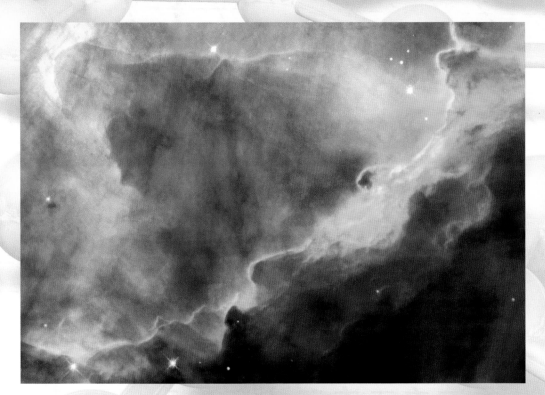

*Fiery firmament*
*Radiation emitted from stars within the Omega Nebula causes vast oceans of interstellar hydrogen to resemble an inferno. Some 75 per cent of all matter and as much as 90 per cent by number of atoms in the Universe is composed of hydrogen.*

# TOP 10 **LIGHTEST SOLID ELEMENTS**

| ELEMENT / DISCOVERER / COUNTRY | YEAR DISCOVERED | DENSITY* |
|---|---|---|
| 1 Lithium<br>Johan August Arfvedson, Sweden | 1817 | 0.533 |
| 2 Potassium<br>Sir Humphry Davy, UK | 1807 | 0.859 |
| 3 Sodium<br>Sir Humphry Davy | 1807 | 0.969 |
| 4 Calcium<br>Sir Humphry Davy | 1808 | 1.526 |
| 5 Rubidium<br>Robert Wilhelm Bunsen/<br>Gustav Kirchhoff, Germany | 1861 | 1.534 |
| 6 Magnesium<br>Sir Humphry Davy | 1808# | 1.737 |
| 7 Phosphorus<br>Hennig Brandt, Germany | 1669 | 1.825 |
| 8 Beryllium<br>Friedrich Wöhler, Germany/Antoine-<br>Alexandré Brutus Bussy, France | 1828† | 1.846 |
| 9 Caesium<br>Robert Wilhelm Bunsen/<br>Gustav Kirchhoff, Germany | 1860 | 1.896 |
| 10 Sulphur | Prehist. | 2.070 |

* Grams per cm³ at 20°C
# Recognized by Joseph Black, 1755, but not isolated
† Recognized by Nicholas Vauquelin, 1797, but not isolated

Lithium, the lightest solid element, is 42 times lighter than osmium, the heaviest. Although a metal, lithium is so soft that it can be easily cut with a knife. It is half as heavy as water, and lighter than certain types of wood. It is used in the aerospace industry to make lightweight alloys and in the air-filtration systems of spacecraft.

# TOP 10 **HEAVIEST ELEMENTS**

| ELEMENT / DISCOVERER / COUNTRY | YEAR DISCOVERED | DENSITY* |
|---|---|---|
| 1 Osmium<br>Smithson Tennant, UK | 1803 | 22.59 |
| 2 Iridium<br>Smithson Tennant | 1803 | 22.56 |
| 3 Platinum<br>Julius Caesar Scaliger#, Italy/France/<br>Antonio de Ulloa, Spain/<br>Charles Wood, UK† | 1557<br>1735<br>1741 | 21.45 |
| 4 Rhenium<br>Walter K. Noddack *et al*, Germany | 1925 | 21.01 |
| 5 Neptunium<br>Edwin Mattison McMillan/<br>Philip H. Abelson, USA | 1940 | 20.47 |
| 6 Plutonium<br>Glenn Theodore Seaborg *et al*, USA | 1940 | 20.26 |
| 7 Gold | Prehist. | 19.29 |
| 8 Tungsten<br>Juan José and Fausto de Elhuijar, Spain | 1783 | 19.26 |
| 9 Uranium<br>Martin Heinrich Klaproth, Germany | 1789 | 19.05 |
| 10 Tantalum<br>Anders Gustav Ekeberg, Sweden | 1802 | 16.67 |

* Grams per cm³ at 20°C
# Made earliest reference to
† Discovered

The two heaviest elements, the metals osmium and iridium, were discovered by British chemist Smithson Tennant (1761–1815). A 30-cm (1-ft) cube of osmium weighs 640 kg (1,410 lb) – equivalent to 10 people each weighing 64 kg (141 lb).

# Waterworld

## TOP 10 GREATEST* WATERFALLS

| | WATERFALL | COUNTRY | AVERAGE FLOW M³/SEC | FT³/SEC |
|---|---|---|---|---|
| 1 | Inga | Dem. Rep. of Congo | 42,476 | 1,500,000 |
| 2 | Livingstone | Dem. Rep. of Congo | 35,113 | 1,240,000 |
| 3 | Boyoma (Stanley) | Dem. Rep. of Congo | 16,990 | 600,000 |
| 4 | Guíra | Brazil/Paraguay | 13,909 | 491,190 |
| 5 | Khône | Laos | 10,783 | 410,000 |
| 6 | Niagara (Horseshoe) | Canada/USA | 6,009 | 212,200 |
| 7 | Celilo | USA | 5,415 | 191,215 |
| 8 | Salto Pará | Venezuela | 3,540 | 125,000 |
| 9 | Paulo Afonso | Brazil | 2,832 | 100,000 |
| 10 | Iguaçu | Argentina/Brazil | 1,746 | 61,660 |

* Based on volume of water

With an average flow rate of 13,000 m³/sec (459,090 ft³/sec) and a peak of 50,000 m³/sec (1,765,000 ft³/sec), the Guaíra, or Salto das Sete Quedas, between Brazil and Paraguay, once occupied second place in this list, and the Urubupungá, with a discharge rate of 2,747 m³/sec (97,000 ft³/sec) was in 6th position. Following the completion of the Itaipú dam in 1982, however, both are now 'lost'. At 10.8 km (6.7 miles), the Khône Falls are the widest in the world.

## TOP 10 DEEPEST OCEANS AND SEAS

| | SEA/OCEAN | AVERAGE DEPTH M | FT |
|---|---|---|---|
| 1 | Pacific Ocean | 3,939 | 12,925 |
| 2 | Indian Ocean | 3,840 | 12,598 |
| 3 | Atlantic Ocean | 3,575 | 11,730 |
| 4 | Caribbean Sea, Atlantic Ocean | 2,575 | 8,448 |
| 5 | Sea of Japan, Pacific Ocean | 1,666 | 5,468 |
| 6 | Gulf of Mexico, Atlantic Ocean | 1,614 | 5,297 |
| 7 | Mediterranean Sea, Atlantic Ocean | 1,501 | 4,926 |
| 8 | Bering Sea, Pacific Ocean | 1,491 | 4,893 |
| 9 | South China Sea, Pacific Ocean | 1,463 | 4,802 |
| 10 | Black Sea, Atlantic Ocean | 1,190 | 3,906 |

The deepest point in the deepest ocean is the Marianas Trench in the Pacific. In the first ever descent of the Marianas Trench, on 23 January 1960 by Jacques Piccard (Switzerland) and Donald Walsh (USA) in their 17.7-m (58-ft) bathyscaphe *Trieste 2*, a depth of 10,916 m (35,813 ft) was recorded. A more recent survey, on 24 March 1995 by Japanese unmanned probe *Kaikō*, recorded the slightly shallower depth of 10,911 m (35,798 ft). Whichever is the more precise, it is close to 11 km (6.8 miles) down, or almost 29 times the height of the Empire State Building.

## TOP 10 DEEPEST FRESHWATER LAKES

| | LAKE | LOCATION | GREATEST DEPTH M | FT |
|---|---|---|---|---|
| 1 | Baikal | Russia | 1,741 | 5,712 |
| 2 | Tanganyika | Burundi/Tanzania/Dem. Rep. of Congo/Zambia | 1,471 | 4,826 |
| 3 | Malawi | Malawi/Mozambique/Tanzania | 706 | 2,316 |
| 4 | Great Slave | Canada | 614 | 2,014 |
| 5 | Crater | Oregon, USA | 594 | 1,949 |
| 6 | Matana | Celebes, Indonesia | 590 | 1,936 |
| 7 | Toba | Sumatra, Indonesia | 529 | 1,736 |
| 8 | Hornindals | Norway | 514 | 1,686 |
| 9 | Sarezskoye (Sarez) | Tajikistan | 505 | 1,657 |
| 10 | Tahoe | California/Nevada, USA | 501 | 1,643 |

## TOP 10 DEEPEST DEEP-SEA TRENCHES

| | TRENCH* | DEEPEST POINT M | FT |
|---|---|---|---|
| 1 | Marianas | 10,911 | 35,798 |
| 2 | Tonga# | 10,882 | 35,702 |
| 3 | Philippine | 10,540 | 34,580 |
| 4 | Kuril-Kamchatka | 10,500 | 34,449 |
| 5 | Kermadec# | 10,047 | 32,963 |
| 6 | Bonin | 9,994 | 32,789 |
| 7 | New Britain | 9,940 | 32,612 |
| 8 | Izu | 9,780 | 32,087 |
| 9 | Puerto Rico | 8,605 | 28,232 |
| 10 | Yap | 8,527 | 27,976 |

* With the exception of the Puerto Rico (Atlantic), all the trenches are in the Pacific
# Some authorities consider these parts of the same feature

Each of the eight deepest ocean trenches would be deep enough to submerge Mount Everest, which is 8,850 m (29,035 ft) above sea level.

## TOP 10 **COUNTRIES WITH THE GREATEST AREAS OF INLAND WATER**

| COUNTRY | % OF TOTAL AREA | WATER AREA SQ KM | SQ MILES |
|---|---|---|---|
| **1** Canada | 8.93 | 891,163 | 344,080 |
| **2** USA* | 6.76 | 664,707 | 256,645 |
| **3** India | 9.56 | 314,400 | 121,391 |
| **4** China | 2.82 | 270,550 | 104,460 |
| **5** Sudan | 5.18 | 129,810 | 50,120 |
| **6** Colombia | 8.80 | 100,210 | 38,691 |
| **7** Indonesia | 4.85 | 93,000 | 35,908 |
| **8** Russia | 0.47 | 79,400 | 30,657 |
| **9** Dem. Rep. of Congo | 3.32 | 77,810 | 30,427 |
| **10** Australia | 0.90 | 68,920 | 26,610 |
| *UK* | *1.32* | *3,230* | *1,247* |

\* 50 states and District of Columbia

Source: CIA, *The World Factbook 2007*

Large areas of some countries are occupied by major rivers and lakes. Lake Victoria, for example, raises the water area of Uganda to 15.39 per cent of its total. Several European countries have considerable areas of water, among them Sweden's 39,036 sq km (15,072 sq miles) and Finland's 31,560 sq km (12,185 sq miles).

*Amazing Amazon*
*Although slightly shorter than the Nile, the Amazon basin covers a greater area – some 5.9 million sq km (2.3 million sq miles) – and discharges more water at its mouth than any other.*

## TOP 10 **GREATEST\* RIVER SYSTEMS**

| RIVER SYSTEM | CONTINENT | AVERAGE DISCHARGE AT MOUTH M³/SEC | FT³/SEC |
|---|---|---|---|
| **1** Amazon | South America | 219,000 | 7,733,912 |
| **2** Congo (Zaïre) | Africa | 41,800 | 1,476,153 |
| **3** Yangtze (Chang Jiang) | Asia | 31,900 | 1,126,537 |
| **4** Orinoco | South America | 28,000 | 988,810 |
| **5** Brahmaputra (Tsangpo) | Asia | 20,000 | 706,293 |
| **6** Yenisei-Angara | Asia | 19,600 | 692,167 |
| **7** Río de la Plata-Paraná-Uruguay | South America | 19,500 | 688,636 |
| **8** Mississippi-Missouri | North America | 17,545 | 619,595 |
| **9** Lena | Asia | 16,400 | 579,160 |
| **10** Mekong | Asia | 15,900 | 561,503 |

\* Based on rate of discharge at mouth

Source: River Systems of the World

# Down Below

**Low life**
*The Dead Sea is not only the lowest-lying place on Earth, but also so saline that swimmers float with ease.*

## TOP 10 DEEPEST DEPRESSIONS

| DEPRESSION / LOCATION | MAXIMUM DEPTH BELOW SEA LEVEL | |
|---|---|---|
| | M | FT |
| **1 Dead Sea**, Israel/Jordan | 400 | 1,312 |
| **2 Lake Assal**, Djibouti | 156 | 511 |
| **3 Turfan Depression**, China | 154 | 505 |
| **4 Qattâra Depression**, Egypt | 133 | 436 |
| **5 Mangyshlak Peninsula**, Kazakhstan | 132 | 433 |
| **6 Danakil Depression**, Ethiopia | 117 | 383 |
| **7 Death Valley**, California, USA | 86 | 282 |
| **8 Salton Sink**, California, USA | 72 | 235 |
| **9 Zapadny Chink Ustyurta**, Kazakhstan | 70 | 230 |
| **10 Prikaspiyskaya Nizmennost'**, Kazakhstan/Russia | 67 | 220 |

The shore of the Dead Sea is the lowest exposed ground below sea level, but the bed of the sea actually reaches 728 m (2,388 ft) below sea level, and that of Lake Baikal, Russia, attains 1,485 m (4,872 ft) below sea level. Much of Antarctica is below sea level (some as low as 2,538 m/8,326 ft) – but the land there is covered by an ice cap that averages 2,100 m (6,890 ft) in depth. The lowest points on continents outside those appearing in the Top 10 include South America's Peninsula Valdés, Argentina (40 m/131 ft below sea level), Europe's Caspian Sea shore (28 m/92 ft) and Australia's Lake Eyre (12 m/52 ft).

## TOP 10 LONGEST CAVES

CAVE / LOCATION / TOTAL KNOWN LENGTH KM/MILES

**1** Mammoth Cave System, Kentucky, USA  590.6 / 367

**2** Jewel Cave, South Dakota, USA  218.2 / 135

**3** Optimisticeskaja, Ukraine  215.0 / 134

**4** Wind Cave, South Dakota, USA  198.0 / 124

**5** Hölloch, Switzerland  193.6 / 120

**6** Lechuguilla Cave, New Mexico, USA  193.4 / 120

**7** Fisher Ridge System, Kentucky, USA  177.3 / 110

**8** Sistema Sac Actun, Mexico  155.4 / 97

**9** Siebenhengste-hohgant, Switzerland  154.0 / 96

**10** Sistema Ox Bel Ha, Mexico  146.8 / 91

**Going underground**
*The Mammoth Cave System has been explored for over 200 years and is visited by over two million people annually.*

# TOP 10 COUNTRIES WITH THE LOWEST ELEVATIONS

| COUNTRY* | HIGHEST POINT | ELEVATION M | FT |
|---|---|---|---|
| **1** Maldives | Unnamed on Wilingili island in the Addu Atoll | 2.4 | 7.8 |
| **2** Tuvalu | Unnamed | 5 | 16.4 |
| **3** Marshall Islands | Unnamed on Likiep | 10 | 32.8 |
| **4** The Gambia | Unnamed | 53 | 173.9 |
| **5** Nauru | Unnamed on plateau rim | 61 | 200.1 |
| **6** The Bahamas | Mount Alvernia on Cat Island | 63 | 206.7 |
| **7** Vatican City | Unnamed | 75 | 246.1 |
| **8** Kiribati | Unnamed on Banaba | 81 | 265.7 |
| **9** Qatar | Qurayn Abu al Bawl | 103 | 337.9 |
| **10** Singapore | Bukit Timah | 166 | 544.6 |

* Excludes overseas possessions, territories and dependencies

Source: CIA, *The World Factbook 2007*

These 10 countries are definitely off the agenda if you are planning a climbing holiday, none of them possessing a single elevation taller than a medium-sized skyscraper. Compared with these, even the Netherlands' 321-m (1,050-ft) Vaalserberg Hill makes the country's appellation as one of the 'Low Countries' sound somewhat unfair. The low elevations of some countries make them vulnerable to the effects of tsunamis.

# TOP 10 DEEPEST CAVES

The world's deepest cave is a comparatively recent discovery: in January 2001 a team of Ukrainian cave explorers in the Arabikskaja system in the western Caucasus mountains of the Georgian Republic found a branch of the Voronja or 'Crow's Cave' and established that its depth far exceeded anything previously known. Progressively deeper penetrations have taken its extent to more than seven times the height of the Eiffel Tower.

| | CAVE SYSTEM / LOCATION | DEPTH M | FT |
|---|---|---|---|
| **10** | Sistema Huautla, Mexico | 1,475 | 4,839 |
| **9** | Sistema Cheve (Cuicateco), Mexico | 1,484 | 4,869 |
| **8** | Cehi 2, Slovenia | 1,502 | 4,928 |
| **7** | Shakta Vjacheslav Pantjukhina, Georgia | 1,508 | 4,948 |
| **6** | Sarma, Georgia | 1,543 | 5,062 |
| **5** | Torca del Cerro del Cuevon/ Torca de las Saxifragas, Spain | 1,589 | 5,213 |
| **4** | Réseau Jean Bernard, France | 1,602 | 5,256 |
| **3** | Gouffre Mirolda, France | 1,626 | 5,335 |
| **2** | Lamprechtsofen Vogelschacht Weg Schacht, Austria | 1,632 | 5,354 |
| **1** | Krubera (Voronja), Georgia | 2,170 | 7,119 |

# On Top of the World

## TOP 10 **HIGHEST MOUNTAINS**

| MOUNTAIN / LOCATION / FIRST ASCENT / TEAM NATIONALITY | M | FT |
|---|---|---|
| **1** | | |
| **Everest**, Nepal/China, 29 May 1953<br>British/New Zealand | 8,850 | 29,035 |
| **2** | | |
| **K2** (Chogori), Pakistan/China, 31 Jul 1954<br>Italian | 8,611 | 28,251 |
| **3** | | |
| **Kangchenjunga**, Nepal/India, 25 May 1955<br>British | 8,586 | 28,169 |
| **4** | | |
| **Lhotse**, Nepal/China, 18 May 1956<br>Swiss | 8,516 | 27,940 |
| **5** | | |
| **Makalu I**, Nepal/China, 15 May 1955<br>French | 8,485 | 27,838 |
| **6** | | |
| **Cho Oyu**, Nepal/China, 19 Oct 1954<br>Austrian | 8,188 | 26,864 |
| **7** | | |
| **Dhaulagiri I**, Nepal, 13 May 1960<br>Swiss/Austrian | 8,167 | 26,795 |
| **8** | | |
| **Manaslu I** (Kutang I), Nepal, 9 May 1956<br>Japanese | 8,163 | 26,781 |
| **9** | | |
| **Nanga Parbat** (Diamir), Pakistan, 3 Jul 1953<br>German/Austrian | 8,125 | 26,657 |
| **10** | | |
| **Annapurna I**, Nepal, 3 Jun 1950<br>French | 8,091 | 26,545 |

\* Height of principal peak; lower peaks of the same mountain are excluded

## TOP 10 **HIGHEST ACTIVE VOLCANOES**\*

| VOLCANO / LOCATION | LAST ERUPTION | HEIGHT M | FT |
|---|---|---|---|
| **1** Tupungato, Chile/Argentina | 1986 | 6,570 | 21,555 |
| **2** Pular, Chile | 1990 | 6,233 | 20,449 |
| **3** San Pedro, Chile | 1960 | 6,145 | 20,161 |
| **4** Aracar, Argentina | 1993 | 6,082 | 19,954 |
| **5** Guallatiri, Chile | 1985 | 6,071 | 19,918 |
| **6** Tacora, Chile | 1937 | 5,980 | 19,619 |
| **7** Sabancaya, Peru | 2003 | 5,967 | 19,576 |
| **8** Cotopaxi, Ecuador | 1942 | 5,911 | 19,393 |
| **9** Putana, Chile | 1972 | 5,890 | 19,324 |
| **10** San Jose, Chile | 1960 | 5,856 | 19,213 |

\* Eruption during past 100 years

## TOP 10 **HIGHEST MOUNTAINS IN THE UK**

| MOUNTAIN | M | HEIGHT FT |
|---|---|---|
| **1** Ben Nevis, Highland | 1,344 | 4,408 |
| **2** Ben Macdhui, Moray | 1,309 | 4,296 |
| **3** Braeriach, Aberdeenshire/Highland | 1,296 | 4,252 |
| **4** Cairn Toul, Aberdeenshire | 1,293 | 4,241 |
| **5** Cairn Gorm, Moray/Highland | 1,245 | 4,084 |
| **6** Aonach Beag, Highland | 1,236 | 4,054 |
| **7** Carn Mór Dearg, Highland | 1,223 | 4,012 |
| **8** Aonach Mór, Highland | 1,219 | 3,999 |
| **9** Ben Lawers, Perth and Kinross | 1,214 | 3,984 |
| **10** Beinn a' Bhùird, Aberdeenshire | 1,196 | 3,924 |

All 10 of the UK's tallest mountains are in Scotland. The tallest in England, Wales and Northern Ireland are:

| | | |
|---|---|---|
| *England: Scafell Pike* | *977* | *3,206* |
| *Wales: Snowdon* | *1,085* | *3,560* |
| *Northern Ireland: Slieve Donard* | *852* | *2,795* |

### Measuring Everest

In 1852 the Great Trigonometrical Survey of India revealed that Everest (then called 'Peak XV') was the world's tallest peak at 8,840 m (29,002 ft). Errors in measurement were corrected in 1955 to 8,848 m (29,029 ft) and in 1993 to 8,847.7 m (29,028 ft). In 1999 data beamed from sensors on Everest's summit to GPS (Global Positioning System) satellites established a new height of 8,850 m (29,035 ft), which geographers accept as the current 'official' figure.

*African heights*
*The world's tallest animal, the giraffe, poses against Kilimanjaro, Africa's highest mountain.*

## TOP 10 **HIGHEST MOUNTAINS IN AFRICA**

| | MOUNTAIN | COUNTRY | HEIGHT M | HEIGHT FT |
|---|---|---|---|---|
| 1 | Kilimanjaro | Tanganyika/Tanzania | 5,895 | 19,340 |
| 2 | Kenya | Kenya | 5,199 | 17,058 |
| 3 | Ngaliema | Uganda/Dem. Rep. of Congo | 5,109 | 16,763 |
| 4 | Duwoni | Uganda | 4,896 | 16,062 |
| 5 | Baker | Uganda | 4,843 | 15,889 |
| 6 | Emin | Dem. Rep. of Congo | 4,798 | 15,741 |
| 7 | Gessi | Uganda | 4,715 | 15,470 |
| 8 | Sella | Uganda | 4,627 | 15,179 |
| 9 | Ras Dashen | Ethiopia | 4,620 | 15,158 |
| 10 | Wasuwameso | Dem. Rep. of Congo | 4,581 | 15,030 |

Kilimanjaro is the world's tallest freestanding mountain – one that is not part of a more extensive range. It was known to ancient writers such as Ptolemy as early as the 2nd century AD. It was first climbed in 1889 by Hans Meyer (Germany). Mount Kenya, also volcanic, first scaled 10 years later by Halford Mackinder (UK).

## TOP 10 **HIGHEST MOUNTAINS IN EUROPE**

| | MOUNTAIN | COUNTRY | HEIGHT* M | HEIGHT* FT |
|---|---|---|---|---|
| 1 | Mont Blanc | France/Italy | 4,807 | 15,771 |
| 2 | Monte Rosa | Switzerland | 4,634 | 15,203 |
| 3 | Zumsteinspitze | Italy/Switzerland | 4,564 | 14,970 |
| 4 | Signalkuppe | Italy/Switzerland | 4,555 | 14,941 |
| 5 | Dom | Switzerland | 4,545 | 14,911 |
| 6 | Liskamm | Italy/Switzerland | 4,527 | 14,853 |
| 7 | Weisshorn | Switzerland | 4,505 | 14,780 |
| 8 | Täschorn | Switzerland | 4,491 | 14,733 |
| 9 | Matterhorn | Italy/Switzerland | 4,477 | 14,688 |
| 10 | Mont Maudit | France/Italy | 4,466 | 14,649 |

* Height of principal peak; lower peaks of the same mountain are excluded

All 10 of Europe's highest mountains are in the Alps; there are, however, at least 15 mountains in the Caucasus (the mountain range that straddles Europe and Asia) that are taller than Mont Blanc. The highest of them, the west peak of Mount Elbrus, measures 5,642 m (18,510 ft).

# Islands

## TOP 10 **MOST ISOLATED ISLANDS**

ISLAND / LOCATION / ISOLATION INDEX

The United Nations' isolation index is calculated by adding together the square roots of the distances to the nearest island, group of islands and continent. The higher the number, the more remote the island.

**Easter Island**, South Pacific  149

**Rapa Iti**, Tubuai Islands, South Pacific  130

**Kiritimati**, Line Islands, Central Pacific  129

**Jarvis Island**, Central Pacific  128

**Kosrae**, Micronesia, Pacific  126
**Malden**, Line Islands, Central Pacific
**Starbuck**, Line Islands, Central Pacific
**Vostok**, Line Islands, Central Pacific  1

**Bouvet Island**, South Atlantic  125
**Gough Island**, South Atlantic  125
**Palmyra Island**, Central Pacific  125

## TOP 10 **LARGEST ISLANDS IN EUROPE**

| ISLAND / LOCATION | AREA SQ KM | SQ MILES |
|---|---|---|
| 1 Great Britain | 218,077 | 84,200 |
| 2 Iceland | 102,820 | 39,699 |
| 3 Ireland | 82,462 | 31,838 |
| 4 Spitsbergen, Norway | 39,044 | 15,075 |
| 5 Sicily, Italy | 25,708 | 9,925 |
| 6 Sardinia, Italy | 24,090 | 9,301 |
| 7 Nordaustlande, Norway | 14,443 | 5,576 |
| 8 Cyprus, Greece | 9,251 | 3,571 |
| 9 Corsica, France | 8,680 | 3,351 |
| 10 Crete, Greece | 8,336 | 3,218 |

## TOP 10 **SMALLEST ISLAND COUNTRIES**

| COUNTRY / LOCATION | AREA SQ KM | SQ MILES |
|---|---|---|
| 1 Nauru, Pacific Ocean | 21.2 | 8.2 |
| 2 Tuvalu, Pacific Ocean | 26.0 | 10.0 |
| 3 Marshall Islands, Pacific Ocean | 181.3 | 70.0 |
| 4 Saint Kitts and Nevis, Caribbean Sea | 261.0 | 100.8 |
| 5 Maldives, Indian Ocean | 298.0 | 115.1 |
| 6 Malta, Mediterranean Sea | 316.0 | 122.0 |
| 7 Grenada, Caribbean Sea | 344.0 | 132.8 |
| 8 Saint Vincent and the Grenadines, Caribbean Sea | 389.0 | 150.2 |
| 9 Barbados, Caribbean Sea | 431.0 | 166.4 |
| 10 Antigua and Barbuda, Caribbean Sea | 442.6 | 170.9 |

# TOP 10 **LARGEST ISLANDS**

| ISLAND / LOCATION | AREA* SQ KM | SQ MILES |
|---|---|---|
| **1** Greenland (Kalaatdlit Nunaat) | 2,175,600 | 840,004 |
| **2** New Guinea, Papua New Guinea/Indonesia | 785,753 | 303,381 |
| **3** Borneo, Indonesia/Malaysia/Brunei | 748,168 | 288,869 |
| **4** Madagascar | 587,713 | 226,917 |
| **5** Baffin Island, Canada | 503,944 | 194,574 |
| **6** Sumatra, Indonesia | 443,065 | 171,068 |
| **7** Honshu, Japan | 227,413 | 87,805 |
| **8** Great Britain | 218,077 | 84,200 |
| **9** Victoria Island, Canada | 217,292 | 83,897 |
| **10** Ellesmere Island, Canada | 196,236 | 75,767 |

\* Mainlands, including areas of inland water, but excluding offshore islands

Australia is regarded as a continental land mass rather than an island, otherwise it would rank first, at 7,618,493 sq km (2,941,517 sq miles), or 35 times the size of Great Britain.

### Small island
*Comino, with Gozo and Malta, is one of the three inhabited islands that comprise the state of Malta. Together they form Europe's smallest island country and the smallest country in the EC.*

# TOP 10 **LARGEST LAKE ISLANDS**

| ISLAND | LAKE / LOCATION | AREA SQ KM | SQ MILES |
|---|---|---|---|
| **1** Manitoulin | Huron, Ontario, Canada | 2,766 | 1,068 |
| **2** René-Lavasseur | Manicouagan Reservoir, Quebec, Canada | 2,020 | 780 |
| **3** Olkhon | Baikal, Russia | 730 | 282 |
| **4** Samosir | Toba, Sumatra, Indonesia | 630 | 243 |
| **5** Isle Royale | Superior, Michigan, USA | 541 | 209 |
| **6** Ukerewe | Victoria, Tanzania | 530 | 205 |
| **7** St Joseph | Huron, Ontario, Canada | 365 | 141 |
| **8** Drummond | Huron, Michigan, USA | 347 | 134 |
| **9** Idjwi | Kivu, Dem. Rep. of Congo | 285 | 110 |
| **10** Ometepe | Nicaragua, Nicaragua | 276 | 107 |

Not all islands are surrounded by sea: many sizeable islands are situated in lakes. Vozrozhdeniya Island, Uzbekistan, previously second in this list with an area of approximately 2,300 sq km (900 sq miles), has grown as the Aral Sea contracts, and has now linked up with the surrounding land to become a peninsula. There are even larger islands in freshwater river outlets, including Marajó, in the mouth of the Amazon, Brazil (48,000 sq km/ 18,533 sq miles), and Bananal, in the River Araguaia, Brazil (20,000 sq km/7,722 sq miles).

# Extreme World Weather

## TOP 10 **COLDEST PLACES**

| | LOCATION* | LOWEST RECORDED TEMPERATURE | |
|---|---|---|---|
| | | °C | °F |
| 1 | Vostok#, Antarctica | −89.2 | −128.6 |
| 2 | Sovietskaya#, Antarctica | −86.7 | −124.1 |
| 3 | Oymyakon, Russia | −71.2 | −96.2 |
| 4 | Verkhoyansk, Russia | −69.8 | −93.6 |
| 5 | Northice#, Greenland | −66.0 | −87.0 |
| 6 | Eismitte#, Greenland | −64.9 | −85.0 |
| 7 =Snag, Yukon, Canada | | −63.0 | −81.4 |
| =Bulunkul Lake, Tajikistan | | −63.0 | −81.4 |
| 9 | Mayo, Yukon, Canada | −62.2 | −80.0 |
| 10 | Prospect Creek, Alaska, USA | −62.1 | −79.8 |

\* Maximum of two places per country listed
\# Present or former scientific research base

Source: Philip Eden/Roland Bert

Vostok, a Russian research station, recorded the lowest temperature on Earth on 21 July 1983, and, though unofficial, an even colder one of −91°C (−132°F) in 1997. It is situated at an altitude of 3,420 m (11,220 ft) and is susceptible to high-speed katabatic (downhill) winds that can reach up to 322 km/h (200 mph).

**Cold comfort**
*The Siberian village of Oymyakon recorded the lowest temperature in the Northern Hemisphere and of any inhabited place on Earth.*

## TOP 10 **PLACES WITH THE MOST RAINY DAYS**

LOCATION* / RAINY DAYS PER ANNUM#

\* Maximum of two places per country listed
\# Averaged over a long period of years

Source: Philip Eden

1 Waialeale, Hawaii, USA 335
2 Marion Island, South Africa 312
3 Pohnpei, Federated States of Micronesia 311
4 Andagoya, Colombia 306
5 Macquarie Island, Australia 299
6 Gough Island, Tristan da Cunha group, South Atlantic 291
7 Palau, Federated States of Micronesia 286
8 Heard Island, Australia 279
9 Camp Jacob, Guadeloupe 274
10 Atu Nau, Alaska, USA 268

# TOP 10 HOTTEST PLACES

| | LOCATION* | HIGHEST TEMPERATURE °C | °F |
|---|---|---|---|
| 1 | Al'Aziziyah, Libya | 58.0 | 136.4 |
| 2 | Greenland Ranch, Death Valley, USA | 56.7 | 134.0 |
| 3 | = Ghudamis, Libya | 55.0 | 131.0 |
| | = Kebili, Tunisia | 55.0 | 131.0 |
| 5 | Tombouctou, Mali | 54.5 | 130.1 |
| 6 | = Araouane, Mali | 54.4 | 130.0 |
| | = Mammoth Tank#, California, USA | 54.4 | 130.0 |
| 8 | Tirat Tavi, Israel | 54.0 | 129.0 |
| 9 | Ahwaz, Iran | 53.5 | 128.3 |
| 10 | Agha Jari, Iran | 53.3 | 128.0 |

\* Maximum of two places per country listed
\# Former weather station

Source: Philip Eden/Roland Bert

**Dead hot**
*Death Valley, California, and the Western Hemisphere's record highest temperature was measured at the ironically named Greenland Ranch (now Furnace Creek) weather station on 10 July 1913.*

# TOP 10 SUNNIEST PLACES*

| | LOCATION# | % OF MAXIMUM POSSIBLE | AVERAGE ANNUAL HOURS SUNSHINE |
|---|---|---|---|
| 1 | Yuma, Arizona, USA | 91 | 4,127 |
| 2 | Phoenix, Arizona, USA | 90 | 4,041 |
| 3 | Wadi Halfa, Sudan | 89 | 3,964 |
| 4 | Bordj Omar Driss, Algeria | 88 | 3,899 |
| 5 | Keetmanshoop, Namibia | 88 | 3,876 |
| 6 | Aoulef, Algeria | 86 | 3,784 |
| 7 | Upington, South Africa | 86 | 3,766 |
| 8 | Atbara, Sudan | 85 | 3,739 |
| 9 | Mariental, Namibia | 84 | 3,707 |
| 10 | Bilma, Niger | 84 | 3,699 |

\* Highest yearly sunshine total, averaged over a long period of years
\# Maximum of two places per country listed

Source: Philip Eden

# TOP 10 PLACES WITH THE FEWEST RAINY DAYS

| | LOCATION* | NO. OF RAINY DAYS# |
|---|---|---|
| 1 | Arica, Chile | 1 day every 6 years |
| 2 | Asyût, Egypt | 1 day every 5 years |
| 3 | Dakhla Oasis, Egypt | 1 day every 4 years |
| 4 | Al'Kufrah, Libya | 1 day every 2 years |
| 5 | = Bender Qaasim, Somalia | 1 day per year |
| | = Wadi Halfa, Sudan | 1 day per year |
| 7 | Iquique, Chile | 2 days per year |
| 8 | = Dongola, Sudan | 3 days per year |
| | = Faya-Largeau, Chad | 3 days per year |
| | = Masirah Island, Oman | 3 days per year |

\* Maximum of two places per country listed
\# Lowest number of days with rain per year, averaged over a long period of years

Source: Philip Eden

# Natural Disasters

## THE 10 **MOST EXPENSIVE TYPES OF DISASTER**\*

TYPE OF DISASTER / ESTIMATED DAMAGE 1900–2005 ($)

1 **Wind storms**  499,554,558,000

2 **Floods**  353,338,772,000

3 **Earthquakes**  305,890,593,000

4 **Droughts**  63,602,469,000

5 **Extreme temperatures**  62,715,997,000

6 **Forest/scrub fires**  34,804,550,000

7 **Industrial accidents**  28,094,717,000

8 **Tsunamis**  7,767,077,000

9 **Avalanches/ landslides**  4,850,232,000

10 **Volcanoes**  3,808,546,000

\* Includes natural and non-natural

Source: EM-DAT, CRED, University of Louvain, Belgium

*Sri Lankan tragedy*
*Although less severely affected than Indonesia, over 30,000 people died in Sri Lanka, with great damage to coastal property as a result of the 2004 tsunami.*

## THE 10 **WORST FLOODS**

| | LOCATION | DATE | ESTIMATED NO. KILLED |
|---|---|---|---|
| 1 | Huang He River, China | Aug 1931 | 3,700,000 |
| 2 | Huang He River, China | Spring 1887 | 1,500,000 |
| 3 | Holland | 1 Nov 1530 | 400,000 |
| 4 | Kaifong, China | 1642 | 300,000 |
| 5 | Henan, China | Sep–Nov 1939 | >200,000 |
| 6 | Bengal, India | 1876 | 200,000 |
| 7 | Yangtze River, China | Aug–Sep 1931 | 140,000 |
| 8 | Holland | 1646 | 110,000 |
| 9 | North Vietnam | 30 Aug 1971 | >100,000 |
| 10 = | Friesland, Holland | 1228 | 100,000 |
| = | Dort, Holland | 16 Apr 1421 | 100,000 |
| = | Canton, China | 12 Jun 1915 | 100,000 |
| = | Yangtze River, China | Sep 1911 | 100,000 |

Records of floods caused by China's Huang He, or Yellow River, date back to 2297 BC. Since then, it has flooded at least 1,500 times, inundating entire towns and villages, causing millions of deaths and giving it the apt nickname of 'China's Sorrow'.

## THE 10 **WORST TSUNAMIS**

| | LOCATIONS AFFECTED | DATE | ESTIMATED NO. KILLED |
|---|---|---|---|
| 1 | Southeast Asia | 26 Dec 2004 | >186,983 |
| 2 | Krakatoa, Sumatra/Java* | 27 Aug 1883 | 36,380 |
| 3 | Sanriku, Japan | 15 Jun 1896 | 28,000 |
| 4 | Agadir, Morocco# | 29 Feb 1960 | 12,000 |
| 5 | Lisbon, Portugal | 1 Nov 1755 | 10,000 |
| 6 | Papua New Guinea | 18 Jul 1998 | 8,000 |
| 7 | Chile/Pacific islands/Japan | 22 May 1960 | 5,700 |
| 8 | Philippines | 17 Aug 1976 | 5,000 |
| 9 | Hyuga to Izu, Japan | 28 Oct 1707 | 4,900 |
| 10 | Sanriku, Japan | 3 Mar 1933 | 3,000 |

\* Combined effect of volcanic eruption and tsunamis
\# Combined effect of earthquake and tsunamis

Tsunamis (from the Japanese *tsu*, port and *nami*, wave), are powerful waves caused by undersea disturbances such as earthquakes and volcanic eruptions. Tsunamis can be so intense that they frequently cross oceans, devastating islands and coastal regions in their paths. Triggered by a massive undersea earthquake in the Indian Ocean, the 2004 tsunami was exceptionally destructive. It destroyed coastal settlements in low-lying areas of Indonesia, Sri Lanka, Thailand and other countries, resulting in loss of life on an unprecedented scale.

## THE 10 **WORST AVALANCHES AND LANDSLIDES***

| | LOCATION | INCIDENT | DATE | ESTIMATED NO. KILLED |
|---|---|---|---|---|
| 1 | Alps, Italy | Avalanche | Oct 218 BC | 18,000 |
| 2 | Yungay, Peru | Landslide | 31 May 1970 | 17,500 |
| 3 | Italian Alps | Avalanche | 13 Dec 1916 | 10,000 |
| 4 | Huarás, Peru | Avalanche | 13 Dec 1941 | 5,000 |
| 5 | Nevada Huascaran, Peru | Avalanche | 10 Jan 1962 | 3,500 |
| 6 | Chiavenna, Italy | Landslide | 4 Sep 1618 | 2,427 |
| 7 | Plurs, Switzerland | Avalanche | 4 Sep 1618 | 1,496 |
| 8 | Goldau Valley, Switzerland | Landslide | 2 Sep 1806 | 800 |
| 9 | Medellin, Colombia | Landslide | 27 Sep 1987 | 683 |
| 10 | Chungar, Peru | Avalanche | 19 Mar 1971 | 600 |

\* Excluding those where most deaths resulted from flooding, earthquakes, volcanoes, etc., associated with landslides

This list is headed by the catastrophe that befell Carthaginian troops under Hannibal as they descended the Alps, probably in the region of the Col de la Traversette, a pass between France and Italy, when 18,000 men, 2,000 horses and a number of elephants fell victim to a series of avalanches on a single day.

## THE 10 **WORST EARTHQUAKES**

| | LOCATION | DATE | ESTIMATED NO. KILLED |
|---|---|---|---|
| 1 | Near East/Mediterranean | 20 May 1202 | 1,100,000 |
| 2 | Shenshi, China | 2 Feb 1556 | 820,000 |
| 3 | Calcutta, India | 11 Oct 1737 | 300,000 |
| 4 | Antioch, Syria | 20 May 526 | 250,000 |
| 5 | Tang-shan, China | 28 Jul 1976 | 242,419 |
| 6 | Nan-Shan, China | 22 May 1927 | 200,000 |
| 7 | Yeddo, Japan | 30 Dec 1703 | 190,000 |
| 8 | Kansu, China | 16 Dec 1920 | 180,000 |
| 9 | Messina, Italy | 28 Dec 1908 | 160,000 |
| 10 | Tokyo/Yokohama, Japan | 1 Sep 1923 | 142,807 |

There are some discrepancies between the 'official' death tolls in many of the world's worst earthquakes and the estimates of other authorities: a figure of 750,000 is sometimes quoted for the Tang-shan earthquake of 1976. Several other earthquakes in China and Turkey resulted in deaths of 100,000 or more. In recent times, the Armenian earthquake of 7 December 1988, and that which struck north-west Iran on 21 June 1990, resulted in the deaths of more than 55,000 (official estimate 28,854) and 50,000 respectively. For comparison, the earthquakes that destroyed San Francisco on 18 April 1906 killed between 500 and 1,000.

## 100 YEARS AGO: THE MESSINA EARTHQUAKE

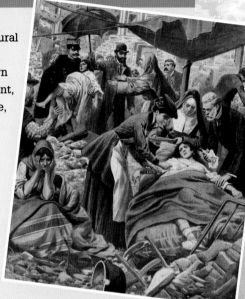

Two cataclysmic natural disasters occurred in 1908. The first, known as the Tunguska Event, took place on 30 June, when a meteorite or asteroid exploded above Siberia, flattening 60 million trees in an area of 2,150 sq km (830 sq miles) – but the forest was so sparsely inhabited that no human loss of life was recorded.

In contrast, the death toll in the second disaster was huge, when, early in the morning of 28 December 1908, a series of earthquakes struck Messina, Sicily – Italy's eighth-largest city. Within minutes, 80,000 of its 147,000 inhabitants were killed, along with 25,000 of the 34,000 in Reggio di Calabria. Some 25 towns and villages within a radius of 193 km (120 miles) were completely destroyed. A 15-m (50-ft) 800 km/h (500 mph) tsunami struck coastal towns, water mains burst and fires raged as gas mains fractured, causing yet more destruction. At least 160,000 and possibly as many as 250,000 died in the region, making it Europe's worst earthquake of modern times.

Messina had suffered a tsunami in 1169 and a severe earthquake in 1783, in which 60,000 had been killed. The buildings had been poorly reconstructed and in this second event virtually every structure, including the city's theatres, hotels, churches and its magnificent cathedral, were reduced to rubble, burying thousands beneath them. The prison walls collapsed, allowing 750 prisoners to escape. They and survivors looted, fought for food and rioted until Russian and British warships arrived to restore law and order and provide assistance in one of the biggest relief operations ever undertaken.

*Above: Aftershock*
*Rescuers tend to the wounded and homeless of Messina amid the devastation caused by the earthquake of 1908.*

# 2
# LIFE ON EARTH

# Extinct & Endangered

## TOP 10 LONGEST DINOSAURS EVER DISCOVERED

| NAME | ESTIMATED WEIGHT (TONNES) | ESTIMATED LENGTH (M) |
|---|---|---|
| **1** Argentinosaurus huinculensis | 80–100 | 35–45 |

An Argentinean farmer discovered a 1.8 m (6 ft) bone in 1988. It was the shinbone of a previously unknown dinosaur, which was named Argentinosaurus.

| | | |
|---|---|---|
| **2** Seismosaurus | 50–80 | 33 |

A skeleton of this colossal plant-eater was excavated in 1985 near Albuquerque, New Mexico, and given a name that means 'earth-shaking lizard'.

| | | |
|---|---|---|
| **3** Sauroposeidon | 50–60 | 30 |

From vertebrae discovered in 1994, it has been estimated that this creature was probably the tallest ever to walk on Earth, able to extend its neck to 18 m (60 ft).

| | | |
|---|---|---|
| **4** = Giraffatitan brancai | Uncertain | 25–30 |

This lightly built but long dinosaur was found in Tanzania and named by Gregory S. Paul in 1988.

| | | |
|---|---|---|
| = Paralititan stromeri | 70 | 25–30 |

Remains discovered in 2001 suggest that this was a plant-eater. Its name, 'Stromer's tidal giant', commemorates geologist Ernst Stromer von Reichenbach.

| | | |
|---|---|---|
| **6** Supersaurus vivianae | 50 | 24–30 |

The remains of Supersaurus were found in Colorado in 1972. Some scientists have suggested a length of up to 42 m (138 ft).

| | | |
|---|---|---|
| **7** Andesaurus delgadoi | 12.5 | 18–30 |

Found in Argentina and named in 1991 by Calvo and José Bonaparte, its vertebrae alone measure 0.6 m (2 ft).

| | | |
|---|---|---|
| **8** Diplodocus | 10–18 | 27 |

A relative lightweight in the dinosaur world, Diplodocus was also probably one of the most stupid dinosaurs, having the smallest brain in relation to its body size.

| | | |
|---|---|---|
| **9** Barosaurus | 40 | 20–27 |

Barosaurus ('heavy lizard') has been found in North America and Africa, thus proving the existence of a land link in Jurassic times (205–140 million years ago).

| | | |
|---|---|---|
| **10** Brachiosaurus | 30–80 | 26 |

Its name means 'arm lizard'. The mounted skeleton in the Humboldt Museum, Berlin, is the largest in the world.

## TOP 10 SMALLEST DINOSAURS

| DINOSAUR | MAXIMUM SIZE CM | IN |
|---|---|---|
| **1** Micropachycephalosaurus | 50 | 20 |
| **2** =Saltopus | 60 | 23 |
| =Yandangornis | 60 | 23 |
| **4** Microraptor | 77 | 30 |
| **5** Lesothosaurus | 90 | 35 |
| =Nanosaurus | 90 | 35 |
| **7** Bambiraptor | 91 | 36 |
| =Sinosauropteryx | 91 | 36 |
| **9** Wannanosaurus | 99 | 39 |
| **10** Procompsognathus | 120 | 47 |

Discovered in Argentina, Mussaurus (meaning 'mouse lizard') is the smallest complete dinosaur skeleton found, but all known specimens are of infants and measure just 18 to 37 cm (7 to 15 in); adults may have attained 300 cm (118 in). The partial remains of a Microraptor ('little plunderer') found in China and measuring 40 cm (16 in) may be those of an adult.

*Dead as a dodo*
*Discovered by European travellers in 1507, the dodo's name comes from the Portuguese for 'stupid'.*

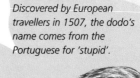

## TOP 10 TIMELINE: LAST SEEN ALIVE

These are the years when some notable creatures became extinct, especially as a result of human intervention. In the case of those that occurred in captivity, the precise date can be stated.

### 1627
**Aurochs**
Extensively hunted, the last of these large oxen died in the Jaktorow Forest in Poland.

### 1649
**Aepyornis**
Also known as the 'Elephant bird', this wingless bird was a native of Madagascar.

### 1681
**Dodo**
The last of these flightless birds was observed on Mauritius by Benjamin Harry.

### 1768
**Steller's sea cow**
This large marine mammal, named after its 1741 discoverer, was hunted to extinction.

### 1844
**Great auk**
The last surviving pair was killed on Eldey island for Icelandic collector Carl Siemsen.

# THE 10 COUNTRIES WITH THE MOST THREATENED ANIMAL SPECIES*

| COUNTRY | MAMMALS | BIRDS | REPTILES | AMPHIBIANS | FISH | INVERTEBRATES | TOTAL |
|---|---|---|---|---|---|---|---|
| **1** USA | 41 | 79 | 27 | 53 | 159 | 576 | 935 |
| **2** Australia | 64 | 65 | 39 | 47 | 85 | 283 | 583 |
| **3** Mexico | 74 | 62 | 21 | 204 | 109 | 40 | 510 |
| **4** Indonesia | 146 | 121 | 28 | 39 | 105 | 31 | 470 |
| **5** Colombia | 38 | 88 | 16 | 217 | 28 | 2 | 389 |
| **6** China | 84 | 88 | 34 | 91 | 59 | 6 | 362 |
| **7** Ecuador | 34 | 76 | 11 | 165 | 14 | 48 | 348 |
| **8** Brazil | 73 | 124 | 22 | 28 | 58 | 34 | 339 |
| **9** India | 89 | 82 | 26 | 68 | 35 | 22 | 322 |
| **10** South Africa | 28 | 38 | 20 | 21 | 58 | 141 | 306 |
| *UK* | *10* | *13* | *0* | *0* | *14* | *10* | *47* |

\* Identified by the IUCN as Critically Endangered, Endangered or Vulnerable

Source: International Union for Conservation of Nature, *2006 Redlist of Threatened Species*

# THE 10 MOST THREATENED SPECIES OF ANIMAL

| TYPE | NO. EVALUATED | NO. THREATENED* |
|---|---|---|
| **1** Amphibians | 5,918 | 1,811 |
| **2** Birds | 9,934 | 1,206 |
| **3** Mammals | 4,864 | 1,093 |
| **4** Actinopterygii (bony fish) | 2,351 | 1,058 |
| **5** Gastropods (snails, etc.) | 1,951 | 880 |
| **6** Insects | 1,192 | 623 |
| **7** Crustaceans | 537 | 459 |
| **8** Reptiles | 664 | 341 |
| **9** Chondrichthyes (sharks, etc.) | 547 | 110 |
| **10** Bivalves (clams, etc.) | 212 | 95 |
| *Total (including classes not in Top 10)* | *28,270* | *7,723* |

\* Identified by the IUCN as Critically Endangered, Endangered or Vulnerable

Source: International Union for Conservation of Nature, *2006 Redlist of Threatened Species*

In many instances, the IUCN has evaluated a very small proportion of the total known species – for example, some 950,000 species of insect have been described, but only 1,192 have been evaluated, of which 623 are regarded as threatened.

*Last of the quaggas*
*After being hunted for meat and leather, the last known quagga died in an Amsterdam zoo.*

## 1875
**Tarpan**
The last pure-bred tarpan, a European wild horse, died in a Moscow zoo.

## 1883
**Quagga**
Found in South Africa, this zebra-like creature, became extinct in the wild by 1883.

## 1914
**Passenger pigeon**
Once seen in vast flocks, the last specimen died in Cincinnati Zoo on 1 September 1914.

## 1932
**Heath hen**
The grouse-like prairie chicken was extensively hunted in New England.

## 1936
**Tasmanian wolf**
Also known as the thylacine, the last specimen died in captivity.

# Mammals

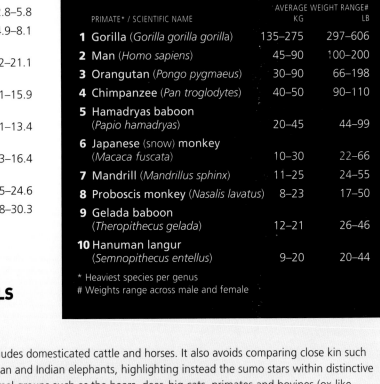

## TOP 10 SMALLEST PRIMATES

| PRIMATE* / SCIENTIFIC NAME | WEIGHT# | |
| --- | --- | --- |
| | G | OZ |
| 1 Pygmy mouse lemur (*Microcebus myoxinus*) | 30 | 1.0 |
| 2 Hairy-eared dwarf lemur (*Allocebus trichotis*) | 70–100 | 2.4–3.5 |
| 3 Tarsius pumilus | 80–165 | 2.8–5.8 |
| 4 Lesser bush baby (*Galago moholi*) | 140–230 | 4.9–8.1 |
| 5 Greater dwarf lemur (*Cheirogaleus major*) | 177–600 | 6.2–21.1 |
| 6 Buffy-headed marmoset (*Callithrix flaviceps*) | 230–453 | 8.1–15.9 |
| 7 Cotton-top tamarin (*Saguinus oedipus*) | 260–380 | 9.1–13.4 |
| 8 Golden potto (*Arctocebus calabarensis*) | 266–465 | 9.3–16.4 |
| 9 Golden-rumped lion tamarin (*Leontopithecus chrysopygus*) | 300–700 | 10.5–24.6 |
| 10 Callimico goeldii | 393–860 | 13.8–30.3 |

\* Lightest species per genus
\# Weights range across male and female; ranked by lightest

## TOP 10 HEAVIEST PRIMATES

| PRIMATE* / SCIENTIFIC NAME | AVERAGE WEIGHT RANGE# | |
| --- | --- | --- |
| | KG | LB |
| 1 Gorilla (*Gorilla gorilla gorilla*) | 135–275 | 297–606 |
| 2 Man (*Homo sapiens*) | 45–90 | 100–200 |
| 3 Orangutan (*Pongo pygmaeus*) | 30–90 | 66–198 |
| 4 Chimpanzee (*Pan troglodytes*) | 40–50 | 90–110 |
| 5 Hamadryas baboon (*Papio hamadryas*) | 20–45 | 44–99 |
| 6 Japanese (snow) monkey (*Macaca fuscata*) | 10–30 | 22–66 |
| 7 Mandrill (*Mandrillus sphinx*) | 11–25 | 24–55 |
| 8 Proboscis monkey (*Nasalis lavatus*) | 8–23 | 17–50 |
| 9 Gelada baboon (*Theropithecus gelada*) | 12–21 | 26–46 |
| 10 Hanuman langur (*Semnopithecus entellus*) | 9–20 | 20–44 |

\* Heaviest species per genus
\# Weights range across male and female

## TOP 10 HEAVIEST TERRESTRIAL MAMMALS

MAMMAL* / SCIENTIFIC NAME / LENGTH M/FT / WEIGHT KG/LB

The list excludes domesticated cattle and horses. It also avoids comparing close kin such as the African and Indian elephants, highlighting instead the sumo stars within distinctive large mammal groups such as the bears, deer, big cats, primates and bovines (ox-like mammals). The elephant is 357,000 times as heavy as smallest mammal, the pygmy shrew.

African elephant
(*Loxodonta africana*)
7.5 / 24.6   7,500 / 16,534

Hippopotamus
(*Hippopotamus amphibius*)
5.0 / 16.4   4,500 / 9,920

White rhinoceros
(*Ceratotherium simum*)
4.2 / 13.7   3,600 / 7,937

Giraffe
(*Giraffa cameloparda*
4.7 / 15.4   1,930 / 4,

\* Heaviest species per genus

# TOP 10 **FASTEST MAMMALS**

| MAMMAL* / SCIENTIFIC NAME | MAXIMUM RECORDED SPEED KM/H | MPH |
|---|---|---|
| 1 Cheetah (*Acinonyx jubatus*) | 114 | 71 |
| 2 Pronghorn antelope (*Antilocapra americana*) | 95 | 57 |
| 3 = Blue wildebeest (brindled gnu) (*Connochaetes taurinus*) | 80 | 50 |
| = Lion (*Panthera leo*) | 80 | 50 |
| = Springbok (*Antidorcas marsupialis*) | 80 | 50 |
| 6 = Brown hare (*Lepus capensis*) | 77 | 48 |
| = Red fox (*Vulpes vulpes*) | 77 | 48 |
| 8 = Grant's gazelle (*Gazella granti*) | 76 | 47 |
| = Thomson's gazelle (*Gazella thomsonii*) | 76 | 47 |
| 10 Horse (*Equus caballus*) | 72 | 45 |

\* Of those species for which data available

**The cat's away**
*Cheetahs are the speediest mammals over short distances.*

# TOP 10 **LIGHTEST TERRESTRIAL MAMMALS**

| MAMMAL* / SCIENTIFIC NAME | LENGTH# MM | IN | WEIGHT† G | OZ |
|---|---|---|---|---|
| 1 Pygmy shrew (*Sorex hoyi*) | 46–100 | 1.8–3.9 | 2.1–18 | 0.07–0.63 |
| 2 Pygmy shrew (*Suncus etruscus*) | 35–48 | 1.4–1.9 | 2.5 | 0.22 |
| 3 African pygmy mouse (*Mus minutoides*) | 45–82 | 1.8–3.2 | 2.5–12.0 | 0.09–0.42 |
| 4 Desert shrew (*Notiosorex crawfordi*) | 48–69 | 1.9–2.7 | 3.0–5.0 | 0.1–0.17 |
| 5 Forest musk shrew (*Sylvisorex species*) | 45–100 | 1.8–3.9 | 3.0–12.0 | 0.1–0.42 |
| 6 White-toothed shrew (*Crocidura suaveolens*) | 40–100 | 1.6–3.9 | 3.0–13.0 | 0.1–0.46 |
| 7 Asiatic shrew (*Soriculus salenskii*) | 44–99 | 1.7–3.9 | 5.0–6.0 | 0.17–0.21 |
| 8 Delany's swamp mouse (*Delanymys brooksi*) | 50–63 | 1.9–2.5 | 5.2–6.5 | 0.18–0.23 |
| 9 Birch mouse (*Sicista species*) | 50–90 | 1.9–3.5 | 6.0–14 | 0.21–0.49 |
| 10 Pygmy mouse (*Baiomys species*) | 50–81 | 1.9–3.2 | 7.0–8.0 | 0.24–0.59 |

\* Lightest species per genus, excluding bats
\# Some jerboas are smaller, but no precise weights have yet been recorded
† Ranked by lightest in range

# TOP 10 **COUNTRIES WITH THE MOST MAMMAL SPECIES**

| COUNTRY | MAMMAL SPECIES |
|---|---|
| 1 Indonesia | 667 |
| 2 Brazil | 578 |
| 3 Mexico | 544 |
| 4 China | 502 |
| 5 USA | 468 |
| 6 Colombia | 467 |
| 7 Peru | 441 |
| 8 Dem. Rep. of Congo | 430 |
| 9 India | 422 |
| 10 Kenya | 407 |
| UK | 103 |

Source: EarthTrends/World Conservation Monitoring Centre of the United Nations Environment Programme (UNEP-WCMC)

American buffalo
(*Bison bison*)
3.5 / 11.4
1,000 / 2,205

Moose
(*Alces alces*)
3.1 / 10.1
825 / 1,820

Grizzly bear
(*Ursus arctos*)
3.0 / 9.8
780 / 1,720

Arabian camel
(dromedary)
(*Camelus dromedarius*)
3.45 / 11.3
690 / 1,521

Siberian tiger
(*Panthera tigris altaica*)
3.3 / 10.8
360 / 793

Gorilla
(*Gorilla gorilla gorilla*)
2.0 / 6.5
275 / 606

# Birds

## TOP 10 FASTEST BIRDS

| | BIRD / SCIENTIFIC NAME | MAXIMUM RECORDED SPEED | |
|---|---|---|---|
| | | KM/H | MPH |
| 1 | Common eider (*Somateria mollissima*) | 76 | 47 |
| 2 | Bewick's swan (*Cygnus columbianus*) | 72 | 44 |
| 3 = | Barnacle goose (*Branta leucopsis*) | 68 | 42 |
| = | Common crane (*Grus grus*) | 68 | 42 |
| 5 | Mallard (*Anas platyrhynchos*) | 65 | 40 |
| 6 = | Red-throated diver (*Gavia stellata*) | 61 | 38 |
| = | Wood pigeon (*Columba palumbus*) | 61 | 38 |
| 8 | Oystercatcher (*Haematopus ostralegus*) | 58 | 36 |
| 9 = | Ring-necked pheasant (*Phasianus colchichus*) | 54 | 33 |
| = | White-fronted goose (*Anser albifrons*) | 54 | 33 |

Source: Chris Mead

## TOP 10 HEAVIEST FLIGHTED BIRDS

| | BIRD / SCIENTIFIC NAME* | WEIGHT | | |
|---|---|---|---|---|
| | | KG | LB | OZ |
| 1 | Mute swan (*Cygnus olor*) | 22.50 | 49 | 6 |
| 2 | Kori bustard (*Ardeotis kori*) | 19.00 | 41 | 8 |
| 3 = | Andean condor (*Vultur gryphus*) | 15.00 | 33 | 1 |
| = | Great white pelican (*Pelecanus onocrotalus*) | 15.00 | 33 | 1 |
| 5 | Eurasian black vulture (*Aegypius monachus*) | 12.50 | 27 | 5 |
| 6 | Sarus crane (*Grus antigone*) | 12.24 | 26 | 9 |
| 7 | Himalayan griffon (vulture) (*Gyps himalayensis*) | 12.00 | 26 | 5 |
| 8 | Wandering albatross (*Diomedea exulans*) | 11.30 | 24 | 9 |
| 9 | Steller's sea eagle (*Haliaeetus pelagicus*) | 9.00 | 19 | 8 |
| 10 | Marabou stork (*Leptoptilos crumeniferus*) | 8.90 | 19 | 6 |

* By species

Source: Chris Mead

## TOP 10 HEAVIEST FLIGHTLESS BIRDS

| | BIRD / SCIENTIFIC NAME* | WEIGHT | | |
|---|---|---|---|---|
| | | KG | LB | OZ |
| 1 | Ostrich (male) (*Struthio camelus*) | 156.0 | 343 | 9 |
| 2 | Northern cassowary (*Casuarius unappendiculatus*) | 58.0 | 127 | 9 |
| 3 | Emu (female) (*Dromaius novaehollandiae*) | 55.0 | 121 | 6 |
| 4 | Emperor penguin (female) (*Aptenodytes forsteri*) | 46.0 | 101 | 4 |
| 5 | Greater rhea (*Rhea americana*) | 25.0 | 55 | 2 |
| 6 | Flightless steamer# (duck) (*Tachyeres brachypterus*) | 6.2 | 13 | 7 |
| 7 | Flightless cormorant (*Nannopterum harrisi*) | 4.5 | 9 | 15 |
| 8 | Kiwi (female) (*Apteryx haastii*) | 3.8 | 8 | 4 |
| 9 | Takahe (rail) (*Porphyrio mantelli*) | 3.2 | 7 | 2 |
| 10 | Kakapo (parrot) (*Strigops habroptilus*) | 3.2 | 7 | 1 |

* By species
# The flightless steamer is 84 cm (33 in) long, but does not stand upright

Source: Chris Mead

The flightless great auk, extinct since 1844, weighed about 8 kg (17 lb 6 oz) and stood about 90 cm (35.4 in) high. Other flightless birds were much bigger. The two heaviest, at almost 500 kg (1,102 lb 5 oz) were the elephant bird (*Aepyornis maximus*) that became extinct from Madagascar 350 years ago, and the emu-like *Dromornis stirtoni* from Australia. The tallest, but more lightly built, was the biggest of the moas of New Zealand, *Dinornis maximus*, that became extinct when the Maoris colonized the country, but prior to European settlement; there is thus no account of any living moa, and all evidence is based on discoveries of bones.

**Earthbound athlete**
*Despite its size, the ostrich is capable of running faster – as much as 65 km/h (40 mph) – than the air speeds of many of its flighted cousins.*

# TOP 10 **LONGEST BIRD MIGRATIONS**

SPECIES / SCIENTIFIC NAME / APPROXIMATE DISTANCE KM/MILES

**1** Pectoral sandpiper (*Calidris melanotos*) 19,000* / 11,806

**2** Wheatear (*Oenanthe oenanthe*) 18,000 / 11,184

**3** Slender-billed shearwater (*Puffinus tenuirostris*) 17,500* / 10,874

**4** Ruff (*Philomachus pugnax*) 16,600 / 10,314

**5** Willow warbler (*Phylloscopus trochilus*) 16,300 / 10,128

**6** Arctic tern (*Sterna paradisaea*) 16,200 / 10,066

**7** Arctic skua (*Stercorarius parasiticus*) 15,600 / 9,693

**8** Swainson's hawk (*Buteo swainsoni*) 15,200 / 9,445

**9** Knot (*Calidris canutus*) 15,000 / 9,320

**10** Swallow (*Hirundo rustica*) 14,900 / 9,258

\* Thought to be only half of the path taken during a whole year

Source: Chris Mead

This list is of the likely extremes for a normal migrant, not one that has become lost and wandered into new territory. All migrant birds fly far longer than is indicated by the direct route. Many species fly all year, except when they come to land to breed, or, in the case of seabirds such as the albatross, to rest on the sea.

# TOP 10 **LARGEST OWLS**

| OWL* / SCIENTIFIC NAME | WINGSPAN | | WEIGHT | | |
|---|---|---|---|---|---|
| | CM | IN | KG | LB | OZ |
| **1** Eurasian eagle-owl (*Bubo bubo*) | 75 | 29 | 4.20 | 9 | 4 |
| **2** Verraux's eagle-owl (*Bubo lacteus*) | 65 | 26 | 3.11 | 6 | 14 |
| **3** Snowy owl (*Bubo scandiacus*) | 70 | 28 | 2.95 | 6 | 8 |
| **4** Great horned owl (*Bubo virginianus*) | 60 | 24 | 2.50 | 5 | 8 |
| **5** Pel's fishing-owl (*Scotopelia peli*) | 63 | 25 | 2.32 | 5 | 2 |
| **6** Pharaoh eagle-owl (*Bubo ascalaphus*) | 50 | 20 | 2.30 | 5 | 1 |
| **7** Cape eagle-owl (*Bubo capensis*) | 58 | 23 | 1.80 | 3 | 15 |
| **8** Great grey owl (*Strix nebulosa*) | 69 | 27 | 1.70 | 3 | 12 |
| **9** Powerful owl (*Ninox strenua*) | 60 | 24 | 1.50 | 3 | 5 |
| **10** Ural owl (*Strix uralensis*) | 62 | 24 | 1.30 | 2 | 14 |

\* Some owls closely related to these species may be of similar size; most measurements are from female owls as they are usually larger

Source: Chris Mead

*Eagle-eyed hunter*
*The Eurasian eagle owl is a formidable predator, capable of preying on mammals as large as fox and deer.*

# Reptiles & Amphibians

## TOP 10 **LONGEST SNAKES**

| SNAKE / SCIENTIFIC NAME | MAXIMUM LENGTH M | FT |
|---|---|---|
| **1** Reticulated (royal) python (*Python regius*) | 10.7 | 35 |
| **2** Anaconda (*Eunectes murinus*) | 8.5 | 28 |
| **3** Indian python (*Python molurus molurus*) | 7.6 | 25 |
| **4** Diamond python (*Morelia spilota spilota*) | 6.4 | 21 |
| **5** King cobra (*Opiophagus hannah*) | 5.8 | 19 |
| **6** Boa constrictor (*Boa constrictor*) | 4.9 | 16 |
| **7** Bushmaster (*Lachesis muta*) | 3.7 | 12 |
| **8** Giant brown snake (*Oxyuranus scutellatus*) | 3.4 | 11 |
| **9** Diamondback rattlesnake (*Crotalus atrox*) | 2.7 | 9 |
| **10** Indigo or gopher snake (*Drymarchon corais*) | 2.4 | 8 |

Although the South American anaconda is sometimes claimed to be the longest snake, and reports of monsters up to 36.5 m (120 ft) have been published, none has never been authenticated – despite offers of substantial rewards for material evidence.

## THE 10 **MOST VENOMOUS REPTILES AND AMPHIBIANS**

| | CREATURE* | TOXIN | FATAL AMOUNT (MG)# |
|---|---|---|---|
| **1** | Indian cobra | Peak V | 0.009 |
| **2** | Mamba | Toxin 1 | 0.02 |
| **3** | Brown snake | Texilotoxin | 0.05 |
| **4** = | Inland taipan | Paradotoxin | 0.10 |
| = | Mamba | Dendrotoxin | 0.10 |
| **6** | Taipan | Taipoxin | 0.11 |
| **7** = | Indian cobra | Peak X | 0.12 |
| = | Poison arrow frog | Batrachotoxin | 0.12 |
| **9** | Indian cobra | Peak 1X | 0.17 |
| **10** | Krait | Bungarotoxin | 0.50 |

\* Excluding bacteria
# Quantity required to kill an average-sized human adult

The venom of these creatures is almost unbelievably powerful: mambas have a mortality rate approaching 100 per cent – 1 mg (the approximate weight of a banknote) of mamba Toxin 1 would be sufficient to kill 50 people. Deadly poisons such as strychnine (35 mg), and cyanide (700 mg), seem relatively innocuous in comparison.

## TOP 10 **COUNTRIES WITH THE MOST REPTILE SPECIES**

COUNTRY / REPTILE SPECIES

| | | | |
|---|---|---|---|
| **1** Australia 880 | | **6** Colombia 518 | |
| **2** Mexico 837 | | **7** China 424 | |
| **3** Indonesia 749 | | **8** Ecuador 419 | |
| **4** Brazil 651 | | **9** Malaysia 388 | |
| **5** India 521 | | **10** Madagascar 383 | |
| | | *UK 16* | |

Source: World Conservation Monitoring Centre of the United Nations Environment Programme (UNEP-WCMC)

*Friendly dragon*
*The bearded dragon, one of Australia's numerous native reptile species, has become popular worldwide as a pet.*

## TOP 10 **HEAVIEST TURTLES**

| TURTLE / SCIENTIFIC NAME | MAXIMUM WEIGHT | |
|---|---|---|
| | KG | LB |
| **1** Pacific leatherback turtle (*Dermochelys coriacea*)\* | 704.4 | 1,552 |
| **2** Atlantic leatherback turtle (*Dermochelys coriacea*)\* | 463.0 | 1,018 |
| **3** Green sea turtle (*Chelonia mydas*) | 355.3 | 783 |
| **4** Loggerhead turtle (*Caretta caretta*) | 257.8 | 568 |
| **5** Alligator snapping turtle (*Macroclemys temmincki*)# | 100.0 | 220 |
| **6** Flatback (sea) turtle (*Natator depressus*) | 78.2 | 171 |
| **7** Hawksbill (sea) turtle (*Eretmochelys imbricata*) | 62.7 | 138 |
| **8** Kemps Ridley turtle (*Lepidochelys kempi*) | 60.5 | 133 |
| **9** Olive Ridley turtle (*Lepidochelys olivacea*) | 49.9 | 110 |
| **10** Common snapping turtle (*Chelydra serpentina*)# | 38.5 | 85 |

\* One species, differing in size according to where they live
# Freshwater species

Source: Lucy T. Verma

The sizes and the longevity of turtles and tortoises are hotly debated by zoologists and there are many claims of even larger specimens among the 265 species of *Chelonia* (turtles and tortoises). All living examples would be dwarfed in size by prehistoric monster turtles such as *Stupendemys geographicus*, which measured up to 3 m (10 ft) in length and weighed over 2,040 kg (4,497 lb).

## TOP 10 **COUNTRIES WITH THE MOST AMPHIBIAN SPECIES**

| COUNTRY / AMPHIBIAN SPECIES | |
|---|---|
| **1** | Brazil 695 |
| **2** | Colombia 623 |
| **3** | Ecuador 428 |
| **4** | Peru 361 |
| **5** | Mexico 358 |
| **6** | China 340 |
| **7** | Venezuela 288 |
| **8** = | Indonesia 285 |
| = | USA 285 |
| **10** | Papua New Guinea 253 |
| | *UK 12* |

Source: World Conservation Monitoring Centre of the United Nations Environment Programme (UNEP-WCMC)

The world total of amphibian species (frogs toads, newts, salamanders and caecilians) is put at 6,074, so representatives of over 11 per cent of them are found in Brazil. In contrast, there are countries such as Jordan, and islands including Barbados, Cyprus and Malta, that have just one native amphibian species.

*Pacific leatherback*
*Numbers of Pacific leatherbacks, the largest of all turtles, have declined in recent years and the species is considered endangered.*

# Sea Creatures

## TOP 10 **FASTEST FISH**

FISH / SCIENTIFIC NAME / MAXIMUM RECORDED SPEED KM/H / MPH

**1** Sailfish (*Istiophorus platypterus*)  112 / 69

**2** Striped marlin (*Tetrapturus audax*)  80 / 50

**3** Wahoo (peto, jack mackerel)
(*Acanthocybium solandri*)  77 / 48

**4** Southern bluefin tuna (*Thunnus maccoyii*)  76 / 47

**5** Yellowfin tuna (*Thunnus albacares*)  74 / 46

**6** Blue shark (*Prionace glauca*)  69 / 43

**7** = Bonefish (*Albula vulpes*)  64 / 40
= Swordfish (*Xiphias gladius*)  64 / 40

**9** Tarpon (ox-eye herring)
(*Megalops cyprinoides*)  56 / 35

**10** Tiger shark (*Galeocerdo cuvier*)  53 / 33

Source: Lucy T. Verma

Flying fish are excluded: they have a top speed in the water of only 37 km/h (23 mph), but airborne they can reach 56 km/h (35 mph). Many sharks qualify for the list, but only two are listed here to prevent the Top 10 becoming overly shark-infested. Just in case you thought it was safe to go back in the water, the great white shark (of *Jaws* fame), the largest of all predatory fish, cruises at just 3.2 km/h (2 mph) but can manage bursts of 48 km/h (30 mph).

## TOP 10 **HEAVIEST SHARKS**

| | | MAXIMUM WEIGHT | |
|---|---|---|---|
| SHARK / SCIENTIFIC NAME | | KG | LB |
| **1** Whale shark (*Rhincodon typus*) | | 30,500 | 67,240 |
| **2** Basking shark (*Cetorhinus maximus*) | | 9,258 | 20,410 |
| **3** Great white shark (*Carcharodon carcharias*) | | 3,507 | 7,731 |
| **4** Greenland shark (*Somniosus microcephalus*) | | 1,009 | 2,224 |
| **5** Tiger shark (*Galeocerdo cuvieri*) | | 927 | 2,043 |
| **6** Great hammerhead shark (*Sphyrna mokarran*) | | 857 | 1,889 |
| **7** Six-gill shark (*Hexanchus griseus*) | | 602 | 1,327 |
| **8** Grey nurse shark (*Carcharias taurus*) | | 564 | 1,243 |
| **9** Mako shark (*Isurus oxyrinchus*) | | 554 | 1,221 |
| **10** Thresher shark (*Alopias vulpinus*) | | 498 | 1,097 |

Source: Lucy T. Verma

As well as specimens that have been caught, estimates have been made of beached examples, but such is the notoriety of sharks that many accounts of their size are exaggerated, and this list should be taken as an approximate ranking based on the best available evidence.

## TOP 10 **LONGEST-LIVED MARINE MAMMALS**\*

| MARINE MAMMAL / SCIENTIFIC NAME | LIFESPAN (YEARS) |
|---|---|
| **1** Bowhead whale (*Balaena mysticetus*) | 200 |
| **2** Dugong (*Dugong dugon*) | 60 |
| **3** Bottlenose dolphin (*Tursiops truncatus*) | 48 |
| **4** Grey seal (*Halichoerus grypus*) | 46 |
| **5** = Beluga whale (*Delphinapterus leucas*) | 30 |
| = Californian sea lion (*Zalophus californianus*) | 30 |
| = Walrus (*Odobenus rosmarus*) | 30 |
| **8** Canadian otter (*Lontra canadensis*) | 21 |
| **9** Polar bear (*Ursus maritimus*) | 20 |
| **10** Harbour porpoise (*Phocoena phocoena*) | 8 |

\* Longest-lived of each genus listed

Source: Lucy T. Verma

*Tail of a whale*
*Found exclusively in Arctic waters and second only to the blue whale in size, there are believed to be fewer than 10,000 bowhead whales worldwide, and it is considered as under threat of extinction.*

## TOP 10 **COUNTRIES WITH THE MOST FISH SPECIES**

| | COUNTRY | FISH SPECIES |
|---|---|---|
| **1** | India | 5,749 |
| **2** | Indonesia | 4,080 |
| **3** | Australia | 1,489 |
| **4** | USA | 1,101 |
| **5** | Japan | 1,007 |
| **6** | Philippines | 952 |
| **7** | Papua New Guinea | 858 |
| **8** | Taiwan | 816 |
| **9** | Mexico | 674 |
| **10** | Palau | 631 |
| | *UK* | *427* |

Source: World Conservation Monitoring Centre (WCMC)

*Left: Tropical totals*
*The warm waters of the tropics are host to the world's most diverse fish populations.*

## TOP 10 **HEAVIEST MARINE MAMMALS**

| MAMMAL / SCIENTIFIC NAME | LENGTH M | FT | WEIGHT (TONNES) |
|---|---|---|---|
| **1** Blue whale (*Balaenoptera musculus*) | 33.5 | 110.0 | 137.0 |
| **2** Bowhead whale (Greenland right) (*Balaena mysticetus*) | 20.0 | 65.0 | 86.0 |
| **3** Northern right whale (black right) (*Balaena glacialis*) | 18.6 | 60.0 | 77.7 |
| **4** Fin whale (common rorqual) (*Balaenoptera physalus*) | 25.0 | 82.0 | 63.4 |
| **5** Sperm whale (*Physeter catodon*) | 18.0 | 59.0 | 43.7 |
| **6** Grey whale (*Eschrichtius robustus*) | 14.0 | 46.0 | 34.9 |
| **7** Humpback whale (*Megaptera novaeangliae*) | 15.0 | 49.2 | 34.6 |
| **8** Sei whale (*Balaenoptera borealis*) | 18.5 | 60.0 | 29.4 |
| **9** Bryde's whale (*Balaenoptera edeni*) | 14.6 | 47.9 | 20.0 |
| **10** Baird's whale (*Berardius bairdii*) | 5.5 | 18.0 | 12.1 |

Source: Lucy T. Verma

Probably the largest animal that ever lived, the blue whale dwarfs even the other whales listed here, all but one of which far outweigh the biggest land animal, the elephant. The elephant seal, with a weight of 3.5 tonnes, is the largest marine mammal that is not a whale.

# Insects & Spiders

## TOP 10 FASTEST INSECT FLYERS

| SPECIES* / SCIENTIFIC NAME | MAXIMUM RECORDED SPEED | |
|---|---|---|
| | KM/H | MPH |
| **1** Hawkmoth (*Sphingidae*) | 53.6 | 33.3 |
| **2** = Deer bot fly (*Cephenemyia pratti*) | 48.0 | 30.0 |
| = West Indian butterfly (*Nymphalidae prepona*) | 48.0 | 30.0 |
| **4** Deer bot fly (*Chrysops*) | 40.0 | 25.0 |
| **5** West Indian butterfly (*Hesperiidae species*) | 30.0 | 18.6 |
| **6** Lesser Emperor dragonfly (*Anax parthenope*) | 28.6 | 17.8 |
| **7** = Dragonfly (*Aeschna*) | 25.2 | 15.6 |
| = Hornet (*Vespa*) | 25.2 | 15.6 |
| **9** = Honey bee (*Apis millefera*) | 22.4 | 13.9 |
| = Horsefly (*Tabanus bovinus*) | 22.4 | 13.9 |

\* Of those for which data available

Few accurate assessments of insect flying speeds have ever been attempted, and this Top 10 represents only the results of the handful of scientific studies that are widely recognized by entomologists. Some experts have also suggested that the male horsefly (*Hybomitra linei wrighti*) is capable of travelling at 145 km/h (90 mph) when in pursuit of a female, while there are exceptional one-off examples such as that of a dragonfly allegedly recorded in 1917 by Dr Robert J. Tilyard as flying at a speed of 98 km/h (61 mph). Many so-called records are clearly flawed, however. For example, Charles Townsend estimated the flying speed of the deer bot fly at an unbelievable 1,317 km/h (818 mph). If true, it would have broken the sound barrier!

**Buzzing along**
*Various species of hawkmoth have been claimed to achieve exceptional wingbeat and flying speeds.*

## TOP 10 LARGEST MOTHS

| MOTH / SCIENTIFIC NAME | WINGSPAN | |
|---|---|---|
| | MM | IN |
| **1** Atlas moth (*Attacus atlas*) | 300 | 11.8 |
| **2** Owlet moth (*Thysania agrippina*)* | 290 | 11.4 |
| **3** Haematopis grataria | 260 | 10.2 |
| **4** Hercules emperor moth (*Coscinocera hercules*) | 210 | 8.3 |
| **5** Malagasy silk moth (*Argema mitraei*) | 180 | 7.1 |
| **6** Eacles imperialis | 175 | 6.9 |
| **7** = Common emperor moth (*Bunaea alcinoe*) | 160 | 6.3 |
| = Giant peacock moth (*Saturnia pyri*) | 160 | 6.3 |
| **9** Gray moth (*Brahmaea wallichii*) | 155 | 6.1 |
| **10** = Black witch (*Ascalapha odorata*) | 150 | 5.9 |
| = Regal moth (*Citheronia regalis*) | 150 | 5.9 |
| = Polyphemus moth (*Antheraea polyphemus*) | 150 | 5.9 |

\* Exceptional specimen measured at 308 mm (12.2 in)

## TOP 10 SMALLEST BUTTERFLIES

| BUTTERFLY / SCIENTIFIC NAME | AVERAGE WINGSPAN | |
|---|---|---|
| | MM | IN |
| **1** Dwarf blue (*Brephidium barberae*) | 14 | 0.55 |
| **2** Western pygmy blue (*Brephidium exilis*) | 15 | 0.62 |
| **3** Western square-dotted blue (*Euphilotes battoides*) | 17 | 0.66 |
| **4** Pallid dotted-blue (*Euphilotes pallescens*) | 18 | 0.70 |
| **5** = Bernardino dotted-blue (*Euphilotes bernardino*) | 19 | 0.74 |
| = Cyna blue (*Zizula cyna*) | 19 | 0.74 |
| = Intermediate dotted-blue (*Euphilotes intermedia*) | 19 | 0.74 |
| = Little metalmark (*Calephelis virginiensis*) | 19 | 0.74 |
| = Rita dotted-blue (*Euphilotes rita*) | 19 | 0.74 |
| = Small dotted-blue (*Philotiella speciosa*) | 19 | 0.74 |
| = Telea hairstreak (*Chlorostrymon teleai*) | 19 | 0.74 |

## TOP 10 LARGEST BUTTERFLIES

| BUTTERFLY / SCIENTIFIC NAME | APPROX. WINGSPAN | |
|---|---|---|
| | MM | IN |
| **1** Queen Alexandra's birdwing (*Ornithoptera alexandrae*) | 280 | 11.0 |
| **2** African giant swallowtail (*Papilio antimachus*) | 230 | 9.1 |
| **3** Goliath birdwing (*Ornithoptera goliath*) | 210 | 8.3 |
| **4** = Buru opalescent birdwing (*Troides prattorum*) | 200 | 7.9 |
| = (Birdwing) Trogonoptera trojana | 200 | 7.9 |
| = (Birdwing) Troides hypolitus | 200 | 7.9 |
| **7** = Chimaera birdwing (*Ornithoptera chimaera*) | 190 | 7.5 |
| = Ornithoptera lydius | 190 | 7.5 |
| = Troides magellanus | 190 | 7.5 |
| = Troides miranda | 190 | 7.5 |

# TOP 10 **DEADLIEST SPIDERS**

COUNTRY / ESTIMATED PET REPTILE POPULATION (2005)

*Chinese whistlers*
*The total number of birds and other pets in China has escalated by*
*20 per cent in the past five years.*

**1** USA  18,371,000

**2** China  4,682,100

# TOP 10 **PET-OWNING COUNTRIES**\*

# TOP 10 **PET BIRD POPULATIONS**

# TOP 10 **PET FISH POPULATIONS**

COUNTRY / ESTIMATED PET FISH POPULATION (2005)

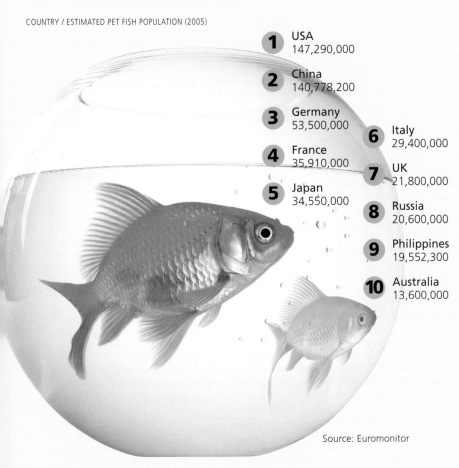

**1** USA 147,290,000

**2** China 140,778,200

**3** Germany 53,500,000

**4** France 35,910,000

**5** Japan 34,550,000

**6** Italy 29,400,000

**7** UK 21,800,000

**8** Russia 20,600,000

**9** Philippines 19,552,300

**10** Australia 13,600,000

Source: Euromonitor

# TOP 10 **PET DOG POPULATIONS**

COUNTRY / ESTIMATED PET DOG POPULATION (2005)

**1** USA 63,010,000

**2** Brazil 31,408,300

**3** China 26,153,600

**4** Mexico 16,581,800

**5** Japan 12,780,000

**6** Russia 11,200,000

**7** France 8,495,000

**8** Philippines 7,690,000

**9** Thailand 7,440,000

**10** South Africa 7,300,000

Source: Euromonitor

### Oldest Pet
Adwayita, an Aldabra Giant Tortoise that died at the Alipore Zoo, Kolkata (Calcutta) on 23 March 2006, was claimed to have been the pet of Robert Clive (1725–74), known as 'Clive of India'. If true, it could have been as much as 250 years old.

# TOP 10 **PET CAT POPULATIONS**

COUNTRY / ESTIMATED PET CAT POPULATION (2005)

**1** USA 81,420,000

**2** China 58,180,100

**3** Russia 17,100,000

**4** Brazil 12,234,000

**5** Japan 11,500,000

**6** France 9,960,000

**7** UK 9,200,000

**8** Germany 7,600,000

**9** Ukraine 7,470,000

**10** Italy 7,430,000

Source: Euromonitor

# Livestock

## TOP 10 **TYPES OF LIVESTOCK**

| | ANIMAL | WORLD STOCKS (2005) |
|---|---|---|
| **1** | Chickens | 16,695,877,000 |
| **2** | Cattle | 1,372,250,974 |
| **3** | Sheep | 1,079,005,851 |
| **4** | Ducks | 1,044,736,450 |
| **5** | Pigs | 960,847,340 |
| **6** | Goats | 808,903,601 |
| **7** | Rabbits | 535,379,620 |
| **8** | Geese | 301,905,920 |
| **9** | Turkeys | 276,821,650 |
| **10** | Buffaloes | 173,921,455 |

Source: Food and Agriculture Organization of the United Nations

The 23,249,649,861 animals accounted for by the Top 10 outnumber the world's human population by almost four to one. The world chicken population is more than double the human population, while the world's cattle population outnumbers the population of China. There are almost as many pigs in the world as the entire population of India, nearly enough turkeys for every citizen of the USA to have one each for Thanksgiving, and – though just outside the Top 10 – sufficient horses for every inhabitant of the UK to go riding.

## TOP 10 **CATTLE COUNTRIES**

| | COUNTRY | CATTLE (2005) |
|---|---|---|
| **1** | Brazil | 207,000,000 |
| **2** | India | 185,000,000 |
| **3** | China | 115,229,500 |
| **4** | USA | 95,848,000 |
| **5** | Argentina | 50,768,000 |
| **6** | Ethiopia | 38,500,000 |
| **7** | Sudan | 38,325,000 |
| **8** | Mexico | 31,800,000 |
| **9** | Australia | 27,730,000 |
| **10** | Colombia | 25,000,000 |
| | *UK* | *10,378,023* |
| | *World total* | *1,372,250,974* |

Source: Food and Agriculture Organization of the United Nations

Since the 1960s, growing and increasingly wealthy populations have raised the demand for milk and meat, prompting an increase in the world's cattle populations: the world total has risen by over 45 per cent since 1961, while that of China has more than doubled. India, which long held first place in this list, was overtaken by Brazil in 2003, prompting concern that the latter's increase was linked to severe deforestation to provide grazing lands.

## TOP 10 **PIG COUNTRIES**

| | COUNTRY | PIGS (2005) |
|---|---|---|
| **1** | China | 488,809,978 |
| **2** | USA | 60,644,500 |
| **3** | Brazil | 33,200,000 |
| **4** | Vietnam | 27,000,000 |
| **5** | Germany | 26,858,000 |
| **6** | Spain | 25,250,000 |
| **7** | Poland | 18,112,380 |
| **8** | France | 15,020,198 |
| **9** | Canada | 14,675,000 |
| **10** | Mexico | 14,625,199 |
| | *UK* | *4,851,000* |
| | *World total* | *960,847,340* |

Source: Food and Agricultural Organization of the United Nations

The distribution of the world's pig population is determined by cultural, religious and dietary factors – few pigs are found in African and Islamic countries, for example – with the result that there is a disproportionate concentration of pigs in those countries that do not have such prohibitions. Denmark, in 12th place, is the country in which the pig population (13,466,283) most outnumbers the human population (5,450,661).

## TOP 10 **BEEHIVE COUNTRIES**

COUNTRY / BEEHIVES (2005)

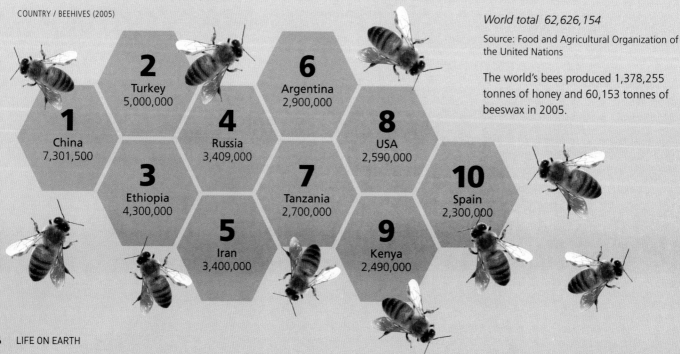

**2** Turkey 5,000,000

**6** Argentina 2,900,000

**1** China 7,301,500

**4** Russia 3,409,000

**8** USA 2,590,000

**3** Ethiopia 4,300,000

**7** Tanzania 2,700,000

**10** Spain 2,300,000

**5** Iran 3,400,000

**9** Kenya 2,490,000

*World total  62,626,154*

Source: Food and Agricultural Organization of the United Nations

The world's bees produced 1,378,255 tonnes of honey and 60,153 tonnes of beeswax in 2005.

*Horses for courses*
Mongolia figures in few Top 10 lists, but is noted for its presence among the world's leading horse-owners. The horse figures prominently in Mongolian culture, with cross-country horse-racing a major part of national festivals.

## TOP 10 **HORSE COUNTRIES**

| COUNTRY | HORSES (2005) |
| --- | --- |
| **1** China | 7,641,320 |
| **2** Mexico | 6,260,000 |
| **3** Brazil | 5,700,000 |
| **4** USA | 5,300,000 |
| **5** Argentina | 3,655,000 |
| **6** Colombia | 2,750,000 |
| **7** Mongolia | 2,005,300 |
| **8** Russia | 1,505,000 |
| **9** Ethiopia | 1,500,000 |
| **10** Kazakhstan | 1,120,000 |
| *UK* | *184,000* |
| *World total* | *54,701,074* |

Source: Food and Agricultural Organization of the United Nations

## TOP 10 **GOAT COUNTRIES**

| COUNTRY | GOATS (2005) |
| --- | --- |
| **1** China | 195,758,954 |
| **2** India | 120,000,000 |
| **3** Pakistan | 56,700,000 |
| **4** Sudan | 42,000,000 |
| **5** Bangladesh | 36,900,000 |
| **6** Nigeria | 28,000,000 |
| **7** Iran | 26,500,000 |
| **8** Indonesia | 13,182,100 |
| **9** Somalia | 12,700,000 |
| **10** Tanzania | 12,550,000 |
| *World total* | *808,903,601* |

Source: Food and Agriculture Organization of the United Nations

The goat is one of the most widely distributed of all domesticated animals, its resilience to diseases and adaptability to harsh conditions making it ideally suited to environments that are unsuitable for livestock such as cattle or sheep.

## TOP 10 **SHEEP COUNTRIES**

| COUNTRY | SHEEP (2005) |
| --- | --- |
| **1** China | 170,882,215 |
| **2** Australia | 102,700,000 |
| **3** India | 62,500,000 |
| **4** Iran | 54,000,000 |
| **5** Sudan | 48,000,000 |
| **6** New Zealand | 39,928,000 |
| **7** UK | 35,253,048 |
| **8** South Africa | 25,316,424 |
| **9** Turkey | 25,201,156 |
| **10** Pakistan | 24,900,000 |
| *USA* | *6,135,000* |
| *World total* | *1,079,005,851* |

Source: Food and Agriculture Organization of the United Nations

This is one of the few world lists in which the UK ranks considerably higher than the USA. The 1900 census put the USA's sheep stocks at an all-time level of over 61 million, since when they have been in decline.

# Living off the Land

## TOP 10 **CEREAL CROPS**

| CROP | PRODUCTION 2005 (TONNES) |
|---|---|
| **1** Maize | 701,666,160 |
| **2** Wheat | 629,566,041 |
| **3** Rice (paddy) | 618,440,644 |
| **4** Barley | 139,043,947 |
| **5** Sorghum | 58,688,212 |
| **6** Millet | 28,559,553 |
| **7** Oats | 23,953,749 |
| **8** Rye | 15,515,206 |
| **9** Triticale (wheat/rye hybrid) | 13,499,822 |
| **10** Mixed grain | 4,841,314 |
| *Total of all cereals (including those not in Top 10)* | *2,239,399,875* |

Source: Food and Agriculture Organization of the United Nations

## TOP 10 **CEREAL-PRODUCING COUNTRIES**

| COUNTRY | PRODUCTION 2005 (TONNES) |
|---|---|
| **1** China | 427,613,440 |
| **2** USA | 366,515,556 |
| **3** India | 235,913,000 |
| **4** Russia | 76,420,000 |
| **5** Indonesia | 65,998,299 |
| **6** France | 64,129,852 |
| **7** Brazil | 55,724,261 |
| **8** Canada | 50,362,600 |
| **9** Germany | 45,995,000 |
| **10** Bangladesh | 41,586,000 |
| *UK* | *21,059,000* |
| *World total* | *2,239,399,875* |

Source: Food and Agriculture Organization of the United Nations

*Rice bowl*
*China's production of rice is 185 million tonnes annually, 30 per cent of the world total.*

## TOP 10 **NON-FOOD CROPS**

| CROP | PRODUCTION 2005 (TONNES) |
|---|---|
| **1** Cotton | 68,297,507 |
| **2** Rubber | 9,123,590 |
| **3** Coffee | 7,779,495 |
| **4** Tobacco | 6,564,017 |
| **5** Tea | 3,436,180 |
| **6** Jute | 2,861,982 |
| **7** Linseed | 2,801,277 |
| **8** Castor beans | 1,393,812 |
| **9** Coir | 954,290 |
| **10** Flax | 887,227 |

Source: Food and Agriculture Organization of the United Nations

# TOP 10 **FRUIT-PRODUCING COUNTRIES**

COUNTRY / PRODUCTION* 2005 (TONNES)

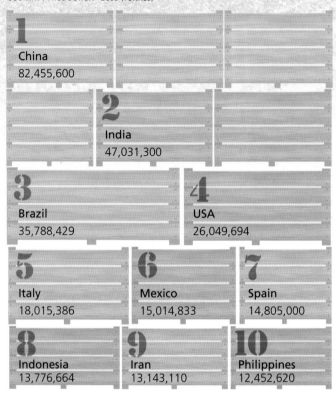

**1** China
82,455,600

**2** India
47,031,300

**3** Brazil
35,788,429

**4** USA
26,049,694

**5** Italy
18,015,386

**6** Mexico
15,014,833

**7** Spain
14,805,000

**8** Indonesia
13,776,664

**9** Iran
13,143,110

**10** Philippines
12,452,620

UK 281,050   World total 504,966,608

* Excluding melons

Source: Food and Agriculture Organization of the United Nations

# TOP 10 **NUT-PRODUCING COUNTRIES**

| | COUNTRY | PRODUCTION 2005 (TONNES) |
|---|---|---|
| 1 | Mexico | 95,150 |
| 2 | Indonesia | 90,000 |
| 3 | Ethiopia | 75,000 |
| 4 | China | 45,000 |
| 5 | Australia | 39,500 |
| 6= | Azerbaijan | 28,000 |
| | Russia | 28,000 |
| 8 | Guatemala | 24,000 |
| 9 | Thailand | 23,000 |
| 10 | Portugal | 21,000 |
| | *World total* | *757,810* |

Source: Food and Agriculture Organization of the United Nations

# TOP 10 **VEGETABLE-PRODUCING COUNTRIES**

| | COUNTRY | PRODUCTION* 2005 (TONNES) |
|---|---|---|
| 1 | China | 435,024,075 |
| 2 | India | 80,528,500 |
| 3 | USA | 36,941,115 |
| 4 | Turkey | 25,395,111 |
| 5 | Egypt | 16,165,402 |
| 6 | Russia | 16,144,000 |
| 7 | Italy | 16,013,954 |
| 8 | Iran | 13,495,000 |
| 9 | Spain | 12,635,273 |
| 10 | South Korea | 12,160,100 |
| | *UK* | *2,659,813* |
| | *World total* | *882,452,051* |

* Including watermelons; only vegetables grown for human consumption, excluding crops from private gardens

Source: Food and Agriculture Organization of the United Nations

# TOP 10 **VEGETABLE CROPS**

| | CROP* | PRODUCTION 2005 (TONNES) |
|---|---|---|
| 1 | Sugar cane | 1,291,685,924 |
| 2 | Potatoes | 323,102,918 |
| 3 | Sugar beets | 240,984,299 |
| 4 | Soybeans | 214,347,289 |
| 5 | Sweet potatoes | 129,392,309 |
| 6 | Cabbages | 69,916,555 |
| 7 | Onions (dry) | 57,400,277 |
| 8 | Cucumbers/gherkins | 41,836,847 |
| 9 | Yams | 39,856,954 |
| 10 | Aubergines | 30,477,775 |

Total of all vegetables (including those not in Top 10)   882,452,051

* Excluding cereals; including only vegetables grown for human and animal consumption

Source: Food and Agriculture Organization of the United Nations

# TOP 10 **NUT CROPS**

CROP / PRODUCTION 2005 (TONNES)

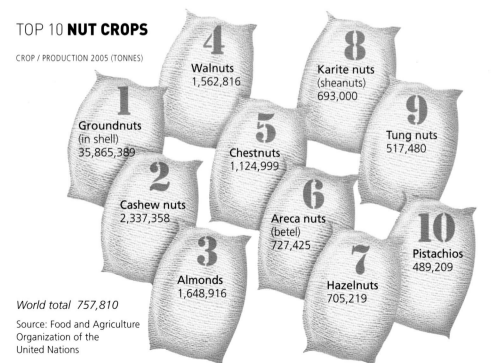

**1** Groundnuts (in shell)
35,865,389

**2** Cashew nuts
2,337,358

**3** Almonds
1,648,916

**4** Walnuts
1,562,816

**5** Chestnuts
1,124,999

**6** Areca nuts (betel)
727,425

**7** Hazelnuts
705,219

**8** Karite nuts (sheanuts)
693,000

**9** Tung nuts
517,480

**10** Pistachios
489,209

World total  757,810

Source: Food and Agriculture Organization of the United Nations

# Trees

## TOP 10 COUNTRIES WITH THE LARGEST AREAS OF FOREST

| COUNTRY | SQ KM | % OF TOTAL | SQ MILES |
|---|---|---|---|
| **1** Russia | 8,087,900 | 47.9 | 3,122,756 |
| **2** Brazil | 4,776,980 | 57.2 | 1,844,402 |
| **3** Canada | 3,101,340 | 33.6 | 1,197,434 |
| **4** USA | 3,030,890 | 33.1 | 1,170,233 |
| **5** China | 1,972,900 | 21.2 | 761,741 |
| **6** Australia | 1,636,780 | 21.3 | 631,964 |
| **7** Dem. Rep. of Congo | 1,336,100 | 58.9 | 515,871 |
| **8** Indonesia | 884,950 | 48.8 | 341,681 |
| **9** Peru | 687,420 | 53.7 | 265,414 |
| **10** India | 677,010 | 22.8 | 261,395 |
| *UK* | *28,450* | *11.8* | *10,985* |
| *World total* | *39,520,250* | *30.3* | *15,258,855* |

Source: Food and Agriculture Organization of the United Nations, *Global Forest Resources Assessment 2005*

## TOP 10 DEFORESTING COUNTRIES*

| COUNTRY | ANNUAL FOREST LOSS 2000–05 SQ KM | SQ MILES |
|---|---|---|
| **1** Brazil | 31,030 | 11,980 |
| **2** Indonesia | 18,710 | 7,223 |
| **3** Sudan | 5,890 | 2,274 |
| **4** Myanmar | 4,660 | 1,799 |
| **5** Zambia | 4,450 | 1,718 |
| **6** Tanzania | 4,120 | 1,590 |
| **7** Nigeria | 4,100 | 1,583 |
| **8** Dem. Rep. of Congo | 3,190 | 1,231 |
| **9** Zimbabwe | 3,130 | 1,208 |
| **10** Venezuela | 2,880 | 1,111 |
| *World total* | *73,170* | *28,251* |

\* Countries for which data available

Source: Food and Agriculture Organization of the United Nations, *Global Forest Resources Assessment 2005*

Some 42,510 sq km (16,413 sq miles) of forest were lost in South America each year between 2000 and 2005, 40,400 sq km (15,598 sq miles) in Africa and 38,400 sq km (14,826 sq miles) in Asia. The total global loss during the period was 439,020 sq km (169,506 sq miles), an area equivalent to more than three times that of the UK.

## TOP 10 TIMBER-PRODUCING COUNTRIES

COUNTRY / WOOD PRODUCTION* 2005 / M³/FT³

\* Roundwood and fuel

**1** USA 540,838,000 / 19,099,515,493

**2** Brazil 290,476,000 / 10,258,064,082

**3** Canada 223,500,000 / 7,892,828,745

**4** Russia 180,000,000 / 6,356,640,600

**5** China 135,435,000 / 4,782,842,331

**6** Ethiopia 111,861,000 / 3,950,334,300

**7** Nigeria 86,627,000 / 3,059,203,918

**8** Dem. Rep. of Congo 82,994,000 / 2,930,905,721

**9** Sweden 76,780,000 / 2,711,460,362

**10** Finland 64,295,000 / 2,270,556,707

*UK 8,895,000 / 314,123,989*

Source: Food and Agriculture Organization of the United Nations, *Global Forest Resources Assessment 2005*

## TOP 10 REFORESTING COUNTRIES*

| COUNTRY | ANNUAL FOREST GAIN 2000–05 SQ KM | SQ MILES |
|---|---|---|
| **1** China | 40,480 | 15,629 |
| **2** Spain | 2,960 | 1,142 |
| **3** Vietnam | 2,410 | 930 |
| **4** USA | 1,590 | 613 |
| **5** Italy | 1,060 | 409 |
| **6** Chile | 570 | 220 |
| **7** Cuba | 560 | 216 |
| **8** Bulgaria | 500 | 193 |
| **9** France | 410 | 158 |
| **10** Portugal | 400 | 154 |
| *UK* | *100* | *38* |

\* Countries for which data available

Source: Food and Agriculture Organization of the United Nations, *Global Forest Resources Assessment 2005*

*Trees top*
*Suriname has a greater proportion of forest areas than any other country, its 16,000-sq km (6,178-sq mile) Central Suriname Nature Reserve, an unspoilt tropical rainforest, being designated as UNESCO World Heritage Site in 2000.*

## TOP 10 **MOST FORESTED COUNTRIES**

| | COUNTRY | AREA SQ KM | SQ MILES | % FOREST COVER |
|---|---|---|---|---|
| **1** | Suriname | 147,760 | 57,050 | 94.7 |
| **2** | French Guiana | 80,630 | 31,131 | 91.9 |
| **3** | Micronesia | 630 | 243 | 90.6 |
| **4** | American Samoa | 180 | 69 | 89.4 |
| **5** | Seychelles | 400 | 154 | 88.9 |
| **6** | Palau | 400 | 154 | 87.6 |
| **7** | Gabon | 217,750 | 84,074 | 84.5 |
| **8** | Pitcairn | 40 | 15 | 83.3 |
| **9** | Turks and Caicos Islands | 340 | 131 | 80.0 |
| **10** | Solomon Islands | 21,720 | 8,386 | 77.6 |
| | *UK* | *28,450* | *10,985* | *11.8* |
| | *World total* | *39,520,250* | *15,258,855* | *30.3* |

Source: Food and Agriculture Organization of the United Nations, *Global Forest Resources Assessment 2005*

These are the 10 countries with the greatest area of forest and woodland as a percentage of their total land area. Although deforestation in tropical countries remains an environmental concern, recent research has indicated that reforestation is also taking place and the 'forest identity' in 22 of the world's 50 most-forested countries has actually increased during the past 15 years.

## TOP 10 **TALLEST TREES IN THE UK***

| | TREE / LOCATION | HEIGHT M | FT |
|---|---|---|---|
| **1** | Douglas fir# Dunans Estate, Argyll and Bute, Scotland | 62 | 203 |
| **2** | Grand fir Ardkinglas Woodland Garden, Argyll and Bute, Scotland | 61 | 200 |
| **3** | Sitka spruce Randolph's Leap, Moray, Scotland | 58 | 190 |
| **4** | Giant sequoia# Benmore Botanical Garden, Argyll and Bute, Scotland | 53 | 174 |
| **5 =** | Norway spruce Reelig Glen Wood, Moniack, Highland, Scotland | 52 | 171 |
| **=** | Noble fir Ardkinglas Woodland Garden, Argyll and Bute, Scotland | 52 | 171 |
| **7** | Western hemlock Benmore Botanical Garden, Argyll and Bute, Scotland | 51 | 167 |
| **8** | European silver fir Benmore Botanical Garden, Argyll and Bute, Scotland | 50 | 164 |
| **9** | Nordmann fir Cragside, Northumberland | 48 | 157 |
| **10** | Coastal redwood Bodnant Garden, Colwyn Bay, Conwy, Wales | 47 | 154 |

* Tallest known example of each of the 10 tallest species
# Further examples of same species match this height

Source: The Tree Register of the British Isles

# THE HUMAN WORLD

# The Human Body

## TOP 10 **MOST COMMON ELEMENTS IN THE HUMAN BODY**

| | | AVERAGE ADULT TOTAL | |
|---|---|---|---|
| | ELEMENT | G | OZ |
| 1 | Oxygen* | 43,000 | 1,517 |
| 2 | Carbon | 16,000 | 564 |
| 3 | Hydrogen* | 7,000 | 247 |
| 4 | Nitrogen | 1,800 | 63 |
| 5 | Calcium | 1,200 | 42 |
| 6 | Phosphorus | 780 | 28 |
| 7 | Sulphur | 140 | 5 |
| 8 | Potassium | 110–140 | 4–5 |
| 9 | Sodium | 100 | 4 |
| 10 | Chlorine | 95 | 3 |

\* Mostly combined as water

The Top 10 elements account for more than 99 per cent of the total, the balance comprising minute quantities of metallic elements including iron, zinc, tin and aluminium.

## TOP 10 **LARGEST HUMAN ORGANS**

| | ORGAN | | AVERAGE WEIGHT G | OZ |
|---|---|---|---|---|
| 1 | Skin | | 10,886 | 384.0 |
| 2 | Liver | | 1,560 | 55.0 |
| 3 | Brain | male | 1,408 | 49.7 |
| | | female | 1,263 | 44.6 |
| 4 | Lungs | right | 580 | 20.5 |
| | | left | 510 | 18.0 |
| | | total | 1,090 | 38.5 |
| 5 | Heart | male | 315 | 11.1 |
| | | female | 265 | 9.3 |
| 6 | Kidneys | right | 140 | 4.9 |
| | | left | 150 | 5.3 |
| | | total | 290 | 10.2 |
| 7 | Spleen | | 170 | 6.0 |
| 8 | Pancreas | | 98 | 3.5 |
| 9 | Thyroid | | 35 | 1.2 |
| 10 | Prostate | male only | 20 | 0.7 |

This list is based on average immediate post-mortem weights. The skin heads the list, at 16 per cent of a body's total weight, an average of 10.9 kg (24 lb).

## TOP 10 **LONGEST BONES IN THE HUMAN BODY**

BONE / AVERAGE LENGTH CM/IN

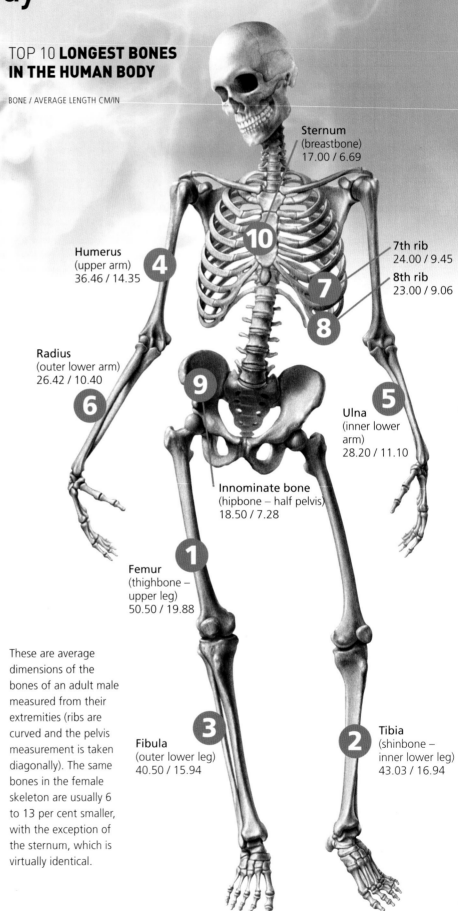

Sternum (breastbone) 17.00 / 6.69

7th rib 24.00 / 9.45

8th rib 23.00 / 9.06

Humerus (upper arm) 36.46 / 14.35

Radius (outer lower arm) 26.42 / 10.40

Ulna (inner lower arm) 28.20 / 11.10

Innominate bone (hipbone – half pelvis) 18.50 / 7.28

Femur (thighbone – upper leg) 50.50 / 19.88

Fibula (outer lower leg) 40.50 / 15.94

Tibia (shinbone – inner lower leg) 43.03 / 16.94

These are average dimensions of the bones of an adult male measured from their extremities (ribs are curved and the pelvis measurement is taken diagonally). The same bones in the female skeleton are usually 6 to 13 per cent smaller, with the exception of the sternum, which is virtually identical.

## TOP 10 **OLDEST PEOPLE**

| | NAME / COUNTRY | BORN | DIED | YEARS | AGE MONTHS | DAYS |
|---|---|---|---|---|---|---|
| 1 | Jeanne Calment (France) | 21 Feb 1875 | 4 Aug 1997 | 122 | 5 | 14 |
| 2 | Sarah Knauss (USA) | 24 Sep 1880 | 30 Dec 1999 | 119 | 3 | 6 |
| 3 | Lucy Hannah (USA) | 16 Jul 1875 | 21 Mar 1993 | 117 | 8 | 5 |
| 4 | Marie-Louise Meilleur (Canada) | 29 Aug 1880 | 16 Apr 1998 | 117 | 7 | 18 |
| 5 | María Capovilla (Ecuador) | 14 Sep 1889 | 27 Aug 2006 | 116 | 11 | 13 |
| 6 | Tane Ikai (Japan) | 18 Jan 1879 | 12 Jul 1995 | 116 | 5 | 24 |
| 7 | Elizabeth Bolden (USA) | 15 Aug 1890 | 11 Dec 2006 | 116 | 3 | 26 |
| 8 | Maggie Barnes (USA) | 6 Mar 1882 | 19 Jan 1998 | 115 | 10 | 13 |
| 9 | Charlotte Hughes (UK) | 1 Aug 1877 | 17 Mar 1993 | 115 | 7 | 16 |
| 10 | Christian Mortensen* (Denmark/USA) | 16 Aug 1882 | 25 Apr 1998 | 115 | 7 | 9 |

* Oldest male – all others female

This list is based on the longevity of supercentenarians (those aged over 110) for whom there is undisputed evidence of their birth date. It thus excludes alleged oldest man Shigechiyo Izumi (Japan), as there is doubt as to whether he was born in 1865 or 1880, and Carrie C. White (USA), whose 1874 birth date cannot be verified, as well as earlier claims like that of Thomas Parr (UK), said to have been 152 at his death in 1635.

## TOP 10 **TALLEST PEOPLE**

| | NAME / DATES / COUNTRY | M | HEIGHT CM | FT | IN |
|---|---|---|---|---|---|
| 1 | Robert Pershing Wadlow (1918–40) USA | 2 | 72 | 8 | 11.1 |
| 2 | John William Rogan (1868–1905) USA | 2 | 68 | 8 | 9.8 |
| 3 | John Aasen (1887–1938) USA | 2 | 67 | 8 | 9.7 |
| 4 | John F. Carroll (1932–69) USA | 2 | 64 | 8 | 7.6 |
| 5 | Al Tomaini (1918–62) USA | 2 | 55 | 8 | 4.4 |
| 6 | Trijntje Keever* (1616–33) Netherlands | 2 | 54 | 8 | 3.3 |
| 7 | Edouard Beaupré (1881–1904) Canada | 2 | 50 | 8 | 2.5 |
| 8 | =Bernard Coyne (1897–1921) USA | 2 | 49 | 8 | 1.2 |
| | =Don Koehler (1925–81) USA | 2 | 49 | 8 | 1.2 |
| 10 | =Jeng Jinlian* (1964–82) China | 2 | 48 | 8 | 1.1 |
| | =Väinö Myllyrinne (1909–63) Finland | 2 | 48 | 8 | 1.1 |

* Female – all others male

*Made to measure*
*Measured shortly before his death at the age of 22, Robert Wadlow still holds the record as the world's tallest person.*

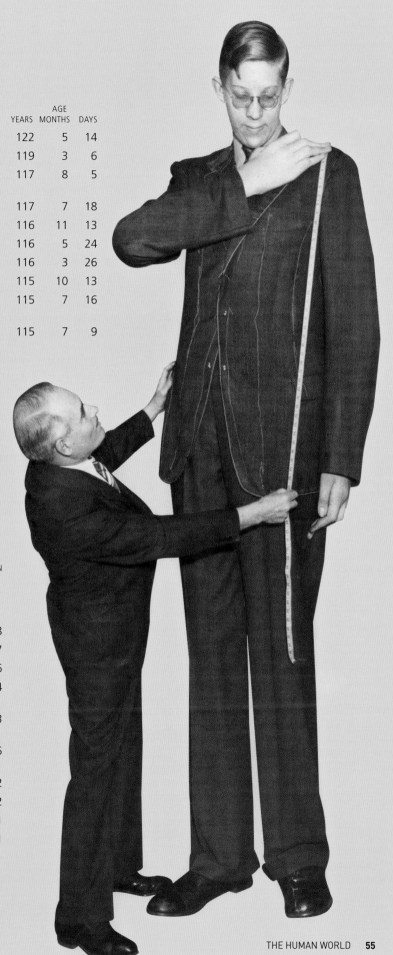

# Health & Healthcare

## TOP 10 MOST COMMON REASONS FOR VISITS TO THE DOCTOR IN THE UK

COMPLAINT / RATE*

**1** Hypertensive diseases 946

**2** Dermatitis and eczema 897

**3** Skin disorders 884

**4** Acute upper-respiratory infections 802

**5** Disorders of the eye 792

**6** Disorders of the ear and mastoid process 731

**7** Other acute lower-respiratory infections 716

**8** Chronic lower-respiratory diseases 696

**9** Dorsopathies (back problems) 640

**10** Non-inflammatory female disorders 543

* Patients consulting per 10,000

Source: Office of Health Economics, *Compendium of Health Statistics*, 17th Edition, 2005–2006

## TOP 10 COUNTRIES WITH THE MOST DENTISTS

| | COUNTRY | DENTISTS PER 1,000 |
|---|---|---|
| 1 | USA | 1.63 |
| 2 | Jordan | 1.29 |
| 3 | = Estonia | 1.28 |
| | = Finland | 1.28 |
| 5 | Lebanon | 1.21 |
| 6 | = Israel | 1.17 |
| | = Seychelles | 1.17 |
| 8 | Uruguay | 1.16 |
| 9 | Greece | 1.13 |
| 10 | Brazil | 1.11 |
| | *UK* | *1.01* |

Source: World Health Organization, *The World Health Report 2006*

## TOP 10 COUNTRIES WITH THE MOST NURSES

| | COUNTRY | NURSES PER 1,000 |
|---|---|---|
| 1 | San Marino | 95.48 |
| 2 | Ireland | 15.20 |
| 3 | Norway | 14.84 |
| 4 | Finland | 14.33 |
| 5 | Netherlands | 13.73 |
| 6 | Iceland | 13.63 |
| 7 | UK | 12.12 |
| 8 | Belarus | 11.63 |
| 9 | Switzerland | 10.75 |
| 10 | Denmark | 10.36 |

Source: World Health Organization, *The World Health Report 2006*

## TOP 10 COUNTRIES WITH THE MOST DOCTORS

COUNTRY / DOCTORS PER 1,000

| | | |
|---|---|---|
| 1 | San Marino | 47.35 |
| 2 | Cuba | 5.91 |
| 3 | Monaco | 5.81 |
| 4 | St Lucia | 5.17 |
| 5 | Belarus | 4.55 |
| 6 | Belgium | 4.49 |
| 7 | Estonia | 4.48 |
| 8 | Greece | 4.38 |
| 9 | Russia | 4.25 |
| 10 | Italy | 4.20 |
| | *UK* | *2.30* |

Source: World Health Organization, *The World Health Report 2006*

## THE 10 MOST UNDERNOURISHED COUNTRIES

| | COUNTRY | % OF POPULATION UNDERNOURISHED 2000–03* |
|---|---|---|
| 1 | Eritrea | 73 |
| 2 | Dem. Rep. of Congo | 72 |
| 3 | Burundi | 67 |
| 4 | Comoros | 62 |
| 5 | Tajikistan | 61 |
| 6 | Sierra Leone | 50 |
| 7 | = Haiti | 47 |
| | = Zambia | 47 |
| 9 | Ethiopia | 46 |
| 10 | = Central African Republic | 45 |
| | = Mozambique | 45 |
| | = Zimbabwe | 45 |

* Food intake that is insufficient to meet dietary requirements continuously

Source: United Nations, *Human Development Report 2006*

## TOP 10 MOST OBESE COUNTRIES

| | COUNTRY | % OF OBESE ADULTS* MEN | WOMEN |
|---|---|---|---|
| 1 | Nauru | 80.2 | 78.6 |
| 2 | Tonga | 46.6 | 70.3 |
| 3 | Samoa | 32.9 | 63.0 |
| 4 | Jordan# | 32.7 | 59.8 |
| 5 | Nieue | 15.0 | 46.0 |
| 6 | Qatar | 34.6 | 45.3 |
| 7 | French Polynesia | 36.3 | 44.3 |
| 8 | Saudi Arabia | 26.4 | 44.0 |
| 9 | Palestine | 23.9 | 42.5 |
| 10 | United Arab Emirates | 25.9 | 39.9 |
| | *England* | *22.2* | *23.0* |
| | *Scotland* | *19.0* | *22.0* |
| | *Wales* | *17.0* | *18.0* |

* Ranked by percentage of obese women (those with a BMI greater than 30) in those countries and latest year for which data available
# Urban population only

Source: International Obesity Task Force (IOTF)

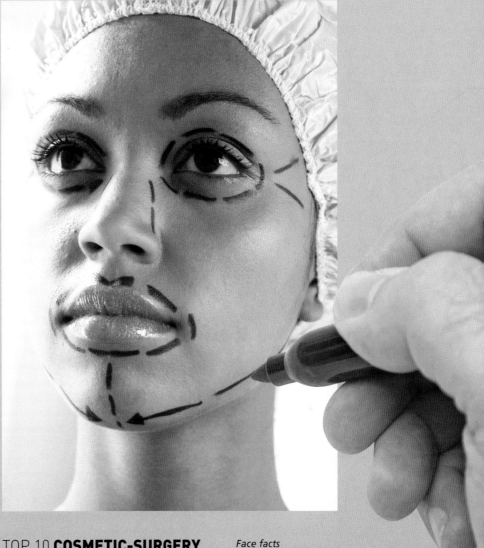

## TOP 10 COSMETIC-SURGERY PROCEDURES PERFORMED IN THE USA

| | PROCEDURE | NO. PERFORMED (2006) |
|---|---|---|
| 1 | Liposuction | 403,604 |
| 2 | Breast augmentation | 383,886 |
| 3 | Cosmetic eyelid surgery | 209,999 |
| 4 | Nose reshaping | 141,912 |
| 5 | Tummy tuck | 172,457 |
| 6 | Breast reduction (women) | 145,822 |
| 7 | Facelift | 138,245 |
| 8 | Breast lift | 125,896 |
| 9 | Forehead lift | 54,149 |
| 10 | Breast reduction (men) | 23,670 |

Source: American Society for Aesthetic Plastic Surgery

*Face facts*
*Over 11 million cosmetic-surgery procedures a year, at a cost of over $8 billion, are undertaken in the USA alone.*

In 2006, 1,922,788 and 9,533,980 non-surgical procedures were performed in the USA. The latter category included 3,181,592 botox injections – a remarkable 4,883 per cent increase over the 65,157 recorded in 1997. The total cost was put at $7,632,270,642 for surgical and $4,542,014,327 non-surgical, a total of $12,174,284,969. Following extensive publicity of unsatisfactory lip-augmentation procedures, the number plummeted by 83 per cent from the 50,237 performed in 2005.

# Birth & Life Expectancy

## TOP 10 **YEARS WITH MOST BIRTHS IN THE UK**

| | YEAR | BIRTHS |
|---|---|---|
| 1 | 1920 | 1,194,068 |
| 2 | 1903 | 1,183,627 |
| 3 | 1904 | 1,181,770 |
| 4 | 1902 | 1,174,639 |
| 5 | 1908 | 1,173,759 |
| 6 | 1906 | 1,170,622 |
| 7 | 1905 | 1,163,535 |
| 8 | 1899 | 1,163,279 |
| 9 | 1901 | 1,162,975 |
| 10 | 1900 | 1,159,922 |

The total number of births in the UK more than doubled in the 19th century. High figures were also experienced in the early years of the 20th century, with an all-time peak in 1920, the so-called post-World War I 'bulge'. This was paralleled in 1947 by a post-World War II surge to 1,025,000 (in 1941 the figure had been just 703,858).

## TOP 10 **COUNTRIES WITH THE HIGHEST BIRTH RATES**

| | COUNTRY | ESTIMATED BIRTH RATE (LIVE BIRTHS PER 1,000, 2008) |
|---|---|---|
| 1 | Niger | 49.62 |
| 2 | Mali | 49.38 |
| 3 | Uganda | 48.15 |
| 4 | Afghanistan | 45.82 |
| 5 | Sierra Leone | 45.07 |
| 6 | Burkina Faso | 44.93 |
| 7 | Chad | 44.88 |
| 8 | Angola | 44.09 |
| 9 | Somalia | 44.08 |
| 10 | Dem. Rep. of Congo | 42.96 |
| | UK | 10.65 |
| | World average | 20.00 |

Source: US Census Bureau, International Data Base

The countries with the highest birth rates are among the poorest countries in the world. In these countries, people often deliberately have large families so that the children can help earn income for the family when they are older. The 10 countries with the highest birth rates therefore corresponds very closely with the list of countries with the highest fertility rates – the average number of children born to each woman in the country.

## TOP 10 **COUNTRIES WITH THE MOST BIRTHS**

| | COUNTRY | ESTIMATED BIRTHS (2008) |
|---|---|---|
| 1 | India | 25,508,469 |
| 2 | China | 18,234,912 |
| 3 | Nigeria | 5,528,564 |
| 4 | Pakistan | 4,900,375 |
| 5 | Indonesia | 4,569,738 |
| 6 | Bangladesh | 4,431,364 |
| 7 | USA | 4,308,233 |
| 8 | Brazil | 3,078,214 |
| 9 | Ethiopia | 2,879,751 |
| 10 | Dem. Rep. of Congo | 2,861,321 |
| | UK | 649,053 |
| | World | 133,975,284 |

Source: US Census Bureau, International Data Base

## THE 10 **COUNTRIES WITH THE LOWEST BIRTH RATES**

| | COUNTRY | ESTIMATED BIRTH RATE (LIVE BIRTHS PER 1,000, 2008) |
|---|---|---|
| 1 | Germany | 8.18 |
| 2 | Andorra | 8.23 |
| 3 | Italy | 8.36 |
| 4 | Austria | 8.66 |
| 5 | Bosnia and Herzegovina | 8.82 |
| 6 | Czech Republic | 8.89 |
| 7 | =Singapore | 8.99 |
| | =Slovenia | 8.99 |
| 9 | Lithuania | 9.00 |
| 10 | Japan | 9.07 |

Source: US Census Bureau, International Data Base

Although not independent countries, several places record similarly low rates, among them Hong Kong (7.37) and Guernsey (8.57).

# TOP 10 COUNTRIES WITH THE HIGHEST LIFE EXPECTANCY

| | COUNTRY | LIFE EXPECTANCY AT BIRTH (2008) |
|---|---|---|
| 1 | Andorra | 83.53 |
| 2 | Singapore | 81.89 |
| 3 | San Marino | 81.88 |
| 4 | Japan | 81.44 |
| 5 | = Sweden | 80.74 |
| | = Switzerland | 80.74 |
| 7 | Australia | 80.73 |
| 8 | Iceland | 80.55 |
| 9 | Canada | 80.46 |
| 10 | Italy | 80.07 |
| | *UK* | *78.85* |
| | *World average* | *66.10* |

Source: US Census Bureau, International Data Base

Several other territories, including Hong Kong, the Cayman Islands, Gibraltar and Guernsey, all have life expectancies of more than 80 years.

# THE 10 COUNTRIES WITH THE LOWEST LIFE EXPECTANCY

| | COUNTRY | LIFE EXPECTANCY AT BIRTH (2008) |
|---|---|---|
| 1 | Swaziland | 31.99 |
| 2 | Botswana | 33.83 |
| 3 | Lesotho | 34.61 |
| 4 | Angola | 37.92 |
| 5 | Zambia | 38.59 |
| 6 | Zimbabwe | 39.73 |
| 8 | Mozambique | 41.04 |
| 9 | Liberia | 41.17 |
| 10 | South Africa | 42.37 |

Source: US Census Bureau, International Data Base

*Life span*
*Diet, medical and other factors have resulted in a progressive increase in life expectancy in Japan: over half those born since 2000 are expected to live beyond 90.*

# Quality of Life

**Best and worst**
*Despite the efforts of governments and international agencies, the graphic contrast between countries where most people are healthy, wealthy and well-educated and those where they are not – as here, in Norway (left) and Niger (below) – is one of the biggest challenges of the 21st century.*

## TOP 10 **MOST LIVABLE COUNTRIES**

COUNTRY / HDI RANK (2003)

 1 Norway
0.963

 2 Iceland
0.956

3 Australia
0.955

4 = Canada 0.949
= Luxembourg 0.949
= Sweden 0.949

7 Switzerland
0.947

8 Ireland
0.946

9 Belgium
0.945

10 USA
0.944

*UK 0.939*

Source: United Nations, *Human Development Report 2005*

The UN Human Development Index ranks countries by their quality of life. Criteria for the ranking include life expectancy, adult literacy, school enrolment, educational attainment and per capita GDP.

## THE 10 **LEAST LIVABLE COUNTRIES**

COUNTRY / HDI RANK (2003)

 1 Niger
0.281

 2 Sierra Leone
0.298

 3 Burkina Faso
0.317

 4 Mali
0.333

 5 Chad
0.341

 6 Guinea Bissau
0.348

 7 Central African Republic
0.355

 8 Ethiopia
0.367

 9 Burundi
0.378

 10 Mozambique
0.379

Source: United Nations, *Human Development Report 2005*

## TOP 10 **BEST PLACES TO LIVE IN THE UK**

**1** Epsom and Ewell

**2** City of Westminster

**3** Harrogate

**4** Ashford, Kent

**5** Stratford-on-Avon

**6** East Hertfordshire

**7** South Cambridgeshire

**8** Mole Valley

**9** Guildford

**10** West Oxfordshire

Source: Channel 4

This survey examined 434 UK local authorities, basing its rankings on statistics for crime, education, employment, environment and lifestyle.

### The Great Stink

The worst place to live in the UK 150 years ago was London: the summer of 1858 was dubbed 'The Great Stink', when untreated sewage discharged into the Thames created an unbearable smell. It prompted the development of a modern sewerage system that transformed the capital.

## THE 10 **WORST PLACES TO LIVE IN THE UK**

**1** Hull

**2** Nottingham

**3** Strabane

**4** Hackney

**5** Middlesbrough

**6** Mansfield

**7** Blaenau Gwent

**8** Merthyr Tydfil

**9** Salford

**10** Easington

Source: Channel 4

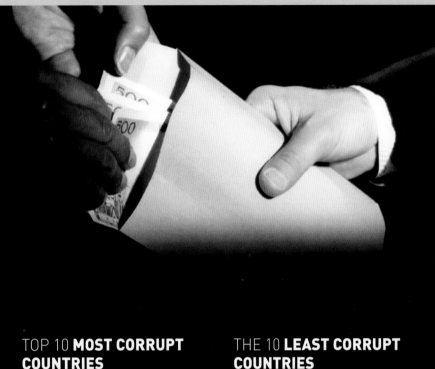

## TOP 10 **MOST CORRUPT COUNTRIES**

| | COUNTRY | RATING |
|---|---|---|
| **1** | = Bangladesh | 1.7 |
| | = Chad | 1.7 |
| **3** | = Haiti | 1.8 |
| | = Myanmar | 1.8 |
| | = Turkmenistan | 1.8 |
| **6** | = Côte d'Ivoire | 1.9 |
| | = Equatorial Guinea | 1.9 |
| | = Nigeria | 1.9 |
| **9** | Angola | 2.0 |
| **10** | = Dem. Rep. of Congo | 2.1 |
| | = Kenya | 2.1 |
| | = Pakistan | 2.1 |
| | = Paraguay | 2.1 |
| | = Somalia | 2.1 |
| | = Sudan | 2.1 |
| | = Tajikistan | 2.1 |

## THE 10 **LEAST CORRUPT COUNTRIES**

| | COUNTRY | RATING |
|---|---|---|
| **1** | Iceland | 9.7 |
| **2** | = Finland | 9.6 |
| | = New Zealand | 9.6 |
| **4** | Denmark | 9.5 |
| **5** | Singapore | 9.4 |
| **6** | Sweden | 9.2 |
| **7** | Switzerland | 9.1 |
| **8** | Norway | 8.9 |
| **9** | Australia | 8.8 |
| **10** | Austria | 8.7 |
| | *UK* | *8.6* |

Source: Transparency International, *Corruption Perceptions Index 2005*

The Corruption Perceptions Index ranks countries by how likely they are to accept bribes, as perceived by the general public, business people and risk analysts. They are ranked on a scale of 0–10, the higher the score, the 'cleaner', or less corrupt the country. A total of 159 countries were covered by the latest survey.

# First Names First

| BOYS | | GIRLS |
|---|---|---|
| William | 1 | Mary |
| John | 2 | Florence |
| George | 3 | Doris |
| Thomas | 4 | Edith |
| Arthur | 5 | Dorothy |
| James | 6 | Annie |
| Charles | 7 | Margaret |
| Frederick | 8 | Alice |
| Albert | 9 | Elizabeth |
| Ernest | 10 | Elsie |

| BOYS | | GIRLS |
|---|---|---|
| John | 1 | Mary |
| William | 2 | Margaret |
| George | 3 | Doris |
| Thomas | 4 | Dorothy |
| James | 5 | Kathleen |
| Arthur | 6 | Florence |
| Frederick | 7 | Elsie |
| Albert | 8 | Edith |
| Charles | 9 | Elizabeth |
| Robert | 10 | Winifred |

| BOYS | | GIRLS |
|---|---|---|
| John | 1 | Margaret |
| William | 2 | Mary |
| George | 3 | Joan |
| James | 4 | Joyce |
| Thomas | 5 | Dorothy |
| Ronald | 6 | Kathleen |
| Kenneth | 7 | Doris |
| Robert | 8 | Irene |
| Arthur | 9 | Elizabeth |
| Frederick | 10 | Eileen |

| BOYS | | GIRLS |
|---|---|---|
| John | 1 | Margaret |
| Peter | 2 | Jean |
| William | 3 | Mary |
| Brian | 4 | Joan |
| David | 5 | Patricia |
| James | 6 | Sheila |
| Michael | 7 | Barbara |
| Ronald | 8 | Doreen |
| Kenneth | 9 | June |
| George | 10 | Shirley |

| BOYS | | GIRLS |
|---|---|---|
| John | 1 | Margaret |
| David | 2 | Patricia |
| Michael | 3 | Christine |
| Peter | 4 | Mary |
| Robert | 5 | Jean |
| Anthony | 6 | Ann |
| Brian | 7 | Susan |
| Alan | 8 | Janet |
| William | 9 | Maureen |
| James | 10 | Barbara |

| BOYS | | GIRLS |
|---|---|---|
| David | 1 | Susan |
| John | 2 | Linda |
| Stephen | 3 | Christine |
| Michael | 4 | Margaret |
| Peter | 5 | Janet |
| Robert | 6 | Patricia |
| Paul | 7 | Carol |
| Alan | 8 | Elizabeth |
| Christopher | 9 | Mary |
| Richard | 10 | Anne |

## TOP 10 FIRST NAMES IN ENGLAND AND WALES, 1960s

| BOYS | | GIRLS |
|---|---|---|
| David | 1 | Susan |
| Paul | 2 | Julie |
| Andrew | 3 | Karen |
| Mark | 4 | Jacqueline |
| John | 5 | Deborah |
| Michael | 6 | Tracey |
| Stephen | 7 | Jane |
| Ian | 8 | Helen |
| Robert | 9 | Diane |
| Richard | 10 | Sharon |

## TOP 10 FIRST NAMES IN ENGLAND AND WALES, 1970s

| BOYS | | GIRLS |
|---|---|---|
| Paul | 1 | Sarah |
| Mark | 2 | Claire |
| David | 3 | Nicola |
| Andrew | 4 | Emma |
| Richard | 5 | Lisa |
| Christopher | 6 | Joanne |
| James | 7 | Michelle |
| Simon | 8 | Helen |
| Michael | 9 | Samantha |
| Matthew | 10 | Karen |

## TOP 10 FIRST NAMES IN ENGLAND AND WALES, 1980s

| BOYS | | GIRLS |
|---|---|---|
| Christopher | 1 | Sarah |
| James | 2 | Laura |
| David | 3 | Gemma |
| Daniel | 4 | Emma |
| Michael | 5 | Rebecca |
| Matthew | 6 | Claire |
| Andrew | 7 | Victoria |
| Richard | 8 | Samantha |
| Paul | 9 | Rachel |
| Mark | 10 | Amy |

## TOP 10 FIRST NAMES IN ENGLAND AND WALES, 1990s

| BOYS | | GIRLS |
|---|---|---|
| Thomas | 1 | Rebecca |
| James | 2 | Lauren |
| Jack | 3 | Jessica |
| Daniel | 4 | Charlotte |
| Matthew | 5 | Hannah |
| Ryan | 6 | Sophie |
| Joshua | 7 | Amy |
| Luke | 8 | Emily |
| Samuel | 9 | Laura |
| Jordan | 10 | Emma |

## TOP 10 FIRST NAMES IN ENGLAND AND WALES, 2000s

| BOYS | | GIRLS |
|---|---|---|
| Jack | 1 | Emily |
| Joshua | 2 | Ellie |
| Thomas | 3 | Jessica |
| James | 4 | Sophie |
| Daniel | 5 | Chloe |
| Samuel | 6 | Lucy |
| Oliver | 7 | Olivia |
| William | 8 | Charlotte |
| Benjamin | 9 | Katie |
| Joseph | 10 | Megan |

### You Called Him What?

British and American Puritans of the late 16th and early 17th centuries abandoned first names they considered 'heathen' in favour of those with biblical associations, baptizing their children with names that included Be-faithful, Small-hope, Praise-god, Kill-sin, Thankful, Search-the-scriptures, Hope-on-high, Increase and Weep-not.

# Marriage & Divorce

## TOP 10 **COUNTRIES WITH THE HIGHEST PROPORTION OF TEENAGE BRIDES**

| COUNTRY | % OF 15–19-YEAR-OLD GIRLS WHO HAVE EVER BEEN MARRIED* |
|---|---|
| 1 Dem. Rep. of Congo | 74.2 |
| 2 Congo | 55.0 |
| 3 Afghanistan | 53.7 |
| 4 Bangladesh | 51.3 |
| 5 Uganda | 49.8 |
| 6 Mali | 49.7 |
| 7 Guinea | 49.0 |
| 8 Chad | 48.6 |
| 9 Mozambique | 47.1 |
| 10 Senegal | 43.8 |
| *UK* | *1.7* |

\* In latest year for which data available

Source: United Nations

*Young love*
*A teenage bride and groom celebrate their marriage in traditional Afghan style by exchanging a sweet drink. The world average age for marriage is 27.8.*

## TOP 10 **MONTHS FOR MARRIAGES IN ENGLAND AND WALES**

MONTH / MARRIAGES

1 August  46,086
2 September  32,923
3 July  32,860
4 May  28,994
5 June  28,092
6 October  20,432
7 April  18,066
8 November  14,685
9 March  14,166
10 December  13,946

These figures are for 2003, when there was a total of 270,109 marriages in England and Wales. January was the least popular (7,988), followed by February (11,861). As Saturday is the favoured day for weddings, the number of Saturdays in the month – there were five in August, for example – can boost its apparent popularity.

## TOP 10 **COUNTRIES WITH THE HIGHEST PROPORTION OF TEENAGE HUSBANDS**

| COUNTRY | % OF 15–19-YEAR-OLD BOYS WHO HAVE EVER BEEN MARRIED* |
|---|---|
| 1 Iraq | 14.9 |
| 2 Nepal | 13.5 |
| 3 Congo | 11.8 |
| 4 Uganda | 11.4 |
| 5 Central African Republic | 8.1 |
| 6 India | 9.5 |
| 7 Afghanistan | 9.2 |
| 8 Guinea | 8.2 |
| 9 Guatemala | 7.8 |
| 10 Columbia | 7.7 |
| *UK* | *0.5* |

\* In latest year for which data available

Source: United Nations

## TOP 10 **COUNTRIES WHERE MOST WOMEN MARRY**

| | COUNTRY | % OF WOMEN MARRIED BY AGE 50* |
|---|---|---|
| **1** = | Comoros | 100.0 |
| = | Gambia | 100.0 |
| = | Ghana | 100.0 |
| = | Nauru | 100.0 |
| **5** | Chad | 99.9 |
| **6** = | China | 99.8 |
| = | Guinea | 99.8 |
| = | Mali | 99.8 |
| = | Papua New Guinea | 99.8 |
| **10** | Benin | 99.7 |
| | *UK* | *95.1* |

\* In latest year for which data available

Source: United Nations

Marriage in these countries can be considered only marginally above the norm, contrasting with a relatively small number where almost half the female population opts never to marry.

## TOP 10 **COUNTRIES WHERE MOST MEN MARRY**

| | COUNTRY | % OF MEN MARRIED BY AGE 50* |
|---|---|---|
| **1** = | Chad | 100.0 |
| = | Gambia | 100.0 |
| **3** | Guinea | 99.7 |
| **4** = | Mali | 99.6 |
| = | Niger | 99.6 |
| **6** = | Bangladesh | 99.3 |
| = | Mozambique | 99.3 |
| **8** | Cameroon | 99.2 |
| **9** | Nepal | 99.1 |
| **10** = | Central African Republic | 99.0 |
| = | Eritrea | 99.0 |
| = | Tajikistan | 99.0 |
| | *UK* | *91.2* |

\* In latest year for which data available

Source: United Nations

## THE 10 **COUNTRIES WITH THE LOWEST DIVORCE RATES**

| | COUNTRY | DIVORCE RATE PER 1,000* |
|---|---|---|
| **1** | Guatemala | 0.12 |
| **2** | Belize | 0.17 |
| **3** | Mongolia | 0.28 |
| **4** | Libya | 0.32 |
| **5** | Georgia | 0.40 |
| **6** | Chile | 0.42 |
| **7** | St Vincent and the Grenadines | 0.43 |
| **8** | Jamaica | 0.44 |
| **9** | Armenia | 0.47 |
| **10** | Turkey | 0.49 |

\* In those countries/latest year for which data available

Source: United Nations

The countries that figure among those with the lowest rates represent a range of cultures and religions that either condone or condemn divorce to varying extents, thus affecting its prevalence or otherwise. In some countries, legal and other obstacles make divorce difficult or costly, while in certain societies, such as Jamaica, where the marriage rate is also low, partners often separate without the formality of divorce.

## TOP 10 **COUNTRIES WITH THE HIGHEST DIVORCE RATES**

| | COUNTRY | DIVORCE RATE PER 1,000* |
|---|---|---|
| **1** | Russia | 5.30 |
| **2** | Aruba | 5.27 |
| **3** | USA | 4.19 |
| **4** | Ukraine | 3.79 |
| **5** | Belarus | 3.77 |
| **6** | Moldova | 3.50 |
| **7** | Cuba | 3.16 |
| **8** | Czech Republic | 3.11 |
| **9** = | Lithuania | 3.05 |
| = | South Korea | 3.05 |
| | *UK* | *2.58* |

\* In those countries/latest year for which data available

Source: United Nations

The demographics of divorce are more complex than the Top 10 suggests, varying according to age at marriage (highest among those who marry in their early twenties), higher for second and higher still for third marriages.

# Death

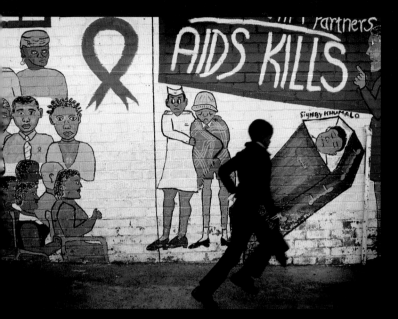

**The writing on the wall**
*Worldwide, AIDS has claimed over 25 million lives in 25 years, making it one of the most devastating epidemics of all time.*

## THE 10 MOST COMMON CAUSES OF DEATH BY INFECTIOUS AND PARASITIC DISEASES

| CAUSE | APPROX. DEATHS (2002) |
|---|---|
| 1 Lower-respiratory infections | 3,884,000 |
| 2 HIV/AIDS | 2,777,000 |
| 3 Diarrhoeal diseases | 1,798,000 |
| 4 Tuberculosis | 1,566,000 |
| 5 Malaria | 1,272,000 |
| 6 Measles | 611,000 |
| 7 Whooping cough (pertussis) | 294,000 |
| 8 Neonatal tetanus | 214,000 |
| 9 Meningitis | 173,000 |
| 10 Syphilis | 157,000 |

Source: World Health Organization, *World Health Report 2004*

In 2002, infectious and parasitic diseases accounted for some 10,904,000 of the 57,029,000 deaths worldwide. After declining, certain childhood diseases – including measles and whooping cough – showed an increase in this year.

## THE 10 MOST COMMON CAUSES OF DEATH IN THE UK

CAUSE / DEATHS (2004)

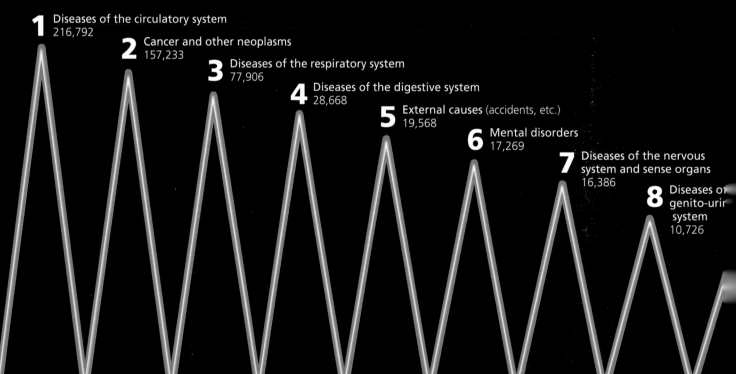

**1** Diseases of the circulatory system
216,792

**2** Cancer and other neoplasms
157,233

**3** Diseases of the respiratory system
77,906

**4** Diseases of the digestive system
28,668

**5** External causes (accidents, etc.)
19,568

**6** Mental disorders
17,269

**7** Diseases of the nervous system and sense organs
16,386

**8** Diseases of genito-urinary system
10,726

*The Chinese way of death*
*China has almost 20 per cent of the global population and accounts for some 17 per cent of annual deaths worldwide.*

# TOP 10 **COUNTRIES WITH THE MOST DEATHS**

| COUNTRY / ESTIMATED DEATHS (2008) | |
|---|---|
| **1** China | 9,350,214 |
| **2** India | 7,347,174 |
| **3** USA | 2,512,630 |
| **4** Nigeria | 2,269,228 |
| **5** Russia | 2,259,676 |
| **6** Indonesia | 1,482,077 |
| **7** Pakistan | 1,355,937 |
| **8** Bangladesh | 1,228,375 |
| **9** Japan | 1,222,013 |
| **10** Brazil | 1,193,671 |
| *UK* | *612,486* |
| *World* | *55,771,877* |

Endocrine, nutritional and metabolic diseases and immunity disorders
8,739

**10** Infectious and parasitic diseases
5,846

*Total deaths from all causes (including some that do not appear in the Top 10)
583,082*

# THE 10 **COUNTRIES WITH THE LOWEST DEATH RATES**

| COUNTRY | ESTIMATED DEATH RATE (DEATHS PER 1,000, 2008) |
|---|---|
| **1** Kuwait | 2.37 |
| **2** Saudi Arabia | 2.52 |
| **3** Jordan | 2.72 |
| **4** Libya | 3.46 |
| **5** Brunei | 3.54 |
| **6** Oman | 3.74 |
| **7** Solomon Islands | 3.82 |
| **8** Ecuador | 4.21 |
| **9** Bahrain | 4.29 |
| **10** Nicaragua | 4.39 |

Source: US Census Bureau, International Data Base

The crude death rate is derived by dividing the total number of deaths in a given year by the total population and multiplying by 1,000. Age-standardized death rates take account of the age structure of the population to produce a more accurate assessment.

# THE 10 **MOST SUICIDAL COUNTRIES**

| COUNTRY | SUICIDES PER 100,000 PER ANNUM* | | |
|---|---|---|---|
| | MALE | FEMALE | TOTAL |
| **1** Lithuania | 74.3 | 13.9 | 42.1 |
| **2** Russia | 69.3 | 11.9 | 38.7 |
| **3** Belarus | 63.3 | 10.3 | 35.1 |
| **4** Kazakhstan | 50.2 | 8.8 | 28.8 |
| **5** Slovenia | 45.0 | 12.0 | 28.1 |
| **6** Hungary | 44.9 | 12.0 | 27.7 |
| **7** Estonia | 47.7 | 9.8 | 27.3 |
| **8** Ukraine | 46.7 | 8.4 | 26.1 |
| **9** Latvia | 45.0 | 9.7 | 26.0 |
| **10** Japan | 35.2 | 12.8 | 23.8 |
| *UK* | *10.8* | *3.1* | *6.9* |

* In those countries/latest year for which data available

Source: World Health Organization

Suicide rates in certain countries appear low, partly because of extended family support networks and because of the cultural taboos attached to suicide.

# World Religions

## TOP 10 **RELIGIOUS BELIEFS**

| | RELIGION | FOLLOWERS |
|---|---|---|
| **1** | Christianity | 2,135,784,198 |
| **2** | Islam | 1,313,983,654 |
| **3** | Hinduism | 870,047,346 |
| **4** | Chinese folk religions | 404,922,244 |
| **5** | Buddhism | 378,809,103 |
| **6** | Ethnic religions | 256,340,652 |
| **7** | New religions | 108,131,713 |
| **8** | Sikhism | 25,373,879 |
| **9** | Judaism | 15,145,702 |
| **10** | Spiritists | 13,030,538 |

Source: World Christian Database

While some mainstream religious groups have experienced a decline in formal attendance, certain fringe religions have grown. Today, about one-third of the world's population are nominally (self-declared), if not practising, Christians, and one-fifth are followers of Islam. At least 15 per cent of the world's population profess no religious beliefs of any kind.

## TOP 10 **LARGEST MUSLIM POPULATIONS**

| | COUNTRY | MUSLIMS |
|---|---|---|
| **1** | Pakistan | 154,563,023 |
| **2** | India | 134,149,817 |
| **3** | Bangladesh | 132,868,312 |
| **4** | Indonesia | 121,606,358* |
| **5** | Turkey | 71,322,513 |
| **6** | Iran | 67,724,004 |
| **7** | Egypt | 63,503,397 |
| **8** | Nigeria | 54,665,801 |
| **9** | Algeria | 31,858,555 |
| **10** | Morocco | 31,000,895 |
| | *UK* | *1,336,074* |
| | *World* | *1,313,983,654* |

\* An additional 46 million people are considered Muslims by the Indonesian government but are more properly categorized as New Religionists (Islamisized syncretistic religions)

Source: World Christian Database

## TOP 10 **LARGEST ROMAN CATHOLIC POPULATIONS**

| | COUNTRY | ROMAN CATHOLICS |
|---|---|---|
| **1** | Brazil | 155,929,000 |
| **2** | Mexico | 99,200,000 |
| **3** | Philippines | 68,252,000 |
| **4** | USA | 65,900,000 |
| **5** | Italy | 55,300,000 |
| **6** | France | 46,274,000 |
| **7** | Colombia | 42,200,000 |
| **8** | Spain | 38,473,000 |
| **9** | Poland | 35,300,000 |
| **10** | Argentina | 35,000,000 |
| | *UK* | *5,712,000* |
| | *World* | *1,118,991,707* |

Source: World Christian Database

*Below: High church*
*The statue of Christ towers over Rio de Janeiro. Brazil is home to one in seven of the world's Roman Catholics.*

## TOP 10 **LARGEST JEWISH POPULATIONS**

| | COUNTRY | JEWS |
|---|---|---|
| 1 | USA | 5,764,208 |
| 2 | Israel | 4,772,138 |
| 3 | France | 607,111 |
| 4 | Argentina | 520,130 |
| 5 | Palestine | 451,001 |
| 6 | Canada | 414,452 |
| 7 | Brazil | 383,837 |
| 8 | UK | 312,173 |
| 9 | Russia | 244,719 |
| 10 | Germany | 222,689 |
| | *World* | *15,145,702* |

Source: World Christian Database

The Diaspora, or scattering, of Jewish people has established Jewish communities in almost every country in the world. In 1939 the estimated total Jewish population was 17 million. Some six million fell victim to Nazi persecution, reducing the figure to about 11 million, since when it has grown to over 15 million.

## TOP 10 **LARGEST HINDU POPULATIONS**

| | COUNTRY | HINDUS |
|---|---|---|
| 1 | India | 810,387,411 |
| 2 | Nepal | 19,020,312 |
| 3 | Bangladesh | 17,029,336 |
| 4 | Indonesia | 7,632,941 |
| 5 | Sri Lanka | 2,173,114 |
| 6 | Pakistan | 2,100,342 |
| 7 | Malaysia | 1,855,194 |
| 8 | USA | 1,143,864 |
| 9 | South Africa | 1,078,667 |
| 10 | Myanmar | 1,006,804 |
| | *UK* | *482,983* |
| | *World* | *870,047,346* |

Source: World Christian Database

Hindus constitute some 74 per cent of the population of India and 72 per cent of that of Nepal, but only 11 per cent of Bangladesh's population and as little as three per cent of Indonesia's.

## TOP 10 **LARGEST BUDDHIST POPULATIONS**

| | COUNTRY | BUDDHISTS |
|---|---|---|
| 1 | China | 111,358,666 |
| 2 | Japan | 70,722,505 |
| 3 | Thailand | 53,294,170 |
| 4 | Vietnam | 40,780,825 |
| 5 | Myanmar | 37,151,956 |
| 6 | Sri Lanka | 13,234,600 |
| 7 | Cambodia | 12,697,958 |
| 8 | India | 7,596,701 |
| 9 | South Korea | 7,281,110 |
| 10 | Taiwan | 4,823,361 |
| | *UK* | *166,430* |
| | *World* | *378,809,103* |

Source: World Christian Database

Although India now features in 8th place among countries with high Buddhist populations, the religion originated there in the 6th century BC. Its espousal of peace and tolerant co-existence ensured its appeal and encouraged the spread of Buddhism throughout Asia and beyond.

*Spiritual leader*
*Tenzin Gyatso was declared as the 14th Dalai Lama at the age of five and enthroned when he was 15.*

## THE 10 **LATEST DALAI LAMAS**

NAME / BORN/DIED

1 Tenzin Gyatso (1935– )
2 Thubten Gyatso (1876–1933)
3 Trinley Gyatso (1856–75)
4 Khendrup Gyatso (1838–56)
5 Tsultrim Gyatso (1816–37)
6 Lungtok Gyatso (1806–15)
7 Jamphel Gyatso (1758–1804)
8 Kelzang Gyatso (1708–57)
9 Tsangyang Gyatso (1683–1706)
10 Lobsang Gyatso (1617–82)

The current Dalai Lama is the 14th in line since the first, Gedun Truppa (1391–1475). Each is believed to be the reincarnation of his predecessor and proclaimed as a child soon after the previous incumbent's death – although they do not take office until they are older.

# Rulers & Leaders

**72 years in the saddle**
*Discounting the doubtful 95 years claimed for king Mihti of Arakan (Myanmar), 94 for Egyptian pharaoh Phiops (Pepi) II and long reigns of other early monarchs, that of French 'Sun King' Louis XIV establishes him as the world's longest-serving ruler.*

## TOP 10 LONGEST-REIGNING MONARCHS*

| MONARCH / COUNTRY / REIGN | AGE AT ACCESSION | REIGN YEARS | MONTHS | DAYS |
|---|---|---|---|---|
| **1 King Louis XIV**, France<br>14 May 1643–1 Sep 1715 | 5 | 72 | 3 | 18 |
| **2 King John II**, Liechtenstein<br>12 Nov 1858–11 Feb 1929 | 18 | 70 | 2 | 30 |
| **3 Emperor Franz-Josef**, Austria-Hungary<br>2 Dec 1848–21 Nov 1916 | 18 | 67 | 11 | 19 |
| **4 Queen Victoria**, UK<br>20 Jun 1837–22 Jan 1901 | 18 | 63 | 7 | 2 |
| **5 James I**, Aragon<br>12 Sep 1213–27 Jul 1276 | 5 | 62 | 10 | 15 |
| **6 Emperor Hirohito**, Japan<br>25 Dec 1926–7 Jan 1989 | 25 | 62 | 0 | 13 |
| **7 Emperor K'ang Hsi**, China<br>5 Feb 1661–20 Dec 1722 | 7 | 61 | 10 | 15 |
| **8 King Sobhuza II#**, Swaziland<br>22 Dec 1921–21 Aug 1982 | 22 | 60 | 7 | 30 |
| **9 Emperor Ch'ien Lung**, China<br>18 Oct 1735–9 Feb 1796 | 25 | 60 | 3 | 22 |
| **10 King Christian IV**, Denmark<br>4 Apr 1588–21 Feb 1648 | 11 | 59 | 10 | 17 |

\* During past 1,000 years, excluding earlier rulers of dubious authenticity
\# Paramount chief until 1967, when Great Britain recognized him as king with the granting of internal self-government

## THE 10 YOUNGEST BRITISH MONARCHS

| MONARCH | REIGN | AGE AT ACCESSION YEARS | MONTHS | DAYS |
|---|---|---|---|---|
| **1 Henry VI** | 1422–61 | 0 | 8 | 25 |
| **2 Henry III** | 1216–72 | 9 | 0 | 18 |
| **3 Edward VI** | 1547–53 | 9 | 3 | 16 |
| **4 Richard II** | 1377–99 | 10 | 5 | 16 |
| **5 Edward V** | 1483 | 12 | 5 | 14 |
| **6 Edward III** | 1327–77 | 14 | 2 | 12 |
| **7 Jane** | 1553 | 15 | 8 | 23* |
| **8 Henry VIII** | 1509–47 | 17 | 9 | 25 |
| **9 Victoria** | 1837–1901 | 18 | 0 | 27 |
| **10 Charles II** | 1649–85# | 18 | 8 | 1 |

\* Circa – precise birthdate unknown
\# Succeeded on death of father, but did not reign until 1660

Henry VI was born on 6 December 1421 and became king of England on 1 September 1422 after the death of his father, Henry V. At the age of 10 months 15 days, following the death of his grandfather, Charles VI, he also became king of France. Before the Norman Conquest, Edward the Martyr became king in AD 975 aged about 12 and Ethelred II ('the Unready') in AD 978 at the age of about 10.

## TOP 10 LONGEST-REIGNING QUEENS

| QUEEN* | COUNTRY | REIGN | YEARS |
|---|---|---|---|
| **1 Victoria** | UK | 1837–1901 | 63 |
| **2 Wilhelmina** | Netherlands | 1890–1948 | 58 |
| **3 Elizabeth II** | UK | 1952– | 55# |
| **4 Wu Chao** | China | AD 655–705 | 50 |
| **5 Salote Tubou** | Tonga | 1918–65 | 47 |
| **6 Elizabeth I** | England | 1558–1603 | 44 |
| **7 Maria Theresa** | Hungary | 1740–80 | 40 |
| **8 Maria I** | Portugal | 1777–1816 | 39 |
| **9 Joanna I** | Italy | 1343–81 | 38 |
| **10 Suiko Tenno** | Japan | AD 592–628 | 36 |

\* Queens and empresses who ruled in their own right, not as consorts of kings or emperors
\# As at 6 February 2007

*Desert reign*
Colonel Gaddafi towers over his rivals as one of Africa's most durable leaders.

## TOP 10 LONGEST-SERVING PRESIDENTS TODAY

| PRESIDENT / COUNTRY | TOOK OFFICE |
|---|---|
| **1** El Hadj Omar Bongo, Gabon | 2 Dec 1967 |
| **2** Colonel Mu'ammar Gaddafi, Libya | 1 Sep 1969* |
| **3** Fidel Castro, Cuba | 2 Nov 1976 |
| **4** Ali Abdullah Saleh, Yemen | 17 Jul 1978 |
| **5** Maumoon Abdul Gayoom, Maldives | 11 Nov 1978 |
| **6** Teodoro Obiang Nguema Mbasogo, Equatorial Guinea | 3 Aug 1979 |
| **7** José Eduardo dos Santos, Angola | 21 Sep 1979 |
| **8** Hosni Mubarak, Egypt | 6 Oct 1981 |
| **9** Paul Biya, Cameroon | 7 Nov 1982 |
| **10** Lansana Conté, Guinea | 3 Apr 1984 |

* Since a reorganization in 1979, Colonel Gaddafi has held no formal position, but continues to rule under the ceremonial title of 'Leader of the Revolution'

All the presidents in this list have been in power for more than 20 years. Fidel Castro became prime minister of Cuba in February 1959. He was chief of the army and as there was no opposition party, he effectively ruled as dictator from then, but was not technically president until the Cuban constitution was revised in 1976.

## THE 10 FIRST FEMALE PRIME MINISTERS AND PRESIDENTS

| PRIME MINISTER/PRESIDENT / COUNTRY | FIRST PERIOD IN OFFICE |
|---|---|
| **1** Sirimavo Bandaranaike (PM), Sri Lanka | 21 Jul 1960–27 Mar 1965 |
| **2** Indira Gandhi (PM), India | 19 Jan 1966–24 Mar 1977 |
| **3** Golda Meir (PM), Israel | 17 Mar 1969–3 Jun 1974 |
| **4** Maria Estela Perón (President), Argentina | 1 Jul 1974–24 Mar 1976 |
| **5** Elisabeth Domitien (PM), Central African Republic | 3 Jan 1975–7 Apr 1976 |
| **6** Margaret Thatcher (PM), UK | 4 May 1979–28 Nov 1990 |
| **7** Dr Maria Lurdes Pintasilgo (PM), Portugal | 1 Aug 1979–3 Jan 1980 |
| **8** Mary Eugenia Charles (PM), Dominica | 21 Jul 1980–14 Jun 1995 |
| **9** Vigdís Finnbogadóttir (President), Iceland | 1 Aug 1980–1 Aug 1996 |
| **10** Gro Harlem Brundtland (PM), Norway | 4 Feb–14 Oct 1981 |

Following the assassination of her husband Solomon West Ridgeway Dias Bandaranaike, Sirimavo Ratwatte Dias Bandaranaike (1916–2000) took over as leader of the Ceylon (later Sri Lanka) Freedom Party, won the election and thereby became the world's first female prime minister, serving three terms.

# All the Presidents

## THE 10 US PRESIDENTS WITH THE MOST CHILDREN

| | PRESIDENT / YEARS IN OFFICE / WIFE | CHILDREN |
|---|---|---|
| 1 | John Tyler (1841–45) 1st Letitia Christian (7*) 2nd Julia Gardiner (7) | 14 |
| 2 | William H. Harrison (1841) Anna Tuthill Symmes | 10 |
| 3 | Rutherford B. Hayes (1877–81) Lucy Ware Webb | 8 |
| 4 | James Garfield (1881) Lucretia Rudolph | 7 |
| 5 = | George H. W. Bush (1989–93) Barbara Pierce | 6 |
| = | Thomas Jefferson (1801–09) Martha Wayles Skelton | 6 |
| = | Franklin D. Roosevelt (1933–45) Anna Eleanor Roosevelt# | 6* |
| = | Theodore Roosevelt (1901–09) 1st Alice Hathaway Lee (1) 2nd Edith Kermit Carow (5) | 6 |
| = | Zachary Taylor (1849–50) Margaret Smith | 6 |
| 10 = | John Adams (1797–1801) Abigail Smith | 5 |
| = | Grover Cleveland (1893–97) Frances Folsom | 5 |
| = | Andrew Johnson (1865–69) Eliza McCardle | 5 |

\* Including one child deceased
# Niece of Theodore Roosevelt

Ronald Reagan had five children, but one was adopted. George Washington, James Buchanan (the only unmarried president), Andrew Jackson, James Polk and James Madison did not have any.

### Millard Fillmore's Bathtub

In the *New York Evening Mail* of 28 December 1917, American journalist H. L. Mencken described as 'A Neglected Anniversary' the installation of the first bathtub in the USA, in Cincinnati in 1842, followed by the first in the White House, by President Millard Fillmore in 1851. Mencken's tale of a tub was, of course, entirely invented – baths had been common long before these dates – and he admitted as much in print, but for 90 years the story has appeared as an authentic historical account in numerous articles, reputable reference books and on websites.

## THE 10 SHORTEST-SERVING US PRESIDENTS

| | PRESIDENT / YEARS IN OFFICE | PERIOD IN OFFICE | | |
|---|---|---|---|---|
| | | YEARS | MONTHS | DAYS |
| 1 | William H. Harrison (1841)* | – | – | 30 |
| 2 | James Garfield (1881)* | – | 6 | 15 |
| 3 | Zachary Taylor (1849–50)* | 1 | 4 | 5 |
| 4 | Warren Harding (1921–23)* | 2 | 4 | 29 |
| 5 | Gerald Ford (1974–77) | 2 | 5 | 11 |
| 6 | Millard Fillmore (1850–53) | 2 | 5 | 25 |
| 7 | John F. Kennedy (1961–63)* | 2 | 10 | 2 |
| 8 | Chester A. Arthur (1881–85) | 3 | 5 | 13 |
| 9 | Andrew Johnson (1865–69) | 3 | 10 | 17 |
| 10 | John Tyler (1841–45) | 3 | 11 | 0 |

\* Died in office

## TOP 10 FATTEST US PRESIDENTS

| | PRESIDENT / YEARS IN OFFICE | BMI |
|---|---|---|
| 1 | William H. Taft (1909–13) | 45.4 |
| 2 | Grover Cleveland (1885–89) | 34.6 |
| 3 | William McKinley (1897–1901) | 31.1 |
| 4 = | Theodore Roosevelt (1901–09) | 30.2 |
| = | Zachary Taylor (1849–50) | 30.2 |
| 6 | Chester A. Arthur (1881–85) | 28.7 |
| 7 | Bill Clinton (1993–2001) | 28.3 |
| 8 | Herbert Hoover (1929–33) | 27.7 |
| 9 | James Buchanan (1857–61) | 26.9 |
| 10 | George W. Bush (2001–) | 26.8 |

BMI stands for 'Body-Mass Index'. A person's weight in kilograms is divided by the square of their height in metres. A person with a BMI of over 25 is considered overweight, and more than 30 is regarded as clinically obese. Taft was 1.8 m (5 ft 11 in) tall and weighed 147 kg (325 lb) when he took office. He had to have a giant bath constructed in the White House to accommodate him.

*Left: Senior citizen*
40th US President Ronald Reagan was both the oldest-elected (69) and oldest-serving (77) of all time.

*Below: Young Teddy*
Theodore Roosevelt was 42 when he took office and 45 at the time of his re-election in 1904.

# THE 10 **YOUNGEST US PRESIDENTS**

| PRESIDENT | TOOK OFFICE | AGE ON TAKING OFFICE | | |
|---|---|---|---|---|
| | | YEARS | MONTHS | DAYS |
| **1** Theodore Roosevelt | 14 Sep 1901 | 42 | 10 | 18 |
| **2** John F. Kennedy | 20 Jan 1961 | 43 | 7 | 22 |
| **3** Bill Clinton | 20 Jan 1993 | 46 | 5 | 1 |
| **4** Ulysses S. Grant | 4 Mar 1869 | 46 | 10 | 5 |
| **5** Grover Cleveland | 4 Mar 1893 | 47 | 11 | 14 |
| **6** Franklin Pierce | 4 Mar 1804 | 48 | 3 | 9 |
| **7** James Garfield | 4 Mar 1881 | 49 | 3 | 13 |
| **8** James Polk | 4 Mar 1845 | 49 | 4 | 2 |
| **9** Millard Fillmore | 10 Jul 1850 | 50 | 6 | 3 |
| **10** John Tyler | 6 Apr 1841 | 51 | 0 | 8 |

The US Constitution requires that a president must be at least 35 years old on taking office. Vice-president Theodore Roosevelt assumed the presidency following the assassination of William McKinley. John F. Kennedy was the youngest president to be elected. Polk holds the record for the shortest lifespan after leaving office, ending his four-year term on 3 March 1849 and dying 103 days later at the age of 53 years 6 months 17 days. George W. Bush was aged 54 years 6 months 14 days when he became president.

# TOP 10 **OLDEST US PRESIDENTS**

| PRESIDENT | LEFT OFFICE | AGE ON LEAVING OFFICE | | |
|---|---|---|---|---|
| | | YEARS | MONTHS | DAYS |
| **1** Ronald Reagan | 20 Jan 1989 | 77 | 11 | 14 |
| **2** Dwight D. Eisenhower | 20 Jan 1961 | 70 | 3 | 6 |
| **3** Andrew Jackson | 3 Mar 1837 | 69 | 11 | 16 |
| **4** James Buchanan | 3 Mar 1841 | 69 | 10 | 8 |
| **5** Harry S. Truman | 20 Jan 1953 | 68 | 8 | 10 |
| **6** George H. W. Bush | 20 Jan 1993 | 68 | 7 | 8 |
| **7** William H. Harrison | 4 Apr 1841* | 68 | 1 | 26 |
| **8** Zachary Taylor | 9 Jul 1850* | 65 | 7 | 15 |
| **9** John Adams | 3 Mar 1801 | 65 | 4 | 3 |
| **10** Gerald Ford | 20 Jan 1977 | 63 | 6 | 6 |

* Died in office

Born on 6 February 1911, Ronald Reagan took the record when he completed his second term on 20 January 1989.

# Organizations

## TOP 10 CHARITIES IN THE UK

| | CHARITY | INCOME (2006)* |
|---|---|---|
| 1 | Nuffield Hospitals | 526,200,000 |
| 2 | The British Council | 517,500,000 |
| 3 | Allchurches Trust Ltd | 468,800,000 |
| 4 | Cancer Research UK | 423,400,000 |
| 5 | The Arts Council England | 378,700,000 |
| 6 | The National Trust | 337,200,000 |
| 7 | Wellcome Trust | 324,400,000 |
| 8 | Oxfam | 310,500,000 |
| 9 | Charities Aid Foundation | 272,300,000 |
| 10 | Anchor Trust | 252,800,000 |

* Year ends vary

Source: Charities Direct

The UK has one of the largest and most active voluntary sectors in Europe. As of September 2006, there were 168,115 charities registered with the Charity Commission in England and Wales (this list does not include Scottish charities, which are regulated by Scottish law). They encompass some independent schools and certain arts organizations, such as the Royal Opera House.

## TOP 10 OLDEST GOLF CLUBS IN THE UK

| | CLUB | FOUNDED |
|---|---|---|
| 1 | Royal Burgess Golfing Society of Edinburgh | 1735 |
| 2 | Honourable Company of Edinburgh Golfers (Muirfield) | 1744 |
| 3 | Royal and Ancient (St Andrews) | 1754 |
| 4 | Bruntsfield Links Golfing Society | 1761 |
| 5 | Royal Blackheath | 1766 |
| 6 | Royal Musselburgh | 1774 |
| 7 | Royal Aberdeen | 1780 |
| 8 | =Glasgow Gailes | 1787 |
| | =Glasgow Killermont | 1787 |
| 10 | Cruden Bay (Aberdeenshire) | 1791 |

All but two of these clubs are in Scotland. The oldest in Northern Ireland is Royal Belfast (1881) and the Republic's oldest is Curragh, Co. Kildare (1883). The oldest Welsh club is Pontnewydd, Cwmbran (1875). The exact date of the formation of the Blackheath Club is uncertain, and some sources record that golf was played there in the 17th century by James VI of Scotland. However, it is generally accepted that the club was formed in 1766.

## TOP 10 OLDEST YACHT CLUBS IN THE WORLD

| | CLUB | FOUNDED |
|---|---|---|
| 1 | Royal Cork Yacht Club (founded as Water Club of the Harbour of Cork; dormant 1763–1803), Cork, Ireland | 1720 |
| 2 | Lough Ree Yacht Club, Athlone, Ireland | 1770 |
| 3 | Starcross Yacht Club, Exeter, Devon, UK | 1772 |
| 4 | Cumberland Sailing Society (Royal Thames Yacht Club since 1830), London, UK | 1775 |
| 5 | Royal Yacht Squadron, Cowes, Isle of Wight, UK | 1815 |
| 6 | Royal Northern Yacht Club, Glasgow, UK | 1824 |
| 7 | Republic of Singapore Yacht Club, Singapore | 1826 |
| 8 | Port of Plymouth Royal Clarence Regatta Club (Royal Western Yacht Club of England since 1842), Plymouth, UK | 1827 |
| 9 | Royal Gibraltar Yacht Club (Royal since 1933), Gibraltar | 1829 |
| 10 | Kungliga Svenska Segel Sällskapet (Royal Swedish Yacht Club), Stockholm, Sweden | 1830 |

*Sail of the centuries*
*A regatta of the Royal Northern. Yacht clubs are among the world's longest-established membership organizations.*

## TOP 10 COUNTRIES WITH THE HIGHEST GIRL-GUIDE AND GIRL-SCOUT MEMBERSHIP

| | COUNTRY | GUIDING FOUNDED | MEMBERSHIP* |
|---|---|---|---|
| 1 | USA | 1912 | 3,854,202 |
| 2 | India | 1911 | 1,170,262 |
| 3 | Philippines | 1919 | 671,267 |
| 4 | UK | 1909 | 555,420 |
| 5 | Canada | 1910 | 149,387 |
| 6 | Kenya | 1920 | 120,805 |
| 7 | Nigeria | 1919 | 100,198 |
| 8 | Egypt | 1913 | 92,000 |
| 9 | Poland | 1910 | 86,591 |
| 10 | Italy | 1912 | 83,601 |

\* Latest year for which data available

Source: World Association of Girl Guides and Girl Scouts

## 100 YEARS AGO: BOY SCOUTS FOUNDED

Robert Baden-Powell (1857–1941), the hero of the Siege of Mafeking during the Boer War (1899), organized an experimental camp attended by 20 boys, held from 29 July to 9 August 1907 on Brownsea Island, Poole, Dorset, England. His book, *Scouting for Boys*, outlining the principles of scouting, much of it based on Baden-Powell's army career in Africa, was published in six two-weekly parts from 15 January 1908. The first edition of the magazine *The Scout* appeared on 14 April 1908, and the first official camp was held at Humshaugh, Northumberland later that year. By 1909 the scouting movement had gained such momentum that a rally held at Crystal Palace, London, attracted 11,000 scouts. The Boy Scouts of America, Sea Scouts and Girl Guides were all established the following year, by which time there were over 100,000 scouts worldwide. The current figure exceeds 38 million.

*Stamp of success*
*A 1960 postage stamp celebrates 50 years of scouting in the USA.*

## TOP 10 COUNTRIES WITH THE HIGHEST SCOUT MEMBERSHIP

COUNTRY / FOUNDED / MEMBERSHIP AS AT SEPTEMBER 2005

**1** Indonesia 1912
8,909,435

**2** USA 1910
6,239,435

**3** India 1909
2,138,015

**4** Philippines 1923
1,956,131

**5** Thailand 1911
1,305,027

**6** Bangladesh 1972
908,435

**7** Pakistan 1947
526,403

**8** UK 1907
498,888

**9** South Korea 1922
252,157

**10** Japan 1913
220,223

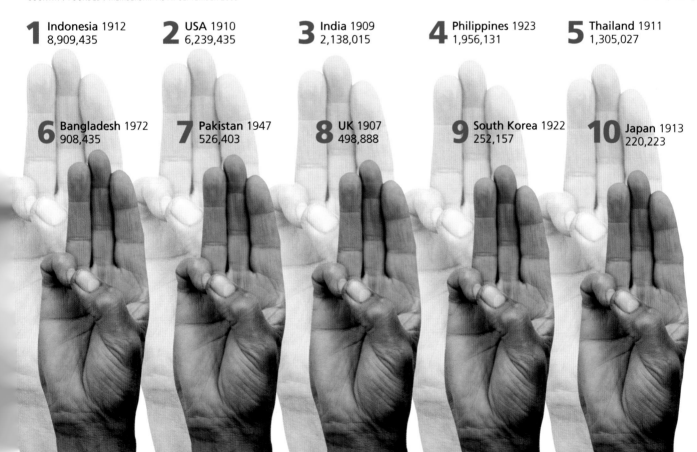

# Endeavour & Achievement

## THE 10 FIRST WOMEN TO WIN A NOBEL PRIZE

| | WINNER | COUNTRY | PRIZE | YEAR |
|---|---|---|---|---|
| 1 | Marie Curie* (1867–1934) | Poland | Physics | 1903 |
| 2 | Bertha von Suttner (1843–1914) | Austria | Peace | 1905 |
| 3 | Selma Lagerlöf (1858–1940) | Sweden | Literature | 1909 |
| 4 | Marie Curie (1867–1934) | Poland | Chemistry | 1911 |
| 5 | Grazia Deledda (1875–1936) | Italy | Literature | 1926# |
| 6 | Sigrid Undset (1882–1949) | Norway | Literature | 1928 |
| 7 | Jane Addams† (1860–1935) | USA | Peace | 1931 |
| 8 | Irène Joliot-Curie§ (1897–1956) | France | Chemistry | 1935 |
| 9 | Pearl Buck (1892–1973) | USA | Literature | 1938 |
| 10 | Gabriela Mistral (1899–1957) | Chile | Literature | 1945 |

\* Shared half with husband Pierre Curie; other half to Henri Becquerel
\# Awarded 1927
† Shared with Nicholas Murray Butler
§ Shared with husband Frédéric Joliot-Curie

## THE 10 YOUNGEST NOBEL PRIZE WINNERS

| | WINNER / COUNTRY / BORN | AWARD | AGE |
|---|---|---|---|
| 1 | William Lawrence Bragg, UK 31 Mar 1890 | Physics 1915 | 25 |
| 2 | Paul Adrien Maurice Dirac, UK 8 Aug 1902 | Physics 1933 | 31 |
| 3 | Carl David Anderson, USA 3 Sep 1905 | Physics 1936 | 31 |
| 4 | Werner Karl Heisenberg, Germany 5 Dec 1901 | Physics 1932 | 31 |
| 5 | Tsung-Dao Lee, China 24 Nov 1926 | Physics 1957 | 31 |
| 6 | Rudolf Ludwig Mössbauer, West Germany, 31 Jan 1929 | Physics 1961 | 32 |
| 7 | Frederick Grant Banting, Canada 14 Nov 1891 | Medicine 1923 | 32 |
| 8 | Brian David Josephson, UK 4 Jan 1940 | Physics 1973 | 33 |
| 9 | Joshua Lederberg, USA 23 May 1925 | Medicine 1958 | 33 |
| 10 | James Dewey Watson, USA 6 Apr 1928 | Medicine 1962 | 34 |

**Nobel first**
*The first of Marie Curie's two Nobel Prizes, for Physics in 1903, is one of only two by women in this field. Maria Goeppert-Mayer (Germany/USA) won the other in 1963.*

## THE 10 FIRST MOUNTAINEERS TO CLIMB EVEREST

| | MOUNTAINEER / COUNTRY | DATE |
|---|---|---|
| 1 | Edmund Hillary, New Zealand | 29 May 1953 |
| 2 | Tenzing Norgay, Nepal | 29 May 1953 |
| 3 | Jürg Marmet, Switzerland | 23 May 1956 |
| 4 | Ernst Schmied, Switzerland | 23 May 1956 |
| 5 | Hans-Rudolf von Gunten, Switzerland | 24 May 1956 |
| 6 | Adolf Reist, Switzerland | 24 May 1956 |
| 7 | Wang Fu-chou, China | 25 May 1960 |
| 8 | Chu Ying-hua, China | 25 May 1960 |
| 9 | Konbu, Tibet | 25 May 1960 |
| 10 = | Nawang Gombu, India | 1 May 1963 |
| = | James Whittaker, USA | 1 May 1963 |

Some 15 reconnaissance expeditions and attempts on Everest – several resulting in the deaths of the mountaineers – preceded the first successful conquest of the world's tallest peak. Nawang Gombu and James Whittaker are 10th equal because, neither wishing to deny the other the privilege of being first, they ascended the last steps to the summit side by side.

*Above: Pole position*
*Jean-Louis Etienne trekked for 63 days solo 1,200 km (750 miles) overland, hauling a sledge, to reach the North Pole.*

*Below: Over a barrel*
*After becoming the first man to survive Niagara Falls, Bobby Leach (1858–1925) died after tripping on an orange peel.*

## THE 10 FIRST EXPEDITIONS TO REACH THE NORTH POLE OVERLAND*

| NAME# / COUNTRY | | DATE |
|---|---|---|
| **1** | Ralph S. Plaisted, USA | 19 Apr 1968 |
| **2** | Wally W. Herbert, UK | 5 Apr 1969 |
| **3** | Naomi Uemura, Japan | 1 May 1978 |
| **4** | Dmitri Shparo, USSR | 31 May 1979 |
| **5** | Sir Ranulph Fiennes/ Charles Burton, UK | 11 Apr 1982 |
| **6** | Will Steger/ Paul Schurke, USA | 1 May 1986 |
| **7** | Jean-Louis Etienne, France | 11 May 1986 |
| **8** | Fukashi Kazami, Japan | 20 Apr 1987 |
| **9** | Helen Thayer, USA† | 20 Apr 1988 |
| **10** | Robert Swan, UK | 14 May 1989 |

\* Confirmed only
\# Expedition leader or co-leader
† New Zealand-born

## THE 10 FIRST PEOPLE TO GO OVER NIAGARA FALLS AND SURVIVE

| | NAME / COUNTRY | METHOD | DATE |
|---|---|---|---|
| **1** | Annie Edson Taylor, USA | Wooden barrel | 24 Oct 1901 |
| **2** | Bobby Leach, UK | Steel barrel | 25 Jul 1911 |
| **3** | Jean Lussier, Canada | Steel and rubber ball fitted with oxygen cylinders | 4 Jul 1928 |
| **4** | Nathan Boya (aka William Fitzgerald), USA | Steel and rubber ball fitted with oxygen cylinders | 15 Jul 1961 |
| **5** | Karel Soucek, Canada | Wood and plastic barrel | 3 Jul 1984 |
| **6** | Steven Trotter, USA | Metal barrel with inner tubes | 18 Aug 1985 |
| **7** | Dave Mundy, Canada | Steel container | 5 Oct 1985 |
| **8** | = Peter deBernardi, Canada | Steel container | 28 Sep 1989 |
| | = Jeffrey Petkovich, Canada | Steel container | 28 Sep 1989 |
| **10** | Dave Mundy | Steel diving bell | 26 Sep 1993 |

Source: Niagara Falls Museum

# Criminal Records

## TOP 10 **MOST COMMON CRIMES IN ENGLAND AND WALES**

CRIME / NO. RECORDED (2005–06)

**1** Theft and handling stolen goods (excluding car theft) 1,297,815

**2** Criminal damage 1,184,683

**3** Violence against the person 1,059,913

**4** Car theft (including theft from vehicles) 721,569

**5** Burglary (excluding domestic) 344,563

**6** Domestic burglary 300,555

**7** Fraud and forgery 233,005

**8** Drug offences 178,502

**9** Robbery 98,204

**10** Sexual offences 62,081

*Total (including those not in Top 10 5,556,513*

Source: Home Office, Crime in England and Wales 2005/2006

## TOP 10 **COUNTRIES WITH THE HIGHEST REPORTED CAR-THEFT RATES**

COUNTRY / RATE PER 100,000 (2000*)

**1** Switzerland 962.80

**2** New Zealand 818.01

**3** England and Wales 752.95

**4** Sweden 738.47

**5** Australia 726.19

**6** Denmark 604.18

**7** Scotland 555.33

**8** Italy 537.00

**9** Canada 521.20

**10** Norway 518.25

* Or latest year for which data available

Source: Interpol

## TOP 10 **MOST STOLEN MAKES OF CAR**

MAKE / NO. STOLEN*

**1** TOYOTA 404,217

**2** VOLKSWAGEN 307,680

**3** FORD 264,017

**4** FIAT 215,225

**5** NISSAN 185,292

**6** RENAULT 148,767

**7** LADA 148,239

**8** MITSUBISHI 137,627

**9** PEUGEOT 126,157

**10** HONDA 125,766

* On Interpol's database as at May 2006

Source: Interpol

# TOP 10 COUNTRIES WITH THE HIGHEST REPORTED CRIME RATES

COUNTRY / REPORTED CRIMES PER 100,000 POPULATION

**1** Dominica 11,382

**2** New Zealand 10,588

**3** Finland 10,153

**4** Denmark 9,283

**5** Chile 8,823

**6** UK 8,555

**7** Montserrat 8,040

**8** USA 8,007

**9** Netherlands 7,958

**10** South Africa 7,719

Source: United Nations

An appearance in this list does not confirm these as the most crime-ridden countries, since the rate of reporting relates closely to such factors as confidence in local law-enforcement authorities. In certain countries crime is so common and law enforcement so inefficient or corrupt that countless incidents go unreported, while for propaganda purposes, many countries do not publish accurate figures. However, a rate of approximately 1,000 per 100,000 may be considered average, so those in the Top 10 are well above it.

*Powder burns*
*Armed drug-enforcement authorities in Chile destroy a quantity of cocaine seized in raids.*

# TOP 10 COUNTRIES WITH THE HIGHEST PRISON POPULATIONS

| | COUNTRY | PRISONERS PER 100,000 POPULATION | TOTAL PRISONERS* |
|---|---|---|---|
| **1** | USA | 737 | 2,193,798 |
| **2** | China | 118 | 1,548,498 |
| **3** | Russia | 613 | 871,693 |
| **4** | Brazil | 203 | 385,317 |
| **5** | India | 30 | 332,112 |
| **6** | Mexico | 197 | 214,452 |
| **7** | Thailand | 256 | 164,443 |
| **8** | Ukraine | 350 | 162,602 |
| **9** | South Africa | 336 | 160,198 |
| **10** | Iran | 214 | 147,926 |
| | *England and Wales* | *147* | *79,537* |
| | *Scotland* | *141* | *7,210* |
| | *Northern Ireland* | *83* | *1,450* |

* As at date of most recent data

Source: International Centre for Prison Studies

# TOP 10 LARGEST PRISONS IN THE UK*

| | PRISON | CAPACITY |
|---|---|---|
| **1** | Wandsworth, London | 1,476 |
| **2** | Winson Green, Birmingham | 1,454 |
| **3** | Walton, Liverpool | 1,340 |
| **4** | Wormwood Scrubs, London | 1,282 |
| **5** | Strangeways, Manchester | 1,244 |
| **6** | Doncaster | 1,138 |
| **7** | Pentonville, London | 1,131 |
| **8** | Altcourse, Liverpool | 1,105 |
| **9** | Risley, Cheshire | 1,072 |
| **10** | Blakenhurst, Redditch | 1,054 |

* As at February 2007

# Murder File

## TOP 10 COUNTRIES WITH THE HIGHEST MURDER RATES

COUNTRY / MURDERS PER 100,000 POPULATION

1 Colombia 61.8
2 South Africa 49.6
3 Jamaica 32.4
4 Venezuela 31.6
5 Russia 20.2
6 Mexico 13.0
7 Estonia 10.7
8 Latvia 10.4
9 Lithuania 10.3
10 Belarus 9.8

Source: United Nations

## THE 10 WORST YEARS FOR MURDER IN ENGLAND AND WALES*

| | YEAR# | MURDER RATE PER MILLION POPULATION | TOTAL |
|---|---|---|---|
| 1 | 2003 | 18.2 | 952 |
| 2 | 2002 | 15.4 | 803 |
| 3 | 2005 | 15.5 | 793 |
| 4 | 2004 | 15.0 | 788 |
| 5 | 2001 | 14.9 | 771 |
| 6 | 2006 | 14.0 | 746 |
| 7 | 2000 | 13.0 | 675 |
| 8 | 1995 | 13.0 | 662 |
| 9 | 1994 | 12.4 | 632 |
| 10 | 1991 | 12.3 | 623 |

* Since 1946; some offences initially recorded as homicide are later reclassified, so figures may reduce over time
# Prior to 1997, data relate to calendar year, from 1997 to financial year

Source: Home Office

Since the 1960s, the number of murders per million population has more than doubled.

## TOP 10 MURDER CIRCUMSTANCES IN THE USA

REASON / MURDERS (2005)

1 Argument (unspecified) 3,692
2 Robbery 921
3 Juvenile gang killing 754
4 Contravention of narcotic drug laws 589
5 Argument over money or property 211
6 Brawl due to influence of alcohol 120
7 Romantic triangle 117
8 Brawl due to influence of narcotics 97
9 Gangland killings 96
10 Burglary 88

Source: *FBI Uniform Crime Reports*

## THE 10 MOST COMMON MURDER WEAPONS AND METHODS IN ENGLAND AND WALES

| WEAPON/METHOD | MEN | VICTIMS (2005–06) WOMEN | TOTAL |
|---|---|---|---|
| 1 Sharp instrument | 156 | 56 | 212 |
| 2 Hitting and kicking | 90 | 20 | 110 |
| 3 Unknown | 65 | 38 | 103 |
| 4 Blunt instrument | 42 | 19 | 61 |
| 5 Strangulation | 15 | 41 | 56 |
| 6 Explosion* | 22 | 30 | 52 |
| 7 Shooting | 39 | 11 | 50 |
| 8 Other | 33 | 12 | 45 |
| 9 Poison or drugs | 20 | 9 | 29 |
| 10 Burning | 16 | 11 | 27 |

* Victims of 7 July 2005 London bombings

Source: Home Office

# THE 10 **MOST PROLIFIC SERIAL KILLERS***

MURDERER / COUNTRY / VICTIMS

**1** **Behram** (India) 931
Behram (or Buhram) was the leader of the Thugee cult in India, which it is reckoned was responsible for the deaths of up to two million people. At his trial Behram was found guilty of personally committing 931 murders between 1790 and 1830.

**2** **Countess Erszébet Báthory** (Hungary) up to 650
In the period up to 1610 in Hungary, Báthory, known as 'Countess Dracula' was alleged to have murdered between 300 and 650 girls in the belief that drinking their blood would prevent her from ageing.

**3** **Pedro Alonso López** (Colombia) 300
Captured in 1980, López, nicknamed the 'Monster of the Andes', led police to 53 graves, but probably murdered at least 300 in Colombia, Ecuador and Peru.

**4** **Dr Harold Shipman** (UK) 215
In January 2000, Dr Shipman was found guilty of the murder of 15 women patients; the official enquiry into his crimes put the figure at 215, with 45 possible further cases.

*Doctor Death*
*Harold Shipman (1946–2004) of Hyde, Manchester, is Britain's worst serial killer.*

**5** **Henry Lee Lucas** (USA) 200
Lucas (1936–2001) admitted in 1983 to 360 murders, many committed with his partner-in-crime Ottis Toole. He died while on Death Row in Huntsville Prison, Texas.

**6** **Gilles de Rais** (France) up to 200
A fabulously wealthy French aristocrat, Gilles de Laval, Baron de Rais (1404–40) committed murders as sacrifices during black-magic rituals. He was accused of having kidnapped and killed between 60 and 200 children.

**7** **Hu Wanlin** (China) 196
Posing as a doctor specializing in ancient Chinese medicine, Hu Wanlin was sentenced on 1 October 2000 to 15 years imprisonment for three deaths, but authorities believe he was responsible for considerably more.

**8** **Luis Alfredo Garavito** (Colombia) 189
Garavito confessed in 1999 to a spate of murders. On 28 May 2000 he was sentenced to a total of 835 years imprisonment.

**9** **Hermann Webster Mudgett** (USA) up to 150
Mudgett (1860–96), was believed to have lured over 150 women to his Chicago 'castle', which he operated as a hotel. It was fully equipped for torturing, murdering and dissecting his victims and disposing of their bodies in furnaces or an acid bath.

**10** **Dr Jack Kevorkian** (USA) 130
In 1999 Kevorkian, who admitted to assisting in 130 suicides since 1990, was convicted of second-degree murder.

* Includes only individual murderers; excludes murders by bandits, those carried out by terrorist groups, political and military atrocities, and gangland slayings

# The World at War

## TOP 10 **LARGEST ARMED FORCES OF WORLD WAR I**

| | COUNTRY | PERSONNEL* |
|---|---|---|
| 1 | Russia | 12,000,000 |
| 2 | Germany | 11,000,000 |
| 3 | British Empire | 8,904,467 |
| 4 | France | 8,410,000 |
| 5 | Austria-Hungary | 7,800,000 |
| 6 | Italy | 5,615,000 |
| 7 | USA | 4,355,000 |
| 8 | Turkey | 2,850,000 |
| 9 | Bulgaria | 1,200,000 |
| 10 | Japan | 800,000 |

\* Total at peak strength

Russia's armed forces were relatively small in relation to the country's population – some six per cent, compared with 17 per cent in Germany. Several other European nations had forces that were similarly substantial in relation to their populations: Serbia's army comprised some 14 per cent of its population. In total, more than 65 million combatants were involved.

*Historic ship*
*Commissioned in 1944, the USS* Missouri *was the ship on which the Japanese signed their surrender document on 2 September 1945. It is now an exhibit at Pearl Harbor, Hawaii.*

## TOP 10 **LARGEST BATTLESHIPS OF WORLD WAR II**

| | NAME | COUNTRY | STATUS | LENGTH M | FT | TONNAGE |
|---|---|---|---|---|---|---|
| 1 | = Musashi | Japan | Sunk 25 Oct 1944 | 263 | 862 | 72,809 |
| | = Yamato | Japan | Sunk 7 Apr 1945 | 263 | 862 | 72,809 |
| 3 | = Iowa | USA | Decommissioned 26 Oct 1990 | 270 | 887 | 55,710 |
| | = Missouri | USA | Decommissioned 31 Mar 1992 | 270 | 887 | 55,710 |
| | = New Jersey | USA | Decommissioned 8 Feb 1991 | 270 | 887 | 55,710 |
| | = Wisconsin | USA | Decommissioned 30 Sep 1991 | 270 | 887 | 55,710 |
| 7 | = Bismarck | Germany | Sunk 27 May 1941 | 251 | 823 | 50,153 |
| | = Tirpitz | Germany | Sunk 12 Nov 1944 | 251 | 823 | 50,153 |
| 9 | = Jean Bart | France | Survived WWII, later scrapped | 247 | 812 | 47,500 |
| | = Richelieu | France | Survived WWII, later scrapped | 247 | 812 | 47,500 |

## THE 10 **HIGHEST PROPORTIONS OF MILITARY VICTIMS IN WORLD WAR I**

| | COUNTRY | DEAD* |
|---|---|---|
| 1 | Romania | 44.76 |
| 2 | France | 16.36 |
| 3 | Germany | 16.12 |
| 4 | Austria-Hungary | 15.38 |
| 5 | Russia | 14.17 |
| 6 | Italy | 11.58 |
| 7 | Turkey | 11.40 |
| 8 | Great Britain | 10.20 |
| 9 | Bulgaria | 7.29 |
| 10 | Portugal | 7.22 |

\* As percentage of troops mobilized

# THE 10 COUNTRIES SUFFERING THE GREATEST AIRCRAFT LOSSES IN WORLD WAR II

| COUNTRY | AIRCRAFT LOST |
|---|---|
| **1** Germany | 116,584 |
| **2** USSR | 106,652 |
| **3** USA | 59,296 |
| **4** Japan | 49,485 |
| **5** UK | 33,090 |
| **6** Australia | 7,160 |
| **7** Italy | 5,272 |
| **8** Canada | 2,389 |
| **9** France | 2,100 |
| **10** New Zealand | 684 |

Reports of aircraft losses vary considerably from country to country, some including aircraft damaged, lost as a result of accidents, or scrapped, as well as those destroyed during combat.

**Bomb damage**
*Frankfurt am Main, one of the German cities devastated by Allied bombing during World War II.*

# THE 10 AREAS OF EUROPE MOST BOMBED BY ALLIED AIRCRAFT*, 1939–45

AREA / BOMBS DROPPED (TONNES)                    * British and US

**1** Germany  1,350,321

**2** France  583,318

**3** Italy  366,524

**4** Austria, Hungary and the Balkans  180,828

**5** Belgium and Netherlands  88,739

**6** Southern Europe and Mediterranean  76,505

**7** Czechoslovakia and Poland  21,419

**8** Norway and Denmark  5,297

**9** Sea targets  564

**10** British Channel Islands  93

# Modern Military

## TOP 10 LARGEST ARMED FORCES

| COUNTRY | ARMY | ESTIMATED ACTIVE FORCES NAVY | AIR | TOTAL |
|---|---|---|---|---|
| **1** China | 1,600,000 | 255,000 | 400,000 | 2,255,000 |
| **2** USA | 595,946 | 376,750 | 347,400 | 1,506,757* |
| **3** India | 1,100,000 | 46,000 | 161,000 | 1,316,000 |
| **4** North Korea | 950,000 | 46,000 | 110,000 | 1,106,000 |
| **5** Russia | 395,000 | 142,000 | 160,000 | 1,027,000# |
| **6** South Korea | 560,000 | 63,000 | 64,000 | 687,000 |
| **7** Pakistan | 550,000 | 24,000 | 45,000 | 619,000 |
| **8** Iran | 350,000 | 18,000 | 52,000 | 545,000† |
| **9** Turkey | 402,000 | 52,750 | 60,100 | 514,850 |
| **10** Egypt | 340,000 | 18,500 | 30,000 | 468,500§ |
| *UK* | *104,980* | *40,840* | *45,210* | *191,030* |

\* Includes 186,661 Marine Corps, 40,500 Coast Guard
\# Includes 80,000 Strategic Deterrent Forces, 250,000 Command and Support
† Includes 125,000 Revolutionary Guard Corps
§ Includes 70,000 Air Defence Command

Source: The International Institute for Strategic Studies, *The Military Balance 2007*

Several countries also have substantial reserves on standby: South Korea's has been estimated at some 4.5 million plus 3.5 Paramilitary, Vietnam's at 5 million and China's at 800,000. North Korea has the highest number of troops in relation to it population – 47.85 per 1,000.

## TOP 10 ARMOUR COUNTRIES*

| | COUNTRY | UNITS |
|---|---|---|
| **1** | Russia | 48,270 |
| **2** | USA | 29,920 |
| **3** | Israel | 14,200 |
| **4** | China | 13,200 |
| **5** | Syria | 9,650 |
| **6** | Egypt | 9,357 |
| **7** | Germany | 8,384 |
| **8** | Iraq | 7,430 |
| **9** | Turkey | 7,165 |
| **10** | France | 6,875 |
| | *UK* | *5,121* |

\* Tracked and wheeled MBTs (Main Battle Tanks) and APCs (Armoured Personnel Carriers)

Source: GlobalFirePower.com

## TOP 10 MILITARY EXPENDITURE COUNTRIES

| | COUNTRY | $ (2005) |
|---|---|---|
| **1** | USA | 518,100,000,000 |
| **2** | China | 81,480,000,000 |
| **3** | France | 45,000,000,000 |
| **4** | Japan | 44,310,000,000 |
| **5** | UK | 42,836,500,000 |
| **6** | Germany | 35,063,000,000 |
| **7** | Italy | 28,182,800,000 |
| **8** | South Korea | 21,060,000,000 |
| **9** | India | 19,040,000,000 |
| **10** | Saudi Arabia | 18,000,000,000 |

Source: GlobalFirePower.com

## TOP 10 WORLD MILITARY RANKING*

1 USA
2 Russia
3 China
4 India
5 Germany
6 France
7 Japan
8 Turkey
9 Brazil
10 UK

\* Based on GlobalFirePower's collective averages across a range of military criteria

Source: GlobalFirePower.com

*Air power*
*The USA operates over 500 F-15 fighters in an armoury of more than 18,000 military aircraft – almost double that of China, its closest rival.*

## TOP 10 **MILITARY AIRCRAFT COUNTRIES**

| | COUNTRY | MILITARY AIRCRAFT IN SERVICE |
|---|---|---|
| 1 | USA | 18,169 |
| 2 | China | 9,218 |
| 3 | Russia | 7,331 |
| 4 | India | 3,382 |
| 5 | Ukraine | 2,451 |
| 6 | France | 2,175 |
| 7 | Turkey | 1,964 |
| 8 | Japan | 1,957 |
| 9 | UK | 1,891 |
| 10 | Germany | 1,641 |

Source: GlobalFirePower.com

## TOP 10 **MISSILE DEFENCE SYSTEMS COUNTRIES**\*

| | COUNTRY | SYSTEMS |
|---|---|---|
| 1 | USA | 35,324 |
| 2 | Russia | 19,250 |
| 3 | China | 18,500 |
| 4 | North Korea | 16,075 |
| 5 | Syria | 11,233 |
| 6 | India | 7,125 |
| 7 | South Korea | 7,032 |
| 8 | Iraq | 5,210 |
| 9 | Egypt | 3,334 |
| 10 | Israel | 3,153 |
| | *UK* | *1,575* |

\* Including Heavy Anti-Tank and SAM Missile Systems

Source: GlobalFirePower.com

## TOP 10 **NAVAL SHIPS COUNTRIES**\*

| | COUNTRY | NAVAL VESSELS IN SERVICE |
|---|---|---|
| 1 | USA | 1,866 |
| 2 | North Korea | 708 |
| 3 | Russia | 701 |
| 4 | China | 284 |
| 5 | Turkey | 182 |
| 6 | Japan | 172 |
| 7 | UK | 164 |
| 8 | India | 145 |
| 9 | France | 140 |
| 10 | Germany | 129 |

\* Includes all military, logistical, survey and research craft under military control

Source: GlobalFirePower.com

# 4
# TOWN & COUNTRY

# Countries – Size

**State within a state**
*Vatican City is the world's smallest and least populated state, and the country with the shortest (virtual) border.*

## THE 10 **SMALLEST COUNTRIES**

| COUNTRY | AREA SQ KM | SQ MILES |
|---|---|---|
| **1** Vatican City | 0.44 | 0.17 |
| **2** Monaco | 1.95 | 0.75 |
| **3** Nauru | 21.20 | 8.18 |
| **4** Tuvalu | 25.63 | 9.89 |
| **5** San Marino | 61.20 | 23.63 |
| **6** Liechtenstein | 160.00 | 61.77 |
| **7** Marshall Islands | 181.43 | 70.05 |
| **8** Saint Kitts and Nevis | 269.40 | 104.01 |
| **9** Maldives | 298.00 | 115.05 |
| **10** Malta | 315.10 | 121.66 |

## TOP 10 **LARGEST COUNTRIES**

| COUNTRY | AREA SQ KM | SQ MILES | % OF WORLD TOTAL |
|---|---|---|---|
| **1** Russia | 17,075,200 | 6,592,772 | 11.5 |
| **2** Canada | 9,984,670 | 3,855,103 | 6.7 |
| **3** USA | 9,631,420 | 3,718,712 | 6.5 |
| **4** China | 9,596,960 | 3,705,407 | 6.4 |
| **5** Brazil | 8,511,965 | 3,286,488 | 5.7 |
| **6** Australia | 7,686,850 | 2,967,910 | 5.2 |
| **7** India | 3,287,590 | 1,269,346 | 2.2 |
| **8** Argentina | 2,766,890 | 1,068,302 | 2.1 |
| **9** Kazakhstan | 2,717,300 | 1,049,156 | 1.9 |
| **10** Sudan | 2,505,810 | 967,499 | 1.7 |
| *UK* | *244,820* | *94,526* | *0.2* |
| *World total* | *148,940,000* | *57,506,062* | *100.0* |

Source: CIA, *The World Factbook 2007*

This list is based on the area of a country within its borders, including offshore islands and inland water, and may thus differ from versions in which these are excluded. The countries in the Top 10 collectively comprise 50 per cent of the total Earth's land surface.

# TOP 10 **COUNTRIES WITH THE MOST NEIGHBOURS**

| COUNTRY / NEIGHBOURS | NO. OF NEIGHBOURS |
|---|---|
| **1** = China<br>Afghanistan, Bhutan, India, Kazakhstan, Kyrgyzstan, Laos, Mongolia, Myanmar, Nepal, North Korea, Pakistan, Russia, Tajikistan, Vietnam | 14 |
| = Russia<br>Azerbaijan, Belarus, China, Estonia, Finland, Georgia, Kazakhstan, Latvia, Lithuania, Mongolia, North Korea, Norway, Poland, Ukraine | 14 |
| **3** Brazil<br>Argentina, Bolivia, Colombia, French Guiana, Guyana, Paraguay, Peru, Suriname, Uruguay, Venezuela | 10 |
| **4** = Dem. Rep. of Congo<br>Angola, Burundi, Central African Republic, Congo, Rwanda, Sudan, Tanzania, Uganda, Zambia | 9 |
| = Germany<br>Austria, Belgium, Czech Republic, Denmark, France, Luxembourg, Netherlands, Poland, Switzerland | 9 |
| = Sudan<br>Central African Republic, Chad, Dem. Rep. of Congo, Egypt, Eritrea, Ethiopia, Kenya, Libya, Uganda | 9 |
| **7** = Austria<br>Czech Republic, Germany, Hungary, Italy, Liechtenstein, Slovakia, Slovenia, Switzerland | 8 |
| = France<br>Andorra, Belgium, Germany, Italy, Luxembourg, Monaco, Spain, Switzerland | 8 |
| = Serbia<br>Albania, Bosnia-Herzegovina, Bulgaria, Croatia, Hungary, Republic of Macedonia, Montenegro, Romania | 8 |
| = Tanzania<br>Burundi, Dem. Rep. of Congo, Kenya, Malawi, Mozambique, Rwanda, Uganda, Zambia | 8 |
| = Turkey<br>Armenia, Azerbaijan, Bulgaria, Georgia, Greece, Iran, Iraq, Syria | 8 |

# TOP 10 **LONGEST BORDERS**

| COUNTRY | TOTAL BORDERS | |
|---|---|---|
| | KM | MILES |
| **1** China | 22,117 | 13,642 |
| **2** Russia | 20,017 | 12,437 |
| **3** Brazil | 14,691 | 9,128 |
| **4** India | 14,103 | 8,763 |
| **5** USA | 12,034 | 7,477 |
| **6** Kazakhstan | 12,012 | 7,463 |
| **7** Dem. Rep. of Congo | 10,730 | 6,667 |
| **8** Argentina | 9,665 | 6,005 |
| **9** Canada | 8,893 | 5,525 |
| **10** Mongolia | 8,220 | 5,107 |

Source: CIA, *The World Factbook 2007*

The total length of the world's land boundaries is approximately 250,472 km (155,636 miles), with shared boundaries counted once.

# THE 10 **SHORTEST BORDERS**

| COUNTRIES | LAND BORDERS | |
|---|---|---|
| | KM | MILES |
| **1** Vatican/Italy | 3.2 | 2.0 |
| **2** Monaco/France | 4.4 | 2.7 |
| **3** Azerbaijan/Turkey | 9.0 | 5.6 |
| **4** North Korea/Russia | 19.0 | 11.8 |
| **5** Cuba/USA (Guantánamo Bay) | 29.0 | 18.0 |
| **6** Liechtenstein/Austria | 34.9 | 21.7 |
| **7** Armenia/Iran | 35.0 | 21.7 |
| **8** San Marino/Italy | 39.0 | 24.2 |
| **9** Liechtenstein/Switzerland | 41.1 | 25.5 |
| **10** Andorra/France | 56.6 | 35.2 |

Source: CIA, *The World Factbook 2007*

*Line of defence*
*The Great Wall of China once marked China's border with Mongolia.*

# Countries – Population

## TOP 10 **MOST DENSELY POPULATED COUNTRIES**

| | COUNTRY | AREA (SQ KM) | POPULATION (2008 EST.) | POPULATION PER SQ KM |
|---|---|---|---|---|
| 1 | Macau | 25 | 460,823 | 18,432.9 |
| 2 | Monaco | 1.95 | 32,796 | 16,818.5 |
| 3 | Singapore | 693 | 4,608,167 | 6,649.6 |
| 4 | Hong Kong | 1,092 | 7,018,636 | 6,427.3 |
| 5 | Vatican City | 0.44 | 932* | 2,118.2 |
| 6 | Malta | 315.10 | 403,532 | 1,280.6 |
| 7 | Maldives | 298.00 | 379,174 | 1,272.4 |
| 8 | Bangladesh | 133,911 | 153,546,901 | 1,146.6 |
| 9 | Bahrain | 665 | 718,306 | 1,080.2 |
| 10 | Nauru | 21 | 13,770 | 655.7 |
| | *UK* | *244,820* | *60,943,912* | *248.9* |
| | *World* | *148,940,000* | *6,682,477,937* | *44.9* |

\* July 2006 estimate

Source: US Census Bureau, International Data Base

Both Macau and Hong Kong are special administrative regions within China, but are still considered countries for the purposes of statistical comparison. Other territories with high population densities include the Gaza Strip with its population of 1,537,269 occupying a land area of 360 sq km (4,270.2 people per sq km), Gibraltar with a population of 28,002 occupying 7 sq km (4,000.3 people per sq km) and Bermuda with 66,536 people occupying 53 sq km (1,255.4 people per sq km).

## THE 10 **LEAST DENSELY POPULATED COUNTRIES**

| | COUNTRY | AREA (SQ KM) | POPULATION (2008 EST.) | POPULATION PER SQ KM |
|---|---|---|---|---|
| 1 | Mongolia | 1,564,116 | 2,916,865 | 1.86 |
| 2 | Namibia | 825,418 | 2,063,927 | 2.50 |
| 3 | Australia | 7,686,850 | 20,600,856 | 2.68 |
| 4 | Suriname | 163,270 | 475,996 | 2.69 |
| 5 | Botswana | 600,370 | 1,638,393 | 2.72 |
| 6 | Iceland | 103,000 | 304,367 | 2.95 |
| 7 | Mauritania | 1,030,700 | 3,364,940 | 3.26 |
| 8 | Canada | 9,984,670 | 33,679,263 | 3.37 |
| 9 | Libya | 1,759,540 | 6,173,579 | 3.50 |
| 10 | Guyana | 214,970 | 770,794 | 3.58 |

Source: US Census Bureau, International Data Base

Greenland is not an independent country, but if included it would be in first place with an area of 2,166,086 sq km and a population of 56,326 – a density of just 0.03 people per square kilometre.

*Above: Population explosion*
*India currently has more than 16 per cent of the world's population on 2.4 per cent of the land area. It is predicted that by 2035 its population will exceed 1.46 billion, overtaking China's – which by then will be declining.*

*Background: Namib Desert*
*Although Namibia is larger than Pakistan, its harsh terrain – one-sixth is desert – is occupied by a population one-eighty-fourth the size of Pakistan's, making it, after Mongolia, the least densely populated country on the planet.*

# TOP 10 **MOST POPULATED COUNTRIES**

| COUNTRY | POPULATION (2008 EST.) |
|---|---|
| 1 China | 1,330,044,605 |
| 2 India | 1,147,995,898 |
| 3 USA | 303,824,646 |
| 4 Indonesia | 237,512,355 |
| 5 Brazil | 191,908,598 |
| 6 Pakistan | 172,730,891 |
| 7 Bangladesh | 153,546,901 |
| 8 Russia | 140,702,094 |
| 9 Nigeria | 138,283,240 |
| 10 Japan | 127,425,722 |
| *UK* | *60,943,912* |
| *World* | *6,682,477,937* |

Source: US Census Bureau, International Data Base

The population of the USA – which had reached 100 million in 1915 and 200 million in 1967 – passed 300 million on 17 October 2006. On average, one American is born every seven seconds and one dies every 13 seconds. Taking account of immigration and emigration, its population increases by one every 10 seconds.

# THE 10 **LEAST POPULATED COUNTRIES**

| COUNTRY | POPULATION (2008 EST.) |
|---|---|
| 1 Vatican City | 932* |
| 2 Tuvalu | 12,181 |
| 3 Nauru | 13,770 |
| 4 Palau | 21,093 |
| 5 San Marino | 29,973 |
| 6 Monaco | 32,796 |
| 7 Liechtenstein | 34,498 |
| 8 Saint Kitts and Nevis | 39,619 |
| 9 Marshall Islands | 63,139 |
| 10 Dominica | 69,080 |

* July 2006 estimate

Source: US Census Bureau, International Data Base/CIA, *The World Factbook 2007*

# TOP 10 **COUNTRIES IN WHICH WOMEN MOST OUTNUMBER MEN**

| COUNTRY | ESTIMATED WOMEN PER 100 MEN (2008) |
|---|---|
| 1 Estonia | 118.9 |
| 2 Ukraine | 116.8 |
| 3 Russia | 116.7 |
| 4 Latvia | 116.0 |
| 5 Belarus | 114.7 |
| 6 Lithuania | 112.6 |
| 7 Armenia | 112.0 |
| 8 Hungary | 110.1 |
| 9 Georgia | 109.8 |
| 10 = Moldova | 109.6 |
| = Monaco | 109.6 |
| *UK* | *101.9* |

Source: US Census Bureau, International Data Base

The male/female ratio of the world is balanced virtually 50:50 – in Mongolia, the Philippines and Senegal precisely so – although in many Western countries male births slightly outnumber female by a very small percentage. There are certain countries, however, where one sex dominates more markedly for reasons that may include imprecise recording or the non-enumeration of women in countries where their status is considered inferior, or the presence of large numbers of immigrant male workers.

# TOP 10 **COUNTRIES IN WHICH MEN MOST OUTNUMBER WOMEN**

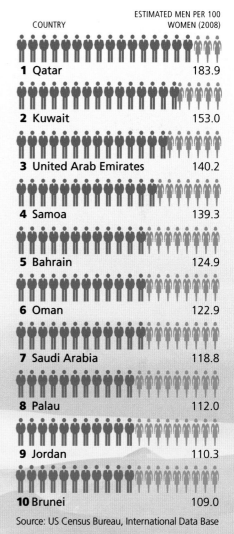

| COUNTRY | ESTIMATED MEN PER 100 WOMEN (2008) |
|---|---|
| 1 Qatar | 183.9 |
| 2 Kuwait | 153.0 |
| 3 United Arab Emirates | 140.2 |
| 4 Samoa | 139.3 |
| 5 Bahrain | 124.9 |
| 6 Oman | 122.9 |
| 7 Saudi Arabia | 118.8 |
| 8 Palau | 112.0 |
| 9 Jordan | 110.3 |
| 10 Brunei | 109.0 |

Source: US Census Bureau, International Data Base

# The United Kingdom

## TOP 10 **LARGEST ENGLISH COUNTIES**

| | COUNTY | AREA SQ KM | SQ MILES |
|---|---|---|---|
| 1 | North Yorkshire | 8,038 | 3,103 |
| 2 | Cumbria | 6,768 | 2,613 |
| 3 | Devon | 6,564 | 2,534 |
| 4 | Lincolnshire | 5,921 | 2,286 |
| 5 | Norfolk | 5,371 | 2,073 |
| 6 | Northumberland | 5,013 | 1,970 |
| 7 | Suffolk | 3,801 | 1,467 |
| 8 | Hampshire | 3,679 | 1,420 |
| 9 | Cornwall and the Isles of Scilly | 3,563 | 1,410 |
| 10 | Kent | 3,544 | 1,368 |

## THE 10 **SMALLEST ENGLISH COUNTIES**

| | COUNTY | AREA SQ KM | SQ MILES |
|---|---|---|---|
| 1 | Bedfordshire | 1,192 | 460 |
| 2 | Buckinghamshire | 1,565 | 604 |
| 3 | Hertfordshire | 1,643 | 634 |
| 4 | Surrey | 1,663 | 642 |
| 5 | East Sussex | 1,709 | 659 |
| 6 | Worcestershire | 1,741 | 672 |
| 7 | Warwickshire | 1,975 | 762 |
| 8 | West Sussex | 1,991 | 768 |
| 9 = | Cheshire | 2,083 | 804 |
| = | Leicestershire | 2,083 | 804 |

## TOP 10 **MOST POPULATED COUNTIES IN ENGLAND**

| | COUNTY* | POPULATION |
|---|---|---|
| 1 | Kent | 1,369,900 |
| 2 | Essex | 1,340,000 |
| 3 | Hampshire | 1,259,400 |
| 4 | Lancashire | 1,156,100 |
| 5 | Surrey | 1,075,600 |
| 6 | Hertfordshire | 1,048,200 |
| 7 | Norfolk | 824,200 |
| 8 | Staffordshire | 816,700 |
| 9 | West Sussex | 764,300 |
| 10 | Nottinghamshire | 762,600 |

\* Non-metropolitan counties only

Source: National Statistics

### Popular Place Names

The most common place name (of towns and villages and other named locations) in Britain is Newton, with over 150 occurrences. The Cottage is the most popular house name, and The Red Lion the most common pub name.

## TOP 10 **LARGEST CITIES IN THE UK 100 YEARS AGO**

| | CITY | POPULATION, 1907 |
|---|---|---|
| 1 | London | 4,758,218 |
| 2 | Glasgow | 847,584 |
| 3 | Liverpool | 746,144 |
| 4 | Manchester | 643,148 |
| 5 | Birmingham | 553,155 |
| 6 | Leeds | 470,268 |
| 7 | Sheffield | 455,553 |
| 8 | Dublin* | 375,350 |
| 9 | Bristol | 367,979 |
| 10 | Belfast | 349,180 |

\* Ireland then part of UK

## TOP 10 **LARGEST CITIES IN THE UK**

| CITY | AREA SQ KM | AREA SQ MILES | POPULATION, 2004 DENSITY PER SQ KM | TOTAL POPULATION |
|---|---|---|---|---|
| **1** London | 1,572 | 606 | 4,726 | 7,429,200 |
| **2** Birmingham | 268 | 103 | 3,703 | 992,400 |
| **3** Leeds | 552 | 213 | 1,304 | 719,600 |
| **4** Glasgow | 175 | 67 | 3,301 | 577,670 |
| **5** Sheffield | 368 | 142 | 1,402 | 516,100 |
| **6** Bradford | 366 | 141 | 1,314 | 481,100 |
| **7** Edinburgh | 264 | 101 | 1,718 | 453,670 |
| **8** Liverpool | 112 | 43 | 3,969 | 444,500 |
| **9** Manchester | 116 | 45 | 3,762 | 437,000 |
| **10** Bristol | 110 | 42 | 3,581 | 393,900 |

Source: National Statistics/General Register Office for Scotland

## TOP 10 **TALLEST BUILDINGS IN THE UK**

| BUILDING / LOCATION* | COMPLETED | STOREYS | HEIGHT M | HEIGHT FT |
|---|---|---|---|---|
| **1** One Canada Square (Canary Wharf Tower) | 1991 | 50 | 235 | 770 |
| **2** = 8 Canada Square (HSBC Building) | 2002 | 45 | 200 | 656 |
| = 25 Canada Square (Citigroup Centre) | 2001 | 45 | 200 | 656 |
| **4** BT Tower (formerly Post Office Tower) | 1965 | 43 | 188 | 616 |
| **5** Tower 42 (formerly NatWest Tower) | 1980 | 43 | 183 | 600 |
| **6** 30 St Mary Axe (Swiss Re Building/'The Gherkin') | 2003 | 40 | 180 | 590 |
| **7** Beetham Tower, Manchester | 2006 | 48 | 171 | 561 |
| **8** Broadgate Tower | 2007 | 36 | 164 | 538 |
| **9** One Churchill Place (Barclays Bank HQ) | 2004 | 32 | 156 | 511 |
| **10** = 25 Bank Street | 2003 | 33 | 153 | 501 |
| = 40 Bank Street | 2003 | 33 | 153 | 501 |

* All London unless otherwise stated

# China

## TOP 10 EXPORTS FROM CHINA

COMMODITY / VALUE ($) (2005)

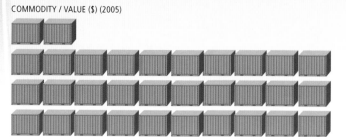

**1** Electrical goods  322,008,000,000

**2** Textiles and products  107,661,000,000

**3** Metals  57,086,000,000

**4** Chemicals  31,853,000,000

**5** Vehicles and transport  28,410,000,000

**6** Scientific, etc. instruments  28,398,000,000

**7** Plastics  23,286,000,000

**8** Footwear and accessories  22,773,000,000

**9** Minerals  20,920,000,000

**10** Leather products  15,601,000,000

Total  761,953,000,000

Source: *China Statistical Yearbook 2006*

## TOP 10 PATENT CATEGORIES IN CHINA

| CATEGORY | PATENT APPLICATIONS | PATENTS GRANTED (2005) |
|---|---|---|
| **1** Electrical | 18,911 | 10,251 |
| **2** Medical and veterinary science and hygiene | 24,875 | 10,179 |
| **3** Telecommunications | 21,578 | 7,013 |
| **4** Measuring and testing | 11,507 | 5,421 |
| **5** Furniture, domestic items | 10,865 | 5,313 |
| **6** Computing, calculating, counting | 12,441 | 4,316 |
| **7** Packing/conveying inflammable materials | 7,143 | 4,175 |
| **8** Engineering, general | 9,047 | 3,988 |
| **9** Stoves, ranges and ventilation | 6,491 | 3,400 |
| **10** Organic chemistry | 6,507 | 3,248 |
| *Total* | *287,162* | *132,654* |

Source: *China Statistical Yearbook 2006*

## TOP 10 TYPES OF BOOK PUBLISHED IN CHINA

| CATEGORY | TITLES PUBLISHED | COPIES PRINTED (2005) |
|---|---|---|
| **1** Culture, science, education, sports | 85,668 | 4,896,590,000 |
| **2** History and geography | 8,525 | 294,020,000 |
| **3** Industrial technology | 29,511 | 196,980,000 |
| **4** Arts | 10,622 | 179,760,000 |
| **5** Languages | 11,659 | 169,860,000 |
| **6** Economics | 18,389 | 142,990,000 |
| **7** Literature | 13,428 | 139,740,000 |
| **8** Politics and law | 10,104 | 119,340,000 |
| **9** Medicine and healthcare | 9,565 | 65,150,000 |
| **10** Mathematics and chemistry | 4,669 | 42,810,000 |
| *Total* | *222,473* | *6,465,970,000* |

Source: *China Statistical Yearbook 2006*

### Little Emperors

In the 1980s, as the population of China passed the one billion mark, fears of overpopulation led to an official policy of one-child families. Without it the current population would be as much as 400 million greater. One consequence, as social commentators have observed, has been the emergence of 'little emperors' – a generation of over-indulged only children.

# TOP 10 ETHNIC GROUPS IN CHINA

| | GROUP | POPULATION |
|---|---|---|
| 1 | Han | 1,136,703,824 |
| 2 | Zhuang | 15,555,800 |
| 3 | Manchu | 8,846,800 |
| 4 | Hui | 8,612,000 |
| 5 | Miao | 7,383,600 |
| 6 | Uygur | 7,207,000 |
| 7 | Yi | 6,578,500 |
| 8 | Tujia | 5,725,000 |
| 9 | Mongolian | 4,802,400 |
| 10 | Tibetan | 4,593,100 |

*Miao women*
*Members of one of the 55 minority ethnic groups officially recognized in China, distinctively dressed Miao women prepare for a festival in Guizhou, the southern province that is home to about half the Miao population of China.*

# TOP 10 SUNNIEST MAJOR CITIES IN CHINA

| | CITY | AVERAGE ANNUAL SUNSHINE HOURS |
|---|---|---|
| 1 | Lhasa | 3,100.0 |
| 2 | Hohhot | 2,816.8 |
| 3 | Yinchuang | 2,813.4 |
| 4 | Dalian | 2,749.7 |
| 5 | Taiyuan | 2,620.9 |
| 6 | Beijing | 2,576.1 |
| 7 | Urumqi | 2,528.7 |
| 8 | Xining | 2,477.5 |
| 9 | Lanzhou | 2,469.9 |
| 10 | Jinan | 2,369.5 |

Source: *China Statistical Yearbook 2006*

Lhasa, the former capital of Tibet, is popularly known as the 'sunlit city'. It benefits from being one of the highest in the world, at 3,650 m (11,975 ft) and has an equable climate, without extreme temperatures or daytime cloud cover.

# TOP 10 TALLEST BUILDINGS IN CHINA

| | BUILDING / LOCATION | YEAR COMPLETED | STOREYS | HEIGHT M | HEIGHT FT |
|---|---|---|---|---|---|
| 1 | Shanghai World Financial Center, Shanghai | 2007* | 101 | 492 | 1,613 |
| 2 | International Commerce Centre, Hong Kong | 2007* | 108 | 484 | 1,587 |
| 3 | Oriental Pearl Tower, Shanghai | 1994 | 14 | 468 | 1,535 |
| 4 | Guangzhou TV & Sightseeing Tower, Guangzhou | 2009* | 37 | 454 | 1,490 |
| 5 | Guangzhou Twin Towers, Guangzhou | 2009* | 103 | 432 | 1,417 |
| 6 | Jin Mao Tower, Shanghai | 1998 | 88 | 421 | 1,381 |
| 7 | Dailian International Trade Center, Dalian | 2007* | 78 | 420 | 1,377 |
| 8 | Two International Finance Centre, Hong Kong | 2003 | 88 | 415 | 1,362 |
| 9 | CITIC Plaza, Guangzhou | 1997 | 80 | 391 | 1,283 |
| 10 | Shun Hing Square, Shenzhen | 1996 | 69 | 384 | 1,260 |

* Under construction – scheduled completion date

# India

## TOP 10 LARGEST STATES IN INDIA

| STATE | AREA KM² | MILES² |
|---|---|---|
| 1 Rajasthan | 342,236 | 132,138 |
| 2 Madhya Pradesh | 308,144 | 118,975 |
| 3 Maharashtra | 307,713 | 118,809 |
| 4 Andhra Pradesh | 275,068 | 106,204 |
| 5 Uttar Pradesh | 238,566 | 92,111 |
| 6 Jammu and Kashmir | 222,236 | 85,806 |
| 7 Gujarat | 196,024 | 75,685 |
| 8 Karnataka | 191,791 | 74,051 |
| 9 Orissa | 155,707 | 60,119 |
| 10 Chhattisgarh | 135,194 | 52,199 |
| *India total* | *3,287,590* | *1,269,346* |

## TOP 10 MOST POPULATED STATES IN INDIA

| STATE | POPULATION* |
|---|---|
| 1 Uttar Pradesh | 166,197,921 |
| 2 Maharashtra | 96,878,627 |
| 3 Bihar | 82,998,509 |
| 4 West Bengal | 80,176,197 |
| 5 Andhra Pradesh | 76,210,007 |
| 6 Tamil Nadu | 62,405,679 |
| 7 Madhya Pradesh | 60,348,023 |
| 8 Rajasthan | 56,507,188 |
| 9 Karnataka | 52,850,562 |
| 10 Gujarat | 50,671,017 |

\* As at 2001 census

## TOP 10 LANGUAGES IN INDIA

| LANGUAGE | SPEAKERS |
|---|---|
| 1 Hindi | 363,839,000 |
| 2 Bengali | 70,561,000 |
| 3 Telugu | 69,634,000 |
| 4 Marathi | 68,030,000 |
| 5 Tamil | 61,527,000 |
| 6 Urdu | 48,062,000 |
| 7 Gujarati | 45,479,000 |
| 8 Malayalam | 35,351,000 |
| 9 Kannada | 35,346,000 |
| 10 Oriya | 31,666,000 |

Source: Central Institute of Indian Languages

**Ancient and modern**
*21st-century India has a technologically skilled labour force, but faces the challenges of a huge population and disparity between the very rich and very poor.*

# TOP 10 **RICHEST INDIANS**

| | NAME | COMPANY / INDUSTRY | NET WORTH ($) |
|---|---|---|---|
| 1 | Lakshmi Mittal | Mittal Steel/metals | 32,000,000,000 |
| 2 | Mukesh Ambani | Reliance/diversified | 20,100,000,000 |
| 3 | Anil Ambani | ADAG/diversified | 18,200,000,000 |
| 4 | Azim Premji | Wipro/ITeS, Software | 17,100,000,000 |
| 5 | Kushal Pal Singh | DLF/property | 10,000,000,000 |
| 6 | Sunil Mittal | Airtel (Bharti Televentures)/ telecoms | 9,500,000,000 |
| 7 | Kumar Birla | Aditya Birla Group/ diversified | 8,000,000,000 |
| 8 | Ramesh Chandra | Unitech/property | 6,400,000,000 |
| 9 | Pallonji Mistry | Shapoorji Pallonji Group/ textiles, construction | 5,600,000,000 |
| 10 | Adi Godrej | Godrej/manufacturing | 4,100,000,000 |

Source: *Forbes* magazine, *The World's Richest People 2006*

# TOP 10 **TALLEST HABITABLE BUILDINGS IN INDIA**\*

| | BUILDING | YEAR COMPLETED | STOREYS | HEIGHT M | FT |
|---|---|---|---|---|---|
| 1 | MVRDC World Trade Centre | 2008# | 35 | 156 | 511 |
| 2 | Shreepati Arcade | 2002 | 45 | 153 | 500 |
| 3 | Belvedere Court | 2000 | 40 | 149 | 490 |
| 4 | Kalpataru Heights | 2000 | 39 | 144 | 472 |
| 5 | Heritage (Hiranandani Gardens) | 2005 | 36 | 138 | 452 |
| 6 | Verona (Hiranandani Gardens) | 2004 | 30 | 129 | 422 |
| 7 | Avalon (Hiranandani Gardens) | 2004 | 30 | 128 | 419 |
| 8 | ITC Grand Central Sheraton & Towers | 2005 | 30 | 127 | 417 |
| 9 | Phiroze Jeejeebhoy Towers | 1980 | 28 | 118 | 387 |
| 10 | Hilton Towers | 1973 | 35 | 117 | 383 |

\* All Mumbai (Bombay)
# Under construction – scheduled completion date

While skyscrapers have become commonplace elsewhere in Asia, tall buildings are rare in India. All those in the Top 10 are in Mumbai, where land is at a premium and population density high.

# Megacities

CITY / COUNTRY / % OF TOTAL COUNTRY POPULATION

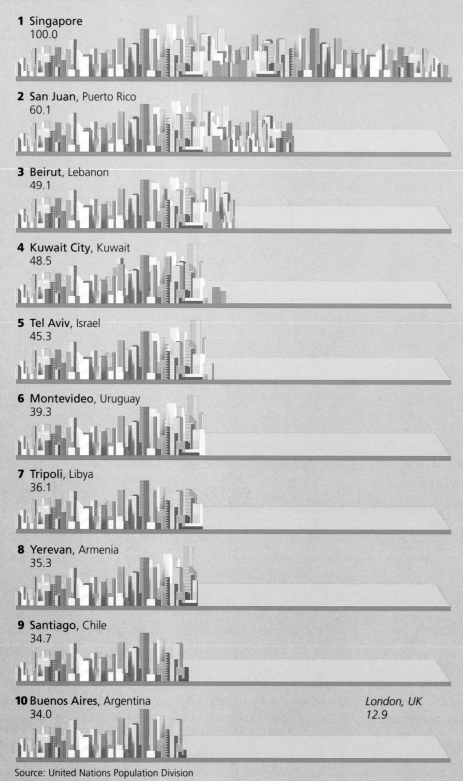

**1** Singapore
100.0

**2** San Juan, Puerto Rico
60.1

**3** Beirut, Lebanon
49.1

**4** Kuwait City, Kuwait
48.5

**5** Tel Aviv, Israel
45.3

**6** Montevideo, Uruguay
39.3

**7** Tripoli, Libya
36.1

**8** Yerevan, Armenia
35.3

**9** Santiago, Chile
34.7

**10** Buenos Aires, Argentina
34.0

*London, UK*
*12.9*

Source: United Nations Population Division

## THE 10 **FIRST CITIES WITH POPULATIONS OF MORE THAN ONE MILLION**

CITY / COUNTRY

**1** Rome, Italy
**2** Alexandria, Egypt
**3** Angkor, Cambodia
**4** Hangchow (Hangzhou), China
**5** London, UK
**6** Paris, France
**7** Peking (Beijing), China
**8** Canton (Guangzhou), China
**9** Berlin, Prussia
**10** New York, USA

Rome's population was reckoned to have exceeded one million some time in the second century BC, and Alexandria soon after. Angkor reached this figure by about AD 900, but was abandoned in the 15th century, and Hangchow in c.1200. London passed the million mark early in the 19th century, followed by others between about 1850 and the late 1870s.

## TOP 10 **COUNTRIES WITH THE MOST MILLION-PLUS CITIES**

| | COUNTRY | CITIES WITH POPULATIONS OF OVER ONE MILLION |
|---|---|---|
| **1** | = China | 52 |
| | = USA | 52 |
| **3** | India | 45 |
| **4** | Brazil | 20 |
| **5** | Russia | 15 |
| **6** | Japan | 13 |
| **7** | Germany | 11 |
| **8** | Mexico | 10 |
| **9** | = Pakistan | 8 |
| | = UK | 8 |

Some 437 cities in the world have populations of more than one million. Although such megacities are found in 100 different countries, many of them contain only one with a population of one million-plus – usually its capital.

**Seoul mate**
*The population of Seoul, South Korea is second only to that of Tokyo, with over 23 million people in the metropolitan area.*

## TOP 10 **LARGEST CITIES**

| CITY / COUNTRY | ESTIMATED POPULATION, 2006 |
|---|---|
| **1 Tokyo**, Japan | 33,400,000 |
| **2 Seoul**, South Korea | 23,100,000 |
| **3 Mexico City**, Mexico | 22,000,000 |
| **4 New York**, USA | 21,800,000 |
| **5 Mumbai** (Bombay), India | 21,100,000 |
| **6 Delhi**, India | 20,800,000 |
| **7 São Paulo**, Brazil | 20,300,000 |
| **8 Shanghai**, China | 18,600,000 |
| **9 Los Angeles**, USA | 17,900,000 |
| **10 Jakarta**, Indonesia | 16,900,000 |

Source: Th. Brinkhoff: The Principal Agglomerations of the World, http://www.citypopulation.de, 2006-11-22

This is based on 'urban agglomerations' as defined by the United Nations, which disregards administrative boundaries in favour of often very extensive built-up areas stretching across densely populated suburbs.

## TOP 10 **LARGEST CAPITAL CITIES**

| CITY / COUNTRY | ESTIMATED POPULATION, 2006 |
|---|---|
| **1 Tokyo** (including Yokohama and Kawasaki), Japan | 34,400,000 |
| **2 Seoul** (including Bucheon, Goyang, Incheon, Seongnam and Suweon), South Korea | 23,100,000 |
| **3 Mexico City** (including Nezahualcóyotl, Ecatepec and Naucalpan), Mexico | 22,000,000 |
| **4 Delhi** (including Faridabad and Ghaziabad), India | 20,800,000 |
| **5 Jakarta** (including Bekasi, Bogor, Depok and Tangerang), Indonesia | 16,900,000 |
| **6 Cairo** (including Al-Jizah and Shubra al-Khaymah), Egypt | 15,800,000 |
| **7 Manila** (including Kalookan and Quezon City), Philippines | 15,200,000 |
| **8 Dhaka**, Bangladesh | 13,600,000 |
| **9 Buenos Aires** (including San Justo and La Plata), Argentina | 13,500,000 |
| **10 Moscow**, Russia | 13,400,000 |

Source: Th. Brinkhoff: The Principal Agglomerations of the World, http://www.citypopulation.de, 2006-11-22

# Tall Buildings & Structures

## TOP 10 HIGHEST DAMS

| | DAM / RIVER / LOCATION | YEAR COMPLETED | HEIGHT M | FT |
|---|---|---|---|---|
| 1 | **Rogun**, Vakhsh, Tajikistan | 1985 | 335 | 1,099 |
| 2 | **Nurek**, Vakhsh, Tajikistan | 1980 | 300 | 984 |
| 3 | **Xiaowan**, Lancangjiang, China | 2012* | 292 | 958 |
| 4 | **Grande Dixence**, Dixence, Switzerland | 1962 | 285 | 935 |
| 5 | **Inguri**, Inguri, Georgia | 1984 | 272 | 892 |
| 6 | **Vaiont**, Vaiont, Italy | 1961 | 262 | 860 |
| 7 | = **Manuel M. Torres**, Chicoasén,Grijalva, Mexico | 1981 | 261 | 856 |
| | = **Tehri**, Bhagirathi, India | 2006 | 261 | 856 |
| 9 | **Alvaro Obregón**, Mextiquic, Mexico | 1946 | 260 | 853 |
| 10 | **Mauvoisin**, Drance de Bagnes, Switzerland | 1957 | 250 | 820 |

\* Under construction – scheduled completion date

Source: International Commission on Large Dams (ICOLD), *World Register of Dams*

## THE 10 LAST BUILDINGS AND STRUCTURES TO HOLD THE TITLE OF 'WORLD'S TALLEST'

| | STRUCTURE | YEAR | HEIGHT M | FT |
|---|---|---|---|---|
| 1 | **Warszawa Radio Mast**, Konstantynow, Poland. Operational 30 July 1974, collapsed 8 August 1991 during renovation, killing 3 and injuring 12 | 1974 | 645 | 2,118 |
| 2 | **KVLY (formerly-KTHI) TV Mast**, Blanchard, North Dakota, USA. Since the destruction of the Warszawa Radio Mast, it is again the world's tallest structure | 1963 | 628 | 2,063 |
| 3 | **Nexstar Broadcasting Tower Vivian**, Vivian, Louisiana, USA | 1961 | 534 | 1,752 |
| 4 | **KFVS TV Mast**, Egypt Mills, Missouri, USA | 1960 | 511 | 1,677 |
| 5 | **KOBR-TV Tower (KSWS-TV Transmitter)** Caprock, New Mexico, USA | 1960 | 490 | 1,608 |
| 6 | **KWTV Mast**, Oklahoma City, Oklahoma, USA | 1954 | 479 | 1,572 |
| 7 | **Empire State Building**, New York, USA | 1930 | 381 | 1,250 |
| 8 | **Chrysler Building**, New York, USA | 1930 | 319 | 1,046 |
| 9 | **Eiffel Tower**, Paris, France | 1889 | 300 | 984 |
| 10 | **Washington Monument**, Washington D.C., USA | 1884 | 169 | 555 |

The Great Pyramid, Giza, Egypt (c. 2580 BC), originally 146 m (479 ft), held the record as the world's tallest structure until 1311, when Lincoln Cathedral (159.7 m/524 ft) overtook it. A succession of cathedrals held the title until the completion of the Washington Monument. All the 'world's tallests' for over 50 years have been guyed masts.

## SINGER CENTENARY

Although the Eiffel Tower was taller, at its completion in 1908 the 186.5-m (612-ft) Singer Building, Manhattan, New York, built for the Singer sewing-machine company, became the tallest habitable building in the world – but only briefly, as the 213-m (700-ft) Metropolitan Life Insurance Company Tower overtook it the following year. It was demolished in 1968 and the 226-m (743-ft) One Liberty Plaza (1973) built on the site. The Singer Building was the tallest ever destroyed prior to the collapse of the twin towers of the World Trade Center in the 9/11 attacks of 2001.

## TOP 10 **CITIES WITH MOST SKYSCRAPERS**\*

| | CITY / LOCATION | SKYSCRAPERS |
|---|---|---|
| 1 | Hong Kong, China | 195 |
| 2 | New York City, USA | 186 |
| 3 | Chicago, USA | 87 |
| 4 | Shanghai, China | 72 |
| 5 | Tokyo, Japan | 65 |
| 6 | Singapore City, Singapore | 38 |
| 7 | Houston, USA | 29 |
| 8 | Seoul, South Korea | 27 |
| 9 | Sydney, Australia | 25 |
| 10 | Kuala Lumpur, Malaysia | 24 |
| | *London* | 9 |

\* Completed habitable buildings of more than 152 m (500 ft)

## TOP 10 **TALLEST CHURCHES**

| | CHURCH / LOCATION | YEAR COMPLETED | HEIGHT\* M | FT |
|---|---|---|---|---|
| 1 | Sagrada Família, Barcelona, Spain | 2020# | 170 | 558 |
| 2 | Ulm Cathedral, Ulm, Germany | 1890 | 162 | 530 |
| 3 | Notre-Dame Cathedral, Rouen, France | 1876 | 158 | 518 |
| 4 | Cologne Cathedral, Cologne, Germany | 1880 | 157 | 516 |
| 5 | Our Lady of Peace Basilica, Yamoussoukro, Côte d'Ivoire | 1990 | 149 | 489 |
| 6 | St Nicholas, Hamburg, Germany | 1847 | 147 | 482 |
| 7 | Notre Dame Cathedral, Strasbourg, France | 1439 | 144 | 472 |
| 8 | St Peter's, Rome, Italy | 1626 | 138 | 452 |
| 9 | St Stephen's Cathedral, Vienna, Austria | 1570 | 137 | 448 |
| 10 | Neuer Dom, Linz, Austria | 1924 | 134 | 439 |

\* To tip of spire
# Under construction – scheduled completion date

The Chicago Methodist Temple, Chicago, USA is 173 m (568 ft) high, but is sited atop a 25-storey, 100-m (328-ft) building. Salisbury Cathedral at 123 m (404 ft) is the UK's tallest religious building. St Paul's Cathedral and Liverpool Anglican Cathedral are the only others over 100 m (328 ft) tall.

## TOP 10 **TALLEST TWIN TOWERS**

| | BUILDING / LOCATION / YEAR COMPLETED | STOREYS | HEIGHT M | FT |
|---|---|---|---|---|
| 1 | Petronas Towers, Kuala Lumpur, Malaysia, 1997 | 96 | 452 | 1,482 |
| | roof height | | 379 | 1,244 |
| 2 | Guangzhou Twin Towers, Guangzhou, China, 2009\* | 104 | 432 | 1,417 |
| 3 | Emirates Park Tower, Dubai, UAE, 2009\* | 77 | 395 | 1,296 |
| 4 | The Imperial, Mumbai, India, 2007\* | 60 | 249 | 815 |
| 5 | Al Fattan Towers, Dubai, UAE, 2006 | 60 | 245 | 802 |
| 6 | Dalian Futures Square, Dalian, China, 2007\* | 62 | 230 | 755 |
| 7 | Grand Gateway, Shanghai, China, 2005 | 52 | 225 | 738 |
| 8 | Atlantic Richfield, Tower, Los Angeles, USA, 1972 | 52 | 213 | 699 |
| 9 | Huaxia Financial Square, Shanghai, China, 2003/2005 | 42 | 202 | 670 |
| 10 | Parque Central Offinicas, Caracas, Venezuela, 1986 | 56 | 200 | 656 |

\* Under construction – scheduled completion date

*Tall twins*
The Petronas Towers were the world's tallest overall from 1984 to 2004.

# Bridges & Tunnels

*The Akashi-Kaikyo, currently the world's longest bridge.*

## TOP 10 LONGEST SUSPENSION BRIDGES

| BRIDGE / LOCATION | YEAR COMPLETED* | LENGTH OF MAIN SPAN M | FT |
|---|---|---|---|
| 1 = Kitan Straight, Japan | u/c | 2,500 | 8,202 |
| = Qiongzhou Haixia, China | u/c | 2,500 | 8,202 |
| 3 Akashi-Kaikyo, Kobe-Naruto, Japan | 1998 | 1,991 | 6,532 |
| 4 Izmit Bay, Turkey | 2002 | 1,668 | 5,472 |
| 5 Donmgfang, China | u/c | 1,650 | 5,413 |
| 6 Great Belt, Denmark | 1997 | 1,624 | 5,328 |
| 7 Ryungyang, China | 2005 | 1,490 | 4,888 |
| 8 Ging Lon Da Qiao, China | 2007# | 1,418 | 4,652 |
| 9 Humber Estuary, UK | 1980 | 1,410 | 4,625 |
| 10 Jiangyin, China | 1998 | 1,385 | 4,543 |

\* u/c – under construction
\# Scheduled completion date

The design of a suspension bridge, in which the weight of the deck is borne by cables, enables single spans to be longer than any other type of bridge. The proposed Messina Strait Bridge between Sicily and Calabria, Italy, would have broken all records with a centre span of 3,300 m (10,827 ft), but the project was cancelled.

## TOP 10 LONGEST CABLE-STAYED BRIDGES

| BRIDGE / LOCATION | YEAR COMPLETED* | LENGTH OF MAIN SPAN M | FT |
|---|---|---|---|
| 1 Suzhou-Nantong, China | u/c | 1,088 | 3,569 |
| 2 Stonecutters, Hong Kong | 2008# | 1,018 | 3,339 |
| 3 = Dongfang, China | u/c | 900 | 2,952 |
| = Linding, China | u/c | 900 | 2,952 |
| 5 Tatara, Onomichi-Imabari, Japan | 1999 | 890 | 2,920 |
| 6 Pont de Normandie, Le Havre, France | 1994 | 856 | 2,808 |
| 7 Zhenyang, China | u/c | 850 | 2,788 |
| 8 Gaopu, China | u/c | 700 | 2,296 |
| 9 Nancha (Second Nanjing), China | 2001 | 628 | 2,060 |
| 10 Wuhan Baishazhou, China | 2000 | 618 | 2,027 |

\* u/c – under construction
\# Scheduled completion date

The towers of a cable-stayed bridge bear the weight of the deck, to which they are connected by cables. Multiple towers enable them to be very long – the Hanzhou Bay Bridge, China (2008), will measure 36 km (22 miles) overall.

## TOP 10 LONGEST BRIDGES IN THE UK

| BRIDGE / LOCATION | TYPE* | YEAR COMPLETED | LENGTH OF MAIN SPAN M | FT |
|---|---|---|---|---|
| 1 Humber Estuary, Hessle–Barton-on-Humber | S | 1980 | 1,410 | 4,626 |
| 2 Forth Road, North Queensferry–South Queensferry | S | 1964 | 1,006 | 3,300 |
| 3 Severn Bridge, Bristol | S | 1966 | 988 | 3,240 |
| 4 Firth of Forth, North Queensferry–South Queensferry | CT | 1890 | 521 | 1,710 |
| 5 Second Severn Crossing, Bristol | CSG | 1996 | 456 | 1,496 |
| 6 Queen Elizabeth II, Dartford | CSG | 1991 | 450 | 1,476 |
| 7 Tamar, Saltash–Plymouth | S | 1961 | 335 | 1,100 |
| 8 Runcorn-Widnes | SA | 1961 | 330 | 1,082 |
| 9 Erskine, Glasgow | CSG | 1971 | 305 | 1,000 |
| 10 Skye, Kyleakin-Kyle of Lochalsh | PCG | 1995 | 250 | 820 |

\* S – Suspension; CT – Cantilever truss; CSG – Cable-stayed steel girder and truss; SA – Steel arch; PCG – Pre-stressed concrete girder

### Brunel's Suspension Bridge
One of the first projects of the great engineer Isambard Kingdom Brunel, the 214–m (702-ft) Clifton Suspension Bridge, Bristol, UK, was started in 1831, but took until 1864 – five years after Brunel's death – to complete. It was Britain's longest suspension bridge for almost 100 years, until the construction of the 335-m (1,100-ft) Tamar Bridge in 1962.

# TOP 10 **LONGEST RAIL TUNNELS**

| TUNNEL / LOCATION / YEAR COMPLETED | LENGTH | |
|---|---|---|
| | M | FT |
| **1** **AlpTransit Gotthard**, Switzerland, 2015* | 57,072 | 187,244 |
| **2** **Seikan**, Japan, 1988 | 53,850 | 176,673 |
| **3** **Channel Tunnel**, France/England, 1994 | 50,450 | 165,518 |
| **4** **Moscow Metro** (Serpukhovsko-Timiryazevskaya line), Russia, 1983 | 38,900 | 127,625 |
| **5** **Guadarrama**, Spain, 2007* | 28,377 | 97,100 |
| **6** **London Underground** (East Finchley/Morden, Northern Line), UK, 1939 | 27,840 | 91,339 |
| **7** **Hakkouda**, Japan, 2013* | 26,455 | 86,795 |
| **8** **Iwate**, Japan, 2013* | 25,810 | 84,678 |
| **9** **Lainzer/Wienerwald**, Austria, 2015* | 23,844 | 78,228 |
| **10** **Iiyama**, Japan, 2013* | 22,225 | 72,917 |

* Under construction –
scheduled completion date

The world's longest rail tunnel, the AlpTransit Gotthard, Switzerland, was proposed as early as 1947 and given the go-ahead in 1998 after a referendum of the Swiss electorate. When completed, trains will travel through it at 250 km/h (155 mph).

## TOP 10 **LONGEST ROAD TUNNELS**

# 5
## CULTURE

# World Culture

## THE 10 **FIRST EUROPEAN CAPITALS OF CULTURE**

| | CITY / COUNTRY | YEAR |
|---|---|---|
| 1 | Athens, Greece | 1985 |
| 2 | Florence, Italy | 1986 |
| 3 | Amsterdam, Netherlands | 1987 |
| 4 | West Berlin, West Germany | 1988 |
| 5 | Paris, France | 1989 |
| 6 | Glasgow, UK | 1990 |
| 7 | Dublin, Ireland | 1991 |
| 8 | Madrid, Spain | 1992 |
| 9 | Antwerp, Belgium | 1993 |
| 10 | Lisbon, Portugal | 1994 |

Each year since 1985, a European city has been designated European Capital (originally 'City') of Culture, providing it with an opportunity to draw attention to its cultural attractions for the year. Each country in the European Union has an opportunity to participate in turn, with two capitals being selected from 2008.

*Left: Cultural icon*
*Michelangelo's statue of David is one of the world's most widely recognized works of art. Completed in 1504, the 5.17-m (17-ft) sculpture is housed in the Gallereria dell'Accademia, Florence, Italy.*

## THE 10 **LATEST ARAB CULTURAL CAPITALS**

| YEAR | CITY / COUNTRY |
|---|---|
| 2007 | Algiers, Algeria |
| 2006 | Muscat, Oman |
| 2005 | Khartoum, Sudan |
| 2004 | Sana'a, Yemen |
| 2003 | Rabat, Morocco |
| 2002 | Amman, Jordan |
| 2001 | Kuwait City, Kuwait |
| 2000 | Riyadh, Saudi Arabia |
| 1999 | Beirut, Lebanon |
| 1998 | Sharjah, United Arab Emirates |

Source: UNESCO

Initiated by the Cultural Capitals Programme of the United Nations Educational, Scientific and Cultural Organization (UNESCO) to promote Arab culture and foster cooperation throughout the Arab world, Cairo, Egypt, was declared the first Arab Cultural Capital in 1996.

*Below: Cultural capital*
*Athens, Greece, was the pioneering European City (now Capital) of Culture, since when, up to 2007, over 30 cities have been designated.*

# TOP 10 **MOST-VISITED NATIONAL TRUST PROPERTIES IN THE UK**

| PROPERTY / LOCATION | VISITORS, 2005–06 |
|---|---|
| **1** Wakehurst Place, West Sussex | 423,819 |
| **2** Stourhead House and Garden, Wiltshire | 344,179 |
| **3** Fountains Abbey and Studley Royal, North Yorkshire | 312,326 |
| **4** Waddesdon Manor, Buckinghamshire | 310,555 |
| **5** Polesden Lacey, Surrey | 288,119 |
| **6** St Michael's Mount, Cornwall | 197,874 |
| **7** Lanhydrock, Cornwall | 187,525 |
| **8** Chartwell, Kent | 186,699 |
| **9** Sheffield Park, East Sussex | 185,351 |
| **10** Corfe Castle, Dorset | 173,829 |

Source: National Trust

# THE 10 **LATEST UNESCO WORLD HERITAGE SITES IN THE UK**

| SITE | YEAR |
|---|---|
| **1** Cornwall and West Devon Mining Landscape | 2006 |
| **2** Liverpool – Maritime Mercantile City | 2004 |
| **3** Royal Botanic Gardens, Kew | 2003 |
| **4** = Derwent Valley Mills | 2001 |
| = Dorset and East Devon Coast | 2001 |
| = New Lanark | 2001 |
| = Saltaire | 2001 |
| **8** Blaenavon Industrial Landscape | 2000 |
| **9** Orkney Neolithic sites | 1999 |
| **10** Maritime Greenwich | 1997 |

# TOP 10 **OLDEST MUSEUMS AND ART GALLERIES IN THE UK**

MUSEUM/ART GALLERY / FOUNDED

**1** Ashmolean Museum, Oxford  1683

**2** British Museum, London  1753

**3** National Museum of Antiquities, Edinburgh  1780

**4** Hunterian Museum, Glasgow  1807

**5** = Museum of Antiquities, Newcastle upon Tyne  1813

= Royal College of Surgeons Museum, London  1813

**7** Dulwich Picture Gallery, London  1814

**8** Fitzwilliam Museum, Cambridge  1816

**9** Leeds City Museum  1820

**10** Manchester Museum  1821

There are some arguments for stating that the Tower Armouries at the Tower of London are the UK's oldest museum. However, although they were established during the reign of Henry VIII (1509–47) and became a showplace for the collection of royal armour, they were not open to the public until much later.

# Words & Language

## TOP 10 **LANGUAGES SPOKEN IN THE UK**

| | LANGUAGE | APPROX. SPEAKERS* |
|---|---|---|
| 1 | English | 58,190,000 |
| 2 | Welsh | 582,000 |
| 3 | Eastern Panjabi | 471,000 |
| 4 | =Bengali | 400,000 |
| | =Urdu | 400,000 |
| 6 | =Chinese (Cantonese) | 300,000 |
| | =Sylheti# | 300,000 |
| 8 | =Greek | 200,000 |
| | =Italian | 200,000 |
| 10 | Caribbean Creole | 170,000 |

\* As primary language
\# Spoken in Bangladesh

*Studying the* Qu'ran
*Widely spoken in North Africa and the Middle East, Arabic is the first language of upwards of 200 million people.*

## TOP 10 **LANGUAGES OFFICIALLY SPOKEN IN THE MOST COUNTRIES**

| | LANGUAGE | COUNTRIES |
|---|---|---|
| 1 | English | 51 |
| 2 | French | 31 |
| 3 | Arabic | 26 |
| 4 | Spanish | 22 |
| 5 | Portuguese | 10 |
| 6 | German | 7 |
| 7 | Italian | 6 |
| 8 | =Dutch | 5 |
| | =Russian | 5 |
| 10 | =Croatian | 4 |
| | =Turkish | 4 |

There are many countries in the world with more than one official language – both English and French are recognized officially in Canada, for example. English is used in numerous countries as the *lingua franca*, the common language that enables people who speak mutually unintelligible languages to communicate with each other.

## TOP 10 **LANGUAGES THAT WILL BE SPOKEN BY THE YOUTH OF 2050**

| | LANGUAGE | ESTIMATED NO. OF 15–24-YEAR-OLD SPEAKERS, 2050 |
|---|---|---|
| 1 | Chinese | 166,000,000 |
| 2 | Hindu/Urdu | 73,700,000 |
| 3 | Arabic | 72,200,000 |
| 4 | English | 65,000,000 |
| 5 | Spanish | 62,800,000 |
| 6 | Portuguese | 32,500,000 |
| 7 | Bengali | 31,600,000 |
| 8 | Russian | 22,500,000 |
| 9 | Japanese | 18,200,000 |
| 10 | Malay | 10,500,000 |

Source: David Graddol, *The Future of English?*, British Council

## TOP 10 MOST COMMON WORDS IN ENGLISH

| WRITTEN | | SPOKEN |
|---|:---:|---|
| the | **1** | be |
| of | **2** | the |
| and | **3** | I |
| a | **4** | you |
| in | **5** | and |
| to | **6** | it |
| is | **7** | have |
| was | **8** | a |
| it | **9** | not |
| for | **10** | do |

Source: British National Corpus

A survey of a wide range of texts containing a total of almost 90 million words indicated that, in written English, one word in every 16 is 'the'.

## TOP 10 COUNTRIES WITH THE MOST SPANISH-LANGUAGE SPEAKERS

| | COUNTRY | APPROX. NO. OF NATIVE SPEAKERS |
|---|---|---|
| 1 | Mexico | 106,255,000 |
| 2 | Colombia | 45,600,000 |
| 3 | Spain | 44,400,000 |
| 4 | Argentina | 41,248,000 |
| 5 | USA | 31,000,000 |
| 6 | Venezuela | 26,021,000 |
| 7 | Peru | 23,191,000 |
| 8 | Chile | 15,795,000 |
| 9 | Cuba | 11,285,000 |
| 10 | Ecuador | 10,946,000 |

## TOP 10 ONLINE LANGUAGES

| | LANGUAGE | % OF ALL INTERNET USERS | INTERNET USERS* |
|---|---|---|---|
| 1 | English | 29.5 | 328,666,386 |
| 2 | Chinese | 14.3 | 159,001,513 |
| 3 | Spanish | 8.0 | 89,077,232 |
| 4 | Japanese | 7.7 | 86,300,000 |
| 5 | German | 5.3 | 58,711,687 |
| 6 | French | 5.0 | 55,521,294 |
| 7 | Portuguese | 3.6 | 40,216,760 |
| 8 | Korean | 3.1 | 34,120,000 |
| 9 | Italian | 2.8 | 30,763,940 |
| 10 | Arabic | 2.6 | 28,540,700 |
| | *Top 10 languages* | *81.8* | *910,919,512* |
| | *Rest of world languages* | *18.2* | *203,354,914* |
| | *World total* | *100.0* | *1,114,274,426* |

* As at March 2007

Source: Internet World Stats
http://www.internetworldstats.com/

### Cornish Speakers

Once spoken by 38,000 people, the Cornish language died out with Dolly Pentreath (c. 1692–1777), claimed to be its last native speaker. In 1860 Prince Louis Lucien Bonaparte erected a monument to her in Mousehole, since when various initiatives have led to the revival of Cornish, which is today spoken by over 300 people.

# Education

## TOP 10 COUNTRIES WITH THE MOST PRIMARY SCHOOL PUPILS

| | COUNTRY / PRIMARY SCHOOL PUPILS | |
|---|---|---|
| 1 | India | 125,568,597 |
| 2 | China | 120,998,605 |
| 3 | Indonesia | 29,050,834 |
| 4 | USA | 24,848,518 |
| 5 | Nigeria | 21,110,707 |
| 6 | Brazil | 19,380,387 |
| 7 | Bangladesh | 17,953,300 |
| 8 | Pakistan | 16,207,286 |
| 9 | Mexico | 14,857,191 |
| 10 | Philippines | 12,970,635 |
| | UK | 4,488,162 |
| | World total | 682,646,764 |

Source: UNESCO, *Global Education Digest 2006*

## TOP 10 COUNTRIES WITH THE MOST SECONDARY SCHOOL PUPILS

| | COUNTRY | % FEMALE | SECONDARY SCHOOL PUPILS |
|---|---|---|---|
| 1 | China | 47 | 98,762,802 |
| 2 | India | 43 | 81,050,129 |
| 3 | Brazil | 52 | 26,789,210 |
| 4 | USA | 49 | 23,854,458 |
| 5 | Indonesia | 49 | 15,872,535 |
| 6 | Russia | 49 | 14,521,818 |
| 7 | Bangladesh | 51 | 11,051,234 |
| 8 | Iran | 47 | 10,312,561 |
| 9 | Mexico | 51 | 10,188,185 |
| 10 | Vietnam | 48 | 9,588,698 |
| | UK | 54 | 9,219,054 |

Source: UNESCO, *Global Education Digest 2006*

## TOP 10 OLDEST SCHOOLS IN THE UK

| | SCHOOL | FOUNDED |
|---|---|---|
| 1 | King's School, Canterbury | AD 597 |
| 2 | King's School, Rochester | AD 604 |
| 3 | St Peter's School, York | AD 627 |
| 4 | Warwick School | AD 914 |
| 5 | St Alban's School | AD 948 |
| 6 | King's School, Ely | AD 970 |
| 7 | Norwich School | 1096 |
| 8 | Abingdon School | 1100 |
| 9 | Thetford Grammar School | 1119 |
| 10 | High School of Glasgow | 1124 |

# TOP 10 **LARGEST UNIVERSITIES**

UNIVERSITY / COUNTRY / STUDENTS

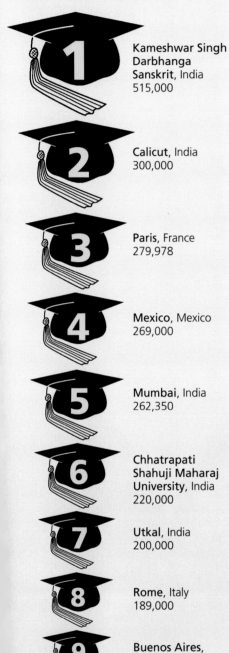

**1** Kameshwar Singh Darbhanga Sanskrit, India
515,000

**2** Calicut, India
300,000

**3** Paris, France
279,978

**4** Mexico, Mexico
269,000

**5** Mumbai, India
262,350

**6** Chhatrapati Shahuji Maharaj University, India
220,000

**7** Utkal, India
200,000

**8** Rome, Italy
189,000

**9** Buenos Aires, Argentina
183,397

**10** Guadalajara, Mexico
180,776

Some distance-learning establishments, such as the Indira Gandhi National Open University, India, with 1.43 million students, are considerably larger than these.

*Paris University*
*Founded in the mid-12th century, the University of Paris was reorganized in 1970 and today comprises 13 separate bodies located across the city, each of which offers a range of specialized subjects.*

# TOP 10 **LARGEST UNIVERSITIES IN THE UK** *

UNIVERSITY / UNDERGRADUATES

**1** University of London  82,732

**2** University of Wales  66,672

**3** Leeds Metropolitan University  41,660

**4** University of Manchester  36,907

**5** University of Leeds  35,963

**6** Thames Valley University  34,000

**7** London Metropolitan University  33,451

**8** Manchester Metropolitan University  31,800

**9** University of Nottingham  29,727

**10** Anglia Ruskin University  28,154

* Excluding Open University (approximately 180,000 students)

# TOP 10 **OLDEST UNIVERSITIES** *

| | UNIVERSITY | COUNTRY | FOUNDED |
|---|---|---|---|
| **1** | Parma | Italy | 1064 |
| **2** | Bologna | Italy | 1088 |
| **3** | Paris | France | 1150 |
| **4** | Oxford | England | 1167 |
| **5** | Modena | Italy | 1175 |
| **6** | Cambridge | England | 1209 |
| **7** | Salamanca | Spain | 1218 |
| **8** | Padua | Italy | 1222 |
| **9** | Naples | Italy | 1224 |
| **10** | Toulouse | France | 1229 |

* Only those in continuous operation since founding

# Books & Libraries

## TOP 10 **BESTSELLING NON-FICTION BOOKS**

| | BOOK / FIRST PUBLISHED | MINIMUM ESTIMATED SALES* |
|---|---|---|
| **1** | The Bible | 6,000,000,000 |
| **2** | Quotations from the Works of Mao Tse-tung, 1966 | 900,000,000 |
| **3** | Xinhua Zidian (Chinese dictionary), 1953 | 400,000,000 |
| **4** | Qur'an (Koran) | 200,000,000 |
| **5** | Noah Webster, The American Spelling Book, 1783 | 100,000,000 |
| **6** | William Holmes McGuffey, The McGuffey Readers, 1836 | 60,000,000 |
| **7** | Benjamin Spock, The Common Sense Book of Baby and Child Care, 1946 | 50,000,000 |
| **8** | Elbert Hubbard, A Message to Garcia, 1899 | 45,000,000 |
| **9** = | Rev Charles Monroe Sheldon, In His Steps: 'What Would Jesus Do?', 1896 | 30,000,000 |
| = | Napoleon Hill, Think and Grow Rich, 1918 | 30,000,000 |
| = | A. S. Hornby, et al, Oxford Advanced Learner's Dictionary, 1948 | 30,000,000 |

\* Including translations; excluding annual publications and series

## TOP 10 **BESTSELLING NOVELS**

| | BOOK / FIRST PUBLISHED | MINIMUM ESTIMATED SALES* |
|---|---|---|
| **1** | J. R. R. Tolkien, The Lord of the Rings, 1954–55 | 100,000,000 |
| **2** | J. K. Rowling, Harry Potter and the Philosopher's Stone, 1997 | 87,000,000 |
| **3** = | Dan Brown, The Da Vinci Code, 2003 | 65,000,000 |
| = | J. K. Rowling, Harry Potter and the Half-Blood Prince, 2005 | 65,000,000 |
| **5** = | J. D. Salinger, The Catcher in the Rye, 1951 | 60,000,000 |
| = | J. K. Rowling, Harry Potter and the Chamber of Secrets, 1998 | 60,000,000 |
| **7** = | J. K. Rowling, Harry Potter and the Prisoner of Azkaban, 1999 | 55,000,000 |
| = | J. K. Rowling, Harry Potter and the Goblet of Fire, 2000 | 55,000,000 |
| = | J. K. Rowling, Harry Potter and the Order of the Phoenix, 2003 | 55,000,000 |
| **10** = | Johanna Spyri, Heidi, 1880 | 50,000,000 |
| = | Antoine de Saint-Exupéry, Le Petit Prince (The Little Prince), 1943 | 50,000,000 |

\* Including translations

**Pottermania**
*The launch of each new Harry Potter title has generated a frenzy of publicity and multi-million sales in over 60 languages.*

# TOP 10 MOST EXPENSIVE BOOKS AND MANUSCRIPTS

BOOK / MANUSCRIPT / SALE*                                              PRICE (£)#

**1  The Codex Hammer** (formerly Codex Leicester), 1506–10   19,263,602 ($30,802,500)
Christie's New York, 11 Nov 1994
This is one of Leonardo da Vinci's notebooks, which includes many scientific drawings
and diagrams. It was purchased by Bill Gates, the billionaire founder of Microsoft.

**2  The Rothschild Prayerbook**, c. 1503                              8,581,500
Christie's London, 8 Jul 1999
This holds the world-record price for an illuminated manuscript.

**3  The Gospels of Henry the Lion**, c. 1173–75                       7,400,000
Sotheby's London, 6 Dec 1983
At the time of its sale, it became the most expensive manuscript, book or work of art
other than a painting ever sold.

**4  John James Audubon's The Birds of America**, 1827–38   6,042,768 ($8,802,500)
Christie's New York, 10 Mar 2000
The record for any printed book. Further copies of the same book, a collection of more
than 400 large, hand-coloured engravings, have also fetched high prices. A facsimile
reprint of *The Birds of America* published in 1985 by Abbeville Press, New York, was
listed at $30,000 (£15,000), making it the most expensive book ever published.

**5  The Canterbury Tales**, Geoffrey Chaucer, c. 1476–77              4,621,500
Christie's London, 8 Jul 1998
Printed by William Caxton and purchased by Sir Paul Getty, it set the record for a work
of English literature. In 1776, the same volume had changed hands for just £6.

**6  Comedies, Histories, and Tragedies,**
**The First Folio of William Shakespeare**, 1623          4,171,854 ($6,166,000)
Christie's New York, 8 Oct 2001
This sale marks the world auction record for a 17th-century book. Another was sold
privately in 2003 (by Oriel College Oxford to Sir Paul Getty) for a rumoured £3,500,000,
and one owned by Dr Williams's Library at Sotheby's, London, on 13 July 2006 for
£2,800,000.

**7  The Gutenberg Bible**, 1455                           3,264,688 ($5,390,000)
Christie's New York, USA, 22 Oct 1987
One of the first books ever printed, by Johann Gutenberg and Johann Fust.

**8  The Northumberland Bestiary**, c. 1250–60                         2,700,000
Sotheby's London, 29 Nov 1990

**9  The Cornaro Missal**, c. 1503                                     2,600,000
Christie's, London, 8 Jul 1999
This manuscript, formerly owned by the Barons Nathaniel and Albert von Rothschild,
achieved a world-record price for an Italian manuscript.

**10 The Burdett Psalter and Hours**, c. 1282–86                       2,500,000
Sotheby's London, 23 Jun 1998

\* Excludes collections
# Includes buyer's premium

# THE 10 LATEST MAN BOOKER PRIZE WINNERS

| YEAR | AUTHOR / TITLE |
| --- | --- |
| **2006** | Kiran Desai, *The Inheritance of Loss* |
| **2005** | John Banville, *The Sea* |
| **2004** | Alan Hollinghurst, *The Line of Beauty* |
| **2003** | D. B. C. Pierre, *Vernon God Little* |
| **2002** | Yann Martel, *Life of Pi* |
| **2001** | Peter Carey, *True History of the Kelly Gang* |
| **2000** | Margaret Atwood, *The Blind Assassin* |
| **1999** | J. M. Coetzee, *Disgrace* |
| **1998** | Ian McEwan, *Amsterdam* |
| **1997** | Arundhati Roy, *The God of Small Things* |

# THE 10 FIRST PUBLIC LIBRARIES IN THE UK

LIBRARY / FOUNDED

| | | |
| --- | --- | --- |
| **1** | Canterbury | 1847 |
| **2** | Warrington | 1848 |
| **3** | Salford | 1849 |
| **4** | Winchester | 1851 |
| **5** | = Liverpool | 1852 |
| | = Manchester Free | 1852 |
| **7** | = Bolton | 1853 |
| | = Ipswich | 1853 |
| **9** | Oxford | 1854 |
| **10** | = Cambridge | 1855 |
| | = Kidderminster | 1855 |

Some specialist institutions, such as
theological libraries, opened their doors
to the public as early as the 17th century,
but charged a fee to borrowers. Following
the 1850 Public Libraries Act, the
Manchester Free Library, which opened
on 2 September 1852, was the country's
first free municipally supported lending
library open to the public.

# The Press

## TOP 10 **OLDEST NEWSPAPERS IN THE WORLD**

| | NEWSPAPER | COUNTRY | FOUNDED |
|---|---|---|---|
| 1 | Haarlems Dagblad | Netherlands | 1656 |
| 2 | Gazzetta di Mantova | Italy | 1664 |
| 3 | The London Gazette | UK | 1665 |
| 4 | Wiener Zeitung | Austria | 1703 |
| 5 | Hildesheimer Allgemeine Zeitung | Germany | 1705 |
| 6 | Berrow's Worcester Journal | UK | 1709 |
| 7 | Newcastle Journal | UK | 1711 |
| 8 | Stamford Mercury | UK | 1712 |
| 9 | Northampton Mercury | UK | 1720 |
| 10 | Hanauer Anzeiger | Germany | 1725 |

This list includes only newspapers that have been published continuously since their founding. The former No. 1 on this list, the *Swedish Post-och Inrikes Tidninga*r, founded in 1645, ceased publication on paper on 1 January 2007 and is now available only online.

*The word on the street*
*Despite the wide choice of alternative media, from TV to the Internet, traditional newspapers have maintained their importance, with some 50 worldwide selling more than a million copies a day.*

## THE 10 **OLDEST PERIODICALS STILL IN PRINT IN THE UK**

| | PERIODICAL* | FOUNDED |
|---|---|---|
| 1 | Philosophical Transactions of the Royal Society | 1665 |
| 2 | The Scots Magazine | 1739 |
| 3 | Archaeologia (Journal of the Society of Antiquaries) | 1770 |
| 4 | Curtis's Botanical Magazine | 1787 |
| 5 | The Lancet# | 1823 |
| 6 | The Spectator | 1828 |
| 7 | = Nautical Magazine | 1832 |
| | = Royal Society of Edinburgh Proceedings | 1832 |
| 9 | Gospel Standard | 1835 |
| 10 | Justice of the Peace | 1837 |

\* Includes only those continuously published under their original titles
\# The oldest British weekly

*The Philosophical Transactions of the Royal Society* was first published on 6 March 1665. Among other British periodicals dating back more than 150 years are such specialist publications as the *Numismatic Chronicle* (1839), the *British Medical Journal* (1840), the *Pharmaceutical Journal* (1841) and the *Archaeological Journal* (1844). Several religious magazines have a similarly long history, among them the Catholic publication *The Tablet* (1840) and the Quaker journal *The Friend* (1843). *Notes & Queries*, founded in 1849 as a monthly journal (it is now published quarterly), contains letters raising questions on almost any topic posed by readers that are answered, often in great detail, by other readers. *The Bookseller*, 'The Organ of the Book Trade', was first published by Joseph Whitaker in January 1858 and thus celebrates its 150th anniversary in 2008.

## TOP 10 DAILY NEWSPAPERS IN THE UK

| NEWSPAPER | AVERAGE NET CIRCULATION* |
|---|---|
| 1 The Sun | 3,144,567 |
| 2 The Daily Mail | 2,357,878 |
| 3 The Mirror | 1,608,367 |
| 4 The Daily Telegraph | 899,806 |
| 5 Daily Express | 803,454 |
| 6 Daily Star | 786,627 |
| 7 The Times | 662,487 |
| 8 Financial Times | 430,469 |
| 9 Daily Record | 420,486 |
| 10 The Guardian | 376,271 |

* July–December 2006

Source: Audit Bureau of Circulations Ltd

## TOP 10 MAGAZINES IN THE UK

| TITLE | AVERAGE NET CIRCULATION* |
|---|---|
| 1 What's on TV | 1,436,873 |
| 2 TV Choice | 1,352,090 |
| 3 Radio Times | 1,066,686 |
| 4 Take a Break | 1,015,010 |
| 5 Reader's Digest | 662,417 |
| 6 Closer | 604,149 |
| 7 Saga Magazine | 592,075 |
| 8 Heat | 586,081 |
| 9 OK! Magazine | 544,430 |
| 10 Glamour | 527,317 |

* Actively purchased July–December 2006

Source: Periodical Publishers Association

## TOP 10 DAILY NEWSPAPERS IN THE WORLD

| NEWSPAPER | COUNTRY | AVERAGE DAILY CIRCULATION, 2006 |
|---|---|---|
| 1 Yomiuri Shimbun | Japan | 14,246,000 |
| 2 Asahi Shimbun | Japan | 12,326,000 |
| 3 Mainichi Shimbun | Japan | 5,635,000 |
| 4 Nihon Keizai Shimbun | Japan | 4,737,000 |
| 5 Chunichi Shimbun | Japan | 4,571,000 |
| 6 Bild | Germany | 4,220,000 |
| 7 The Sun | UK | 3,461,000 |
| 8 Sankei Shimbun | Japan | 2,665,000 |
| 9 USA Today | USA | 2,603,000 |
| 8 Canako Xiaoxi (Beijing) | China | 2,530,000 |

Source: World Association of Newspapers

*Yomiuri Shimbun* was founded in Japan 1874. In 1998 it became the country's and the world's bestselling daily newspaper, achieving a record average sale of 14,532,694 copies a day.

## TOP 10 MAGAZINES IN THE WORLD

| MAGAZINE | COUNTRY | AVERAGE CIRCULATION |
|---|---|---|
| 1 Reader's Digest | USA | 12,078,000 |
| 2 Better Homes and Gardens | USA | 7,605,000 |
| 3 Family Circle | USA | 4,634,000 |
| 4 Women's Day | USA | 4,205,000 |
| 5 Time | USA | 4,112,000 |
| 6 Ladies' Home Journal | USA | 4,101,000 |
| 7 Kampioen | Netherlands | 3,756,000 |
| 8 People | USA | 3,625,000 |
| 9 Playboy | USA | 3,215,000 |
| 10 Newsweek | UK | 3,183,000 |

Source: International Federation of Audit Bureaux of Circulations

# Art on Show

## TOP 10 BEST-ATTENDED ART EXHIBITIONS, 2006

| | EXHIBITION | VENUE / CITY / DATES | ATTENDANCE* DAILY | TOTAL |
|---|---|---|---|---|
| 1 | Tutankhamun and the Golden Age of the Pharaohs | Museum of Art, Fort Lauderdale, Florida, USA, 15 Dec 2005– 23 Apr 2006 | 5,443 | 707,534 |
| 2 | Russia! | Guggenheim Museum, Bilbao, Spain, 29 Mar–10 Sep | 4,392 | 621,188 |
| 3 | Klimt, Schiele, Moser, Kokoschka | Grand Palais, Paris, France, 5 Oct 2005–23 Jan 2006 | 6,297 | 600,000 |
| 4 | Gauguin/Van Gogh: The Adventure of Colour | Museo Santa Giulia, Breshia, Italy, 22 Oct 2005–26 Mar 2006 | 3,517 | 541,547 |
| 5 = | Egypt's Sunken Treasures | Martin-Gropius-Bau Museum, Berlin, Germany, 13 May–4 Sep | 4,559 | 450,000 |
| = | The Phillips Collection in Paris | Musée du Luxembourg, Paris, France, 20 Nov 2005–26 Mar 2006 | 3,543 | 450,000 |
| 7 | The King's Jewels | Green Vault, Residenzschloss, Dresden, Germany, 3 Dec 2005– 24 Jul 2006 | 2,165 | 434,506 |
| 8 | Edvard Munch: The Modern Life of the Soul | Museum of Modern Art, New York, USA, 19 Feb–8 May | 6,184 | 419,653 |
| 9 | Cézanne and Pissarro, 1865–85 | Musée d'Orsay, Paris, France, 28 Feb–28 May | 5,242 | 405,165 |
| 10 | Picasso: Tradition and Avant-garde | Reina Sofia, Madrid, Spain, 6 Jun–25 Sep | 4,211 | 404,879 |

* Includes exhibitions spanning 2005–2006

Source: *The Art Newspaper*

## TOP 10 BEST-ATTENDED ART EXHIBITIONS IN THE UK, 2006

| | EXHIBITION | VENUE / CITY / DATES* | ATTENDANCE DAILY | TOTAL |
|---|---|---|---|---|
| 1 | China: The Three Emperors, 1662–1795 | Royal Academy of Arts, 12 Nov 2005–14 Apr 2006 | 2,105 | 320,016 |
| 2 | Kandinsky: The Path to Abstraction | Tate Modern, 22 Jun–1 Oct | 2,700 | 275,425 |
| 3 | Icons and Idols | National Portrait Gallery, 9 Nov 2005–12 Feb 2006 | 1,938 | 211,264 |
| 4 | Degas, Sickert and Toulouse-Lautrec | Tate Britain, 5 Oct 2005– 15 Jan 2006 | 2,008 | 200,837 |
| 5 | BP Portrait Award | National Portrait Gallery, 15 Jun–17 Sep | 2,081 | 197,687 |
| 6 | Henri Rousseau | Tate Modern, 3 Nov 2005– 5 Feb 2006 | 2,073 | 190,725 |
| 7 | Modigliani and His Models | Royal Academy of Arts, 8 Jul–15 Oct | 1,886 | 188,551 |
| 8 | Photographic Portrait Prize | National Portrait Gallery, 9 Nov 2005–12 Feb 2006 | 1,960 | 184,211 |
| 9 | Modernism: Designing a New World | Victoria & Albert Museum, 6 Apr–23 Jul | 1,491 | 162,452 |
| 10 | Michelangelo Drawings: Closer to the Master | British Museum, 23 Mar–25 Jun | 1,691 | 160,635 |

* All London; includes exhibitions spanning 2005–06  Source: *The Art Newspaper*

## TOP 10 ART GALLERIES AND MUSEUMS IN THE UK

ATTRACTION / LOCATION* / VISITORS (2006)

1 British Museum  4,837,878
2 Tate Modern  4,915,000
3 National Gallery  4,562,471
4 Natural History Museum  3,754,496
5 Science Museum  2,421,440
6 Victoria & Albert Museum  2,372,919
7 National Portrait Gallery  1,601,448
8 Tate Britain  1,597,000
9 National Maritime Museum  1,572,310
10 National Gallery of Scotland, Edinburgh  942,788

*All London, except where indicated

Source: Association of Leading Visitor Attractions (ALVA)

## TOP 10 **BEST-ATTENDED EXHIBITIONS AT THE BRITISH MUSEUM, LONDON**

| | EXHIBITION | YEAR | TOTAL ATTENDANCE |
|---|---|---|---|
| 1 | Treasures of Tutankhamun* | 1972–73 | 1,694,117 |
| 2 | Turner Watercolours | 1975 | 585,046 |
| 3 | The Vikings* | 1980 | 465,000 |
| 4 | Thracian Treasures from Bulgaria | 1976 | 424,465 |
| 5 | From Manet to Toulouse-Lautrec: French Lithographs 1860–1900 | 1978 | 355,354 |
| 6 | The Ancient Olympic Games | 1980 | 334,354 |
| 7 | Treasures for the Nation* | 1988–89 | 297,837 |
| 8 | Excavating in Egypt | 1982–83 | 285,736 |
| 9 | Heraldry | 1978 | 262,183 |
| 10 = | Drawings by Michelangelo | 1975 | 250,000 |
| = | Exploring the City: the Foster Studio | 2001 | 250,000 |

* Admission charged, all others free

*Russian art*
*Yuri Pimenov's* New Moscow *(1935), one of more than 250 works of art shown at the Guggenheim's major Russia! exhibition.*

## TOP 10 **TALLEST EGYPTIAN OBELISKS**

| | | HEIGHT | | |
|---|---|---|---|---|
| | OBELISK / LOCATION | M | FT | IN |
| 1 | **Lateran**, Piazza San Giovanni in Laterano, Rome, Italy | 32.18 | 105 | 7 |
| 2 | **Hatsheput**, Karnak, Egypt | 29.56 | 97 | 0 |
| 3 | **Tuthmosis III***, Istanbul, Turkey | 28.95 | 95 | 0 |
| 4 | **St Peter's**, Rome, Italy | 25.37 | 83 | 3 |
| 5 | **Rameses II**, Luxor, Egypt | 25.00 | 82 | 0 |
| 6 | **Piazza del Popolo**, Rome, Italy | 23.20 | 76 | 1 |
| 7 | **Rameses II**, Place de la Concorde, Paris, France | 22.55 | 74 | 0 |
| 8 | **Piazza di Montecitorio**, Rome, Italy | 21.79 | 71 | 6 |
| 9 | **Tuthmosis III**, Central Park, New York, USA | 21.21 | 69 | 7 |
| 10 | **Tuthmosis III** ('Cleopatra's Needle'), Thames Embankment, London, UK | 20.88 | 68 | 6 |

* Broken, total height estimated (actual surviving fragment 19.8 m/65 ft)

There are some 27 surviving ancient Egyptian obelisks – tall columns built at the entrance to temples – only eight of which remain in Egypt. The rest have been plundered by or donated to other countries at various stages of Egypt's history, including 11 in Italy and those from Heliopolis set up in Paris (1833), New York (1881) and London (1878), popularly known as 'Cleopatra's Needles' – despite having no connection with Queen Cleopatra.

*Royal treasure*
*The mask of Tutankhamun was the star attraction of a series of record-breaking exhibitions.*

# Art on Sale

## TOP 10 MOST EXPENSIVE PAINTINGS BY GUSTAV KLIMT

| WORK / YEAR / SALE | PRICE ($) |
|---|---|
| **1 Portrait of Adele Bloch-Bauer II**, 1912 Christie's New York, 8 Nov 2006 | 87,936,000 |
| **2 Birch Forest**, 1903, Christie's New York, 8 Nov 2006 | 40,336,000 |
| **3 Apple Tree I**, 1912, Christie's New York, 8 Nov 2006 | 33,056,000 |
| **4 Houses at Unterach on the Attersee**, 1916, Christie's New York, 8 Nov 2006 | 31,376,000 |
| **5 Landhaus am Attersee**, 1914, Sotheby's New York, 5 Nov 2003 | 29,128,000 |
| **6 Schloss Kammer am Attersee II**, 1909 Christie's London, 9 Oct 1997 (£14,521,500) | 23,490,000 |
| **7 Litzlbergerkeller am Attersee**, 1915–16 Sotheby's New York, 13 May 1997 | 14,742,500 |
| **8 Dame mit Facher**, 1917–18, Sotheby's New York, 11 May 1994 | 11,662,500 |
| **9 Bauergarten**, 1905–07, Christie's London, 28 Nov 1994 (£3,741,500) | 5,844,270 |
| **10 Obstbäume am Attersee (Fruit trees by Lake Attersee)**, 1901, Sotheby's London, 8 Dec 1997 (£3,301,500) | 5,548,740 |

## TOP 10 MOST EXPENSIVE PAINTINGS SOLD PRIVATELY

| ARTIST / PAINTING / YEAR / TRANSACTION LOCATION / YEAR | ESTIMATED PRICE ($) |
|---|---|
| **1 Jackson Pollock, No. 5**, 1948, New York, 2006 | 140,000,000 |
| **2 Willem De Kooning, Woman III**, 1952/53, New York, 2006 | 137,500,000 |
| **3 Gustav Klimt, Portrait of Adele Bloch-Bauer I**, 1907, New York, 2006 | 135,000,000 |
| **4 Jasper Johns, False Start**, 1959, New York, 2006 | 80,000,000 |
| **5 Willem De Kooning, Police Gazette**, 1955, New York, 2006 | 63,500,000 |
| **6 Vincent van Gogh, Champ de blé avec cyprès**, 1889, New York, 1993 | 57,000,000 |
| **7 Vincent Van Gogh, Peasant Woman Against a Background of Wheat**, 1890, New York, 1997 | 47,500,000* |
| **8 Vassily Kandinsky, Composition V**, 1911, unknown, 1998 | 40,000,000 |
| **9 = Paul Cézanne, Nature morte avec pot de gingembre, sucrier et pommes**, 1888–90, London, 1996 | 35,000,000 |
| **= Paul Gauguin, Famille Tahitienne (Promenade au bord de la mer)**, 1902, London, 1996 | 35,000,000 |

\* Re-sold in 2005 with Gauguin's *The Bathers* for total of $100 million

The precise details of private (as contrasted with public auction) sales of works of art range from those that are totally secret to others where the vendor or purchaser deliberately publishes – and perhaps exaggerates – them in order to derive the maximum publicity. This Top 10 is therefore based on those for which reliable evidence is available, and may exclude certain similarly or even higher-priced but unknown transactions. In 2006 Pablo Picasso's *Le rêve*, the 6th most expensive by the artist ever sold, hit the headlines when its new owner, Las Vegas casino magnate Steve Wynn, agreed to sell it in a private transaction for $139 million, which would have made it the world's most expensive work of art. The sale was abandoned when Mr Wynn accidentally damaged it by poking his elbow through the canvas.

**Portrait of Adele Bloch-Bauer II**
*This work, painted in 1912, and the earlier* Portrait of Adele Bloch-Bauer I *(1907), along with other works by Gustav Klimt, were looted by the Nazis during World War II. After a protracted legal battle, they were restored to their owner Maria Altmann, a niece of the sitter. Both paintings were sold for record sums in 2006, this at auction, the other privately.*

# TOP 10 MOST EXPENSIVE PAINTINGS

| | PAINTING / ARTIST | SALE | PRICE* ($) |
|---|---|---|---|
| 1 | Garçon à la pipe, Pablo Picasso (Spanish, 1881–1973) | Sotheby's New York, 5 May 2004 | 104,168,000 |
| 2 | Dora Maar au chat, Pablo Picasso | Sotheby's New York, 3 May 2006 (£46,436,415) | 95,216,000 |
| 3 | Portrait of Adele Bloch-Bauer II, Gustav Klimt (Austrian, 1862–1918) | Christie's New York, 8 Nov 2006 | 87,936,000 |
| 4 | Portrait du Dr Gachet, Vincent van Gogh (Dutch, 1853–90) | Christie's New York, 15 May 1990 | 82,500,000 |
| 5 | Bal au Moulin de la Galette, Montmartre Pierre-Auguste Renoir (French, 1841–1919) | Sotheby's New York, 17 May 1990 | 78,100,000 |
| 6 | Massacre of the Innocents, Sir Peter Paul Rubens (Flemish, 1577–1640) | Sotheby's London, 10 Jul 2002 (£49,506,648/£45,000,000) | 75,930,440 |
| 7 | Portrait de l'Artiste Sans Barbe, Vincent van Gogh | Christie's New York, 19 Nov 1998 | 71,502,496 |
| 8 | Rideau, Cruchon et Compôtier, Paul Cézanne (French, 1839–1906) | Sotheby's New York, 10 May 1999 | 60,502,500 |
| 9 | Femme aux Bras Croises, Pablo Picasso | Christie's New York, 8 Nov 2000 | 55,006,000 |
| 10 | Irises, Vincent van Gogh | Sotheby's New York, 11 Nov 1987 | 53,900,000 |

* Including buyer's premium; if not sold in $ converted at rate prevailing at time of sale

# TOP 10 MOST EXPENSIVE PAINTINGS BY PABLO PICASSO*

| | PAINTING / YEAR / SALE | PRICE ($) |
|---|---|---|
| 1 | Garçon à la pipe, 1905, Sotheby's New York, 5 May 2004 | 104,168,000 |
| 2 | Dora Maar au chat, 1941, Sotheby's New York, 3 May 2006 | 95,216,000 |
| 3 | Femme aux bras croisés, 1901–02, Christie's New York, 8 Nov 2000 | 55,006,000 |
| 4 | Les Noces de Pierrette, Binoche et Godeau, Paris, 30 Nov 1989 (F.Fr315,000,000) | 51,796,432 |
| 5 | Femme assise dans un jardin, 1938, Sotheby's New York, 10 Nov 1999 | 49,502,500 |
| 6 | Le rêve, 1932, Christie's New York, 10 Nov 1997 | 48,402,500 |
| 7 | Self-portrait: Yo Picasso, 1901, Sotheby's New York, 9 May 1989 | 47,850,000 |
| 8 | Nu au fauteuil noir, 1932, Christie's New York, 9 Nov 1999 | 45,102,500 |
| 9 | Au Lapin Agile, 1905, Sotheby's New York, 15 Nov 1989 | 40,700,000 |
| 10 | Acrobate et jeune Arlequin, 1905, Christie's London, 28 Nov 1988 (£20,900,000) | 38,138,700 |

* Sold at auction up to 1 January 2007, including buyer's premium

# TOP 10 MOST EXPENSIVE WORKS BY ANDY WARHOL

| | WORK / YEAR / SALE | PRICE ($) |
|---|---|---|
| 1 | Mao, 1972, Christie's New York, 15 Nov 2006 | 17,376,000 |
| 2 | Orange Marilyn, 1964, Sotheby's New York, 14 May 1998 | 17,327,500 |
| 3 | Orange Marilyn, 1962, Christie's New York, 15 Nov 2006 | 16,256,000 |
| 4 | Sixteen Jackies, 1964, Christie's New York, 15 Nov 2006 | 15,696,000 |
| 5 | Mustard Race Riot (2 panels), 1963, Christie's New York, 10 Nov 2004 | 15,127,500 |
| 6 | Liz, 1963, Sotheby's New York, 10 May 2005 | 12,616,000 |
| 7 | Small Torn Campbell's Soup Can (Pepper pot), 1962, Christie's New York, 9 May 2006 | 11,776,000 |
| 8 | Brigitte Bardot, 1974, Christie's London, 8 Feb 2007 (£5,396,000) | 10,633,047 |
| 8 | Jackie Frieze (13 parts), 1964, Sotheby's New York, 9 Nov 2005 | 9,200,000 |
| 10 | Three Women, 1963, Christie's London, 8 Feb 2007 (£4,444,000) | 8,748,031 |

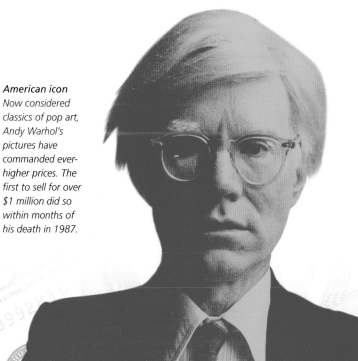

**American icon**
*Now considered classics of pop art, Andy Warhol's pictures have commanded ever-higher prices. The first to sell for over $1 million did so within months of his death in 1987.*

# MUSIC

# Singles

## TOP 10 **SINGLES OF ALL TIME IN THE UK**

| TITLE / ARTIST / YEAR OF ENTRY | EST. UK SALES |
|---|---|
| **1** 'Candle in the Wind (1997)'/'Something About the Way You Look Tonight', Elton John, 1997 | 4,865,000 |
| **2** 'Do They Know It's Christmas?', Band Aid, 1984 | 3,550,000 |
| **3** 'Bohemian Rhapsody', Queen, 1975/91 | 2,130,000 |
| **4** 'Mull of Kintyre', Wings, 1977 | 2,050,000 |
| **5** 'Rivers of Babylon'/'Brown Girl in the Ring', Boney M, 1978 | 1,985,000 |
| **6** 'You're the One that I Want', John Travolta and Olivia Newton-John, 1978 | 1,975,000 |
| **7** 'Relax', Frankie Goes to Hollywood, 1984 | 1,910,000 |
| **8** 'She Loves You', The Beatles, 1963 | 1,890,000 |
| **9** 'Unchained Melody', Robson Green and Jerome Flynn, 1995 | 1,844,000 |
| **10** 'Mary's Boy Child'/'Oh My Lord', Boney M, 1978 | 1,790,000 |

Source: The Official UK Charts Company

Some 80 singles have sold over one million copies apiece in the UK during the last 50 years, and these are the cream of that crop. The Band Aid single had a host of special circumstances surrounding it, and it took the remarkable response to the death of Diana, Princess of Wales, to generate sales capable of overtaking it.

## THE 10 **FIRST SINGLES BY FOREIGN\* ARTISTS TO TOP THE UK CHART**

| TITLE / ARTIST / NATIONALITY | DATE |
|---|---|
| **1** 'Moulin Rouge', Mantovani (Italian) | 15 Aug 1953 |
| **2** 'Let's Have Another Party', Winifred Atwell (Trinidadian) | 4 Dec 1954 |
| **3** 'Cherry Pink and Apple Blossom White', Perez 'Prez' Prado (Cuban) | 30 Apr 1955 |
| **4** 'Poor People of Paris', Winifred Atwell | 14 Apr 1956 |
| **5** 'Diana', Paul Anka (Canadian) | 31 Aug 1957 |
| **6** 'What Do You Want to Make Those Eyes at Me For', Emile Ford and the Checkmates (Saint Lucian) | 19 Dec 1959 |
| **7** 'Moon River', Danny Williams (South African) | 30 Dec 1961 |
| **8** 'The Carnival is Over', The Seekers (Australian) | 27 Nov 1965 |
| **9** 'Cinderella Rockefella', Esther and Abi Ofarim (Israeli) | 2 Mar 1968 |
| **10** 'The Israelites', Desmond Dekker and the Aces (Jamaican) | 19 Apr 1969 |

\* Excluding US

Source: Music Information Database

## TOP 10 **SINGLES OF THE PAST 10 YEARS IN THE UK**

| YEAR | TITLE | ARTIST |
|---|---|---|
| **2006** | 'Crazy' | Gnarls Barkley |
| **2005** | '(Is This the Way to) Amarillo' | Tony Christie featuring Peter Kay |
| **2004** | 'Do They Know It's Christmas?' | Band Aid 20 |
| **2003** | 'Where is the Love' | Black Eyed Peas |
| **2002** | 'Anything is Possible'/'Evergreen' | Will Young |
| **2001** | 'It Wasn't Me' | Shaggy featuring Rikrok |
| **2000** | 'Can We Fix It' | Bob the Builder |
| **1999** | 'Baby One More Time' | Britney Spears |
| **1998** | 'Believe' | Cher |
| **1997** | 'Candle in the Wind (1997)'/'Something About the Way You Look Tonight' | Elton John |

Source: Music Information Database

Of these bestselling artists, only four have had No. 1 hits since – Will Young (3), Britney Spears (2) and Elton John and Shaggy (1 each). 'Where is the Love' was the Black Eyed Peas' sole chart-topper. The proceeds from both Nos. 3 and 10 were donated to charity.

*King of the singles*
*Through numerous posthumous re-releases, Elvis Presley's death in 1977 at the age of 42 failed to end his run of UK hits, with more No. 1s and more chart entries overall than any other artist.*

# TOP 10 **ARTISTS WITH THE MOST NO. 1 SINGLES IN THE UK**

ARTIST (TOTAL CHART HITS) / NO. 1 SINGLES

**1** Elvis Presley (155) 21

**2** The Beatles (54) 17

**3** = Cliff Richard (131) 14

**3** = Westlife (20) 14

**5** Madonna (63) 12

**6** Take That (16) 10

**7** = Abba (27) 9

**7** = The Spice Girls (10) 9

**9** = Oasis (23) 8

**9** = The Rolling Stones (54) 8

Source: Music Information Database

# TOP 10 **SINGLES THAT STAYED LONGEST IN THE UK CHARTS**

| | TITLE / ARTIST | FIRST CHART ENTRY | WEEKS IN CHART |
|---|---|---|---|
| **1** | 'My Way', Frank Sinatra (42) | 1969 | 124 |
| **2** | 'Amazing Grace', Judy Collins (32) | 1970 | 66 |
| **3** | 'Relax', Frankie Goes to Hollywood (48) | 1983 | 59 |
| **4** | ='Rock Around the Clock', Bill Haley and His Comets (17) | 1955 | 57 |
| | ='Release Me', Engelbert Humperdinck (56) | 1967 | 57 |
| **6** | 'Stranger on the Shore', Mr. Acker Bilk (55) | 1961 | 55 |
| **7** | 'Blue Monday', New Order (17) | 1983 | 53 |
| **8** | 'I Love You Because', Jim Reeves (39) | 1964 | 47 |
| **9** | 'Let's Twist Again', Chubby Checker (27) | 1961 | 44 |
| **10** | 'White Lines (Don't Don't Do It)', Grandmaster Flash and Melle Mel (43) | 1984 | 43 |

Source: Music Information Database

These include reissues and remixes. Numbers in parentheses denote the longest consecutive run on the charts.

*Pop princes*
*Although the Beatles' career spanned just 10 years, compared with Elvis Presley's 23, they scored only four fewer No. 1 singles in the UK.*

# Albums

## TOP 10 **ALBUMS IN THE UK**

| TITLE / ARTIST | YEAR |
|---|---|
| 1 Sgt. Pepper's Lonely Hearts Club Band, The Beatles | 1967 |
| 2 (What's the Story) Morning Glory, Oasis | 1995 |
| 3 Bad, Michael Jackson | 1987 |
| 4 Brothers in Arms, Dire Straits | 1985 |
| 5 Abba Gold Greatest Hits, Abba | 1990 |
| 6 The Immaculate Collection, Madonna | 1990 |
| 7 Stars, Simply Red | 1991 |
| 8 Greatest Hits (Volume One), Queen | 1981 |
| 9 Thriller, Michael Jackson | 1982 |
| 10 Come On Over, Shania Twain | 1998 |

Source: BPI

With UK sales alone of over 4.5 million copies, the Beatles' *Sgt. Pepper's Lonely Hearts Club Band* album was both a commercial success and a critical triumph, considered by many as the most influential rock album ever and hailed by *Rolling Stone* magazine as 'the greatest album of all time'. It is the only record on this list that has never received a BPI award, since most of its sales occurred prior to the adoption of Gold and Platinum awards in 1973. Oasis's *(What's the Story) Morning Glory* is the only other album to top the four-million mark. The rest of the Top 10 have sold in excess of three million copies each in the UK.

*Still rolling*
*Mick Jagger and the Rolling Stones have been performing and recording for over 45 years, during which their album releases have put them on a par with Elvis Presley's 10 UK No. 1s – a position mirrored in the US ranking, in which they also follow hard on the heels of Elvis and list-topping Beatles.*

## THE 10 **FIRST US ALBUMS TO TOP THE UK CHART**

| TITLE / ARTIST | DATE |
|---|---|
| 1 The Explosive Freddy Cannon, Freddy Cannon | 12 Mar 1960 |
| 2 Elvis is Back, Elvis Presley | 30 Jul 1960 |
| 3 G.I. Blues, Elvis Presley | 14 Jan 1961 |
| 4 Blue Hawaii, Elvis Presley | 6 Jan 1962 |
| 5 Pot Luck, Elvis Presley | 28 Jul 1962 |
| 6 The Freewheelin' Bob Dylan, Bob Dylan | 17 Apr 1965 |
| 7 Bringing it All Back Home, Bob Dylan | 29 May 1965 |
| 8 The Monkees, The Monkees | 4 Feb 1967 |
| 9 More of the Monkees, The Monkees | 13 May 1967 |
| 10 Greatest Hits, The Four Tops | 10 Feb 1968 |

Source: Music Information Database

## TOP 10 **ALBUMS IN THE UK IN THE PAST 10 YEARS**

YEAR / TITLE / ARTIST

**2006**
Eyes Open, Snow Patrol

**2005**
Back to Bedlam, James Blunt

**2004**
Scissor Sisters, Scissor Sisters

**2003**
Life for Rent, Dido

**2002**
Escapology, Robbie Williams

**2001**
No Angel, Dido

**2000**
1, The Beatles

**1999**
Come on Over, Shania Twain

**1998**
Talk on Corners, The Corrs

**1997**
Be Here Now, Oasis

Source: Music Information Database

**In the pink**
*Pink Floyd in concert: their iconic* The Dark Side of the Moon *never reached UK No. 1, but nonetheless spent 366 weeks in the album chart. It made US No. 1 and holds the record for the longest-ever US chart residence – a total of 741 weeks.*

## TOP 10 **ALBUMS THAT STAYED LONGEST IN THE UK CHARTS**

| TITLE / ARTIST | FIRST CHART ENTRY | WEEKS IN CHART |
|---|---|---|
| **1** Rumours, Fleetwood Mac (120) | 1977 | 478 |
| **2** Bat Out of Hell, Meat Loaf (329) | 1978 | 473 |
| **3** Greatest Hits, Queen (222) | 1981 | 449 |
| **4** The Sound of Music, Soundtrack (318) | 1965 | 382 |
| **5** The Dark Side of the Moon, Pink Floyd (135) | 1973 | 366 |
| **6** Abba Gold Greatest Hits, Abba (101) | 1992 | 352 |
| **7** South Pacific, Soundtrack (153) | 1960 | 319 |
| **8** Bridge Over Troubled Water, Simon and Garfunkel (244) | 1970 | 307 |
| **9** Greatest Hits, Simon and Garfunkel (195) | 1972 | 283 |
| **10** Tubular Bells, Mike Oldfield (128) | 1973 | 276 |

Source: Music Information Database

Figures in parentheses denote the longest consecutive run on the charts.

## TOP 10 **ARTISTS WITH THE MOST NO. 1 ALBUMS IN THE UK**

| | ARTIST | NO. 1 ALBUMS |
|---|---|---|
| **1** | The Beatles (32) | 15 |
| **2** | = Elvis Presley (111) | 10 |
| | = The Rolling Stones (45) | 10 |
| **4** | = Abba (16) | 9 |
| | = Queen (27) | 9 |
| | = U2 (18) | 9 |
| **7** | = David Bowie (41) | 8 |
| | = Michael Jackson | 8 |
| | = Madonna (16) | 8 |
| | = Led Zeppelin (17) | 8 |

Source: Music Information Database

Figures in parentheses denote total chart hits. The comparable list for the USA features the same three artists at Nos. 1, 2 and 3.

# Male Singers

## TOP 10 MALE SOLO ARTISTS WITH THE MOST NO. 1 ALBUMS IN THE UK

| | ARTIST (TOTAL CHART HITS) | NO. 1 ALBUMS |
|---|---|---|
| 1 | Elvis Presley (111) | 10 |
| 2 | = David Bowie (40) | 8 |
| | = Michael Jackson (22) | 8 |
| | = Robbie Williams (9) | 8 |
| 5 | = Cliff Richard (58) | 7 |
| | = Rod Stewart (31) | 7 |
| 7 | = Elton John (39) | 6 |
| | = Bob Dylan (48) | 6 |
| | = Bruce Springsteen (21) | 6 |
| 10 | = Phil Collins (12) | 5 |
| | = George Michael (6) | 5 |
| | = Prince (20) | 5 |

Source: Music Information Database

*Left: Career achievement*
As he approaches his 50th birthday in 2008, Michael Jackson's success appears unassailable.

*Right: Made in the USA*
Bruce Springsteen is one of only five American male artists with five No.1 albums in the UK.

## THE 10 FIRST RECORDS BY A FOREIGN MALE ARTIST TO TOP THE UK ALBUM CHART*

| | TITLE / ARTIST / COUNTRY | DATE |
|---|---|---|
| 1 | Val Doonican Rocks But Gently, Val Doonican (Ireland) | 30 Dec 1967 |
| 2 | Back to Front, Gilbert O'Sullivan (Ireland) | 20 Jan 1973 |
| 3 | Flying Colours, Chris De Burgh (Ireland) | 15 Oct 1988 |
| 4 | Ten Good Reasons, Jason Donovan (Australia) | 20 May 1989 |
| 5 | The Essential Pavarotti, Luciano Pavarotti (Italy) | 23 Jun 1990 |
| 6 | The Essential Pavarotti II, Luciano Pavarotti (Italy) | 10 Aug 1991 |
| 7 | Waking up the Neighbors, Bryan Adams (Canada) | 5 Oct 1991 |
| 8 | So Far So Good, Bryan Adams | 15 Jan 1994 |
| 9 | 18 Til I Die, Bryan Adams | 22 Jun 1996 |
| 10 | Ronan, Ronan Keating (Ireland) | 12 Aug 2000 |

* Excluding US acts

Source: Music Information Database

## TOP 10 BESTSELLING ALBUMS BY A MALE ARTIST IN THE UK

| | TITLE / ARTIST | YEAR |
|---|---|---|
| 1 | Thriller, Michael Jackson | 1982 |
| 2 | Bad, Michael Jackson | 1987 |
| 3 | Back to Bedlam, James Blunt | 2006 |
| 4 | White Ladder, David Gray | 2000 |
| 5 | Bat Out of Hell, Meat Loaf | 1978 |
| 6 | But Seriously..., Phil Collins | 1989 |
| 7 | Tubular Bells, Mike Oldfield | 1973 |
| 8 | I've Been Expecting You, Robbie Williams | 1998 |
| 9 | Ladies & Gentlemen – The Best Of, George Michael | 1998 |
| 10 | The Marshall Mathers LP, Eminem | 2000 |

Source: The Official UK Charts Company

Michael Jackson's *Thriller* and *Bad* have both sold in excess of 3.5 million copies, meaning that approximately one in every six British households, or one in every 15 inhabitants, owns a copy of one or both of these mega-sellers. James Blunt's debut album is a long way behind with sales of 2.8 million. In the bestselling Top 100 albums of all time, Robbie Williams is the king of pop, with six records selling a combined 12.5 million copies.

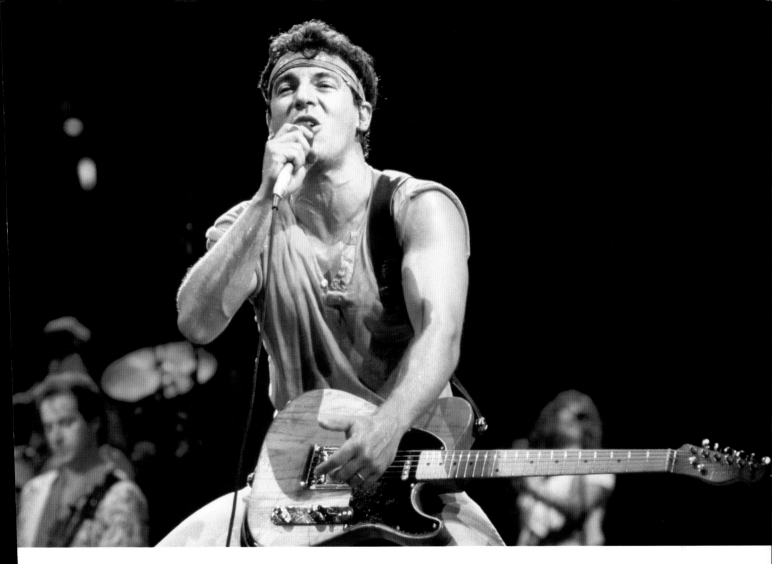

## TOP 10 **SINGLES BY MALE SOLO SINGERS IN THE UK**

| TITLE / ARTIST | YEAR |
|---|---|
| **1** 'Candle in the Wind (1997)'/'Something About the Way You Look Tonight', Elton John | 1997 |
| **2** 'Anything is Possible'/'Evergreen', Will Young | 2002 |
| **3** 'I Just Called to Say I Love You', Stevie Wonder | 1984 |
| **4** '(Everything I Do) I Do It For You', Bryan Adams | 1991 |
| **5** 'Tears', Ken Dodd | 1965 |
| **6** 'Imagine', John Lennon | 1975 |
| **7** 'Careless Whisper', George Michael | 1984 |
| **8** 'Release Me', Engelbert Humperdinck | 1967 |
| **9** 'Unchained Melody', Gareth Gates | 2002 |
| **10** 'Diana', Paul Anka | 1957 |

Source: The Official UK Charts Company

This list represents a timeshaft through the history of British popular music, with singles from each decade reflecting the sometimes unpredictable taste of the British public.

## THE 10 **FIRST RECORDS BY A US MALE ARTIST TO TOP THE UK ALBUM CHART**

| TITLE / ARTIST | DATE |
|---|---|
| **1** The Explosive Freddy Cannon, Freddy Cannon | 12 Mar 1960 |
| **2** Elvis is Back, Elvis Presley | 30 Jul 1960 |
| **3** G.I. Blues, Elvis Presley | 14 Jan 1961 |
| **4** Blue Hawaii, Elvis Presley | 6 Jan 1962 |
| **5** Pot Luck, Elvis Presley | 28 Jul 1962 |
| **6** The Freewheelin' Bob Dylan, Bob Dylan | 17 Apr 1965 |
| **7** Bringing it All Back Home, Bob Dylan | 29 May 1965 |
| **8** John Wesley Harding, Bob Dylan | 9 Mar 1968 |
| **9** Scott 2, Scott Walker | 18 May 1968 |
| **10** Love Andy, Andy Williams | 15 Jun 1968 |

Source: Music Information Database

Although earlier UK charts were published, those issued by *Record Retailer* beginning with its issue dated 10 March 1960, represent the first based on accurate sales figures.

# Female Singers

## TOP 10 **ALBUMS BY A FEMALE ARTIST IN THE UK**

| TITLE / ARTIST | YEAR |
|---|---|
| **1** The Immaculate Collection, Madonna | 1990 |
| **2** Come On Over, Shania Twain | 1998 |
| **3** No Angel, Dido | 2000 |
| **4** Life For Rent, Dido | 2003 |
| **5** Jagged Little Pill, Alanis Morissette | 1995 |
| **6** Come Away With Me, Norah Jones | 2002 |
| **7** Tracy Chapman, Tracy Chapman | 1998 |
| **8** Whitney, Whitney Houston | 1987 |
| **9** Simply The Best, Tina Turner | 1991 |
| **10** Kylie, Kylie Minogue | 1988 |

Source: The Official UK Charts Company

The top three albums listed here have all sold in excess of three million copies – in fact Dido's first two releases have combined sales of almost 5.8 million. Although not featured in this Top 10, Celine Dion is the only female artist with million-plus-selling albums.

*Twain makes her mark*
*Although it combines rock, pop and country genres, Canadian-born Shania Twain's 1998 album* Come On Over *ranks as the all-time bestselling country album in the UK, topping the album chart for 11 weeks and selling over 4.8 million copies.*

## TOP 10 **SINGLES BY FEMALE SOLO SINGERS IN THE UK**

| TITLE / ARTIST | YEAR |
|---|---|
| **1** 'Believe', Cher | 1998 |
| **2** '...Baby One More Time', Britney Spears | 1999 |
| **3** 'I Will Always Love You', Whitney Houston | 1992 |
| **4** 'The Power of Love', Jennifer Rush | 1985 |
| **5** 'My Heart Will Go On', Celine Dion | 1998 |
| **6** 'Think Twice', Celine Dion | 1994 |
| **7** 'Saturday Night', Whigfield | 1994 |
| **8** 'Can't Get You Out Of My Head', Kylie Minogue | 2001 |
| **9** 'Don't Cry For Me Argentina', Julie Covington | 1976 |
| **10** 'Torn', Natalie Imbruglia | 1997 |

Source: The Official UK Charts Company

## THE 10 **FIRST RECORDS BY A FOREIGN FEMALE ARTIST TO TOP THE UK ALBUM CHART***

| TITLE / ARTIST / COUNTRY | DATE |
|---|---|
| **1** Kylie, Kylie Minogue (Australia) | 27 Aug 1988 |
| **2** Cuts Both Ways, Gloria Estefan (Cuba) | 5 Aug 1989 |
| **3** Enjoy Yourself, Kylie Minogue (Australia) | 21 Oct 1989 |
| **4** I Do Not Want What I Haven't Got, Sinead O'Connor (Ireland) | 24 Mar 1990 |
| **5** Shepherd Moons, Enya (Ireland) | 16 Nov 1991 |
| **6** Kylie Greatest Hits, Kylie Minogue (Australia) | 4 Sep 1992 |
| **7** The Colour of My Love, Celine Dion (Canada) | 28 Jan 1995 |
| **8** Falling Into You, Celine Dion | 23 Mar 1996 |
| **9** Jagged Little Pill, Alanis Morissette (Canada) | 4 May 1996 |
| **10** Come On Over, Shania Twain (Canada) | 11 Sep 1999 |

* Excluding US acts

## TOP 10 **FEMALE ARTISTS WITH THE MOST NO. 1 SINGLES IN THE UK**

| | ARTIST (TOTAL CHART HITS)* | NO. 1 SINGLES |
|---|---|---|
| **1** | Madonna (63) | 12 |
| **2** | Spice Girls (10) | 9 |
| **3** | Kylie Minogue (36) | 6 |
| **4** | = All Saints (8) | 5 |
| | = Britney Spears (16) | 5 |
| **6** | = B*witched (6) | 4 |
| | = Geri Halliwell (8) | 4 |
| | = S Club 7 (9) | 4 |
| | = Sugababes (13) | 4 |
| | = Whitney Houston (25) | 4 |

\* Duets and 'featuring' are not included

Source: Music Information Database

*Golden girl*
*Following the success of her 1.2 million-selling debut single '...Baby One More Time', Britney Spears enjoyed spectacular success in the UK chart.*

## TOP 10 **ALBUMS BY FEMALE SOLO ARTISTS IN THE UK IN THE PAST 10 YEARS**

| YEAR | TITLE / ARTIST |
|---|---|
| **2006** | I'm Not Dead, P!nk |
| **2005** | Eye to the Telescope, KT Tunstall |
| **2004** | Call Off the Search, Katie Melua |
| **2003** | Life For Rent, Dido |
| **2002** | M!ssundaztood, P!nk |
| **2001** | No Angel, Dido |
| **2000** | The Greatest Hits, Whitney Houston |
| **1999** | Come On Over, Shania Twain |
| **1998** | Ray of Light, Madonna |
| **1997** | Let's Talk About Love, Celine Dion |

Source: Music Information Database

# Music Awards

## THE 10 LATEST WINNERS OF THE BRIT AWARD FOR BEST SINGLE BY A BRITISH ARTIST

| YEAR | TITLE | ARTIST |
|---|---|---|
| 2007 | 'Patience' | Take That |
| 2006 | 'Speed of Sound' | Coldplay |
| 2005 | 'Your Game' | Will Young |
| 2004 | 'White Flag' | Dido |
| 2003 | 'Just a Little' | Liberty X |
| 2002 | 'Don't Stop Movin' | S Club 7 |
| 2001 | 'Rock DJ' | Robbie Williams |
| 2000 | 'She's the One' | Robbie Williams |
| 1999 | 'Angels' | Robbie Williams |
| 1998 | 'Never Ever' | All Saints |

## THE 10 LATEST WINNERS OF THE BRIT AWARD FOR BEST BRITISH MALE SOLO ARTIST

| YEAR | ARTIST |
|---|---|
| 2007 | James Morrison |
| 2006 | James Blunt |
| 2005 | The Streets |
| 2004 | Daniel Bedingfield |
| 2003 | Robbie Williams |
| 2002 | Robbie Williams |
| 2001 | Robbie Williams |
| 2000 | Tom Jones |
| 1999 | Robbie Williams |
| 1998 | Finlay Quaye |

## THE 10 LATEST WINNERS OF THE BRIT AWARD FOR BEST BRITISH BREAKTHROUGH ACT*

| YEAR | ARTIST |
|---|---|
| 2007 | The Fratellis |
| 2006 | Arctic Monkeys |
| 2005 | Keane |
| 2004 | Busted |
| 2003 | Will Young |
| 2002 | Blue |
| 2001 | A1 |
| 2000 | S Club 7 |
| 1999 | Belle and Sebastian |
| 1998 | Stereophonics |

* 'Best British Newcomer' until 2002

## THE 10 LATEST WINNERS OF THE BRIT AWARD FOR BEST BRITISH GROUP

| YEAR | GROUP |
|---|---|
| 2007 | Arctic Monkeys |
| 2006 | Kaiser Chiefs |
| 2005 | Franz Ferdinand |
| 2004 | The Darkness |
| 2003 | Coldplay |
| 2002 | Travis |
| 2001 | Coldplay |
| 2000 | Travis |
| 1999 | Manic Street Preachers |
| 1998 | The Verve |

## THE 10 LATEST WINNERS OF BEST FEMALE POP VOCAL PERFORMANCE GRAMMYS

| YEAR* | ARTIST / SONG |
|---|---|
| 2007 | Christina Aguilera 'Ain't No Other Man' |
| 2006 | Kelly Clarkson 'Since U Been Gone' |
| 2005 | Norah Jones 'Sunrise' |
| 2004 | Christina Aguilera 'Beautiful' |
| 2003 | Norah Jones 'Don't Know Why' |
| 2002 | Nelly Furtado 'I'm Like a Bird' |
| 2001 | Macy Gray 'I Try' |
| 2000 | Sarah McLachlan 'I Will Remember You' |
| 1999 | Celine Dion 'My Heart Will Go On' |
| 1998 | Sarah McLachlan 'Building a Mystery' |

* Awards are for singles released during the previous year

### Back on track
*Taken from her No. 1 US and UK Back to Basics album, Christina Aguilera's 'Ain't No Other Man' single clocked up over one million downloads in the US and won her the Best Female Pop Vocal Performance Grammy.*

## THE 10 **LATEST GRAMMY RECORDS** OF THE YEAR

| YEAR* | SINGLE | PERFORMING ARTIST(S) |
|---|---|---|
| **2007** | 'Not Ready to Make Nice' | Dixie Chicks |
| **2006** | 'Boulevard of Broken Dreams' | Green Day |
| **2005** | 'Here We Go Again' | Ray Charles & Norah Jones |
| **2004** | 'Clocks' | Coldplay |
| **2003** | 'Don't Know Why' | Norah Jones |
| **2002** | 'Walk On' | U2 |
| **2001** | 'Beautiful Day' | U2 |
| **2000** | 'Smooth' | Rob Thomas & Santana |
| **1999** | 'My Heart Will Go On' | Celine Dion |
| **1998** | 'Sunny Came Home' | Shawn Colvin |

\* Awards are for singles released during the previous year

## THE 10 **LATEST GRAMMY ALBUMS** OF THE YEAR

| YEAR* | ALBUM | PERFORMING ARTIST(S) |
|---|---|---|
| **2007** | Taking the Long Way | Dixie Chicks |
| **2006** | How to Dismantle an Atomic Bomb | U2 |
| **2005** | Genius Loves Company | Ray Charles & various artists |
| **2004** | Speakerboxxx/The Love Below | OutKast |
| **2003** | Come Away with Me | Norah Jones |
| **2002** | O Brother, Where Art Thou? (Soundtrack) | Various artists |
| **2001** | Two Against Nature | Steely Dan |
| **2000** | Supernatural | Santana |
| **1999** | The Miseducation of Lauryn Hill | Lauryn Hill |
| **1998** | Time Out of Mind | Bob Dylan |

\* Awards are for albums released during the previous year

# Classical Music

## TOP 10 CLASSICAL ALBUMS IN THE UK

| | TITLE | PERFORMER/ORCHESTRA | YEAR |
|---|---|---|---|
| 1 | The Three Tenors In Concert | José Carreras, Placido Domingo, Luciano Pavarotti | 1990 |
| 2 | Il Divo | Il Divo | 2004 |
| 3 | The Essential Pavarotti | Luciano Pavarotti | 1990 |
| 4 | Ancora | Il Divo | 2005 |
| 5 | Vivaldi: The Four Seasons | Nigel Kennedy/English Chamber Orchestra | 1989 |
| 6 | The Three Tenors – In Concert 1994 | José Carreras, Placido Domingo, Luciano Pavarotti, Zubin Mehta | 1994 |
| 7 | The Voice | Russell Watson | 2000 |
| 8 | Voice of an Angel | Charlotte Church | 1998 |
| 9 | Pure | Hayley Westenra | 2003 |
| 10 | Encore | Russell Watson | 2002 |

Source: Music Information Database

## TOP 10 CLASSICAL ALBUMS IN THE UK, 2006

| | TITLE | ARTIST |
|---|---|---|
| 1 | Voices of the Valley | Fron Male Voice Choir |
| 2 | Serenade | Katherine Jenkins |
| 3 | The Voice: The Ultimate Collection | Russell Watson |
| 4 | All Angels | All Angels |
| 5 | Odyssey | Hayley Westernra |
| 6 | Living a Dream | Katherine Jenkins |
| 7 | Second Nature | Katherine Jenkins |
| 8 | Premiere | Katherine Jenkins |
| 9 | Songs from the Labyrinth | Sting |
| 10 | You Raise Me Up: The Best Of | Aled Jones |

Source: The Official UK Charts Company

## THE 10 LATEST GRAMMY AWARDS FOR BEST CLASSICAL CONTEMPORARY COMPOSITION

| YEAR | COMPOSER | WORK |
|---|---|---|
| 2007 | Osvaldo Golijov | Ainadamar: Fountain of Tears |
| 2006 | William Bolcom | Songs of Innocence and of Experience |
| 2005 | John Adams | On the Transmigration of Souls |
| 2004 | Dominick Argento | Casa Guidi |
| 2003 | John Tavener | Lamentations and Praises |
| 2002 | Christopher Rouse | Concert de Gaudí for Guitar and Orchestra |
| 2001 | George Crumb | Star Child |
| 2000 | Pierre Boulez | Répons |
| 1999 | Krzysztof Penderecki | Violin Concerto No. 2: Metamorphosen |
| 1998 | John Adams | El Dorado |

*Church music*
*Charlotte Church's debut album* Voice of an Angel *is the UK's bestselling by a female singer.*

# TOP 10 **OPERAS MOST FREQUENTLY PERFORMED AT THE ROYAL OPERA HOUSE, COVENT GARDEN, 1833–2006**

| | OPERA | COMPOSER | FIRST PERFORMANCE | TOTAL* |
|---|---|---|---|---|
| **1** | La Bohème | Giacomo Puccini | 2 Oct 1897 | 545 |
| **2** | Carmen | Georges Bizet | 27 May 1882 | 495 |
| **3** | Aïda | Giuseppi Verdi | 22 Jun 1876 | 481 |
| **4** | Rigoletto | Giuseppi Verdi | 14 May 1853 | 465 |
| **5** | Faust | Charles Gounod | 18 Jul 1863 | 442 |
| **6** | Tosca | Giacomo Puccini | 12 Jul 1900 | 415 |
| **7** | Don Giovanni | Wolfgang Amadeus Mozart | 17 Apr 1834 | 414 |
| **8** | La Traviata | Giuseppi Verdi | 25 May 1858 | 391 |
| **9** | Madama Butterfly | Giacomo Puccini | 10 Jul 1905 | 366 |
| **10** | Norma | Vincenzo Bellini | 12 Jul 1833 | 355 |

\* To 1 January 2006

Most of the works appearing in the ROH Top 10 were first performed at Covent Garden within a few years of their world premiers. Although some were considered controversial at the time, all of them are now regarded as important components of the classic opera repertoire.

# THE 10 **LATEST WINNERS OF THE BEST CLASSICAL ALBUM GRAMMY AWARD**

| YEAR* COMPOSER / TITLE | CONDUCTOR / SOLOIST / ORCHESTRA |
|---|---|
| **2007** Gustav Mahler, Symphony No.7 | Michael Tilson Thomas, San Francisco Symphony Orchestra |
| **2006** William Bolcom, Songs of Innocence and of Experience | Leonard Slatkin, University of Michigan School of Music Symphony Orchestra |
| **2005** John Adams, On the Transmigration of Souls | Lorin Maazel, Brooklyn Youth Chorus and New Choral Artists, New York Philharmonic |
| **2004** Gustav Mahler, Symphony No. 3; Kindertotenlieder | Michael Tilson Thomas, Michelle DeYoung, San Francisco Symphony Orchestra |
| **2003** Vaughan Williams, A Sea Symphony (Symphony No. 1) | Robert Spano, Norman Mackenzie, Brett Polegato, Christine Goerke, Atlanta Symphony Orchestra |
| **2002** Hector Berlioz, Les Troyens | Sir Colin Davis, Ben Heppner, Kenneth Tarver, Michelle De Young, Peter Mattei, Petra Lang, Sara Mingardo, Stephen Milling, London Symphony Orchestra |
| **2001** Dmitri Shostakovich, The String Quartets | Emerson String Quartet |
| **2000** Igor Stravinsky, Firebird; The Right of Spring; Perséphone | Michael Tilson Thomas, Stuart Neill, San Francisco Symphony Orchestra |
| **1999** Samuel Barber, Prayers of Kierkegaard/ Ralph Vaughan Williams, Dona Nobis Pacem/Béla Bartók, Cantata Profana | Robert Shaw, Richard Clement, Nathan Gunn, Atlanta Symphony Orchestra and Chorus |
| **1998** Richard Danielpour, Leon Kirchner, Christopher Rouse, Premieres – Cello Concertos | Yo-Yo Ma, David Zinman, Philadelphia Orchestra |

\* Awards are for albums released during the previous year

Source: NARAS

# TOP 10 **LARGEST OPERA HOUSES**

| | THEATRE / LOCATION | CAPACITY* |
|---|---|---|
| **1** | Arena di Verona# <br> Verona, Italy | 15,000 |
| **2** | Metropolitan Opera House <br> New York, USA | 3,800 |
| **3** | NHK Hall <br> Tokyo, Japan | 3,677 |
| **4** | Civic Opera House <br> Chicago, USA | 3,563 |
| **5** | Music Hall <br> Cincinnati, USA | 3,516 |
| **6** | Music Hall <br> Dallas, USA | 3,420 |
| **7** | War Memorial Opera House <br> San Francisco, USA | 3,176 |
| **8** | The Hummingbird Centre <br> Toronto, Canada | 3,167 |
| **9** | Dorothy Chandler Pavilion <br> Los Angeles, USA | 3,098 |
| **10** | Civic Theatre <br> San Diego, USA | 2,992 |
| | *Royal Opera House <br> London, UK* | *2,267* |

\* Seating capacity only, excluding standing
\# Open-air venue

Although there are many more venues in the world where opera is also performed, such as the 13,000-seat Municipal Opera Theatre ('Muny') open-air auditorium, St Louis, USA, this list is limited to those where the principal performances are opera.

# Movie Music

## TOP 10 **FILM MUSICALS ADAPTED FROM STAGE VERSIONS**

| | MUSICAL | THEATRE OPENING | FILM RELEASE |
|---|---|---|---|
| 1 | Grease | 1972 | 1978 |
| 2 | Chicago | 1975 | 2002 |
| 3 | The Sound of Music | 1959 | 1965 |
| 4 | The Phantom of the Opera | 1986 | 2004 |
| 5 | Evita | 1978 | 1996 |
| 6 | The Rocky Horror (Picture) Show | 1973 | 1975 |
| 7 | Dreamgirls | 1981 | 2006 |
| 8 | Fiddler on the Roof | 1964 | 1971 |
| 9 | My Fair Lady | 1956 | 1964 |
| 10 | The Best Little Whorehouse in Texas | 1978 | 1982 |

The adapting of stage musicals as films has a long history, with these the most successful cinematic versions of, in most instances, long-running theatrical productions. Some followed even longer routes from stage to screen, having been non-musical theatrical productions before being adapted as stage musicals, among them the recent success *Chicago*, which started life in 1926 as a play by Maurine Dallas Watkins and was made into two films, *Chicago* (1927) and *Roxie Hart* (1942), before Bob Fosse wrote the 1975 musical.

*Still alive*
*Over 40 years after its release,* The Sound of Music *maintains its place among the most successful stage-to-film adaptations.*

## TOP 10 **POP STAR FILM DEBUTS**

| | FILM | STAR | YEAR |
|---|---|---|---|
| 1 | The Bodyguard | Whitney Houston | 1992 |
| 2 | Austin Powers in Goldmember | Beyonce Knowles | 2002 |
| 3 | 8 Mile | Eminem | 2002 |
| 4 | Rocky Horror Picture Show | Meat Loaf | 1975 |
| 5 | The Dukes of Hazzard | Jessica Simpson | 2005 |
| 6 | Nine to Five | Dolly Parton | 1980 |
| 7 | Crash | Ludacris | 2005 |
| 8 | Spice World | Spice Girls | 1998 |
| 9 | Money Train | Jennifer Lopez | 1995 |
| 10 | Romeo Must Die | Aaliyah | 2000 |

Since Al Jolson's debut role in the pioneering talkie *The Jazz Singer* (1927), many popular vocalists have made the transition to films, with those listed ranked as the most successful (although some had minor parts, often uncredited, in films before starring in these), the first six of them earning more than $100 million each worldwide. Since the 1930s this catalogue has included artists of the calibre of Bing Crosby, Marlene Dietrich, Elvis Presley, The Beatles, David Bowie, Sting, Madonna and Björk.

## TOP 10 **MGM MUSICALS**

| | FILM | YEAR |
|---|---|---|
| 1 | Victor/Victoria | 1982 |
| 2 | That's Entertainment! | 1974 |
| 3 | The Wizard of Oz | 1939 |
| 4 | De-Lovely | 2004 |
| 5 | Gigi | 1958 |
| 6 | Seven Brides For Seven Brothers | 1954 |
| 7 | I'll Cry Tomorrow | 1955 |
| 8 | High Society | 1956 |
| 9 | The Unsinkable Molly Brown | 1964 |
| 10 | Meet Me in St Louis | 1944 |

From the earliest years of talking pictures, MGM established itself as the pre-eminent studio for musicals, making some 200 and winning the first Best Picture Oscar for *The Broadway Melody* (1929) and subsequently for *The Great Ziegfeld* (1936), *An American in Paris* (1951) and *Gigi* (1958). MGM's *That's Entertainment*, like its two sequels (1976 and 1994), was a compilation of clips rather than a single narrative film, while *De-Lovely* is a musical biopic based on the life and songs of Cole Porter.

## TOP 10 **MUSICIAN FILM BIOPICS**

| | FILM | SUBJECT | YEAR |
|---|---|---|---|
| 1 | Walk the Line | Johnny Cash | 2005 |
| 2 | The Sound of Music | von Trapp family | 1965 |
| 3 | Ray | Ray Charles | 2004 |
| 4 | Shine | David Helfgott | 1996 |
| 5 | Coal Miner's Daughter | Loretta Lynn | 1980 |
| 6 | La Bamba | Ritchie Valens | 1987 |
| 7 | Amadeus | Wolfgang Amadeus Mozart | 1984 |
| 8 | What's Love Got to Do with It | Tina Turner | 1993 |
| 9 | Selena | Selena Quintanilla | 1997 |
| 10 | The Doors | The Doors | 1991 |

Biopics on the lives of famous musicians have been a Hollywood staple for over 50 years. Those within and outside the Top 10 have encompassed both classical and popular musicians, including such artists as Hank Williams (*Your Cheatin' Heart*, 1964), Peter Tchaikovsky (*The Music Lovers*, 1970), Billie Holiday (*Lady Sings the Blues*, 1972), Buddy Holly (*The Buddy Holly Story*, 1978), John Lennon (*Imagine: John Lennon*, 1988) and Jacqueline du Pré (*Hilary and Jackie*, 1998).

## TOP 10 **SOUNDTRACK ALBUMS IN THE UK**

| | ALBUM | YEAR |
|---|---|---|
| 1 | The Bodyguard | 1992 |
| 2 | Dirty Dancing | 1998 |
| 3 | Titanic | 1997 |
| 4 | Bridget Jones's Diary | 2001 |
| 5 | Trainspotting | 1996 |
| 6 | The Commitments | 1991 |
| 7 | The Full Monty | 1997 |
| 8 | Buster | 1988 |
| 9 | Top Gun | 1986 |
| 10 | Evita | 1996 |

Source: Music Information Database

Although predominantly a vehicle for the film's star Whitney Houston, all-time bestselling soundtrack album *The Bodyguard* also features other singers, including Joe Cocker and Lisa Stansfield.

**Profitable line**
*With world earnings approaching $200 million,* Walk the Line *has overtaken* The Sound of Music *as the most successful musical biopic ever.*

# 7

## STAGE & SCREEN

# Stage

**We like it**
*Although possibly unperformed in his lifetime, Shakespeare's comedy* As You Like It *has become the most popular of all his plays in the modern era.*

## TOP 10 **MOST-PRODUCED PLAYS BY SHAKESPEARE, 1878–2005**

| | PLAY | PRODUCTIONS |
|---|---|---|
| **1** | As You Like It | 79 |
| **2** | Twelfth Night | 77 |
| **3** | = Hamlet | 76 |
| | = The Taming of the Shrew | 76 |
| **5** | A Midsummer Night's Dream | 72 |
| **6** | Much Ado About Nothing | 71 |
| **7** | The Merchant of Venice | 70 |
| **8** | Macbeth | 66 |
| **9** | The Merry Wives of Windsor | 61 |
| **10** | Romeo and Juliet | 59 |

Source: Shakespeare Centre

This list is based on an analysis of Shakespearean productions (rather than individual performances) from 31 December 1878 to 31 December 2005 at Stratford upon Avon and by the Royal Shakespeare Company in London and on tour.

## TOP 10 **LONGEST SHAKESPEAREAN ROLES**

| | ROLE | PLAY | LINES |
|---|---|---|---|
| **1** | Hamlet | Hamlet | 1,422 |
| **2** | Falstaff | Henry IV, Parts I and II | 1,178 |
| **3** | Richard III | Richard III | 1,124 |
| **4** | Iago | Othello | 1,097 |
| **5** | Henry V | Henry V | 1,025 |
| **6** | Othello | Othello | 860 |
| **7** | Vincentio | Measure for Measure | 820 |
| **8** | Coriolanus | Coriolanus | 809 |
| **9** | Timon | Timon of Athens | 795 |
| **10** | Antony | Antony and Cleopatra | 766 |

Hamlet's role comprises 11,610 words, but if multiple plays are considered, he is beaten by Falstaff, who appears in *Henry IV, Parts I* and *II* and in *The Merry Wives of Windsor*, his total of 1,614 lines making him the most talkative of all Shakespeare's characters. However, if more than one play (or parts of a play) are taken into account, others would increase their tallies, among them Richard III, who appears (as Richard, Duke of Gloucester) in *Henry VI, Part III*, and *Henry V* who appears (as Prince Hal) in *Henry IV*, where he speaks 117 lines, making his total 1,142. Rosalind's 668-line role in *As You Like It* is the longest female part in the works of Shakespeare.

## TOP 10 **OLDEST LONDON THEATRES**

| | THEATRE / OPENING SHOW | OPENED |
|---|---|---|
| **1** | **Theatre Royal**, Drury Lane<br>The Humorous Lieutenant | 7 May 1663 |
| **2** | **Sadler's Wells**, Rosebery Avenue<br>Musical performances | 3 Jun 1683 |
| **3** | **The Haymarket** (Theatre Royal), Haymarket<br>La Fille à la Mode | 29 Dec 1720 |
| **4** | **Royal Opera House**, Covent Garden<br>The Way of the World | 7 Dec 1732 |
| **5** | **The Adelphi** (originally Sans Pareil), Strand<br>The Rout/Tempest Terrific/Vision in the Holyland | 17 Nov 1806 |
| **6** | **The Old Vic** (originally Royal Coburg)<br>Waterloo Road<br>Trial by Battle/Alzora and Nerine/Midnight Revelry | 11 May 1818 |
| **7** | **The Vaudeville**, Strand<br>For Love or Money | 16 Apr 1870 |
| **8** | **The Criterion**, Piccadilly Circus<br>An American Lady | 21 Mar 1874 |
| **9** | **The Savoy**, Strand<br>Patience | 10 Oct 1881 |
| **10** | **The Comedy**, Panton Street<br>La Mascotte | 15 Oct 1881 |

These are London's 10 oldest theatres operating on their original sites.

*Grand* Opera
*With a run of over 20 years in London and approaching that on Broadway, and numerous productions including a Las Vegas spectacular,* The Phantom of the Opera *has become a global phenomenon.*

## TOP 10 **LONGEST-RUNNING MUSICALS IN THE UK**

| SHOW | PERFORMANCES* |
|---|---|
| **1** Cats (1981–2002) | 8,949 |
| **2** Les Misérables (1985–) | 8,852# |
| **3** The Phantom of the Opera (1986–) | 8,517# |
| **4** Starlight Express (1984–2002) | 7,406 |
| **5** Miss Saigon (1989–99) | 4,263 |
| **6** Jesus Christ, Superstar (1972–80) | 3,357 |
| **7** Evita (1978–86) | 2,900 |
| **8** Oliver! (1960–66) | 2,618 |
| **9** The Sound of Music (1961–67) | 2,386 |
| **10** Salad Days (1954–60) | 2,283 |

\* Continuous runs only
\# Still running, total as at 31 March 2007

*Cats* closed on 12 May 2001, its 21st birthday, having held the record as the UK's longest-running musical since 12 May 1989. Some include runs at different theatres, making *Cats* also the longest continuously running musical at the same venue.

## TOP 10 **LONGEST-RUNNING COMEDIES IN THE UK**

| SHOW | PERFORMANCES |
|---|---|
| **1** No Sex Please – We're British (1971–81; 1982–86; 1986–87) | 6,761 |
| **2** The Complete Works of William Shakespeare (abridged) (1996–2005) | 4,266 |
| **3** Run for Your Wife (1983–91) | 2,638 |
| **4** There's a Girl in My Soup (1966–69; 1969–72) | 2,547 |
| **5** Pyjama Tops (1969–75) | 2,498 |
| **6** Worm's Eye View (1945–51) | 2,245 |
| **7** Boeing Boeing (1962–65; 1965–67) | 2,035 |
| **8** Blithe Spirit (1941–42; 1942; 1942–46) | 1,997 |
| **9** Dirty Linen (1976–80) | 1,667 |
| **10** Reluctant Heroes (1950–54) | 1,610 |

*No Sex Please – We're British* is the world's longest running comedy. It opened at the Strand Theatre, London, on 3 June 1971 and after transfers to the Garrick and Duchess Theatres, finally closed on 5 September 1987.

# Theatre Awards

## THE 10 LATEST WINNERS OF THE LAURENCE OLIVIER AWARD FOR BEST NEW PLAY*

| YEAR# | PLAY / PLAYWRIGHT |
|---|---|
| 2007 | Blackbird, David Harrower |
| 2006 | On the Shore of the Wide World, Simon Stephens |
| 2005 | The History Boys, Alan Bennett |
| 2004 | The Pillowman, Martin McDonagh |
| 2003 | Vincent in Brixton, Nicholas Wright |
| 2002 | Jitney, August Wilson |
| 2001 | Blue/Orange, Marie Jones |
| 2000 | Goodnight Children Everywhere, Richard Nelson |
| 1999 | The Weir, Conor McPherson |
| 1998 | Closer, Patrick Marber |

* BBC Award for Best Play until 1996, Best New Play thereafter
# Awards are for plays staged during the previous year

Presented by The Society of London Theatres (founded 1908), the award is named after Laurence (later Lord) Olivier (1907–89). Several earlier winners went on to become successful films, among them *Whose Life is it Anyway?* (play 1978, film 1981), *Children of a Lesser God* (1981/86), *Les Liaisons Dangereuses* (1986/88 – as *Dangerous Liaisons*) and *The History Boys* (2005/2006).

## THE 10 LATEST WINNERS OF THE LAURENCE OLIVIER AWARD FOR BEST ACTOR

| YEAR* | ACTOR / PLAY |
|---|---|
| 2007 | Rufus Sewell, Rock 'N' Roll |
| 2006 | Brian Dennehy, Death of a Salesman |
| 2005 | Richard Griffiths, The History Boys |
| 2004 | Matthew Kelly, Of Mice and Men |
| 2003 | Simon Russell Beale, Uncle Vanya |
| 2002 | Roger Allam, Privates on Parade |
| 2001 | Conleth Hill, Stones in his Pockets |
| 2000 | Henry Goodman, The Merchant of Venice |
| 1999 | Kevin Spacey, The Iceman Cometh |
| 1998 | Ian Holm, King Lear |

* Awards are for plays staged during the previous year

## THE 10 LATEST WINNERS OF THE EVENING STANDARD AWARD FOR BEST ACTRESS

| YEAR | ACTRESS / PLAY |
|---|---|
| 2006 | Kathleen Turner, Who's Afraid of Virginia Woolf? |
| 2005 | Harriet Walter, Mary Stuart |
| 2004 | Victoria Hamilton, Suddenly Last Summer |
| 2003 | Sandy McDade, Iron |
| 2002 | Clare Higgins, Vincent in Brixton |
| 2001 | Fiona Shaw, Medea |
| 2000 | Paola Dionisotti, Further than the Furthest Thing |
| 1999 | Janie Dee, Comic Potential |
| 1998 | Sinead Cusack, Our Lady of Sligo |
| 1997 | Eileen Atkins, A Delicate Balance |

Maggie Smith has won this prestigious award on no fewer than five occasions. Vanessa Redgrave has won four times, and Peggy Ashcroft and Judi Dench have each received three awards.

## THE 10 LATEST WINNERS OF THE EVENING STANDARD AWARD FOR BEST ACTOR

| YEAR | ACTOR / PLAY |
|---|---|
| 2006 | Rufus Sewell, Rock 'N' Roll |
| 2005 | Simon Russell Beale, The Philanthropist |
| 2004 | Richard Griffiths, The History Boys |
| 2003 | Michael Sheen, Caligula |
| 2002 | Simon Russell Beale, Uncle Vanya and Twelfth Night |
| 2001 | Alex Jennings, The Winter's Tale and The Relapse |
| 2000 | Simon Russell Beale, Hamlet |
| 1999 | Stephen Dillane, The Real Thing |
| 1998 | Kevin Spacey, The Ice Man Cometh |
| 1997 | Ian Holm, King Lear |

The Best Actor award was first presented in 1955, when it was won by Richard Burton. Albert Finney, Ian Holm, Alec McCowen, Laurence Olivier and Paul Scofield each won it three times.

*Production number*
*The stage musical version of Mel Brooks' 1968 film The Producers won an Evening Standard Award for Best Musical.*
*The musical of the film about a musical in turn became a musical film (2005).*

## THE 10 **LATEST WINNERS OF THE LAURENCE OLIVIER AWARD FOR BEST ACTRESS**

| YEAR* | ACTRESS / PLAY |
|---|---|
| **2007** | Tamsin Greig, Much Ado About Nothin |
| **2006** | Eve Best, Hedda Gabler |
| **2005** | Clare Higgins, Hecuba |
| **2004** | Eileen Atkins, Honour |
| **2003** | Clare Higgins, Vincent in Brixton |
| **2002** | Lindsay Duncan, Private Lives |
| **2001** | Julie Walters, All My Sons |
| **2000** | Janie Dee, Comic Potential |
| **1999** | Eileen Atkins, The Unexpected Man |
| **1998** | Zoë Wanamaker, Electra |

* Awards are for plays staged during the previous year

## THE 10 **LATEST WINNERS OF THE EVENING STANDARD AWARD FOR BEST MUSICAL***

| YEAR | MUSICAL |
|---|---|
| **2006** | Caroline, Or Change |
| **2005** | Billy Elliot |
| **2004** | The Producers |
| **2003** | Jerry Springer: The Opera |
| **2002** | The Full Monty |
| **2001** | Kiss Me Kate |
| **2000** | The Car Man |
| **1999** | Spend, Spend, Spend |
| **1998** | Oklahoma! |
| **1997** | Lady in the Dark |

* The Carlton Television Award

## THE 10 **LATEST WINNERS OF THE EVENING STANDARD AWARD FOR BEST PLAY**

| YEAR | PLAY / PLAYWRIGHT |
|---|---|
| **2006** | Rock 'N' Roll, Tom Stoppard |
| **2005** | The Home Place, Brian Friel |
| **2004** | The History Boys, Alan Bennett |
| **2003** | Democracy, Michael Frayn |
| **2002** | A Number, Caryl Churchill |
| **2001** | The Far Side of the Moon, Robert Lepage |
| **2000** | Blue/Orange, Joe Penhall |
| **1998** | Copenhagen, Michael Frayn |
| **1997** | The Invention of Love, Tom Stoppard |
| **1996** | Stanley, Pam Gems |

# Film Industry

## TOP 10 **COUNTRIES WITH THE MOST CINEMA SCREENS**

COUNTRY / SCREENS (2005)

 China  39,425

 USA  38,852

 India  10,500

 France  5,366

 Germany  4,889

 Spain  4,398

 Italy  3,865

 Mexico  3,544

 UK  3,486

 Canada  2,933

Source: *Screen Digest*

STAGE & SCREEN

## TOP 10 **FILM BUDGETS**

| | FILM | YEAR | ESTIMATED BUDGET ($) |
|---|---|---|---|
| **1** | Spider-Man 3 | 2007 | 300,000,000 |
| **2** | Superman Returns | 2006 | 270,000,000 |
| **3** | Pirates of the Caribbean: Dead Man's Chest | 2006 | 225,000,000 |
| **4** | X-Men: The Last Stand | 2006 | 210,000,000 |
| **5** | King Kong | 2005 | 207,000,000 |
| **6** | = Titanic | 1997 | 200,000,000 |
| | = Terminator 3: Rise of the Machines | 2003 | 200,000,000 |
| | = Spider-Man 2 | 2004 | 200,000,000 |
| | = Pirates of the Caribbean: At World's End | 2007 | 200,000,000 |
| | = Avatar | 2008 * | 200,000,000 |
| | = The Curious Case of Benjamin Button | 2008 * | 200,000,000 |
| | = Battle Angel | 2009 * | 200,000,000 |

\* Scheduled

*Budget burden*
*Industry sources claim the production budget of* Superman Returns *to have been $270 million.*

*Bollywood spectacle*
*Hrishitaa Bhatt in* Kisna: The Warrior Poet,
*one of more than 1,000 films produced by
the Indian film industry in 2005.*

## TOP 10 **YEARS FOR CINEMA ADMISSIONS IN THE UK**

| | YEAR | ADMISSIONS |
|---|---|---|
| **1** | 1946 | 1,635,000,000 |
| **2** | 1945 | 1,585,000,000 |
| **3** | 1944 | 1,575,000,000 |
| **4** | 1943 | 1,541,000,000 |
| **5** | 1948 | 1,514,000,000 |
| **6** | 1942 | 1,494,000,000 |
| **7** | 1947 | 1,462,000,000 |
| **8** | 1949 | 1,430,000,000 |
| **9** | 1950 | 1,395,800,000 |
| **10** | 1951 | 1,365,000,000 |

When they were first recorded in 1933, there were 903 million cinema admissions in the UK. The first post-war year, 1946, retains the record for the highest number of cinema admissions. Annual visits of more than one billion were common up to 1956. Even allowing for present-day access to television and DVD, these figures are especially remarkable, since the population in 1946 was estimated at 48,016,000 or under 80 per cent of today's total, but was equivalent to 34 annual visits per person, compared with fewer than three today.

## TOP 10 **FILM-PRODUCING COUNTRIES**

| | COUNTRY | FEATURE FILMS PRODUCED (2005) |
|---|---|---|
| **1** | India | 1,041 |
| **2** | USA | 699 |
| **3** | Japan | 356 |
| **4** | China | 260 |
| **5** | France | 240 |
| **6** | Russia | 160 |
| **7** | Spain | 142 |
| **8** | UK | 124 |
| **9** | Germany | 103 |
| **10** | Bangladesh | 102 |

Source: Screen Digest

Hollywood's 'golden age' was the 1920s and 1930s, with 854 films made in 1921, and its nadir 1978 with just 354. In 2005 the USA made 600 films at a cost of $13,945,000,000, an average of $19,950,000 per film. Total world feature film production reached 4,603, an increase of 7.8 per cent on the previous year, led by growth among European and South American producers. The total cost was $22,598,000,000, an average of less than $5 million per film.

## TOP 10 **COUNTRIES BY BOX-OFFICE REVENUE**

| | COUNTRY | ESTIMATED TOTAL BOX-OFFICE GROSS, 2006 ($) |
|---|---|---|
| **1** | USA | 9,420,000,000 |
| **2** | Japan | 1,839,600,000 |
| **3** | UK | 1,397,000,000 |
| **4** | France | 1,387,600,000 |
| **5** | Germany | 1,018,300,000 |
| **6** | Spain | 788,300,000 |
| **7** | Canada | 685,900,000 |
| **8** | Italy | 680,200,000 |
| **9** | Australia | 661,000,000 |
| **10** | Mexico | 557,900,000 |

Source: *Screen Digest*

# Blockbuster Movies

## TOP 10 FILMS OF ALL TIME

| FILM | YEAR | USA | GROSS INCOME ($) OVERSEAS | WORLD TOTAL |
|---|---|---|---|---|
| 1 Titanic* | 1997 | 600,788,188 | 1,244,246,000 | 1,845,034,188 |
| 2 The Lord of the Rings: The Return of the King | 2003 | 377,027,325 | 752,191,927 | 1,129,219,252 |
| 3 Pirates of the Caribbean: Dead Man's Chest | 2006 | 423,315,812 | 642,344,000 | 1,065,659,812 |
| 4 Harry Potter and the Philosopher's Stone | 2001 | 317,575,550 | 668,242,109 | 985,817,659 |
| 5 The Lord of the Rings: The Two Towers | 2002 | 341,786,758 | 584,500,642 | 926,287,400 |
| 6 Star Wars: Episode I – The Phantom Menace | 1999 | 431,088,301 | 493,229,257 | 924,317,558 |
| 7 Shrek 2# | 2004 | 441,226,247 | 479,439,411 | 920,665,658 |
| 8 Jurassic Park | 1993 | 357,067,947 | 562,632,053 | 919,700,000 |
| 9 Harry Potter and the Goblet of Fire | 2005 | 290,013,036 | 602,200,000 | 892,213,036 |
| 10 Harry Potter and the Chamber of Secrets | 2002 | 261,988,482 | 614,700,000 | 876,688,482 |

\* Won Best Picture Oscar
\# Animated

Prior to the release of *Star Wars* in 1977, no film had ever made more than $500 million worldwide. Since then, some 47 films have done so, 15 of them earning over $800 million each. *Titanic* remains the only film to have made more than this amount in the USA alone, and just 13 films have exceeded this total outside the USA.

*Hot pursuit*
Pirates of the Caribbean: Dead Man's Chest *became only the third film ever to earn more than $1 billion globally, with the 2007 release of* Pirates of the Caribbean: At World's End, *set to consolidate the success of the series.*

## TOP 10 FILMS IN THE UK, 2006

| FILM | UK GROSS (£) |
|---|---|
| 1 Pirates of the Caribbean: Dead Man's Chest | 51,993,705 |
| 2 The Da Vinci Code | 30,415,008 |
| 3 Ice Age: The Meltdown* | 29,450,144 |
| 4 X-Men: The Last Stand | 19,130,046 |
| 5 Cars* | 16,245,451 |
| 6 Superman Returns | 16,118,973 |
| 7 Mission: Impossible III | 15,408,898 |
| 8 Chicken Little* | 13,680,077 |
| 9 Over the Hedge* | 13,015,427 |
| 10 The Break-Up | 10,258,206 |

\* Animated

*Winning the war*
The Star Wars *series has (just) outearned the* Bond *franchise.*

# TOP 10 **FILMS WORLDWIDE, 2006**

FILM / WORLDWIDE GROSS, 2006 ($)

**1** Pirates of the Caribbean: Dead Man's Chest
1,059,696,468

**2** The Da Vinci Code
756,220,423

**3** Ice Age: The Meltdown*
646,593,702

**4** X-Men: The Last Stand
458,602,385

**5** Cars*
456,005,982

**6** Mission: Impossible III
395,695,255

**7** Superman Returns
391,028,903

**8** Over the Hedge*
319,942,172

**9** The Devil Wears Prada
233,210,662

**10** Click
224,319,234

* Animated

# TOP 10 **FILM FRANCHISES OF ALL TIME**

| FRANCHISE | NO. OF FILMS | YEARS | TOTAL WORLD GROSS ($)* |
|---|---|---|---|
| **1** Star Wars | 6 | 1977–2005 | 4,421,000,000 |
| **2** James Bond | 21# | 1963–2006 | 4,325,000,000 |
| **3** Harry Potter | 4 | 2001–06 | 3,545,000,000 |
| **4** The Lord of the Rings | 3 | 2001–03 | 2,927,000,000 |
| **5** Jurassic Park | 3 | 1993–2001 | 1,902,000,000 |
| **6** Pirates of the Caribbean | 2 | 2003–06 | 1,720,000,000 |
| **7** Batman | 5 | 1989–2005 | 1,643,000,000 |
| **8** The Matrix | 3 | 1999–2003 | 1,624,000,000 |
| **9** Spider-Man | 2 | 2002–04 | 1,606,000,000 |
| **10** Shrek | 2 | 2001–04 | 1,405,000,000 |

* Cumulative global earnings of the original film and all its sequels to 20 March 2007
# Excluding 'unofficial' *Casino Royale* and *Never Say Never Again*

# TOP 10 **OPENING WEEKENDS IN THE UK**

| FILM | RELEASE DATE | SCREENS | OPENING WEEKEND GROSS (£) |
|---|---|---|---|
| **1** Harry Potter and the Prisoner of Azkaban | 31 May 2004 | 535 | 23,882,688 |
| **2** Harry Potter and the Chamber of Secrets | 15 Nov 2002 | 524 | 18,871,829 |
| **3** Harry Potter and the Philosopher's Stone | 16 Nov 2001 | 507 | 16,335,627 |
| **4** Shrek 2* | 2 Jul 2004 | 512 | 16,220,752 |
| **5** The Lord of the Rings: The Return of the King | 17 Dec 2003 | 494 | 15,021,761 |
| **6** Harry Potter and the Goblet of Fire | 18 Nov 2005 | 535 | 14,933,901 |
| **7** Star Wars: Episode III – Revenge of the Sith | 19 May 2005 | 490 | 14,361,469 |
| **8** Pirates of the Caribbean: Dead Man's Chest | 6 Jul 2006 | 514 | 13,740,784 |
| **9** Casino Royale | 16 Nov 2006 | 505 | 13,370,969 |
| **10** The Lord of the Rings: The Two Towers | 18 Dec 2002 | 501 | 13,063,560 |

* Animated

# Movies Through the Decades

**Monster hit**
*Despite being released during the Depression, King Kong (1933) was one of the most commercially successful films of the decade and through numerous re-releases.*

## TOP 10 FILMS OF THE 1930s

| | FILM | YEAR | WORLD BOX OFFICE ($) |
|---|---|---|---|
| 1 | Gone with the Wind* | 1939 | 400,176,459 |
| 2 | Snow White and the Seven Dwarfs# | 1937 | 187,670,866 |
| 3 | King Kong | 1933 | 62,815,000 |
| 4 | The Hurricane | 1937 | 17,300,000 |
| 5 | The Wizard of Oz | 1939 | 14,800,000 |
| 6 | Frankenstein | 1931 | 12,000,000 |
| 7 | Ingagi | 1931 | 4,000,000 |
| 8 | Top Hat | 1935 | 3,000,000 |
| 9 | = 42nd Street | 1933 | 2,300,000 |
| | = Ninotchka | 1939 | 2,300,000 |

\* Won Best Picture Oscar
# Animated

## TOP 10 FILMS OF THE 1940s

| | FILM | YEAR | WORLD BOX OFFICE ($) |
|---|---|---|---|
| 1 | Bambi* | 1942 | 267,997,150 |
| 2 | Pinocchio* | 1940 | 84,254,167 |
| 3 | Fantasia* | 1940 | 76,408,097 |
| 4 | Song of the South# | 1946 | 65,000,000 |
| 5 | Samson and Delilah | 1949 | 28,800,000 |
| 6 | The Best Years of Our Lives† | 1946 | 23,650,000 |
| 7 | The Bells of St Mary's | 1945 | 21,333,333 |
| 8 | Duel in the Sun | 1946 | 20,408,163 |
| 9 | This is the Army | 1943 | 19,500,000 |
| 10 | The Jolson Story | 1946 | 19,000,000 |

\* Animated
# Part animated, part live action
† Won Best Picture Oscar

## TOP 10 FILMS OF THE 1950s

| | FILM | YEAR | WORLD BOX OFFICE ($) |
|---|---|---|---|
| 1 | Lady and The Tramp* | 1955 | 93,602,326 |
| 2 | Peter Pan* | 1953 | 87,404,651 |
| 3 | The Ten Commandments | 1956 | 80,000,000 |
| 4 | Ben-Hur# | 1959 | 74,000,000 |
| 5 | Sleeping Beauty* | 1959 | 51,600,000 |
| 6 | Around the World in 80 Days# | 1956 | 42,000,000 |
| 7 | This is Cinerama | 1952 | 41,600,000 |
| 8 | South Pacific | 1958 | 36,800,000 |
| 9 | Rear Window | 1954 | 36,764,313 |
| 10 | = The Greatest Show on Earth# | 1952 | 36,000,000 |
| | = The Robe | 1953 | 36,000,000 |

\* Animated
# Won Best Picture Oscar

## TOP 10 FILMS OF THE 1960s

| | FILM | YEAR | WORLD BOX OFFICE ($) |
|---|---|---|---|
| 1 | One Hundred and One Dalmatians | 1961 | 224,000,000 |
| 2 | The Jungle Book* | 1967 | 205,843,612 |
| 3 | 2001: A Space Odyssey | 1968 | 190,700,000 |
| 4 | The Sound of Music# | 1965 | 163,214,286 |
| 5 | Thunderball | 1965 | 141,195,658 |
| 6 | Goldfinger | 1964 | 124,881,062 |
| 7 | Doctor Zhivago | 1965 | 112,950,721 |
| 8 | You Only Live Twice | 1967 | 111,584,787 |
| 9 | The Graduate | 1967 | 104,397,102 |
| 10 | Butch Cassidy and the Sundance Kid | 1969 | 102,308,889 |

\* Animated
# Won Best Picture Oscar

*Over the moon*
E.T. *was the 1980s' biggest earner, and the 16th of all time.*

## TOP 10 **FILMS OF THE** 1970s

| FILM | YEAR | WORLD BOX OFFICE ($) |
|---|---|---|
| **1** Star Wars: Episode IV – A New Hope | 1977 | 775,398,007 |
| **2** Jaws | 1975 | 470,653,000 |
| **3** The Exorcist | 1973 | 441,071,011 |
| **4** Grease | 1978 | 394,589,888 |
| **5** Close Encounters of the Third Kind | 1977 | 303,788,635 |
| **6** Superman | 1978 | 300,218,018 |
| **7** Saturday Night Fever | 1977 | 285,400,000 |
| **8** The Godfather* | 1972 | 245,044,459 |
| **9** Jaws 2 | 1978 | 209,040,376 |
| **10** Moonraker | 1979 | 202,708,099 |

* Won Best Picture Oscar

## TOP 10 **FILMS OF THE** 1980s

| FILM | YEAR | WORLD BOX OFFICE ($) |
|---|---|---|
| **1** E.T. the Extra-Terrestrial | 1982 | 792,910,554 |
| **2** Star Wars: Episode VI – Return of the Jedi | 1983 | 573,006,177 |
| **3** Star Wars: Episode V – The Empire Strikes Back | 1980 | 538,375,067 |
| **4** Indiana Jones and the Last Crusade | 1989 | 494,771,806 |
| **5** Rain Man* | 1988 | 416,011,462 |
| **6** Batman | 1989 | 413,388,924 |
| **7** Raiders of the Lost Ark | 1981 | 384,140,454 |
| **8** Back to the Future | 1985 | 381,109,762 |
| **9** Top Gun | 1986 | 353,816,701 |
| **10** Indiana Jones and the Temple of Doom | 1984 | 333,107,271 |

* Won Best Picture Oscar

## TOP 10 **FILMS OF THE** 1990s

| FILM | YEAR | WORLD BOX OFFICE ($) |
|---|---|---|
| **1** Titanic* | 1997 | 1,845,034,188 |
| **2** Star Wars: Episode I – The Phantom Menace | 1999 | 924,317,554 |
| **3** Jurassic Park | 1993 | 919,700,000 |
| **4** Independence Day | 1996 | 816,969,255 |
| **5** The Lion King# | 1994 | 783,841,776 |
| **6** Forrest Gump* | 1994 | 677,386,686 |
| **7** The Sixth Sense | 1999 | 672,804,617 |
| **8** Jurassic Park: The Lost World | 1997 | 618,638,999 |
| **9** Men in Black | 1997 | 589,390,539 |
| **10** Armageddon | 1998 | 553,709,788 |

* Won Best Picture Oscar
# Animated

## TOP 10 **FILMS OF THE** 2000s*

| FILM | YEAR | WORLD BOX OFFICE ($) |
|---|---|---|
| **1** The Lord of the Rings: The Return of the King# | 2003 | 1,129,219,252 |
| **2** Pirates of the Caribbean: Dead Man's Chest | 2006 | 1,065,659,812 |
| **3** Harry Potter and the Philosopher's Stone | 2001 | 985,817,659 |
| **4** The Lord of the Rings: The Two Towers | 2002 | 926,287,400 |
| **5** Shrek 2† | 2004 | 920,665,658 |
| **6** Harry Potter and the Goblet of Fire | 2005 | 892,213,036 |
| **7** Harry Potter and the Chamber of Secrets | 2002 | 876,688,482 |
| **8** The Lord of the Rings: The Fellowship of the Ring | 2001 | 871,368,364 |
| **9** Finding Nemo† | 2003 | 864,625,978 |
| **10** Star Wars: Episode III – Revenge of the Sith | 2005 | 848,797,674 |

* To end of 2006
# Won Best Picture Oscar
† Animated

# Film Genres

*Crossing America*
*Borat's tour of the USA crosses the road-trip and mockumentary genres, topping both in world earnings of $250 million.*

## TOP 10 **DISASTER FILMS**

| FILM / YEAR |
| --- |
| **1** Titanic 1997 |
| **2** Armageddon 1998 |
| **3** The Day After Tomorrow 2004 |
| **4** Twister 1996 |
| **5** Die Hard: With a Vengeance 1995 |
| **6** Apollo 13 1995 |
| **7** Deep Impact 1998 |
| **8** The Perfect Storm 2000 |
| **9** Die Hard 2: Die Harder 1990 |
| **10** Outbreak 1995 |

Excluding science-fiction subjects (alien attacks, rampaging dinosaurs and other fantasy themes), disasters involving blazing buildings, natural disasters such as volcanoes, earthquakes, tidal waves, train and air crashes, sinking ships and terrorist attacks, have long been a staple of Hollywood films, while latterly asteroid impacts, tornadoes, exploding space capsules and killer viruses have been added to the genre.

## TOP 10 **MOCKUMENTARIES**

| FILM | YEAR |
| --- | --- |
| **1** Borat: Cultural Learnings of America for Make Benefit Glorious Nation of Kazakhstan | 2006 |
| **2** Best in Show | 2000 |
| **3** A Mighty Wind | 2003 |
| **4** Drop Dead Gorgeous | 1999 |
| **5** Zelig | 1983 |
| **6** Sweet and Lowdown | 1999 |
| **7** Take the Money and Run | 1969 |
| **8** For Your Consideration | 2006 |
| **9** Bob Roberts | 1992 |
| **10** This is Spinal Tap | 1984 |

Spoof comedy documentaries by Christopher Guest (2, 3 and 8) and Woody Allen (5, 6 and 7) feature prominently in this list.

## TOP 10 **COMEDY ROAD-TRIP FILMS**

| FILM | YEAR |
| --- | --- |
| **1** Borat: Cultural Learnings of America for Make Benefit Glorious Nation of Kazakhstan | 2006 |
| **2** Dumb and Dumber | 1994 |
| **3** Road Trip | 2000 |
| **4** The Blues Brothers | 1980 |
| **5** Sideways | 2004 |
| **6** Are We There Yet? | 2005 |
| **7** Little Miss Sunshine | 2006 |
| **8** Forces of Nature | 1999 |
| **9** RV | 2006 |
| **10** Rat Race | 2001 |

## TOP 10 **FILMS ADAPTED FROM COMICS**

| FILM* | COMIC FIRST PUBLISHED | FILM RELEASED |
| --- | --- | --- |
| **1** Spider-Man | 1962 | 2002 |
| **2** Men in Black | 1990 | 1997 |
| **3** X-Men: The Last Stand | 1963 | 2006 |
| **4** Batman | 1939 | 1989 |
| **5** Superman Returns | 1938 | 2006 |
| **6** The Mask | 1991 | 1994 |
| **7** Fantastic Four | 1961 | 2005 |
| **8** Superman | 1938 | 1978 |
| **9** Casper# | 1949 | 1995 |
| **10** Hulk | 1962 | 2003 |

* If series, highest-earning only
# Original film made 1946

The transition from cartoons and comic strips to film has been commonplace since the 1920s, and there are many popular predecessors to those appearing in the Top 10, each of which earned over $245 million at the global box office. Disney's animated *Tarzan* (1999) has been excluded since although Tarzan became a comic strip in 1929, the film derived from Edgar Rice Burroughs' 1914 *Tarzan of the Apes* novel and its sequels.

## TOP 10 **TREASURE-HUNT FILMS**

| FILM | YEAR |
|---|---|
| **1** Pirates of the Caribbean: Dead Man's Chest | 2006 |
| **2** Pirates of the Caribbean: The Curse of the Black Pearl | 2003 |
| **3** Indiana Jones and the Last Crusade | 1989 |
| **4** Raiders of the Lost Ark | 1981 |
| **5** National Treasure | 2004 |
| **6** Lara Croft: Tomb Raider | 2001 |
| **7** Lara Croft Tomb Raider: The Cradle of Life | 2003 |
| **8** Sahara | 2005 |
| **9** Romancing the Stone | 1984 |
| **10** Treasure Planet | 2002 |

## TOP 10 **CHRISTMAS FILMS**

| FILM | YEAR |
|---|---|
| **1** Dr Seuss's How the Grinch Stole Christmas | 2000 |
| **2** The Santa Clause | 1994 |
| **3** The Santa Clause 2: The Mrs Clause | 2002 |
| **4** Jingle All the Way | 1996 |
| **5** The Santa Clause 3: The Escape Clause | 2006 |
| **6** Christmas with the Kranks | 2004 |
| **7** Bad Santa | 2003 |
| **8** The Nightmare Before Christmas | 1993 |
| **9** National Lampoon's Christmas Vacation | 1989 |
| **10** Scrooged | 1988 |

These are films in which Christmas and/or Santa Claus provide the principal theme, rather than films containing Christmas or holiday scenes – which would be led by movies such as *Home Alone*. The top five in the list earned over $100 million each worldwide, with the No.1 scooping a festive $345 million.

## TOP 10 **JAMES BOND FILMS**

| FILM | BOND ACTOR | YEAR |
|---|---|---|
| **1** Casino Royale | Daniel Craig | 2006 |
| **2** Die Another Day | Pierce Brosnan | 2002 |
| **3** The World is Not Enough | Pierce Brosnan | 1999 |
| **4** GoldenEye | Pierce Brosnan | 1995 |
| **5** Tomorrow Never Dies | Pierce Brosnan | 1997 |
| **6** Moonraker | Roger Moore | 1979 |
| **7** For Your Eyes Only | Roger Moore | 1981 |
| **8** The Living Daylights | Timothy Dalton | 1987 |
| **9** The Spy Who Loved Me | Roger Moore | 1977 |
| **10** Octopussy | Roger Moore | 1983 |

Ian Fleming wrote 12 James Bond novels, only two of which – *Moonraker* (1955) and *The Spy Who Loved Me* (1962) – figure in this Top 10. After his death in 1964, *For Your Eyes Only*, *Octopussy*, *The Living Daylights* and *GoldenEye* were developed by other writers from his short stories, while subsequent releases were written without reference to Fleming's writings. The original *Casino Royale* (book 1953, film 1967), featuring 56-year-old David Niven as the retired spy Sir James Bond, is an oddity in that it was presented as a comedy. This and *Never Say Never Again* (1983), effectively a remake of *Thunderball*, are not considered 'official' Bond films, making the 2006 *Casino Royale* the 21st in the canonical series.

*High-yield Bond*
Casino Royale, *Daniel Craig's debut as James Bond, is the highest-earning Bond film to date. Craig is also to star in the 22nd in the series, scheduled for release in 2008.*

# Animated Films

**Ice breaker**
Ice Age: The Meltdown *was made with a budget of $80 million, but has earned more than eight times as much worldwide.*

## TOP 10 ANIMATED FILMS

| | FILM | YEAR | WORLDWIDE TOTAL GROSS ($) |
|---|---|---|---|
| 1 | Shrek 2* | 2004 | 920,665,658 |
| 2 | Finding Nemo# | 2003 | 864,625,978 |
| 3 | The Lion King# | 1994 | 783,841,776 |
| 4 | Ice Age: The Meltdown† | 2006 | 651,552,216 |
| 5 | The Incredibles# | 2004 | 631,436,092 |
| 6 | Monsters, Inc.# | 2001 | 529,061,238 |
| 7 | Madagascar* | 2005 | 528,898,225 |
| 8 | Aladdin# | 1992 | 504,050,219 |
| 9 | Toy Story 2# | 1999 | 485,015,179 |
| 10 | Shrek* | 2001 | 484,409,218 |

\* DreamWorks
\# Disney
† 20th Century Fox Animation

## TOP 10 ANIMATED FILM BUDGETS

| | FILM | YEAR | BUDGET ($) |
|---|---|---|---|
| 1 | The Polar Express | 2004 | 170,000,000 |
| 2 | Tarzan | 1999 | 145,000,000 |
| 3 | Flushed Away | 2006 | 143,000,000 |
| 4 | Treasure Planet | 2002 | 140,000,000 |
| 5 | Final Fantasy: The Spirits Within | 2001 | 137,000,000 |
| 6 | Dinosaur | 2000 | 127,500,000 |
| 7 | Cars | 2006 | 120,000,000 |
| 8 | Monsters, Inc. | 2001 | 115,000,000 |
| 9 | Home on the Range | 2004 | 110,000,000 |
| 10 | The Emperor's New Groove | 2000 | 100,000,000 |

*Snow White and the Seven Dwarfs* (1937) set a record animated film budget of $1.49 million. Subsequent milestones include *Pinocchio* (1940) at $2.28 million, *Sleeping Beauty* (1959) $6 million, *Robin Hood* (1973) $15 million and *The Lion King* (1994) $79.3 million.

## TOP 10 ANIMATED OPENING WEEKENDS IN THE UK

| | FILM | YEAR | WEEKEND GROSS (£) |
|---|---|---|---|
| 1 | Shrek 2 | 2004 | 16,220,752 |
| 2 | The Incredibles | 2004 | 9,874,782 |
| 3 | Ice Age: The Meltdown | 2006 | 9,775,974 |
| 4 | Wallis & Gromit: The Curse of the Were-Rabbit | 2005 | 9,374,932 |
| 5 | Monsters, Inc. | 2002 | 9,200,257 |
| 6 | Toy Story 2 | 2000 | 7,971,539 |
| 7 | Finding Nemo | 2003 | 7,590,845 |
| 8 | Shark Tale | 2004 | 7,545,074 |
| 9 | Madagascar | 2005 | 5,431,639 |
| 10 | Shrek | 2001 | 4,686,210 |

## TOP 10 ANIMATED FILMS IN THE UK

| | FILM | YEAR | UK TOTAL GROSS (£) |
|---|---|---|---|
| 1 | Shrek 2* | 2004 | 48,243,628 |
| 2 | Toy Story 2# | 2000 | 44,306,070 |
| 3 | Monsters, Inc.# | 2002 | 37,907,451 |
| 4 | Finding Nemo# | 2003 | 37,364,251 |
| 5 | The Incredibles# | 2004 | 32,277,041 |
| 6 | Wallace & Gromit: The Curse of the Were-Rabbit* | 2005 | 32,007,310 |
| 7 | Chicken Run* | 2000 | 29,514,237 |
| 8 | Ice Age: The Meltdown† | 2006 | 29,450,144 |
| 9 | A Bug's Life# | 1999 | 29,449,272 |
| 10 | Shrek* | 2001 | 29,004,582 |

* DreamWorks  # Disney  † 20th Century Fox Animation

## THE 10 LATEST WINNERS OF ANNIE AWARDS FOR BEST ANIMATED FEATURE

| YEAR* | FILM |
|---|---|
| **2006** | Cars |
| **2005** | Wallace & Gromit: The Curse of the Were-Rabbit |
| **2004** | The Incredibles |
| **2003** | Finding Nemo |
| **2002** | Spirited Away |
| **2001** | Shrek |
| **2000** | Toy Story 2 |
| **1999** | The Iron Giant |
| **1998** | Mulan |
| **1997** | Cats Don't Dance |

* Of film – awards are made the following year

The Annie Awards have been presented by the International Animated Film Society (ASIFA-Hollywood) since 1972. In addition to the individual and specialist category awards presented from then, it has been honouring Best Animated Features (originally Outstanding Achievement in an Animated Theatrical Feature) since 1992, when it was won by *Beauty and the Beast*. The Academy Award (Oscar) for Best Animated Feature was first presented in 2001.

*Figures of fun*
*First presented in 1992, the International Animated Film Society's Annie Award went to British feature* Wallace & Gromit *in 2005.*

# Actors

## TOP 10 **JOHNNY DEPP FILMS**

| | FILM | YEAR |
|---|---|---|
| 1 | Pirates of the Caribbean: Dead Man's Chest | 2006 |
| 2 | Pirates of the Caribbean: The Curse of the Black Pearl | 2003 |
| 3 | Charlie and the Chocolate Factory | 2004 |
| 4 | Sleepy Hollow | 1999 |
| 5 | Platoon | 1986 |
| 6 | Chocolat | 2000 |
| 7 | Donnie Brasco | 1997 |
| 8 | Finding Neverland | 2004 |
| 9 | Desperado II: Once Upon a Time in Mexico | 2003 |
| 10 | Secret Window | 2004 |

The first eight of Johnny Depp's Top 10 films have earned more than $100 million each, his run of successes led – by a considerable margin – by the first two *Pirates of the Caribbean* films.

## TOP 10 **TOM HANKS FILMS**

| | FILM | YEAR |
|---|---|---|
| 1 | The Da Vinci Code | 2006 |
| 2 | Forrest Gump* | 1994 |
| 3 | Saving Private Ryan | 1998 |
| 4 | Cast Away | 2000 |
| 5 | Apollo 13 | 1995 |
| 6 | Catch Me if You Can | 2002 |
| 7 | The Green Mile | 1999 |
| 8 | You've Got M@il | 1998 |
| 9 | Sleepless in Seattle | 1993 |
| 10 | The Terminal | 2004 |

\* Won Best Actor Oscar

Tom Hanks also appeared in a voice-only part as Woody in *Toy Story* (1995), *Toy Story 2* (1999), *The Polar Express* (2004) and *Cars* (2006). If included, these would be part of his personal Top 10, every one of which has earned more than $200 million worldwide.

## TOP 10 **HARRISON FORD FILMS**

| | FILM | YEAR |
|---|---|---|
| 1 | Star Wars: Episode IV – A New Hope | 1977 |
| 2 | Star Wars: Episode VI – Return of the Jedi | 1983 |
| 3 | Star Wars: Episode V – The Empire Strikes Back | 1980 |
| 4 | Indiana Jones and the Last Crusade | 1989 |
| 5 | Raiders of the Lost Ark | 1981 |
| 6 | The Fugitive | 1993 |
| 7 | Indiana Jones and the Temple of Doom | 1984 |
| 8 | Air Force One | 1997 |
| 9 | What Lies Beneath | 2000 |
| 10 | Presumed Innocent | 1990 |

**Billion-dollar Bloom**
*British actor Orlando Bloom has starred in two of only three films ever to earn more than $1 billion worldwide.*

## TOP 10 **ORLANDO BLOOM FILMS**

| | FILM | YEAR |
|---|---|---|
| 1 | The Lord of the Rings: The Return of the King | 2003 |
| 2 | Pirates of the Caribbean: Dead Man's Chest | 2006 |
| 3 | The Lord of the Rings: The Two Towers | 2002 |
| 4 | The Lord of the Rings: The Fellowship of the Ring | 2001 |
| 5 | Pirates of the Caribbean: The Curse of the Black Pearl | 2003 |
| 6 | Troy | 2004 |
| 7 | Kingdom of Heaven | 2005 |
| 8 | Black Hawk Down | 2001 |
| 9 | Elizabethtown | 2005 |
| 10 | Ned Kelly | 2004 |

Orlando Bloom's role in *Black Hawk Down* was minor; if discounted, the 10th entry in his personal Top 10 would be his first film, *Wilde* (1998) – in which his role was also small – or his most recent, *Haven* (2006).

## TOP 10 **DANIEL CRAIG FILMS**

| | FILM | YEAR |
|---|---|---|
| 1 | Casino Royale | 2006 |
| 2 | Lara Croft: Tomb Raider | 2001 |
| 3 | Road to Perdition | 2002 |
| 4 | Munich | 2005 |
| 5 | Elizabeth | 1998 |
| 6 | The Jacket | 2005 |
| 7 | I Dreamed of Africa | 2000 |
| 8 | A Kid in King Arthur's Court | 1995 |
| 9 | Layer Cake | 2004 |
| 10 | The Power of One | 1992 |

Daniel Wroughton Craig (born 1968) made his film debut in *The Power of One*, but also appeared in numerous TV dramas, including *Our Friends in the North* (1996). His roles in *Lara Croft: Tomb Raider* and *Road to Perdition* secured his fame and led to his casting as the new James Bond in *Casino Royale*. He appears as Lord Asriel in *His Dark Materials: The Golden Compass*, released in 2007.

*On the right track*
Based on a children's book by Milan Trenc, Night at the Museum, *starring Ben Stiller, received a negative critical response, but has made over $500 million worldwide, placing it among the highest-earning comedy films of all time.*

## TOP 10 **BEN STILLER FILMS**

| | FILM | YEAR |
|---|---|---|
| 1 | Night at the Museum | 2006 |
| 2 | Meet the Fockers | 2004 |
| 3 | There's Something About Mary | 1998 |
| 4 | Meet the Parents | 2000 |
| 5 | Along Came Polly | 2004 |
| 6 | Starsky and Hutch | 2004 |
| 7 | DodgeBall: A True Underdog Story | 2004 |
| 8 | The Cable Guy | 1996 |
| 9 | The Royal Tenenbaums | 2001 |
| 10 | Zoolander | 2001 |

## TOP 10 **NICOLAS CAGE FILMS**

| | FILM | YEAR |
|---|---|---|
| 1 | National Treasure | 2004 |
| 2 | The Rock | 1996 |
| 3 | Face/Off | 1997 |
| 4 | Gone in 60 Seconds | 2000 |
| 5 | Con Air | 1997 |
| 6 | City of Angels | 1998 |
| 7 | Ghost Rider | 2006 |
| 8 | The Family Man | 2000 |
| 9 | Snake Eyes | 1998 |
| 10 | 8MM | 1999 |

## TOP 10 **DENZEL WASHINGTON FILMS**

| | FILM | YEAR |
|---|---|---|
| 1 | Philadelphia | 1993 |
| 2 | The Pelican Brief | 1993 |
| 3 | Inside Man | 2006 |
| 4 | Déjà Vu | 2006 |
| 5 | Crimson Tide | 1995 |
| 6 | The Bone Collector | 1999 |
| 7 | Remember the Titans | 2000 |
| 8 | Man on Fire | 2004 |
| 9 | The Siege | 1998 |
| 10 | Training Day* | 2001 |

* Won Best Actor Oscar

# Actresses

## TOP 10 CAMERON DIAZ FILMS

| FILM | YEAR |
|---|---|
| **1** There's Something About Mary | 1998 |
| **2** The Mask | 1994 |
| **3** My Best Friend's Wedding | 1997 |
| **4** Charlie's Angels | 2000 |
| **5** Charlie's Angels: Full Throttle | 2003 |
| **6** Vanilla Sky | 2001 |
| **7** Gangs of New York | 2002 |
| **8** The Holiday | 2006 |
| **9** Any Given Sunday | 1999 |
| **10** In Her Shoes | 2005 |

Cameron Diaz's Top 10 films include some of the highest-earning of recent years, the top nine here having earned between $100 million and $370 million worldwide. She also provided the voice of Princess Fiona in *Shrek* (2001) and *Shrek 2* (2004) – which have outearned all of them.

## TOP 10 RACHEL WEISZ FILMS

| FILM | YEAR |
|---|---|
| **1** The Mummy Returns | 2001 |
| **2** The Mummy | 1999 |
| **3** Constantine | 2005 |
| **4** About a Boy | 2002 |
| **5** Enemy at the Gates | 2001 |
| **6** The Constant Gardener | 2005 |
| **7** Runaway Jury | 2003 |
| **8** Chain Reaction | 1996 |
| **9** Confidence | 2003 |
| **10** Envy | 2004 |

*Song and dance*
*Renée Zellweger stars as Roxie Hart in the film musical* Chicago. *Her first singing and dancing role and her most successful film to date, grossing over $300 million globally,* Chicago *was based on a 1975 stage musical, in turn derived from a 1926 play.*

## TOP 10 SCARLETT JOHANSSON FILMS

| FILM | YEAR |
|---|---|
| **1** The Horse Whisperer | 1998 |
| **2** The Island | 2005 |
| **3** Lost in Translation | 2003 |
| **4** The Prestige | 2006 |
| **5** Home Alone 3 | 1997 |
| **6** Match Point | 2005 |
| **7** Just Cause | 1995 |
| **8** In Good Company | 2004 |
| **9** The Black Dahlia | 2006 |
| **10** Eight Legged Freaks | 2002 |

Scarlett Johansson (born 1984) began her career as a child actress in *North* (1994), making *The Horse Whisperer*, her 7th and to date highest-earning film, by the age of 13. She won the BAFTA Best Actress award for her role in *Lost in Translation*.

## TOP 10 RENÉE ZELLWEGER FILMS

| FILM | YEAR |
|---|---|
| **1** Chicago* | 2002 |
| **2** Bridget Jones's Diary | 2001 |
| **3** Jerry Maguire | 1996 |
| **4** Bridget Jones: The Edge of Reason | 2004 |
| **5** Cold Mountain | 2003 |
| **6** Me, Myself & Irene | 2000 |
| **7** Cinderella Man | 2005 |
| **8** Down with Love | 2003 |
| **9** Nurse Betty | 2000 |
| **10** The Bachelor | 1999 |

* Won Best Picture Oscar

Renée Zellweger gained consecutive Best Actress Oscar nominations for *Bridget Jones's Diary* (2001) and *Chicago* (2002), and won as Best Actress in a Supporting Role for *Cold Mountain* (2003).

## TOP 10 REESE WITHERSPOON FILMS

| FILM | YEAR |
|---|---|
| **1** Sweet Home Alabama | 2002 |
| **2** Walk the Line* | 2005 |
| **3** Legally Blonde | 2001 |
| **4** Legally Blonde 2: Red, White and Blonde | 2003 |
| **5** Just Like Heaven | 2005 |
| **6** Cruel Intentions | 1999 |
| **7** Little Nicky | 2000 |
| **8** Pleasantville | 1998 |
| **9** American Psycho | 2000 |
| **10** Fear | 1996 |

* Won Best Actress Oscar

Reese Witherspoon's role in *Little Nicky* was only a cameo; if discounted, her starring part in *Vanity Fair* (2004) occupies 10th place among her highest-earning films.

*Second spin*
Kirsten Dunst in Spider-Man 2. *The first two films in the franchise earned a total of $1.6 billion at the world box office.*

## TOP 10 **KIRSTEN DUNST** FILMS

| | FILM | YEAR |
|---|---|---|
| 1 | Spider-Man | 2002 |
| 2 | Spider-Man 2 | 2004 |
| 3 | Jumanji | 1995 |
| 4 | Interview with the Vampire: The Vampire Chronicles | 1994 |
| 5 | Mona Lisa Smile | 2003 |
| 6 | Bring It On | 2000 |
| 7 | Small Soldiers | 1998 |
| 8 | Eternal Sunshine of the Spotless Mind | 2004 |
| 9 | Wag the Dog | 1997 |
| 10 | Marie Antoinette | 2006 |

## TOP 10 **KEIRA KNIGHTLEY** FILMS

| | FILM | YEAR |
|---|---|---|
| 1 | Pirates of the Caribbean: Dead Man's Chest | 2006 |
| 2 | Star Wars: Episode I – The Phantom Menace | 1999 |
| 3 | Pirates of the Caribbean: The Curse of the Black Pearl | 2003 |
| 4 | Love Actually | 2003 |
| 5 | King Arthur | 2004 |
| 6 | Pride and Prejudice | 2005 |
| 7 | Bend it Like Beckham | 2003 |
| 8 | Domino | 2005 |
| 9 | The Jacket | 2005 |
| 10 | Pure | 2005 |

## TOP 10 **KATE WINSLET** FILMS

| | FILM | YEAR |
|---|---|---|
| 1 | Titanic* | 1997 |
| 2 | The Holiday | 2006 |
| 3 | Sense and Sensibility | 1995 |
| 4 | Finding Neverland | 2004 |
| 5 | Eternal Sunshine of the Spotless Mind | 2004 |
| 6 | The Life of David Gale | 2003 |
| 7 | Quills | 2000 |
| 8 | Iris | 2001 |
| 9 | Enigma | 2001 |
| 10 | A Kid in King Arthur's Court | 1995 |

* Won Best Picture Oscar

# Best Picture Oscars

## THE 10 FIRST COLOUR FILMS TO WIN BEST PICTURE OSCARS*

| FILM | YEAR |
| --- | --- |
| 1 Gone With the Wind | 1939 |
| 2 An American in Paris | 1951 |
| 3 The Greatest Show on Earth | 1952 |
| 4 Around the World in 80 Days | 1956 |
| 5 The Bridge on the River Kwai | 1957 |
| 6 Gigi | 1958 |
| 7 Ben-Hur | 1959 |
| 8 West Side Story | 1961 |
| 9 Lawrence of Arabia | 1962 |
| 10 Tom Jones | 1963 |

* Oscar® is a Registered Trade Mark

## THE 10 LAST BLACK-AND-WHITE FILMS TO WIN BEST PICTURE OSCARS

| FILM | YEAR |
| --- | --- |
| 1 Schindler's List* | 1993 |
| 2 The Apartment | 1960 |
| 3 Marty | 1955 |
| 4 On the Waterfront | 1954 |
| 5 From Here to Eternity | 1953 |
| 6 All About Eve | 1950 |
| 7 All the King's Men | 1949 |
| 8 Hamlet | 1948 |
| 9 Gentleman's Agreement | 1947 |
| 10 The Best Years of Our Lives | 1946 |

* With colour sequences

## THE 10 LATEST BEST PICTURE OSCAR-WINNERS ADAPTED FROM A NOVEL

| FILM | YEAR |
| --- | --- |
| 1 The Lord of the Rings: The Return of the King | 2003 |
| 2 A Beautiful Mind | 2001 |
| 3 The English Patient | 1996 |
| 4 Forrest Gump | 1994 |
| 5 Schindler's List | 1993 |
| 6 The Silence of the Lambs | 1991 |
| 7 Dances with Wolves | 1990 |
| 8 Out of Africa | 1985 |
| 9 Terms of Endearment | 1983 |
| 10 Ordinary People | 1980 |

The third-ever Oscar-winner, *All Quiet on the Western Front* (1930), based on a novel by Erich Maria Remarque, was the first adapted work of fiction.

*Above: List topper*
Schindler's List *is the only black-and-white film to win a Best Picture Oscar since 1960.*

*Left: Scarlett in colour*
Gone with the Wind *won 10 Oscars, including Best Picture – the first colour film to do so.*

**The Departed** *arrives*

*As well as winning Oscars for Best Picture, Adapted Screenplay and Editing,* The Departed *gained its director Martin Scorsese his first Academy Award after eight nominations since 1980.*

## TOP 10 **LONGEST BEST PICTURE OSCAR FILMS**

| | FILM / YEAR | LENGTH (MINS) |
|---|---|---|
| 1 | Gone with the Wind 1939 | 238 |
| 2 | Lawrence of Arabia 1962 | 216 |
| 3 | Ben-Hur 1959 | 212 |
| 4 | The Lord of the Rings: The Return of the King 2003 | 201 |
| 5 | The Godfather: Part II 1974 | 200 |
| 6 | Schindler's List 1993 | 197 |
| 7 | Titanic 1997 | 194 |
| 8 | Gandhi 1982 | 188 |
| 9 | =Dances with Wolves 1990 | 183 |
| | =The Deer Hunter 1978 | 183 |

## THE 10 **SHORTEST BEST PICTURE OSCAR FILMS**

| | FILM / YEAR | LENGTH (MINS) |
|---|---|---|
| 1 | Marty 1955 | 91 |
| 2 | Annie Hall 1977 | 93 |
| 3 | Driving Miss Daisy 1989 | 99 |
| 4 | The Lost Weekend 1945 | 101 |
| 5 | Casablanca 1942 | 102 |
| 6 | The French Connection 1971 | 104 |
| 7 | =It Happened One Night 1934 | 105 |
| | =Kramer vs. Kramer 1979 | 105 |
| 9 | On the Waterfront 1954 | 108 |
| 10 | =In the Heat of the Night 1967 | 109 |
| | =All the King's Men 1949 | 109 |

## THE 10 **LATEST BEST PICTURE OSCAR-WINNERS**

| YEAR | FILM / DIRECTOR |
|---|---|
| **2006** | The Departed Martin Scorsese |
| **2005** | Crash Paul Haggis* |
| **2004** | Million Dollar Baby Clint Eastwood |
| **2003** | The Lord of the Rings: The Return of the King Peter Jackson |
| **2002** | Chicago Rob Marshall* |
| **2001** | A Beautiful Mind Ron Howard |
| **2000** | Gladiator Ridley Scott* |
| **1999** | American Beauty Sam Mendes |
| **1998** | Shakespeare in Love John Madden* |
| **1997** | Titanic James Cameron |

* Did not also win Best Director Oscar

# Oscar-Winning Actors

## TOP 10 **ACTORS WITH THE MOST NOMINATIONS***

| | ACTOR | WINS | | |
| --- | --- | --- | --- | --- |
| | | SUPPORTING | BEST | NOMINATIONS |
| 1 | Jack Nicholson | 1 | 2 | 12 |
| 2 | Laurence Olivier | 0 | 1 | 10 |
| 3 | = Paul Newman | 0 | 1 | 9 |
| | = Spencer Tracy | 0 | 2 | 9 |
| 5 | = Marlon Brando | 0 | 2 | 8 |
| | = Jack Lemmon | 1 | 1 | 8 |
| | = Al Pacino | 0 | 1 | 8 |
| | = Peter O'Toole | 0 | 0 | 8 |
| 9 | = Richard Burton | 0 | 0 | 7 |
| | = Dustin Hoffman | 0 | 2 | 7 |

* In all acting categories

*Left: Here's Jack!*
Out of his dozen nominations, Jack Nicholson won Oscars for One Flew Over the Cuckoo's Nest *(1975),* Terms of Endearment *(1983) and* As Good as It Gets *(1997).*

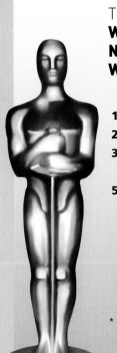

## TOP 10 **ACTORS WITH THE MOST NOMINATIONS WITHOUT A WIN***

| | ACTOR | NOMINATIONS |
| --- | --- | --- |
| 1 | Peter O'Toole | 8 |
| 2 | Richard Burton | 7 |
| 3 | = Albert Finney | 5 |
| | = Arthur Kennedy | 5 |
| 5 | = Warren Beatty | 4 |
| | = Charles Boyer | 4 |
| | = Jeff Bridges | 4 |
| | = Montgomery Clift | 4 |
| | = Ed Harris | 4 |
| | = Claude Rains | 4 |
| | = Mickey Rooney | 4 |

* In any acting categories

## THE 10 **LATEST ACTORS TO WIN A BEST ACTOR OSCAR WITH THEIR ONE AND ONLY NOMINATION**

| | ACTOR | FILM | YEAR |
| --- | --- | --- | --- |
| 1 | Forest Whitaker | The Last King of Scotland | 2006 |
| 2 | Philip Seymour Hoffman | Capote | 2005 |
| 3 | Jamie Foxx | Ray | 2004 |
| 4 | Adrien Brody | The Pianist | 2002 |
| 5 | Roberto Benigni | La Vita è Bela/ Life is Beautiful | 1998 |
| 6 | Jeremy Irons | Reversal of Fortune | 1990 |
| 7 | Michael Douglas | Wall Street | 1987 |
| 8 | F. Murray Abraham | Amadeus | 1984 |
| 9 | Art Carney | Harry and Tonto | 1974 |
| 10 | Cliff Robertson | Charly | 1968 |

In the first year of the Oscars, Emil Jannings won for two films, but since single-film nominations have been the norm, all these actors won the Oscar after being nominated in this category once and never again.

*Last first*
*Best Actor Oscar-winner Forest Whitaker as*
*Idi Amin in* The Last King of Scotland.

## THE 10 **LATEST BEST ACTOR OSCAR-WINNERS**

| YEAR | ACTOR / FILM |
|---|---|
| **2006** | Forest Whitaker<br>The Last King of Scotland |
| **2005** | Philip Seymour Hoffman<br>Capote |
| **2004** | Jamie Foxx<br>Ray |
| **2003** | Sean Penn<br>Mystic River |
| **2002** | Adrien Brody<br>The Pianist |
| **2001** | Denzel Washington<br>Training Day |
| **2000** | Russell Crowe<br>Gladiator* |
| **1999** | Kevin Spacey<br>American Beauty* |
| **1998** | Roberto Benigni<br>Life is Beautiful |
| **1997** | Jack Nicholson<br>As Good as It Gets |

\* Won Best Picture Oscar

## TOP 10 **OLDEST OSCAR-WINNING ACTORS**

| | ACTOR | FILM | YEAR | YEARS | AGE*<br>MONTHS | DAYS |
|---|---|---|---|---|---|---|
| **1** | George Burns | The Sunshine Boys | 1975 | 80 | 2 | 9 |
| **2** | Melvyn Douglas | Being There | 1979 | 79 | 0 | 9 |
| **3** | John Gielgud | Arthur | 1981 | 77 | 11 | 15 |
| **4** | Don Ameche | Cocoon | 1985 | 77 | 9 | 24 |
| **5** | Henry Fonda | On Golden Pond | 1981 | 76 | 10 | 13 |
| **6** | Edmund Gwenn | Miracle on 34th Street | 1947 | 72 | 5 | 24 |
| **7** | Jack Palance | City Slickers | 1991 | 72 | 0 | 1 |
| **8** | John Houseman | The Paper Chase | 1973 | 71 | 6 | 0 |
| **9** | Morgan Freeman | Million Dollar Baby# | 2004 | 67 | 8 | 27 |
| **10** | Charles Coburn | The More the Merrier | 1943 | 66 | 8 | 13 |

\* At the time of the Award ceremony
\# Won Best Picture Oscar

All the Academy Awards listed are for Best Supporting Actor, apart from Henry Fonda's award for Best Actor in *On Golden Pond*. The oldest person to win the Best Actor award prior to Henry Fonda was John Wayne, who was 62 when he received his 1969 award for *True Grit*.

# Oscar-Winning Actresses

## THE 10 YOUNGEST OSCAR-WINNING ACTRESSES

| | ACTRESS | AWARD / FILM (WHERE SPECIFIED) | YEAR | AGE* YRS | MTHS | DAYS |
|---|---|---|---|---|---|---|
| 1 | Shirley Temple | Special Award: Outstanding Contribution during 1934 | 1934 | 6 | 10 | 4 |
| 2 | Margaret O'Brien | Special Award: Outstanding Child Actress of 1944 (Meet Me in St. Louis) | 1944 | 8 | 2 | 0 |
| 3 | Tatum O'Neal | Best Supporting Actress (Paper Moon) | 1973 | 10 | 4 | 28 |
| 4 | Anna Paquin | Best Supporting Actress (The Piano) | 1993 | 11 | 7 | 25 |
| 5 | Hayley Mills | Special Award: Outstanding Juvenile Performance of 1960 (Pollyanna) | 1960 | 13 | 11 | 30 |
| 6 | Peggy Ann Garner | Special Award: Outstanding Child Performer of 1945 (A Tree Grows in Brooklyn) | 1945 | 14 | 4 | 18 |
| 7 | Patty Duke | Best Supporting Actress (The Miracle Worker) | 1962 | 16 | 3 | 25 |
| 8 | Deanna Durbin | Special Award: Juvenile Players Setting a High Standard of Ability and Achievement# | 1938 | 17 | 2 | 19 |
| 9 | Judy Garland | Special Award (Wizard of Oz) | 1939 | 17 | 8 | 19 |
| 10 | Marlee Matlin | Best Actress (Children of a Lesser God) | 1986 | 21 | 7 | 6 |

\* At the time of the Award ceremony
\# Shared with fellow teen star Mickey Rooney

British actress Hayley Mills, the 12th and last winner of the Special Award miniature Oscar, won her award precisely one day before her 14th birthday. Subsequent winners have had to compete on the same basis as adult actors and actresses for the major acting awards. Tatum O'Neal is thus the youngest winner of – as well as the youngest ever nominee for – an 'adult' Oscar. The youngest Best Actress nominee is Keisha Castle-Hughes (Australia), who was 13 in 2004 when she was nominated for her role in *Whale Rider*. The Academy Awards ceremony usually takes place at the end of February in the year following that in which the film was released, so the winners are generally at least a year older when they receive their Oscars than when they acted in their award-winning films.

*Child star*
*Shirley Temple made her first film at the age of three and won a special Oscar at six.*

## TOP 10 ACTRESSES WITH THE MOST OSCAR NOMINATIONS*

| | ACTRESS | WINS SUPPORTING | BEST | NOMS |
|---|---|---|---|---|
| 1 | Meryl Streep | 1 | 1 | 14 |
| 2 | Katharine Hepburn | 0 | 4 | 12 |
| 3 | Bette Davis | 0 | 2 | 10 |
| 4 | Geraldine Page | 0 | 1 | 8 |
| 5 | = Ingrid Bergman | 1 | 2 | 7 |
| | = Jane Fonda | 0 | 2 | 7 |
| | = Greer Garson | 0 | 1 | 7 |
| 8 | = Ellen Burstyn | 0 | 1 | 6 |
| | = Judi Dench | 1 | 0 | 6 |
| | = Deborah Kerr | 0 | 0 | 6 |
| | = Jessica Lange | 1 | 1 | 6 |
| | = Vanessa Redgrave | 1 | 0 | 6 |
| | = Thelma Ritter | 0 | 0 | 6 |
| | = Norma Shearer | 0 | 0 | 6 |
| | = Maggie Smith | 1 | 1 | 6 |
| | = Sissy Spacek | 0 | 1 | 6 |

\* In all acting categories

## THE 10 LATEST BEST SUPPORTING ACTRESS OSCAR-WINNERS

| YEAR | ACTRESS / FILM |
|---|---|
| 2006 | Jennifer Hudson Dreamgirls |
| 2005 | Rachel Weisz The Constant Gardener |
| 2004 | Cate Blanchett The Aviator |
| 2003 | Renée Zellweger Cold Mountain |
| 2002 | Catherine Zeta Jones Chicago* |
| 2001 | Jennifer Connelly A Beautiful Mind* |
| 2000 | Marcia Gay Harden Pollock |
| 1999 | Angelina Jolie Girl, Interrupted |
| 1998 | Judi Dench Shakespeare in Love* |
| 1997 | Kim Basinger L.A. Confidential |

\* Won Best Picture Oscar

*One has won*
Helen Mirren's title role in The Queen *earned her the Best Actress Oscar.*

## THE 10 **LATEST ACTRESSES TO WIN A BEST ACTRESS OSCAR WITH THEIR ONE AND ONLY NOMINATION**

| | ACTRESS | FILM | YEAR |
|---|---|---|---|
| 1 | Reese Witherspoon | Walk the Line | 2005 |
| 2 | Halle Berry | Monster's Ball | 2001 |
| 3 | Gwyneth Paltrow | Shakespeare in Love | 1998 |
| 4 | Helen Hunt | As Good As It Gets | 1997 |
| 5 | Marlee Matlin | Children of a Lesser God | 1986 |
| 6 | Louise Fletcher | One Flew Over the Cuckoo's Nest | 1975 |
| 7 | Grace Kelly | The Country Girl | 1954 |
| 8 | Shirley Booth | Come Back, Little Sheba | 1952 |
| 9 | Judy Holliday | Born Yesterday | 1950 |
| 10 | Ginger Rogers | Kitty Foyle | 1940 |

The first actress to win a Best Actress Oscar with her unique nomination was Mary Pickford for *Coquette* (1929), although in 1976, at the age of 84, she was presented with an honorary award. In the first ceremony in 1929, Janet Gaynor was nominated for and won a Best Actress Oscar for three films.

## THE 10 **LATEST BEST ACTRESS OSCAR-WINNERS**

| YEAR | ACTRESS / FILM |
|---|---|
| 2006 | Helen Mirren, The Queen |
| 2005 | Reese Witherspoon, Walk the Line |
| 2004 | Hilary Swank, Million Dollar Baby* |
| 2003 | Charlize Theron, Monster |
| 2002 | Nicole Kidman, The Hours |
| 2001 | Halle Berry, Monster's Ball |
| 2000 | Julia Roberts, Erin Brockovich |
| 1999 | Hilary Swank, Boys Don't Cry |
| 1998 | Gwyneth Paltrow, Shakespeare in Love* |
| 1997 | Helen Hunt, As Good as It Gets |

* Won Best Picture Oscar

# Other Film Awards

**The Wind That Shakes The Barley**
*Ken Loach's film is the first British Palm d'Or winner since Mike Leigh's* Secrets and Lies *in 1996.*

## THE **AMERICAN FILM INSTUTUTE'S 10 GREATEST ACTORS**

ACTOR

1 Humphrey Bogart
2 Cary Grant
3 James Stewart
4 Marlon Brando
5 Fred Astaire
6 Henry Fonda
7 Clark Gable
8 James Cagney
9 Spencer Tracy
10 Charlie Chaplin

Source: American Film Institute

## THE **AMERICAN FILM INSTUTUTE'S 10 GREATEST FILMS**

FILM

1 Citizen Kane (1941)
2 Casablanca (1942)
3 The Godfather (1972)
4 Gone with the Wind (1939)
5 Lawrence of Arabia (1962)
6 The Wizard of Oz (1939)
7 The Graduate (1967)
8 On the Waterfront (1954)
9 Schindler's List (1993)
10 Singin' in the Rain (1952)

Source: American Film Institute

These are the Top 10 of a long list identified by members of the American movie community for a poll conducted by the American Film Institute.

## THE 10 **LATEST PALM D'OR WINNERS AT THE CANNES FILM FESTIVAL**

YEAR*   FILM

2006  The Wind That Shakes the Barley
2005  The Child
2004  Fahrenheit 9/11
2003  Elephant
2002  The Pianist
2001  The Son's Room
2000  Dancer in the Dark
1999  Rosetta
1998  Eternity and a Day
1997  A Taste of Cherry

* Of award

## THE 10 **LATEST BEST FILM GOLDEN GLOBE WINNERS**\*

| YEAR# | FILM |
|---|---|
| **2006** | Babel |
| **2005** | Brokeback Mountain |
| **2004** | The Aviator |
| **2003** | The Lord of the Rings: The Return of the King |
| **2002** | The Hours |
| **2001** | A Beautiful Mind |
| **2000** | Gladiator |
| **1999** | American Beauty |
| **1998** | Saving Private Ryan |
| **1997** | Titanic |

\* Drama category
# Of film – awards take place the following year

Source: Hollywood Foreign Press Association

## THE 10 **LATEST BEST ACTOR WINNERS AT THE GOLDEN GLOBE AWARDS**\*

| YEAR# | ACTOR |
|---|---|
| **2006** | Forest Whitaker |
| **2005** | Philip Seymour Hoffman |
| **2004** | Leonardo DiCaprio |
| **2003** | Sean Penn |
| **2002** | Jack Nicholson |
| **2001** | Russell Crowe |
| **2000** | Tom Hanks |
| **1999** | Denzel Washington |
| **1998** | Jim Carey |
| **1997** | Peter Fonda |

\* Drama category
# Of film – awards take place the following year

Source: Hollywood Foreign Press Association

### Golden Raspberry Awards

Founded by film critic and writer John J. B. Wilson, the Golden Raspberry Award Foundation™ has been presenting its annual awards, known as the 'Razzies', since 1980. A parody of such established awards as the Oscars, it includes numerous categories, including worst film (or 'cinematic stinkers'), actor and actress.

**Golden double**
*Dubbing it 'Basically, It Stinks, Too', the Golden Raspberries picked Basic Instinct 2 and its star Sharon Stone as its 2006 worst film and worst actress winners.*

## THE 10 **LATEST WORST FILM GOLDEN RASPBERRY WINNERS**

| YEAR | FILM |
|---|---|
| **2006** | Basic Instinct 2 |
| **2005** | Dirty Love |
| **2004** | Catwoman |
| **2003** | Gigli |
| **2002** | Swept Away |
| **2001** | Freddy Got Fingered |
| **2000** | Battlefield Earth |
| **1999** | Wild Wild West |
| **1998** | An Alan Smithee Film: Burn Hollywood Burn |
| **1997** | The Postman |

Source: Golden Raspberry Awards

## THE 10 **LATEST WORST ACTRESS GOLDEN RASPBERRY WINNERS**

| YEAR | ACTRESS |
|---|---|
| **2006** | Sharon Stone |
| **2005** | Jessica McCarthy |
| **2004** | Halle Berry |
| **2003** | Jennifer Lopez |
| **2002** | Madonna |
| **2001** | Mariah Carey |
| **2000** | Madonna |
| **1999** | Heather Donahue |
| **1998** | The Spice Girls |
| **1997** | Demi Moore |

Source: Golden Raspberry Awards

# DVD & Video

## TOP 10 **BESTSELLING DVDS IN THE UK***

**1** The Lord of the Rings: The Fellowship of the Ring
**2** The Lord of The Rings: The Two Towers
**3** The Lord of the Rings – The Return of the King
**4** Pirates of the Caribbean: The Curse of the Black Pearl
**5** Shrek 2
**6** Harry Potter and the Prisoner of Azkaban
**7** Finding Nemo
**8** The Matrix
**9** Harry Potter and the Chamber of Secrets
**10** Love Actually

Source: British Video Association/The Official UK Charts Company

The 1999 release of *The Matrix* marks it out as the earliest DVD in this all-time list. Later releases have benefited from the progressive increase in DVD market penetration: it is estimated that while some 25 per cent of UK homes owned a DVD player in 2002, this figure grew to 45 per cent in 2003, 62 per cent in 2004 and 75 per cent in 2005.

## TOP 10 **BESTSELLING DVDS IN THE UK, 2005**

**1** The Incredibles
**2** Bridget Jones: The Edge of Reason
**3** Madagascar
**4** Star Wars: Episode III – Revenge of the Sith
**5** War of the Worlds
**6** Charlie and the Chocolate Factory
**7** Shark Tale
**8** Meet the Fockers
**9** The Bourne Supremacy
**10** Dodgeball: A True Underdog Story

Source: British Video Association/The Official UK Charts Company

*Three rings to rule them all*
The Lord of the Rings *trilogy dominates the DVD purchase market in the UK, with the first in the series also heading the combined DVD and video list.*

*Animal magic* The animated animal movie Madagascar *proved one of the top-selling DVDs in the UK.*

## TOP 10 **MOST-RENTED VIDEOS IN THE UK**\*

1 Four Weddings and a Funeral
2 Dirty Dancing
3 Basic Instinct
4 Crocodile Dundee
5 Gladiator
6 Sister Act
7 Forrest Gump
8 The Sixth Sense
9 Home Alone
10 Ghost

\* To 1 January 2006; includes VHS and DVD formats

Source: British Video Association/MRIB

In 2005, the most recent year for which statistics are available, 137 million videos and DVDs were rented in the UK. Film represented 99 per cent of rentals with UK films – such as long-time No.1 here – accounting for 22 per cent of all transactions on video and DVD. VHS accounted for only 5 per cent of the total rental market, in both volume and value.

## TOP 10 **BESTSELLING VIDEOS IN THE UK**\*

1 The Lord of the Rings: The Fellowship of the Ring
2 Titanic
3 The Lord of the Rings: The Two Towers
4 Shrek
5 The Lion King
6 The Jungle Book
7 The Matrix
8 Dirty Dancing
9 Gladiator
10 Snow White and the Seven Dwarfs

\* To 1 January 2006; includes VHS and DVD formats

Source: British Video Association/The Official UK Charts Company

Already 55 years old when it appeared on video in 1992, animated Disney classic *Snow White and the Seven Dwarfs* topped the all-time list but has been progressively eclipsed by subsequent releases. DVD is now the format of choice for all the UK's bestselling titles.

## TOP 10 **VIDEO PIRACY COUNTRIES**

| | COUNTRY | EST. LOSSES ($) 2005\* |
|---|---|---|
| 1 | Mexico | 483,000,000 |
| 2 | Russia | 266,000,000 |
| 3 | China | 244,000,000 |
| 4 | Italy | 161,000,000 |
| 5 | Thailand | 149,000,000 |
| 6 | Brazil | 120,000,000 |
| 7 | Canada | 118,000,000 |
| 8 = | Hungary | 102,000,000 |
| = | Poland | 102,000,000 |
| 10 | Taiwan | 98,000,000 |

\* Or latest year for which data available, including illicit broadcasts

Source: International Intellectual Property Alliance (IIPA)

The IIPA calculates that losses affecting the motion picture business – primarily through illicit DVDs, each of them robbing the industry of a legitimate sale – totalled almost $2 billion in 2005.

# TV & Radio

## THE 10 FIRST COUNTRIES TO HAVE TELEVISION*

| | COUNTRY | DATE |
|---|---|---|
| 1 | UK | 2 Nov 1936 |
| 2 | USSR | 31 Dec 1938 |
| 3 | USA | 30 Apr 1939 |
| 4 | France | 29 Jun 1949 |
| 5 | Mexico | 31 Aug 1950 |
| 6 | Brazil | 18 Sep 1950 |
| 7 | Cuba | 24 Oct 1950 |
| 8 | =Denmark | 2 Oct 1951 |
| | =Netherlands | 2 Oct 1951 |
| 10 | Argentina | 17 Oct 1951 |

* High-definition regular public broadcasting service

## TOP 10 COUNTRIES WITH THE MOST TV STATIONS

| | COUNTRY | TELEVISION STATIONS |
|---|---|---|
| 1 | Russia | 7,306 |
| 2 | China | 3,240 |
| 3 | USA | 2,218 |
| 4 | Turkey | 635 |
| 5 | France | 584 |
| 6 | India | 562 |
| 7 | South Africa | 556 |
| 8 | Germany | 373 |
| 9 | Norway | 360 |
| 10 | Italy | 358 |
| | *UK* | *228* |

Source: CIA, *The World Factbook 2007*

## TOP 10 TV CHANNELS IN THE UK

| | CHANNEL | % 2005–06* |
|---|---|---|
| 1 | BBC 1 | 79.7 |
| 2 | ITV1 | 73.0 |
| 3 | Channel 4 | 62.3 |
| 4 | BBC 2 | 59.1 |
| 5 | Five | 43.4 |
| 6 | UKTV | 22.5 |
| 7 | ITV2 | 16.9 |
| 8 | Sky One | 14.2 |
| 9 | E4 | 13.6 |
| 10 | BBC 3 | 11.8 |

* Of viewers watching for at least 15 minutes per week

Source: BBC Annual Report and Accounts 2005/2006

# TOP 10 TELEVISION AUDIENCES IN THE UK

| | PROGRAMME | BROADCAST | AUDIENCE |
|---|---|---|---|
| 1 | 1966 World Cup Final: England v. West Germany | 30 Jul 1966 | 32,300,000 |
| 2 | Funeral of Diana, Princess of Wales | 6 Sep 1997 | 32,100,000 |
| 3 | The Royal Family documentary | 21 Jun 1969 | 30,690,000 |
| 4 | EastEnders Christmas episode (Den divorces Angie) | 25 Dec 1986 | 30,150,000 |
| 5 | Apollo 13 splashdown | 17 Apr 1970 | 28,600,000 |
| 6 | Cup Final Replay: Chelsea v. Leeds United | 28 Apr 1970 | 28,490,000 |
| 7 | Wedding of Prince Charles and Lady Diana Spencer | 29 Jul 1981 | 28,400,000 |
| 8 | Wedding of Princess Anne and Capt Mark Phillips | 14 Nov 1973 | 27,600,000 |
| 9 | Coronation Street (Alan Bradley killed by a tram) | 19 Mar 1989 | 26,930,000 |
| 10 | Only Fools and Horses (Batman and Robin episode) | 29 Dec 1996 | 24,350,000 |

Source: British Film Institute

Other than exceptional events, such as the funeral of Princess Diana, which is reckoned to have been seen by some 2.5 billion people worldwide, the largest audience in television history, such numbers are unlikely to be replicated in the future as multiple channel choices and time-shifting (recording for later watching) reduce overall live viewing figures. The most-watched film of all time on British television is *Live and Let Die*, the eighth James Bond movie. Although already seven years old when it was first broadcast on 20 January 1980, it attracted an audience of 23.5 million.

# TOP 10 TV COUNTRIES*

**1** China 186,679,720

**2** USA 112,884,190

**3** India 83,512,900

**4** Japan 48,842,920

**5** Brazil 48,390,910

**6** Russia 40,822,010

**7** Germany 38,715,850

**8** Indonesia 34,334,330

**9** UK 25,269,160

**10** France 24,369,170

*World total 1,176,019,000*

* Households with colour TVs, 2007 forecast  Source: Euromonitor

# THE 10 LAST BRITISH COMEDY AWARD-WINNING TV SHOWS*

| YEAR | SHOW |
|---|---|
| 2006 | Peep Show |
| 2005 | Little Britain |
| 2004 | Little Britain |
| 2003 | Coupling |
| 2002 | The Office |
| 2001 | One Foot in the Grave |
| 2000 | Dinnerladies |
| 1999 | Dinnerladies |
| 1998 | Goodness Gracious Me |
| 1997 | The Fast Show |

* Best TV Comedy category

# TOP 10 COUNTRIES WITH THE MOST RADIO STATIONS*

| | COUNTRY | AM | FM | TOTAL |
|---|---|---|---|---|
| 1 | USA | 4,789 | 8,961 | 13,750 |
| 2 | France | 41 | 3,500 | 3,541 |
| 3 | Russia | 323 | 1,500 | 1,823 |
| 4 | Brazil | 1,365 | 296 | 1,661 |
| 5 | Mexico | 850 | 545 | 1,395 |
| 6 | Philippines | 369 | 583 | 952 |
| 7 | Spain | 208 | 715 | 923 |
| 8 | Germany | 51 | 787 | 838 |
| 9 | Canada | 245 | 582 | 827 |
| 10 | Poland | 14 | 777 | 781 |
| | *UK* | *219* | *431* | *650* |

* 2006 or latest year for which data available

Source: CIA, *The World Factbook 2007*

**Tiny TV**
Hailed as the 'world's smallest TV', the Seiko TV Watch was launched in 1982 and used by Roger Moore as James Bond in *Octopussy*. Unfortunately, its poor-quality black and white screen, the bulky receiver to which it was connected, and its $495 price tag made it a commercial failure.

# 8

# THE COMMERCIAL WORLD

# Trade

## TOP 10 **GLOBAL RETAILERS**

| COMPANY / BASE | RETAIL SALES, 2005* ($) |
|---|---|
| **1** Wal-Mart Stores, Inc., USA | 312,427,000,000 |
| **2** Carrefour, France | 92,778,000,000 |
| **3** Home Depot, Inc., USA | 81,511,000,000 |
| **4** METRO AG, Germany | 69,134,000,000 |
| **5** Tesco plc, UK | 68,866,000,000 |
| **6** Kroger Co., USA | 60,553,000,000 |
| **7** Target Corp., USA | 52,620,000,000 |
| **8** Costco Wholesale Corp., USA | 51,862,000,000 |
| **9** Sears Holdings, USA | 49,124,000,000 |
| **10** Schwarz Unternehmens Treuhand KG, Germany | 45,891,000,000 |

\* Financial year

Source: *Stores* magazine, 2007 Global Powers of Retailing

## TOP 10 **COMPANIES SPENDING THE MOST ON ADVERTISING**

| COMPANY / COUNTRY | WORLD ADVERTISING* SPENDING, 2005 ($) |
|---|---|
| **1** Procter & Gamble Company, USA | 8,190,000,000 |
| **2** Unilever, UK/Netherlands | 4,272,000,000 |
| **3** General Motors Corporation, USA | 4,173,000,000 |
| **4** Toyota Motor Corporation, Japan | 2,800,000,000 |
| **5** L'Oréal, France | 2,773,000,000 |
| **6** Ford Motor Company, USA | 2,645,000,000 |
| **7** Time Warner, USA | 2,479,000,000 |
| **8** DaimlerChrysler, Germany/USA | 2,104,000,000 |
| **9** Nestlé, Switzerland | 2,033,000,000 |
| **10** Johnson & Johnson, USA | 1,968,000,000 |

\* Includes newspapers, magazines, billboards, television, radio, Internet and Yellow Pages

Source: *Advertising Age Global Marketing Report 2006*

## TOP 10 **IMPORTERS**

| COUNTRY | GOODS AND SERVICES IMPORTS, 2004 ($) |
|---|---|
| **1** USA | 1,769,031,000,000 |
| **2** Germany | 912,587,000,000 |
| **3** China | 606,543,000,000 |
| **4** UK | 604,562,000,000 |
| **5** Japan | 542,380,000,000 |
| **6** France | 526,635,000,000 |
| **7** Italy | 423,241,000,000 |
| **8** Netherlands | 341,622,000,000 |
| **9** Canada | 336,733,000,000 |
| **10** Spain | 307,365,000,000 |
| *World total* | *11,096,960,000,000* |

Source: The World Bank, *World Development Indicators 2006*

## TOP 10 **EXPORTERS**

| COUNTRY | GOODS AND SERVICES EXPORTS, 2004 ($) |
|---|---|
| **1** USA | 1,151,448,000,000 |
| **2** Germany | 1,051,303,000,000 |
| **3** China | 655,827,000,000 |
| **4** Japan | 636,610,000,000 |
| **5** UK | 533,167,000,000 |
| **6** France | 531,488,000,000 |
| **7** Italy | 435,871,000,000 |
| **8** Netherlands | 388,899,000,000 |
| **9** Canada | 377,646,000,000 |
| **10** South Korea | 299,174,000,000 |
| *World total* | *11,238,500,000,000* |

Source: The World Bank, *World Development Indicators 2006*

**The real thing**
*Launched in 1886, Coca-Cola is recognized internationally and considered the world's most valued brand.*

## TOP 10 **MOST VALUABLE GLOBAL BRANDS**

| | BRAND NAME* | INDUSTRY | BRAND VALUE 2006 ($) |
|---|---|---|---|
| 1 | Coca-Cola | Beverages | 67,000,000,000 |
| 2 | Microsoft | Technology | 56,962,000,000 |
| 3 | IBM | Technology | 56,201,000,000 |
| 4 | General Electric | Diversified | 48,907,000,000 |
| 5 | Intel | Technology | 32,319,000,000 |
| 6 | Nokia, Finland | Technology | 30,131,000,000 |
| 7 | Toyota, Japan | Automotive | 27,941,000,000 |
| 8 | Disney | Leisure | 27,848,000,000 |
| 9 | McDonald's | Food retail | 27,501,000,000 |
| 10 | Mercedes | Automotive | 21,795,000,000 |

* All US-owned unless otherwise stated

Source: Interbrand/BusinessWeek

Brand consultants Interbrand use a method of estimating value that takes account of the profitability of individual brands within a business (rather than the companies that own them), as well as such factors as their potential for growth.

## TOP 10 **MOST-ADVERTISED PRODUCTS***

| | CATEGORY | WORLD ADVERTISING SPENDING, 2005 ($) |
|---|---|---|
| 1 | Automotive | 22,761,000,000 |
| 2 | Personal care | 19,491,000,000 |
| 3 | Entertainment and media | 11,029,000,000 |
| 4 | Food | 8,129,000,000 |
| 5 | Pharmaceuticals | 7,470,000,000 |
| 6 | Soft drinks | 3,971,000,000 |
| 7 | Restaurants | 3,349,000,000 |
| 8 | Computers | 3,106,000,000 |
| 9 | Telephone | 3,104,000,000 |
| 10 | Financial | 3,000,000,000 |
| | *World total* | *98,273,000,000* |

* Based on total worldwide spend by Top 100 companies

Source: *Advertising Age Global Marketing Report 2006*

# Rich Lists

## TOP 10 **RICHEST WOMEN** *

| | NAME / COUNTRY | SOURCE | NET WORTH ($) |
|---|---|---|---|
| 1 | Liliane Bettencourt, France | L'Oreal | 20,700,000,000 |
| 2 | Alice L. Walton, USA | Wal-Mart | 16,600,000,000 |
| 3 | Helen R. Walton, USA | Wal-Mart | 16,400,000,000 |
| 4 | Abigail Johnson, USA | Finance | 13,000,000,000 |
| 5 = | Anne Cox Chambers, USA | Media/entertainment | 12,600,000,000 |
| = | Barbara Cox Anthony, USA | Media/entertainment | 12,600,000,000 |
| 7 | Jacqueline Mars, USA | Candy | 10,500,000,000 |
| 8 | Susanne Klatten, Germany | Pharmaceuticals | 9,600,000,000 |
| 9 | Charlene de Carvalho-Heineken, Netherlands | Beverages | 7,200,000,000 |
| 10 | Johanna Quandt, Germany | BMW cars | 6,700,000,000 |

\* Excluding rulers and family fortunes

Source: *Forbes* magazine, *The World's Billionaires, 2007*

## TOP 10 **COUNTRIES WITH THE MOST DOLLAR BILLIONAIRES**

| | COUNTRY* | $ BILLIONAIRES |
|---|---|---|
| 1 | USA | 369 |
| 2 | Germany | 45 |
| 3 | UK | 33 |
| 4 | Russia | 32 |
| 5 | Japan | 27 |
| 6 | Hong Kong | 22 |
| 7 = | Switzerland | 21 |
| = | Turkey | 21 |
| 9 = | Canada | 19 |
| = | India | 19 |
| | *World total* | *746* |

\* Of residence, irrespective of citizenship

Source: *Forbes* magazine, *The World's Billionaires, 2006*

## TOP 10 **HIGHEST-EARNING CELEBRITIES**

| | CELEBRITY* | PROFESSION | EARNINGS# ($) |
|---|---|---|---|
| 1 | Steven Spielberg | Film producer/director | 332,000,000 |
| 2 | Howard Stern | Radio shock jock | 302,000,000 |
| 3 | George Lucas | Film producer/director | 235,000,000 |
| 4 | Oprah Winfrey | Talk-show host/producer | 225,000,000 |
| 5 | Jerry Seinfeld | Actor/producer | 100,000,000 |
| 6 | Tiger Woods | Golfer | 90,000,000 |
| 7 | Dan Brown | Author | 88,000,000 |
| 8 | Jerry Bruckheimer | Film and TV producer | 84,000,000 |
| 9 | J. K. Rowling (UK) | Author | 75,000,000 |
| 10 | Dick Wolf | Director/producer | 70,000,000 |

\* Individuals, excluding groups; US unless otherwise stated
\# 2005–2006

Source: *Forbes* magazine, *The Celebrity 100, 2006*

**Director rules**
*The sale of part of DreamWorks and box-office revenue combine to make Steven Spielberg the highest-earning celebrity.*

## TOP 10 **HIGHEST-EARNING DEAD CELEBRITIES**

| | CELEBRITY | PROFESSION | DEATH | EARNINGS 2005 ($) |
|---|---|---|---|---|
| 1 | Kurt Cobain | Rock star | 5 Apr 1994 | 50,000,000 |
| 2 | Elvis Presley | Rock star | 16 Aug 1977 | 42,000,000 |
| 3 | Charles Schultz | 'Peanuts' cartoonist | 12 Feb 2000 | 35,000,000 |
| 4 | John Lennon | Rock star | 8 Dec 1980 | 24,000,000 |
| 5 | Albert Einstein | Scientist | 18 Apr 1955 | 20,000,000 |
| 6 | Andy Warhol | Artist | 22 Feb 1987 | 19,000,000 |
| 7 = | Theodor 'Dr Seuss' Geisel | Author | 24 Sep 1991 | 10,000,000 |
| = | Ray Charles | Musician | 10 Jun 2004 | 10,000,000 |
| 9 = | Marilyn Monroe | Actress | 5 Aug 1962 | 8,000,000 |
| = | Johnny Cash | Musician | 12 Sep 2003 | 8,000,000 |

Source: *Forbes* magazine, *Top-Earning Dead Celebrities*, 2006

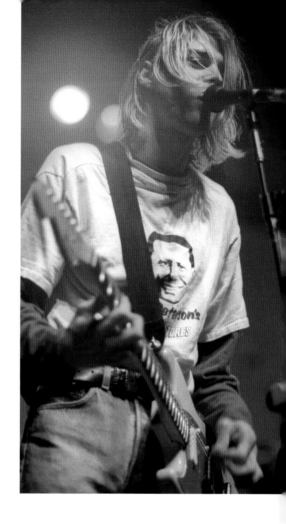

**Dead rich**
*Income from the sale of part of his band Nirvana's song catalogue places Kurt Cobain at the head of the dead rich list.*

## TOP 10 **RICHEST MEN***

| | NAME / COUNTRY (CITIZEN/ RESIDENCE, IF DIFFERENT) | SOURCE | NET WORTH ($) |
|---|---|---|---|
| 1 | William H. Gates III, USA | Microsoft (software) | 56,000,000,000 |
| 2 | Warren Edward Buffett, USA | Berkshire Hathaway (investments) | 52,000,000,000 |
| 3 | Carlos Slim Helu, Mexico | Communications | 49,000,000,000 |
| 4 | Ingvar Kamprad, Sweden/Switzerland | Ikea (home furnishings) | 33,000,000,000 |
| 5 | Lakshmi Mittal, India/UK | Mittal Steel | 32,000,000,000 |
| 6 | Sheldon Adelson, USA | Casinos and hotels | 26,500,000,000 |
| 7 | Bernard Arnault, France | Louis Vuitton, etc. (luxury goods) | 26,000,000,000 |
| 8 | Amancio Ortega, Spain | Zara, etc. (clothing) | 24,000,000,000 |
| 9 | Li Ka-shing, China | Diverse investments | 23,000,000,000 |
| 10 | David Thomson, Canada | Media, entertainment | 22,000,000,000 |

* Excluding rulers and family fortunes

Source: *Forbes* magazine, *The World's Billionaires*, 2007

**Richest 50 Years Ago**

In 1957, *Fortune* magazine published a list of America's 76 richest people. It was headed by oil magnate J. Paul Getty (1892–1976), whose fortune was estimated at between $700 million and $1 billion – worth some six times as much in today's values, yet still little more than one tenth of the wealth of today's richest man, Bill Gates.

# Resources

## TOP 10 **STEEL PRODUCERS**

| COUNTRY | PRODUCTION 2006 (TONNES) |
|---|---|
| 1 China | 418,800,000 |
| 2 Japan | 116,200,000 |
| 3 USA | 98,500,000 |
| 4 Russia | 70,600,000 |
| 5 South Korea | 48,400,000 |
| 6 Germany | 47,200,000 |
| 7 India | 44,000,000 |
| 8 Ukraine | 40,800,000 |
| 9 Italy | 31,600,000 |
| 10 Brazil | 30,900,000 |
| *UK* | *13,900,000* |
| *World total* | *1,239,500,000* |

Source: International Iron & Steel Institute

The world's largest steel producer, Mittal Steel, produced 63 million tonnes of steel in 2005. In 2006, it merged with second largest Arcelor (46.7 million tonnes). Its Indian owner Lakshmi Mittal is the fifth-richest man in the world ($32 billion).

## TOP 10 **URANIUM PRODUCERS**

| COUNTRY | PRODUCTION 2005 (TONNES) |
|---|---|
| 1 Canada | 11,628 |
| 2 Australia | 9,519 |
| 3 Kazakhstan | 4,357 |
| 4 Russia* | 3,431 |
| 5 Namibia | 3,147 |
| 6 Niger | 3,093 |
| 7 Uzbekistan | 2,300 |
| 8 USA | 1,039 |
| 9 Ukraine* | 800 |
| 10 China* | 750 |
| *World total* | *41,595* |

\* Estimated

Source: World Nuclear Association

*Forging ahead*
*As its economy has expanded, China's steel output has grown – the country now makes more than one-third of the world's steel.*

## TOP 10 **PLATINUM PRODUCERS**

| COUNTRY | PRODUCTION 2005 KG | LB |
|---|---|---|
| 1 South Africa | 168,749 | 372,027 |
| 2 Russia* | 30,000 | 66,138 |
| 3 Canada | 6,400 | 14,109 |
| 4 Zimbabwe | 4,834 | 10,657 |
| 5 USA | 3,920 | 8,642 |
| 6 Colombia | 1,082 | 2,385 |
| 7 Finland | 800 | 1,763 |
| 8 Japan | 730 | 1,609 |
| 9 Botswana* | 300 | 661 |
| 10 Australia* | 240 | 529 |
| *World total* | *217,000* | *478,402* |

\* Estimated

Source: US Geological Survey, *Minerals Yearbook*

## TOP 10 **SILVER PRODUCERS**

| | COUNTRY | % OF WORLD TOTAL | PRODUCTION 2005 (TONNES) |
|---|---|---|---|
| 1 | Peru | 16.0 | 3,191 |
| 2 | Mexico | 14.4 | 2,871 |
| 3 | Australia | 12.1 | 2,407 |
| 4 | China | 10.1 | 2,012 |
| 5 | Chile | 6.9 | 1,378 |
| 6 | Russia | 6.6 | 1,313 |
| 7 | Poland | 6.3 | 1,260 |
| 8 | USA | 6.1 | 1,219 |
| 9 | Canada | 5.3 | 1,061 |
| 10 | Kazakhstan | 4.0 | 803 |
| | *World total* | *100.0* | *19,956* |

Source: The Silver Institute, *World Silver Survey 2006*

Total world silver production hit a new record in 2005, up from 14,920 tonnes in the 10 years since 1995, with leading producer Peru's output growing by 67 per cent.

## TOP 10 **GOLD PRODUCERS**

| | COUNTRY | % OF WORLD TOTAL | PRODUCTION 2005 (TONNES) |
|---|---|---|---|
| 1 | South Africa | 15.7 | 396.3 |
| 2 | Australia | 10.4 | 262.9 |
| 3 | USA | 10.3 | 261.7 |
| 4 | China | 8.8 | 224.1 |
| 5 | Peru | 8.2 | 207.8 |
| 6 | Russia | 7.0 | 175.5 |
| 7 | Indonesia | 6.6 | 166.6 |
| 8 | Canada | 4.7 | 118.5 |
| 9 | Uzbekistan | 3.1 | 79.3 |
| 10 | Papua New Guinea | 2.7 | 68.8 |
| | *World total* | *100.0* | *2,519.2* |

Source: Gold Fields Mineral Services Ltd, *Gold Survey 2006*

Although still below its all-time production high of 619.5 tonnes in 1993, South Africa continues to dominate world production. That of Australia peaked at 313.2 tonnes in 1997, but in 2005 just overtook the USA for the first time.

## THE CULLINAN DIAMOND

The largest diamond ever found, the 3,106.75-carat (621.35-g) Cullinan, was discovered in South Africa in 1905. It was presented to King Edward VII on his 66th birthday on 9 November 1907. For security, a fake was carried to London under armed guard, while the real gem was secretly sent by parcel post. Cut into 105 separate gems by Dutch expert Joseph Asscher, it produced the Great Star of Africa (530.20 carats), which is mounted in the Queen's Sceptre, the Second Star of Africa (317.40 carats), set in the Imperial State Crown, and the Third Star of Africa (94.40 carats) and Fourth Star of Africa (63.60 carats), both once set in Queen Mary's Crown, but now set in a brooch which, with other gems cut from the Cullinan, is worn by Queen Elizabeth II.

## TOP 10 **DIAMOND PRODUCERS (BY VOLUME)**

| | COUNTRY | VALUE (2004) ($) | VOLUME (2004) (CARATS) |
|---|---|---|---|
| 1 | Russia | 1,989,000,000 | 35,000,000 |
| 2 | Botswana | 2,940,000,000 | 31,125,000 |
| 3 | Dem. Rep. of Congo | 790,000,000 | 29,000,000 |
| 4 | Australia | 343,000,000 | 20,673,000 |
| 5 | South Africa | 1,458,000,000 | 14,233,000 |
| 6 | Canada | 1,646,000,000 | 12,618,000 |
| 7 | Angola | 1,300,000,000 | 7,500,000 |
| 8 | Namibia | 698,000,000 | 2,011,000 |
| 9 | Ghana | 26,000,000 | 900,000 |
| 10 | Brazil | 35,000,000 | 700,000 |

Source: Northwest Territories, *Diamond Facts 2005*

*Diamond anniversary Fredrick Wells, an official at the Premier Diamond Mine, discovered the world's largest diamond on 25 June 1905. It was purchased from him and named the Cullinan Diamond after Sir Thomas Cullinan, the mine's owner, and cut in 1907, producing a superb collection of gems that are among the British Crown Jewels.*

# Food

## TOP 10 **EGG CONSUMERS**

COUNTRY / CONSUMPTION PER CAPITA PER DAY (2004)/G/OZ

| | Denmark | Netherlands | Japan | China | Hungary | Brunei | France | USA | Paraguay | Belgium |
|---|---|---|---|---|---|---|---|---|---|---|
| | 1 | 2 | 3 | 4 | 5 | 6 | 7 | 8 | 9 | 10 |
| | 61.19 / 2.15 | 52.58 / 1.85 | 52.25 / 1.84 | 48.29 / 1.70 | 47.83 / 1.68 | 47.61 / 1.67 | 46.69 / 1.64 | 46.62 / 1.64 | 44.09 / 1.55 | 42.85 / 1.51 |

*UK 26.37 / 0.93*

Source: Food and Agriculture Organization of
the United Nations

### You Say 'Potato'

English adventurer Sir John
Hawkins first took potatoes
from Florida to Ireland in
about 1565, in the same year
introducing the word in
English when he wrote,
'These potatoes be the most
delicate rootes that may be
eaten, and doe far exceede
our passeneps or carets.'

## TOP 10 **POTATO CONSUMERS**

| COUNTRY | CONSUMPTION (G PER CAPITA PER DAY, 2004) |
|---|---|
| **1** Belarus | 488.63 |
| **2** Kyrgyzstan | 385.59 |
| **3** Rwanda | 381.83 |
| **4** Lithuania | 373.76 |
| **5** Poland | 373.73 |
| **6** Ukraine | 370.85 |
| **7** Latvia | 370.75 |
| **8** Russia | 359.13 |
| **9** Portugal | 351.22 |
| **10** Ireland | 348.01 |
| *UK* | *291.11* |

Source: Food and Agricultural Organization of
the United Nations

## TOP 10 **FOOD, DRINK AND RESTAURANT BRANDS**

| BRAND* | BRAND VALUE (2006) |
|---|---|
| **1** Coca-Cola | 67,000,000,000 |
| **2** McDonald's | 27,501,000,000 |
| **3** Pepsi | 12,690,000,000 |
| **4** Nescafé, Switzerland | 12,507,000,000 |
| **5** Budweiser | 11,662,000,000 |
| **6** Kellogg's | 8,776,000,000 |
| **7** Heinz | 6,223,000,000 |
| **8** Wrigley's | 5,449,000,000 |
| **9** KFC | 5,350,000,000 |
| **10** Nestlé, Switzerland | 4,932,000,000 |

* US unless otherwise stated

Source: *Interbrand's Best Global Brands 2006*

A number of these multi-billion dollar
global brands have a long history, Nestlé
dating back to 1866 and Heinz to 1869.

## TOP 10 **TAKEAWAY FOOD AND DRINK ITEMS IN THE UK**\*

| ITEM | AVERAGE WEEKLY CONSUMPTION PER HEAD | |
|---|---|---|
| | G | OZ |
| **1** Alcoholic drinks | 616 | 21.72 |
| **2** Soft drinks | 350 | 12.34 |
| **3** Other beverages (coffee, etc.) | 141 | 4.97 |
| **4** Meat and meat products | 91 | 3.20 |
| **5** Potatoes (chips, etc.) | 79 | 2.78 |
| **6** Sandwiches | 71 | 2.50 |
| **7** Vegetables | 33 | 1.16 |
| **8** Ice cream, desserts, cakes | 29 | 1.02 |
| **9** Cheese and egg dishes and pizza | 25 | 0.88 |
| **10** Indian, Chinese and Thai meals | 21 | 0.74 |

\* Food and drink eaten out, by weight

Source: Department of Environment, Food and Rural Affairs (DEFRA), *Family Food in 2004/2005*, 2006

## TOP 10 **FOODS CONSUMED IN THE UK**

| COUNTRY | AVERAGE WEEKLY CONSUMPTION PER HEAD | |
|---|---|---|
| | G | OZ |
| **1** Milk and cream | 1,984 | 69.98 |
| **2** Soft drinks | 1,832 | 64.62 |
| **3** Fresh fruit | 1,168 | 41.20 |
| **4** Vegetables (excluding potatoes) | 1,079 | 38.06 |
| **5** Meat and meat products | 1,049 | 37.00 |
| **6** Cereals\* | 882 | 31.11 |
| **7** Fresh and processed potatoes | 822 | 28.99 |
| **8** Alcoholic drinks | 763 | 26.91 |
| **9** Bread | 695 | 24.51 |
| **10** Fats | 186 | 6.56 |

\* Excluding bread

Source: Department of Environment, Food and Rural Affairs (DEFRA), *Family Food in 2004/2005*, 2006

## TOP 10 **FISH CONSUMERS**\*

| COUNTRY | CONSUMPTION PER CAPITA PER DAY (2004) | |
|---|---|---|
| | G | OZ |
| **1** Maldives | 363.51 | 12.82 |
| **2** Samoa | 132.72 | 4.68 |
| **3** Kiribati | 93.27 | 3.29 |
| **4** Malta | 79.15 | 2.79 |
| **5** Grenada | 71.23 | 2.51 |
| **6** Barbados | 68.44 | 2.41 |
| **7** Saint Lucia | 56.99 | 2.01 |
| **8** South Korea | 56.85 | 2.00 |
| **9** Dominica | 53.41 | 1.88 |
| **10** Ghana | 52.46 | 1.85 |
| *UK* | *10.35* | *0.36* |

\* Pelagic (marine) only, excluding crustaceans, molluscs, etc.

Source: Food and Agriculture Organization of the United Nations

# Drink

## TOP 10 COFFEE DRINKERS

COUNTRY / CONSUMPTION PER HEAD (2005) (KG / LB/OZ / CUPS*)

**3** Sweden 8.3/18/4/1,245

**2** Denmark 8.7/19/2/1,305

**1** Finland 9.7/21/6/1,455

**7** Austria 5.8/12/12/870

**6** Switzerland 7.1/15/10/1,065

**5** Netherlands 7.3/16/1/1,095

**4** Norway 8.2/18/1/1,230

**10** Brazil 3.9/8/9/585

**9** Belgium 5.4/11/14/810

**8** Germany 5.5/12/2/825

UK   1.3 / 2 / 13 / 195

World average   0.7 / 1 / 9 / 105

* Based on 150 cups per kg (2 lb 3 oz)  Source: Euromonitor

## TOP 10 SOFT-DRINK BRANDS IN THE UK

| BRAND | SALES, 2006 (£) |
|---|---|
| **1** Coca-Cola | 942,391,000 |
| **2** Nescafé instant coffee | 331,265,000 |
| **3** Robinsons | 277,285,000 |
| **4** Lucozade | 253,300,000 |
| **5** Tropicana | 222,471,000 |
| **6** Pepsi | 216,343,000 |
| **7** Ribena | 153,046,000 |
| **8** Volvic | 148,214,000 |
| **9** Red Bull | 139,120,000 |
| **10** Tetley | 132,778,000 |

Source: *Checkout*/ACNielsen Scantrack

## TOP 10 BREWERS

| BREWERY / COUNTRY | PERCENTAGE OF WORLD TOTAL | PRODUCTION (2005) LITRES | PINTS |
|---|---|---|---|
| **1** InBev, Belgium | 12.6 | 20,210,000,000 | 35,564,000,000 |
| **2** SABMiller, UK | 11.0 | 17,600,000,000 | 30,971,000,000 |
| **3** Anheuser-Busch, USA | 10.9 | 17,350,000,000 | 30,531,000,000 |
| **4** Heineken, Netherlands | 7.4 | 11,860,000,000 | 20,870,000,000 |
| **5** = Carlsberg, Denmark | 3.0 | 4,830,000,000 | 8,499,000,000 |
| = Molson Coors, USA/Canada | 3.0 | 4,830,000,000 | 8,499,000,000 |
| **7** Modelo, Mexico | 2.9 | 4,550,000,000 | 8,006,000,000 |
| **8** Baltik Beverage, Russia | 2.6 | 4,150,000,000 | 7,302,000,000 |
| **9** Tsingtao, China | 2.6 | 4,090,000,000 | 7,197,000,000 |
| **10** Yan Jing, China | 2.0 | 3,120,000,000 | 5,490,000,000 |
| *World total* | *100.0* | *159,808,800,000* | *281,224,000,000* |

Source: The Barth Report 2005/2006

## TOP 10 **CHAMPAGNE CONSUMERS**

COUNTRY / CONSUMPTION (2005) (LITRES/BOTTLES)

Source: Euromonitor

1 France 131,400,000 / 175,200,000

2 UK 22,500,000 / 30,000,000

3 USA 13,200,000 / 17,600,000

4 Germany 7,400,000 / 9,866,000

5 Belgium 5,700,000 / 7,600,000

6 Italy 5,000,000 / 6,666,000

7 Japan 4,500,000 / 6,000,000

8 Switzerland 4,300,000 / 5,733,000

9 Netherlands 2,000,000 / 2,666,000

10 Spain 1,900,000 / 2,533,000

*World total 217,000,000/289,333,000*

## TOP 10 **MILK CONSUMERS**

| COUNTRY | CONSUMPTION PER CAPITA PER DAY (2005) | |
| | G | OZ |
| --- | --- | --- |
| **1** France | 888.05 | 31.33 |
| **2** Albania | 874.76 | 30.86 |
| **3** Switzerland | 857.80 | 30.26 |
| **4** Iceland | 853.33 | 30.10 |
| **5** Ireland | 850.04 | 29.99 |
| **6** Sweden | 833.74 | 29.41 |
| **7** Finland | 828.20 | 29.21 |
| **8** Australia | 762.95 | 26.91 |
| **9** Kazakhstan | 762.82 | 26.90 |
| **10** Romania | 753.39 | 26.58 |
| *UK* | *661.23* | *23.32* |

Source: Food and Agriculture Organization of the United Nations

While these countries are the principal consumers of milk, the USA is the world's leading producer, with more than 80 million tonnes a year. France produces over 26 million tonnes a year and maintains its place as the leading consumer. The UK formerly appeared in both the Top 10 of consumers and (at almost 15 million tonnes per annum) producers, but health concerns have seen its per capita consumption reduce.

## TOP 10 **COLA-DRINK CONSUMERS**

| COUNTRY | CONSUMPTION PER HEAD (2005) | |
| | LITRES | PINTS |
| --- | --- | --- |
| **1** USA | 116.1 | 204.3 |
| **2** Mexico | 97.2 | 171.0 |
| **3** Australia | 73.9 | 130.0 |
| **4** Canada | 71.1 | 125.1 |
| **5** Chile | 70.8 | 124.6 |
| **6** Belgium | 69.9 | 123.0 |
| **7** Norway | 69.2 | 121.8 |
| **8** Spain | 58.9 | 103.6 |
| **9** New Zealand | 57.4 | 101.0 |
| **10** Argentina | 56.4 | 99.3 |
| *UK* | *53.0* | *93.26* |
| *World average* | *17.0* | *29.91* |

Source: Euromonitor

In marked contrast to the countries in the Top 10, India and Vietnam (1.3 litres/ 2.3 pints per capita) and Indonesia (0.8 litres/1.4 pints), and many African nations, fall well below the average in a world market that in 2005 drank 108.7 billion litres (191.3 billion pints) of cola drinks.

# Energy

## TOP 10 **COUNTRIES WITH THE GREATEST NATURAL-GAS RESERVES**

| | COUNTRY | RESERVES 2005 TRILLION M³ | TRILLION FT³ |
|---|---|---|---|
| 1 | Russia | 47.82 | 1,688.0 |
| 2 | Iran | 26.74 | 943.9 |
| 3 | Qatar | 25.78 | 910.1 |
| 4 | Saudi Arabia | 6.90 | 243.6 |
| 5 | United Arab Emirates | 6.04 | 213.0 |
| 6 | USA | 5.45 | 192.5 |
| 7 | Nigeria | 5.23 | 184.6 |
| 8 | Algeria | 4.58 | 161.7 |
| 9 | Venezuela | 4.32 | 152.3 |
| 10 | Iraq | 3.17 | 111.9 |
| | *UK* | *0.53* | *18.7* |
| | *World total* | *179.83* | *6,348.10* |

Source: *BP Statistical Review of World Energy 2006*

*Cold comfort*
*A natural gas plant in Siberia, Russia. The country has the world's greatest proved reserves.*

## TOP 10 **COUNTRIES WITH THE GREATEST COAL RESERVES**

| | COUNTRY | RESERVES AT END OF 2005 (TONNES) |
|---|---|---|
| 1 | USA | 246,643,000,000 |
| 2 | Russia | 157,010,000,000 |
| 3 | China | 114,500,000,000 |
| 4 | India | 92,445,000,000 |
| 5 | Australia | 78,500,000,000 |
| 6 | South Africa | 48,750,000,000 |
| 7 | Ukraine | 34,153,000,000 |
| 8 | Kazakhstan | 31,279,000,000 |
| 9 | Poland | 14,000,000,000 |
| 10 | Brazil | 10,113,000,000 |
| | *UK* | *220,000,000* |
| | *World total* | *909,064,000,000* |

Source: *BP Statistical Review of World Energy 2006*

Coal reserves are quantities of coal that can be economically recovered from known deposits using current techniques.

## TOP 10 **COAL-CONSUMING COUNTRIES**

| | COUNTRY | CONSUMPTION 2005 (TONNES OF OIL EQUIVALENT) |
|---|---|---|
| 1 | China | 1,081,900,000 |
| 2 | USA | 575,400,000 |
| 3 | India | 212,900,000 |
| 4 | Japan | 121,300,000 |
| 5 | Russia | 111,600,000 |
| 6 | South Africa | 91,900,000 |
| 7 | Germany | 82,100,000 |
| 8 | Poland | 56,700,000 |
| 9 | South Korea | 54,800,000 |
| 10 | Australia | 52,200,000 |
| | *UK* | *39,100,000* |
| | *World total* | *2,929,800,000* |

Source: *BP Statistical Review of World Energy 2006*

## TOP 10 **COAL-PRODUCING COUNTRIES**

| | COUNTRY | PRODUCTION 2005 (TONNES OF OIL EQUIVALENT) |
|---|---|---|
| 1 | China | 1,107,700,000 |
| 2 | USA | 576,200,000 |
| 3 | Australia | 202,400,000 |
| 4 | India | 199,600,000 |
| 5 | South Africa | 138,900,000 |
| 6 | Russia | 137,000,000 |
| 7 | Indonesia | 83,200,000 |
| 8 | Poland | 68,700,000 |
| 9 | Germany | 53,200,000 |
| 10 | Kazakhstan | 44,000,000 |
| | *UK* | *12,500,000* |
| | *World total* | *2,887,200,000* |

Source: *BP Statistical Review of World Energy 2006*

## TOP 10 **NATURAL GAS-CONSUMING COUNTRIES**

| | COUNTRY | CONSUMPTION 2005 (TONNES OF OIL EQUIVALENT) |
|---|---|---|
| 1 | USA | 570,100,000 |
| 2 | Russia | 364,600,000 |
| 3 | UK | 85,100,000 |
| 4 | Canada | 82,300,000 |
| 5 | Iran | 79,600,000 |
| 6 | Germany | 77,300,000 |
| 7 | Japan | 73,000,000 |
| 8 | Italy | 71,100,000 |
| 9 | Ukraine | 65,600,000 |
| 10 | Saudi Arabia | 62,600,000 |
| | World total | 2,474,700,000 |

Source: *BP Statistical Review of World Energy 2006*

## TOP 10 **COUNTRIES WITH THE GREATEST OIL RESERVES**

| | COUNTRY | 2005 RESERVES (TONNES) |
|---|---|---|
| 1 | Saudi Arabia | 36,300,000,000 |
| 2 | Iran | 18,900,000,000 |
| 3 | Iraq | 15,500,000,000 |
| 4 | Kuwait | 14,000,000,000 |
| 5 | United Arab Emirates | 13,000,000,000 |
| 6 | Venezuela | 11,500,000,000 |
| 7 | Russia | 10,200,000,000 |
| 8 | Kazakhstan | 5,400,000,000 |
| 9 | Libya | 5,100,000,000 |
| 10 | Nigeria | 4,800,000,000 |
| | UK | 500,000,000 |
| | World total | 163,600,000,000 |

Source: *BP Statistical Review of World Energy 2006*

## TOP 10 **OIL-CONSUMING COUNTRIES**

| | COUNTRY | CONSUMPTION 2005 (TONNES) |
|---|---|---|
| 1 | USA | 944,600,000 |
| 2 | China | 327,300,000 |
| 3 | Japan | 244,200,000 |
| 4 | Russia | 130,000,000 |
| 5 | Germany | 121,500,000 |
| 6 | India | 115,700,000 |
| 7 | South Korea | 105,500,000 |
| 8 | Canada | 100,100,000 |
| 9 | France | 93,100,000 |
| 10 | Saudi Arabia | 87,200,000 |
| | UK | 82,900,000 |
| | World total | 3,767,100,000 |

Source: *BP Statistical Review of World Energy 2006*

## TOP 10 **OIL-PRODUCING COUNTRIES**

COUNTRY / PRODUCTION 2005 (TONNES)

**1** Saudi Arabia 526,200,000

**2** Russia 470,000,000

**3** USA 310,200,000

**4** Iran 200,400,000

**5** Mexico 187,100,000

**6** China 180,800,000

**7** Venezuela 154,700,000

**8** Norway 149,900,000

**9** Canada 138,200,000

**10** Kuwait 130,100,000

UK 84,700,000
World total 3,895,000,000
Source: *BP Statistical Review of World Energy 2006*

# Environmental Issues

## TOP 10 CARBON DIOXIDE-EMITTING COUNTRIES

| | COUNTRY | CO$_2$ EMISSIONS PER CAPITA, 2004 (TONNES OF CO$_2$) |
|---|---|---|
| 1 | United Arab Emirates | 55.92 |
| 2 | Qatar | 46.25 |
| 3 | Bahrain | 33.52 |
| 4 | Kuwait | 30.88 |
| 5 | Trinidad and Tobago | 30.03 |
| 6 | Singapore | 29.73 |
| 7 | Luxembourg | 26.62 |
| 8 | USA | 20.18 |
| 9 | Australia | 19.39 |
| 10 | Canada | 18.09 |
| | UK | 9.62 |
| | World average | 4.24 |

Source: Energy Information Administration

The concentration of atmospheric carbon dioxide varies, but averages 0.0383 per cent by volume or 0.0582 per cent by weight. Any increase is significant as CO$_2$ is a major contributor to the greenhouse effect and global warming. CO$_2$ emissions derive from three principal sources – fossil-fuel burning, cement manufacturing and gas flaring – as well as various industrial processes. In the past 60 years, increasing industrialization in many countries has resulted in huge increases in carbon output, a trend that most countries are now actively attempting to reverse, with some degree of success among the former leaders in this Top 10, although the USA remains the worst offender in total, with over 5.9 billion tonnes released in 2004. Around the world there are a number of island territories with small populations but a high CO$_2$ output resulting from such industries as the production of liquid fuels. Among them, Gibraltar (149.74 tonnes per head) and the US Virgin Islands (146.86 tonnes per head), have greater per capita emissions than those countries in the Top 10.

## THE 10 WORST AIR-QUALITY COUNTRIES

| | COUNTRY | SCORE* |
|---|---|---|
| 1 | Bangladesh | 6.9 |
| 2 | Pakistan | 8.2 |
| 3 | Albania | 14.4 |
| 4 | Egypt | 14.8 |
| 5 | Mali | 21.2 |
| 6 | China | 22.3 |
| 7 | Niger | 22.9 |
| 8 | Chad | 24.4 |
| 9 | Sudan | 24.9 |
| 10 | Indonesia | 25.1 |

* Out of 100

Source: *Pilot 2006 Environmental Performance Index*

## TOP 10 ENVIRONMENTAL PERFORMANCE INDEX COUNTRIES

| | COUNTRY | EPI SCORE* |
|---|---|---|
| 1 | New Zealand | 88.0 |
| 2 | Sweden | 87.8 |
| 3 | Finland | 87.0 |
| 4 | Czech Republic | 86.0 |
| 5 | UK | 85.6 |
| 6 | Austria | 85.2 |
| 7 | Denmark | 84.2 |
| 8 | Canada | 84.0 |
| 9 = | Ireland | 83.3 |
| = | Malaysia | 83.3 |

* Out of 100

Source: *Pilot 2006 Environmental Performance Index*

The Environmental Performance Index is a measure of environmental health and ecosystem vitality based on an assessment of 16 indicators in each country. These include air quality, water resources, biodiversity and habitat, productive natural resources and sustainable energy.

## TOP 10 AIR-QUALITY COUNTRIES

| | COUNTRY | SCORE* |
|---|---|---|
| 1 | Uganda | 98.0 |
| 2 | Gabon | 96.1 |
| 3 | Rwanda | 91.1 |
| 4 | Burundi | 90.9 |
| 5 | Ghana | 87.3 |
| 6 | Kenya | 87.0 |
| 7 | Liberia | 86.5 |
| 8 | Tanzania | 86.2 |
| 9 | New Zealand | 83.7 |
| 10 = | Dem. Rep. of Congo | 82.3 |
| = | Togo | 82.3 |
| | UK | 61.6 |

* Out of 100

Source: *Pilot 2006 Environmental Performance Index*

Air pollution is a major factor in environmental health. It is caused by power generation, industrial production, motor vehicles and residential heating and cooking, especially through the consumption of fossil fuels. Atmospheric pollutants such as sulphur dioxide cause acid rain, which affect fish stocks and agricultural production. Countries with low-level vehicle use and industrialization score the highest on the Environmental Performance Index.

## THE 10 WORST ENVIRONMENTAL PERFORMANCE INDEX COUNTRIES

| | COUNTRY | EPI SCORE* |
|---|---|---|
| **1** | Niger | 25.7 |
| **2** | Chad | 30.5 |
| **3** | Mauritania | 32.0 |
| **4** | Mali | 33.9 |
| **5** | Ethiopia | 36.7 |
| **6** | Angola | 39.3 |
| **7** | Pakistan | 41.1 |
| **8** | Burkina Faso | 43.2 |
| **9** | Bangladesh | 43.5 |
| **10** | Sudan | 44.0 |

* Out of 100

Source: *Pilot 2006 Environmental Performance Index*

## TOP 10 COUNTRIES WITH THE LOWEST OZONE CONCENTRATION

| | COUNTRY | OZONE (PARTS PER BILLION)* |
|---|---|---|
| **1** | São Tomé and Principe | 11.7 |
| **2** | Gabon | 12.3 |
| **3** | = Congo | 12.6 |
| | = Equatorial Guinea | 12.6 |
| **5** | Rwanda | 14.1 |
| **6** | Uganda | 14.2 |
| **7** | Burundi | 14.7 |
| **8** | Kenya | 15.8 |
| **9** | Liberia | 17.1 |
| **10** | Dem. Rep. of Congo | 17.7 |

* In the atmosphere at ground level

Source: *Pilot 2006 Environmental Performance Index*

## TOP 10 RUBBISH PRODUCERS

| | COUNTRY* | DOMESTIC WASTE PER CAPITA 2003# KG | LB |
|---|---|---|---|
| **1** | Ireland | 760 | 1,676 |
| **2** | USA | 740 | 1,631 |
| **3** | Iceland | 730 | 1,609 |
| **4** | Norway | 700 | 1,543 |
| **5** | Australia | 690 | 1,521 |
| **6** | Denmark | 670 | 1,477 |
| **7** | Switzerland | 660 | 1,455 |
| **8** | = Luxembourg | 650 | 1,433 |
| | = Spain | 650 | 1,433 |
| **10** | Germany | 640 | 1,411 |
| | *UK* | *610* | *1,345* |

* In those countries for which data available
# Or latest year for which data available

## TOP 10 COUNTRIES WITH THE HIGHEST OZONE CONCENTRATION

| | COUNTRY | OZONE (PARTS PER BILLION)* |
|---|---|---|
| **1** | Belize | 64.5 |
| **2** | Guatemala | 64.4 |
| **3** | Mexico | 64.2 |
| **4** | China | 63.4 |
| **5** | East Timor | 62.7 |
| **6** | Mongolia | 60.9 |
| **7** | Australia | 60.6 |
| **8** | Bhutan | 58.9 |
| **9** | Nepal | 58.6 |
| **10** | USA | 57.5 |
| | *UK* | *44.9* |

* In the atmosphere at ground level

Source: *Pilot 2006 Environmental Performance Index*

While the ozone layer in the stratosphere protects us from ultraviolet light from the Sun, and its breakdown is therefore a cause for concern, at lower levels of the atmosphere ozone is a pollutant and affects the health of those who breathe it.

# Industrial Disasters

## THE 10 WORST INDUSTRIAL-SITE DISASTERS*

| LOCATION / DATE / INCIDENT | NO. KILLED |
|---|---|
| **1 Bhopal**, India, 3 Dec 1984<br>Methylisocyante gas escape at Union Carbide plant | 3,849 |
| **2 Jesse**, Nigeria, 17 Oct 1998<br>Oil-pipeline explosion | >700 |
| **3 Oppau**, Germany, 21 Sep 1921<br>Bradishe Aniline chemical-plant explosion | 561 |
| **4 San Juanico**, Mexico, 19 Nov 1984<br>Explosion at a PEMEX liquefied petroleum gas plant | 540 |
| **5 Cubatão**, Brazil, 25 Feb 1984<br>Oil-pipeline explosion | 508 |
| **6 Durunkah**, Egypt, 2 Nov 1994<br>Fuel storage depot fire | >500 |
| **7 Mexico City**, Mexico, 19 Nov 1984<br>Butane-storage explosion | >400 |
| **8 Adeje**, Nigeria, 10 Jul 2000<br>Oil-pipeline explosion | >250 |
| **9 Guadalajara**, Mexico, 22 Apr 1992<br>Explosions caused by gas leak into sewers | 230 |
| **10 Oakdale**, Pennsylvania, 18 May 1918<br>TNT explosion at Aetna Chemical Company | 210 |

* Including industrial sites, factories, fuel depots and pipelines; excluding military, munitions, bombs, mining, marine and other transport disasters, dam failures and mass poisonings

Officially, the meltdown of the nuclear reactor at Chernobyl, Ukraine, on 26 April 1986 caused the immediate death of 31 people, but it has been suggested that by 1992 some 6,000 to 8,000 people had died as a result of radioactive contamination, a toll that will continue for many years. Extending the parameters of 'industrial' to include construction work, as many as 25,000 workers may have died during the building of the Panama Canal in the period 1881–1914, largely as a result of diseases such as yellow fever, malaria and cholera, while the building of the Madeira-Mamore railways in Brazil (1870–1912) resulted in over 6,000 deaths from disease, poison-arrow attacks and snakebite. The boring of the Gauley Bridge Water Tunnel, West Virginia, killed some 476 workers in 1935 as a result of inhalation of silica dust, with perhaps 1,500 becoming disabled.

## THE 10 WORST EXPLOSIONS*

| | LOCATION / DATE / INCIDENT | ESTIMATED NO. KILLED |
|---|---|---|
| **1** | **Rhodes**, Greece, 3 Apr 1856<br>Lightning strike of gunpowder store | 4,000 |
| **2** | **Breschia**, Italy, 18 Aug 1769<br>Church of San Nazaire caught fire after being struck by lightning, gunpowder store exploded | >3,000 |
| **3** | **Salang Tunnel**, Afghanistan, 3 Nov 1982<br>Petrol-tanker collision | >2,000 |
| **4** | **Lanchow**, China, 26 Oct 1935<br>Arsenal | 2,000 |
| **5** | **Halifax**, Nova Scotia, 6 Dec 1917<br>Ammunition ship *Mont Blanc* | 1,963 |
| **6** | **Hamont Station**, Belgium, 3 Aug 1918<br>Ammunition trains | 1,750 |
| **7** | **Memphis**, USA, 27 Apr 1865<br>Sultana paddle-steamer boiler explosion | 1,547 |
| **8 =** | **Archangel**, Russia, 20 Feb 1917<br>Munitions ship | 1,500 |
| **=** | **Smederovo**, Yugoslavia, 9 Jun 1941<br>Ammunition dump | 1,500 |
| **10** | **Bombay**, India, 14 Apr 1944<br>Ammunition ship *Fort Stikine* | 1,376 |

* Excluding mining disasters, terrorist and military bombs, and natural explosions, such as volcanoes

All these 'best-estimate' figures should be treated with caution, since, as with fires and shipwrecks, body counts following explosions are notoriously unreliable.

## THE 10 WORST SINGLE-BUILDING FIRES

| | LOCATION / DATE / BUILDING | NO. KILLED |
|---|---|---|
| **1** | **London Bridge**, UK, 11 July 1212 | 3,000* |
| **2** | **Santiago**, Chile, 8 Dec 1863,<br>Church of La Compañía | 2,500# |
| **3** | **Canton**, China, 25 May 1845, theatre | 1,670 |
| **4** | **Shanghai**, China, Jun 1871, theatre | 900 |
| **5** | **Vienna**, Austria, 8 Dec 1881, Ring Theatre | 640–850 |
| **6** | **St Petersburg**, Russia, 14 Feb 1836,<br>Lehmann Circus | 800 |
| **7** | **Antoung**, China, 13 Feb 1937, Cinema | 658 |
| **8** | **Chicago**, USA, 30 Dec 1903, Iroquois Theatre | 602 |
| **9** | **Mandi Dabwali**, India, 23 Dec 1995, school tent | >500 |
| **10** | **Boston**, USA, 28 Nov 1942,<br>Cocoanut Grove Night Club | 491 |

* Burned, crushed and drowned in ensuing panic; some chroniclers give the year as 1213
# Precise figure uncertain

*Sampoong disaster*
*The sudden and catastrophic collapse of the crowded five-year-old Seoul*
*department store left 501 staff and customers dead and 937 injured.*

# THE 10 **WORST MINING DISASTERS**

| | LOCATION / DATE | NO. KILLED |
|---|---|---|
| 1 | Honkeiko, China, 26 Apr 1942 | 1,549 |
| 2 | Courrières, France, 10 Mar 1906 | 1,060 |
| 3 | Omuta, Japan, 9 Nov 1963 | 447 |
| 4 | Senghenydd, Wales, UK, 14 Oct 1913 | 439 |
| 5 | = Coalbrook, South Africa, 21 Jan 1960 | 437 |
| | = Hokkaido, Japan, 1 Dec 1914 | 437 |
| 7 | Wankie, Rhodesia, 6 Jun 1972 | 427 |
| 8 | Tsinan, China, 13 May 1935 | 400 |
| 9 | Dhanbad, India, 28 May 1965 | 375 |
| 10 | Chasnala, India, 27 Dec 1975 | 372 |

A mine disaster at the Fushun mines, Manchuria, on 12 February
1931 may have resulted in up to 3,000 deaths, but information
was suppressed by the Chinese government. Soviet security was
also responsible for obscuring details of an explosion at the East
German Johanngeorgendstadt uranium mine on 29 November
1949, when as many as 3,700 may have died.

# THE 10 **WORST SHOP AND OFFICE DISASTERS**

| | LOCATION / DATE / INCIDENT | NO. KILLED |
|---|---|---|
| 1 | **Seoul**, Korea, 29 Jun 1995<br>Collapse of Sampoong Department Store | 501 |
| 2 | **Asuncíon**, Paraguay, 1 Aug 2004<br>Fire from gas leak in a supermarket | >400 |
| 3 | **Brussels**, Belgium, 22 May 1967<br>L'Innovation department-store fire | 322 |
| 4 | **Luoyang**, China, 25 Dec 2000<br>Fire in shopping-centre disco | >309 |
| 5 | **Lima**, Peru, 29 Dec 2001<br>Fire in the Mesa Redonda shopping area began in an illegal<br>firework shop, rapidly spreading to other buildings | >290 |
| 6 | **São Paulo**, Brazil, 1 Feb 1974<br>Fire in Joelma bank and office building | 188 |
| 7 | **Paris**, France, 4 May 1897<br>Fire in Grand Bazar de Charité | 129 |
| 8 | **Osaka**, Japan, 13 May 1972<br>Fire in night club in Sennichi department store | 119 |
| 9 | **Kumamoto**, Japan, 29 Nov 1973<br>Taiyo department-store fire | 101 |
| 10 | **Bogota**, Colombia, 16 Dec 1958<br>Fire at El Almacen Vida department store | 84 |

# Research & Development

## TOP 10 COUNTRIES FOR HIGH-TECHNOLOGY EXPORTS

| COUNTRY | HIGH-TECHNOLOGY EXPORTS, 2004 ($) |
|---|---|
| 1 China (includes Hong Kong, $80,109,000,000) | 241,712,000,000 |
| 2 USA | 216,016,000,000 |
| 3 Germany | 131,838,000,000 |
| 4 Japan | 124,045,000,000 |
| 5 Singapore | 87,742,000,000 |
| 6 South Korea | 75,742,000,000 |
| 7 France | 64,871,000,000 |
| 8 UK | 64,295,000,000 |
| 9 Netherlands | 55,211,000,000 |
| 10 Malaysia | 52,868,000,000 |

Source: The World Bank, *World Development Indicators 2006*

## TOP 10 COUNTRIES REGISTERING THE MOST PATENTS

| COUNTRY | PATENTS GRANTED (2004)* |
|---|---|
| 1 USA | 164,291 |
| 2 Japan | 124,192 |
| 3 China | 49,360 |
| 4 South Korea | 49,068 |
| 5 Germany | 29,586 |
| 6 Russia | 23,191 |
| 7 Canada | 13,060 |
| 8 Australia | 12,739 |
| 9 France | 11,841 |
| 10 UK | 10,541 |

* Resident and non-resident applications

Source: World Intellectual Property Organization

## TOP 10 COUNTRIES WITH THE MOST INDUSTRIAL ROBOTS

| COUNTRY | NO. OF OPERATIONAL INDUSTRIAL ROBOTS (2005) |
|---|---|
| 1 Japan | 373,481 |
| 2 North America (USA, Canada, Mexico) | 139,553 |
| 3 Germany | 126,725 |
| 4 South Korea | 61,576 |
| 5 Italy | 56,198 |
| 6 France | 30,434 |
| 7 Spain | 24,081 |
| 8 Taiwan | 15,464 |
| 9 UK | 14,948 |
| 10 China | 11,557 |
| *World total* | *922,875* |

Source: International Federation of Robotics

# TOP 10 INTERNATIONAL COMPANIES FOR RESEARCH AND DEVELOPMENT

| COMPANY / COUNTRY | INDUSTRY | R&D SPENDING 2005-06 (£) |
|---|---|---|
| 1 Ford Motor, USA | Automobiles and parts | 4,659,830,000 |
| 2 Pfizer, USA | Pharmaceuticals | 4,334,810,000 |
| 3 General Motors, USA | Automobiles and parts | 3,902,610,000 |
| 4 DaimlerChrysler, Germany | Automobiles and parts | 3,881,410,000 |
| 5 Microsoft, USA | Software and IT services | 3,835,040,000 |
| 6 Toyota, Japan | Automobiles and parts | 3,726,770,000 |
| 7 Johnson & Johnson, USA | Pharmaceuticals | 3,676,610,000 |
| 8 Siemens, Germany | Electronic and electrical | 3,541,980,000 |
| 9 Samsung, South Korea | Electronic and electrical | 3,169,300,000 |
| 10 GlaxoSmithKline, UK | Pharmaceuticals | 3,136,000,000 |

Source: Department of Trade and Industry, *The R&D Scorecard 2006*

A survey of the leading 1,250 global companies indicated that in the year 2005–06 they invested a total of £249 billion in research and development – an increase of seven per cent over the previous year. R&D is concentrated in firms from five countries (82 per cent in the USA, Japan, Germany, France and the UK), in five sectors (70 per cent in technology hardware, pharmaceuticals, automotive, electronics and software) and in the top 100 companies (61 per cent of the total).

*I, robot*
*More than 125,000 new robots are installed worldwide every year.*

# TOP 10 MOST VALUABLE TECHNOLOGY BRANDS*

| BRAND NAME | BRAND VALUE 2006 ($) |
|---|---|
| 1 Microsoft, USA | 67,000,000,000 |
| 2 IBM, USA | 56,201,000,000 |
| 3 Intel, USA | 32,319,000,000 |
| 4 Nokia, Finland | 30,131,000,000 |
| 5 Hewlett-Packard, USA | 20,458,000,000 |
| 6 Cisco, USA | 17,532,000,000 |
| 7 Samsung, South Korea | 16,169,000,000 |
| 8 Dell, USA | 12,256,000,000 |
| 9 Sony, Japan | 11,695,000,000 |
| 10 Oracle, USA | 11,459,000,000 |

* Includes computer, telecommunications and consumer electronics brands

Source: Interbrand/*BusinessWeek*

Brand consultants Interbrand estimates value by taking account of the profitability of individual brands within a business and such factors as their potential for growth.

# TOP 10 MOST-CITED SCIENTIFIC JOURNALS

| JOURNAL | PAPERS 1996-2006 | CITATIONS* |
|---|---|---|
| 1 Journal of Biological Chemistry | 59,061 | 1,761,650 |
| 2 Proceedings of the National Academy of Science, USA | 29,703 | 1,382,162 |
| 3 Nature | 10,947 | 1,217,027 |
| 4 Science | 10,296 | 1,181,938 |
| 5 Physical Review Letters | 32,732 | 843,701 |
| 6 Journal of the American Chemical Society | 27,362 | 717,785 |
| 7 Physical Review B | 52,173 | 601,422 |
| 8 Cell | 3,780 | 573,285 |
| 9 Journal of Immunology | 17,904 | 520,931 |
| 10 New England Journal of Medicine | 3,864 | 511,082 |

* Most-cited of over 7 million scientific-journal articles

Source: *Essential Science Indicators*

*Essential Science Indicators* considers more than seven million papers published in over 11,500 journals over the previous decade, in 22 main fields of science and the social sciences, to arrive at this ranking.

# Wired World

## TOP 10 COUNTRIES WITH THE MOST TELEPHONES

| COUNTRY | TELEPHONE LINES PER 100 | TOTAL (2004) |
|---|---|---|
| 1 China | 23.98 | 311,756,000 |
| 2 USA | 60.60 | 177,947,000 |
| 3 Japan | 46.00 | 58,788,000 |
| 4 Germany | 66.15 | 54,574,000 |
| 5 India | 4.07 | 43,960,000 |
| 6 Brazil | 23.46 | 42,382,000 |
| 7 Russia | 27.47 | 39,616,000 |
| 8 France | 56.04 | 33,870,200 |
| 9 UK | 56.35 | 33,700,000 |
| 10 South Korea | 55.31 | 26,595,100 |
| *World* | *18.89* | *1,206,247,200* |

Source: International Telecommunications Union, *World Telecommunication/ICT Development Report 2006*

Of the world's telephone lines, 538,981,500 are in Asia, 327,580,000 in Europe, 295,306,500 in North and South America, 25,925,000 in Africa and 13,773,000 in Oceania. In many developing countries, mobile phones have replaced often-defunct, inefficient or non-existent fixed lines, enabling their telephone systems rapidly to adopt 21st-century technology.

## TOP 10 COMPUTER COUNTRIES

| COUNTRY | % OF WORLD TOTAL | COMPUTERS (2005) |
|---|---|---|
| 1 USA | 25.49 | 230,400,000 |
| 2 Japan | 8.15 | 73,660,000 |
| 3 China | 7.03 | 63,520,000 |
| 4 Germany | 5.58 | 50,420,000 |
| 5 UK | 4.27 | 38,620,000 |
| 6 France | 3.58 | 32,400,000 |
| 7 South Korea | 3.14 | 28,380,000 |
| 8 Italy | 2.87 | 25,960,000 |
| 9 Canada | 2.63 | 23,770,000 |
| 10 Russia | 2.52 | 22,760,000 |
| *World total* | *100.00* | *903,900,000* |

Source: Computer Industry Almanac Inc.

## TOP 10 MOBILE-PHONE COUNTRIES

COUNTRY / MOBILE-PHONE SUBSCRIBERS

1 — China
398,000,000

2 — USA
202,000,000

3 — Russia
115,000,000

4 — Japan
95,000,000

5 — Brazil
86,000,000

6 — India
79,000,000

7 — Germany
73,000,000

8 — Italy
59,000,000

9 — UK
58,000,000

10 — France
47,000,000

*World total* — 2,065,000,000

Source: Computer Industry Almanac Inc.

## TOP 10 **INTERNET COUNTRIES**

| | COUNTRY | % OF WORLD TOTAL | INTERNET USERS (2007) |
|---|---|---|---|
| 1 | USA | 18.9 | 211,108,086 |
| 2 | China | 12.3 | 137,000,000 |
| 3 | Japan | 7.7 | 86,300,000 |
| 4 | Germany | 4.5 | 50,471,212 |
| 5 | India | 3.6 | 40,000,000 |
| 6 | UK | 3.4 | 37,600,000 |
| 7 | South Korea | 3.1 | 34,120,000 |
| 8 | Brazil | 2.9 | 32,130,000 |
| 9 | France | 2.8 | 30,837,592 |
| 10 | Italy | 2.8 | 30,763,848 |
| | *World total* | *100.0* | *1,114,274,426* |

Source: Internet World Stats

## TOP 10 **BROADBAND COUNTRIES**

| | COUNTRY | BROADBAND SUBSCRIBERS (2006) |
|---|---|---|
| 1 | USA | 54,558,000 |
| 2 | China | 48,576,000 |
| 3 | Japan | 25,843,000 |
| 4 | South Korea | 13,898,000 |
| 5 | Germany | 12,744,000 |
| 6 | France | 12,643,000 |
| 7 | UK | 12,317,000 |
| 8 | Italy | 8,377,000 |
| 9 | Canada | 7,615,000 |
| 10 | Spain | 6,091,000 |
| | *World total* | *263,801,000* |

Source: Point Topic, *World Broadband Statistics*, December 2006

While these represent the leading users of broadband in terms of subscriber numbers, the percentage of the population connecting to the Internet via broadband varies greatly around the world, from more than 25 per cent in Scandinavian countries to about 20 per cent in the UK and USA, down to under four per cent in China and less than one per cent in India.

# 9 TRANSPORT & TOURISM

# Cars & Road Transport

*The car in front...*
*...is a Toyota – the Corolla is the bestselling ever.*

## TOP 10 MOTOR VEHICLE-OWNING COUNTRIES

| | COUNTRY | CARS | COMMERCIAL VEHICLES | TOTAL (2004) |
|---|---|---|---|---|
| 1 | USA | 132,822,614 | 98,575,667 | 231,398,281 |
| 2 | Japan | 55,994,005 | 17,011,782 | 73,005,787 |
| 3 | Germany | 45,375,526 | 3,539,658 | 48,915,184 |
| 4 | Italy | 33,973,147 | 4,250,896 | 38,224,043 |
| 5 | France | 29,990,000 | 6,139,000 | 36,039,000 |
| 6 | UK | 29,378,190 | 3,396,446 | 33,074,636 |
| 7 | Russia | 24,208,000 | 5,536,200 | 29,744,200 |
| 8 | China | 7,900,000 | 19,800,000 | 27,700,000 |
| 9 | Spain | 19,541,900 | 4,660,400 | 24,202,300 |
| 10 | Brazil | 17,600,000 | 4,400,000 | 22,000,000 |
| | *World total* | *603,433,437* | *233,536,876* | *836,970,313* |

Source: Ward's Motor Vehicle Facts & Figures 2006

## TOP 10 BESTSELLING CARS OF ALL TIME

| | MANUFACTURER / MODEL | YEARS IN PRODUCTION | APPROX. SALES* |
|---|---|---|---|
| 1 | Toyota Corolla | 1966– | 31,600,000 |
| 2 | Volkswagen Golf | 1974– | 24,000,000 |
| 3 | Volkswagen Beetle | 1937–2003# | 21,529,464 |
| 4 | Ford Escort/Orion | 1968–2003 | 20,000,000 |
| 5 | Ford Model T | 1908–27 | 16,536,075 |
| 6 | Honda Civic | 1972– | 16,500,000 |
| 7 | Nissan Sunny/Sentra/Pulsar | 1966– | 15,900,100 |
| 8 | Volkswagen Passat | 1973– | 14,000,000 |
| 9 | Lada Riva | 1980– | 13,500,000 |
| 10 | Chevrolet Impala/Caprice | 1958– | 13,000,000 |

\* To 2006, except where otherwise indicated
# Produced in Mexico 1978–2003

## TOP 10 CAR MANUFACTURERS

| | COMPANY / COUNTRY | PASSENGER-CAR PRODUCTION 2005 |
|---|---|---|
| 1 | Toyota (Japan) | 6,157,038 |
| 2 | General Motors (USA) | 5,657,225 |
| 3 | Volkswagen group (Germany) | 4,979,487 |
| 4 | Ford (USA) | 3,514,496 |
| 5 | Honda (Japan) | 3,324,282 |
| 6 | PSA Peugeot Citroën (France) | 2,982,690 |
| 7 | Hyundai-Kia (South Korea) | 2,726,600 |
| 8 | Nissan (Japan) | 2,697,362 |
| 9 | Renault-Dacia-Samsung (France) | 2,195,162 |
| 10 | DaimlerChrysler (Germany) | 1,965,410 |
| | *World total (including manufacturers outside Top 10)* | *45,855,503* |

Source: OICA Statistics Committee

## TOP 10 CAR-PRODUCING COUNTRIES

COUNTRY / CAR PRODUCTION 2005

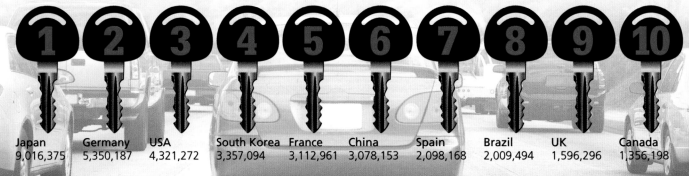

| 1 Japan | 2 Germany | 3 USA | 4 South Korea | 5 France | 6 China | 7 Spain | 8 Brazil | 9 UK | 10 Canada |
|---|---|---|---|---|---|---|---|---|---|
| 9,016,375 | 5,350,187 | 4,321,272 | 3,357,094 | 3,112,961 | 3,078,153 | 2,098,168 | 2,009,494 | 1,596,296 | 1,356,198 |

Source: The International Organization of Motor Vehicle Manufacturers

# TOP 10 COUNTRIES WITH THE LONGEST ROAD NETWORKS

COUNTRY / TOTAL ROAD NETWORK KM/MILES

**1** USA
6,430,366 / 3,995,643

**2** India
3,383,344 / 2,102,312

**3** China
1,870,661 / 1,162,374

**4** Brazil
1,751,868 / 1,088,560

**5** Japan
1,183,000 / 735,982

**6** Canada
1,042,300 / 647,655

**7** France
956,303 / 594,219

**8** Russia
871,000 / 541,214

**9** Australia
810,641 / 503,708

**10** Spain
666,292 / 414,014

*UK  388,008 / 241,096*

*World total  32,345,165 / 20,098,350*

Source: CIA, *The World Factbook 2007*

The CIA's assessment of road lengths includes both paved (mostly tarmac-surfaced) and unpaved highways (gravel and earth-surfaced). In many developing countries the proportion of unpaved is greater than paved. The world total is equivalent to over 800 times the circumference of the Earth at the Equator.

## THE CENTENARY OF THE MODEL T FORD

*The Model T Ford was long the world's most popular car.*

Considered the most influential car of the 20th century, the first Model T Ford left the company's Detroit, Michigan, factory on 27 September 1908. The application of revolutionary production-line methods enabled the Model T, popularly known as the 'Tin Lizzie', to be assembled quickly and hence made it affordable: its original price was $850.50, but fell to under $300 by 1925. The well-known slogan that it was available in 'any colour so long as it's black' was not always true – it was available in various colours in the early and late years of its long life, but restricted to black in the middle period. Model T Fords were also assembled in Canada and the UK.

In 1911, Henry Alexander drove one to the top of Ben Nevis, Britain's highest mountain. So popular did it become that in 1921 642,750, or 50.4 per cent of the world total car production of 1,275,324 vehicles were Model Ts. The last Model T was made on 26 May 1927.

# Fastest on Land

## THE 10 **FIRST HOLDERS OF THE LAND SPEED RECORD**

| DRIVER / CAR | LOCATION | DATE | SPEED KM/H | SPEED MPH |
|---|---|---|---|---|
| **1** Gaston de Chasseloup-Laubat, Jeantaud | Achères, France | 18 Dec 1898 | 62.78 | 39.24 |
| **2** Camille Jenatzy, Jenatzy | Achères, France | 17 Jan 1899 | 66.27 | 41.42 |
| **3** Gaston de Chasseloup-Laubat, Jeantaud | Achères, France | 17 Jan 1899 | 69.90 | 43.69 |
| **4** Camille Jenatzy, Jenatzy | Achères, France | 27 Jan 1899 | 79.37 | 49.92 |
| **5** Gaston de Chasseloup-Laubat, Jeantaud | Achères, France | 4 Mar 1899 | 92.16 | 57.60 |
| **6** Camille Jenatzy, Jenatzy | Achères, France | 29 Apr 1899 | 105.26 | 65.79 |
| **7** Leon Serpollet, Serpollet | Nice, France | 13 Apr 1902 | 120.09 | 75.06 |
| **8** William Vanderbilt, Mors | Albis, France | 5 Aug 1902 | 121.72 | 76.08 |
| **9** Henri Fournier, Mors | Dourdan, France | 5 Nov 1902 | 122.56 | 76.60 |
| **10** M. Augières, Mors | Dourdan, France | 17 Nov 1902 | 123.40 | 77.13 |

The official land speed record was set and broken five times within a year. The first six holders were rival racers Comte Gaston de Chasseloup-Laubat (France) and Camille Jenatzy (Belgium).

## THE 10 **LATEST HOLDERS OF THE LAND SPEED RECORD**

| DRIVER / CAR | DATE | SPEED KM/H | SPEED MPH |
|---|---|---|---|
| **1** Andy Green (UK), ThrustSSC* | 15 Oct 1997 | 1,227.99 | 763.04 |
| **2** Richard Noble (UK), Thrust2* | 4 Oct 1983 | 1,013.47 | 633.47 |
| **3** Gary Gabelich (USA), The Blue Flame | 23 Oct 1970 | 995.85 | 622.41 |
| **4** Craig Breedlove (USA), Spirit of America – Sonic 1 | 15 Nov 1965 | 960.96 | 600.60 |
| **5** Art Arfons (USA), Green Monster | 7 Nov 1965 | 922.48 | 576.55 |
| **6** Craig Breedlove (USA), Spirit of America – Sonic 1 | 2 Nov 1965 | 888.76 | 555.48 |
| **7** Art Arfons (USA), Green Monster | 27 Oct 1964 | 858.73 | 536.71 |
| **8** Craig Breedlove (USA), Spirit of America | 15 Oct 1964 | 842.04 | 526.28 |
| **9** Craig Breedlove (USA), Spirit of America | 13 Oct 1964 | 749.95 | 468.72 |
| **10** Art Arfons (USA), Green Monster | 5 Oct 1964 | 694.43 | 434.02 |

* Location: Black Rock Desert, Nevada, USA; all other speeds were achieved at Bonneville Salt Flats, Utah, USA

*Second pioneer*
*Camille Jenatzy (1868–1913) held successive land speed records and was the first person to exceed the symbolic 100 km/h barrier, in an electric-powered vehicle, La Jamais Contente ('Never Satisfied'). He went on to win major races, but died tragically in a hunting accident.*

*World's fastest car*
*Designed by previous record-holder Richard Noble and driven by RAF pilot Andy Green, the ThrustSSC (SuperSonic Car), powered by two Rolls Royce jet engines from Phantom fighter aircraft, became the first car to break the sound barrier as it set a new land speed record.*

# THE 10 **LATEST HOLDERS OF THE MOTORCYCLE SPEED RECORD**

| | RIDER* | MOTORCYCLE | DATE | SPEED KM/H | MPH |
|---|---|---|---|---|---|
| **1** | Chris Carr | BUB Number Seven | 5 Sep 2006 | 564.68 | 350.88 |
| **2** | Rocky Robinson | Ack Attack, dual-Suzuki-Hayabusa | 3 Sep 2006 | 551.68 | 342.80 |
| **3** | Dave Campos | Twin 91 cu in/1,491 cc Ruxton Harley-Davidson Easyriders | 14 Jul 1990 | 518.45 | 322.15 |
| **4** | Donald A. Vesco | Twin 1,016 cc Kawasaki Lightning Bolt | 25 Aug 1978 | 512.73 | 318.60 |
| **5** | Donald A. Vesco | Twin 1,016 cc Kawasaki Lightning Bolt | 23 Aug 1978 | 507.65 | 315.44 |
| **6** | Donald A. Vesco | 1,496 cc Yamaha Silver Bird | 28 Sep 1975 | 487.51 | 302.93 |
| **7** | Donald A. Vesco | Yamaha | 1 Oct 1974 | 453.36 | 281.71 |
| **8** | Calvin Rayborn | 1,480 cc Harley-Davidson | 16 Oct 1970 | 427.26 | 265.49 |
| **9** | Calvin Rayborn | 1,480 cc Harley-Davidson | 15 Oct 1970 | 410.99 | 255.38 |
| **10** | Donald A. Vesco | 700 cc Yamaha | 17 Sep 1970 | 405.42 | 251.92 |

* All USA

All the records listed here were achieved at the Bonneville Salt Flats, USA. To break a Fédération Internationale Motorcycliste record, the motorcycle has to cover a measured distance, making two runs within one hour, and taking the average of the two. American Motorcycling Association records require a turnround within two hours.

# TOP 10 **FASTEST RAIL JOURNEYS**

| | JOURNEY* | TRAIN | DISTANCE KM | MILES | SPEED KM/H | MPH |
|---|---|---|---|---|---|---|
| **1** | Lyon-St Exupéry to Aix-en-Provence, France | TGV 6171 | 289.6 | 179.9 | 263.3 | 163.6 |
| **2** | Hiroshima to Kokura, Japan | 15 Nozomi | 192.0 | 119.3 | 261.8 | 162.7 |
| **3** | Frankfurt Flughafen to Siegburg/Bonn, Germany | 17 ICE trains | 144.0 | 89.5 | 233.5 | 145.1 |
| **4** | Brussels Midi to Marseilles-St Charles, Belgium/France | ThalysSoleil | 1,054.0 | 654.9 | 233.4 | 145.0 |
| **5** | Madrid Atocha to Cuidad Atocha, Spain | 6 AVE trains | 170.7 | 160.1 | 204.8 | 127.3 |
| **6** | Falköping to Katrineholm, Sweden | X2000 438 | 209.7 | 130.3 | 190.6 | 118.4 |
| **7** | Seoul to Taejeon, South Korea | 5 KTX trains | 155.0 | 96.3 | 189.8 | 117.9 |
| **8** | Stevenage to Grantham, UK | 1 IC255 | 125.3 | 77.9 | 181.1 | 112.5 |
| **9** | Roma (Rome) Termini to Firenze (Florence) SMN, Italy | Eurostar 9458 | 261.0 | 162.2 | 166.6 | 103.5 |
| **10** | Wilmington to Baltimore, USA | 13 Acela Expresses | 110.1 | 68.4 | 165.1 | 102.6 |

* Fastest journey for each country; all those in the Top 10 have other equally or similarly fast services

Source: *Railway Gazette International*, 2005 World Speed Survey

**Fastest Man – On a Sled**
On 10 December 1954, Lt Col John P. Stapp (1910–99) became the fastest man in the world on a rocket-propelled sled, Sonic Wind No. 1, at the Holloman Air Force Base, New Mexico, which attained a speed of 1,017 km/h (632 mph). The fastest speed on land in an unmanned vehicle was achieved on 30 April 2003 by a rocket-powered sled that reached 10,326 km/h (6,416 mph) or Mach 8.5.

*French revolution*
*In service since 1981, the French TGV (Train à Grande Vitesse – high-speed train) has consistently offered some of the world's fastest scheduled services. On 18 May 1990, a specially modified TGV, the Atlantique, set a world speed record of 515.3 km/h (320.3 mph).*

# On the Water

*Queen rules*
The Queen Mary *twice held the Blue Riband for the fastest Atlantic crossing in both directions, seizing the coveted title from the French* Normandie. *She maintained the record until 1952 and retired from service in 1967.*

## TOP 10 **LONGEST CRUISE SHIPS**

| | | LENGTH | |
|---|---|---|---|
| SHIP / YEAR BUILT / COUNTRY | | M | FT |
| **1** Genesis of the Seas 2009*, Finland | | 360 | 1,181 |
| **2** Queen Mary 2 2004, France | | 345 | 1,132 |
| **3** =Freedom of the Seas 2006, Finland | | 339 | 1,112 |
| =Liberty of the Seas 2007, Finland | | 339 | 1,112 |
| **5** =Fantasia 2008*, France | | 333 | 1,092 |
| =Serenata 2009*, France | | 333 | 1,092 |
| **7** =Voyager of the Seas 1999, Finland | | 311 | 1,021 |
| =Explorer of the Seas 2000, Finland | | 311 | 1,021 |
| **9** =Adventure of the Seas 2001, Finland | | 311 | 1,020 |
| =Navigator of the Seas 2003, Finland | | 311 | 1,020 |
| =Mariner of the Seas 2004, Finland | | 311 | 1,020 |

* Scheduled launch

For comparison, the *Great Eastern* (launched 1858) measured 211 m (692 ft), while the *Titanic* was 269 m (882 ft) long, and until the influx of new vessels in 1998, would have ranked 8th in this Top 10. Former entrant in this list the *Queen Mary* (311 m/1,020 ft) is now a floating museum at Long Beach, California, while the 314-m (1,031-ft) *Queen Elizabeth* was taken out of service in 1972. One-time record longest ship, the 316-m (1,035-m) *Norway* (former *France*), ceased sailing in 2003, but plans to scrap her have been halted following protests from environmentalists.

## THE 10 **LATEST BLUE RIBAND WINNERS**\*

| | | | DURATION | | | AVERAGE SPEED |
|---|---|---|---|---|---|---|
| SHIP / COMPANY | | DATE | DAYS | HRS | MINS | (KNOTS) |
| **1** Cat-Link V, Scandlines | | 20 Jul 1998 | 2 | 20 | 9 | 41.28 |
| **2** Catalonia, Buquebus | | 10 Jun 1998 | 3 | 9 | 55 | 38.85 |
| **3** Hoverspeed Great Britain, Hoverspeed | | 24 Jun 1990 | 3 | 7 | 54 | 36.97 |
| **4** United States, US Line | | 7 Jul 1952 | 3 | 10 | 40 | 35.59 |
| **5** Queen Mary, Cunard White Star | | 14 Aug 1938 | 3 | 20 | 42 | 31.69 |
| **6** Normandie, French Line | | 8 Aug 1937 | 3 | 22 | 7 | 31.20 |
| **7** Normandie, French Line | | 22 Mar 1937 | 4 | 0 | 6 | 30.99 |
| **8** Queen Mary, Cunard White Star | | 30 Aug 1936 | 3 | 23 | 57 | 30.63 |
| **9** Normandie, French Line | | 11 Jun 1935 | 4 | 3 | 25 | 30.31 |
| **10** Bremen, Norddeutscher Lloyd | | 15 Jun 1933 | 4 | 16 | 15 | 28.51 |

* Eastbound crossings

Steam ships began carrying passengers across the Atlantic between Europe and the USA from 1838 onwards. In the early years, it could take 18 days or longer to make the journey, a distance – depending on the route – of about 4,828 km (3,000 miles). Shipping companies competed with each other, with the fastest ship carrying a blue flag, or 'Blue Riband'. There were separate Blue Ribands for westbound and eastbound crossings, and after 1934 the Hales Trophy was presented to the ship with the fastest average speed.

## THE 10 LATEST HOLDERS OF THE WATER SPEED RECORD – JET-POWERED

| DRIVER / BOAT / LOCATION / DATE | SPEED KM/H | SPEED MPH |
|---|---|---|
| **1** Ken Warby (Australia), Spirit of Australia, Blowering Dam, Australia 8 Oct 1978 | 317.60 | 511.13 |
| **2** Ken Warby, Spirit of Australia, Blowering Dam, 20 Nov 1977 | 288.18 | 463.78 |
| **3** Lee Taylor (USA), Hustler, Lake Guntersville, Alabama, USA 30 Jun 1967 | 285.22 | 459.02 |
| **4** Donald Campbell (UK), Bluebird K7, Lake Dumbleyung, Australia 31 Dec 1964 | 276.33 | 444.71 |
| **5** Donald Campbell, Bluebird K7, Coniston Water, UK, 14 May 1959 | 260.35 | 418.99 |
| **6** Donald Campbell, Bluebird K7, Coniston Water, 10 Nov 1958 | 248.62 | 400.12 |
| **7** Donald Campbell, Bluebird K7, Coniston Water, 7 Nov 1957 | 239.07 | 384.75 |
| **8** Donald Campbell, Bluebird K7, Coniston Water, 19 Sep 1956 | 225.63 | 363.12 |
| **9** Donald Campbell, Bluebird K7, Lake Mead, Nevada, USA, 16 Nov 1955 | 216.20 | 347.94 |
| **10** Donald Campbell, Bluebird K7, Ullswater, 23 Jul 1955 | 202.32 | 325.60 |

Jet-powered craft have long held the World Unlimited water speed record, with Ken Warby's self-built *Spirit of Australia* unbeaten for 30 years.

## THE 10 LATEST HOLDERS OF THE WATER SPEED RECORD – PROPELLER-DRIVEN

| DRIVER / BOAT / LOCATION / DATE | SPEED KM/H | SPEED MPH |
|---|---|---|
| **1** Dave Villwock, Miss Budweiser, Lake Oroville, California, USA 13 Mar 2004 | 354.849 | 220.493 |
| **2** Russ Wicks, Miss Freei, Lake Washington, Washington, USA 15 Jun 2000 | 330.711 | 205.494 |
| **3** Roy Duby, Miss US1, Lake Guntersville, Alabama, USA 17 Apr 1962 | 322.543 | 200.419 |
| **4** Bill Muncey, Miss Thriftaway, Lake Washington, 16 Feb 1960 | 308.996 | 192.001 |
| **5** Jack Regas, Hawaii Kai III, Lake Washington, 30 Nov 1957 | 301.956 | 187.627 |
| **6** Art Asbury (Canada), Miss Supertest II, Lake Ontario, Canada, 1 Nov 1957 | 296.988 | 184.540 |
| **7** Stanley Sayres, Slo-Mo-Shun IV, Lake Washington, 7 Jul 1952 | 287.263 | 178.497 |
| **8** Stanley Sayres, Slo-Mo-Shun IV, Lake Washington, 26 Jun 1950 | 258.015 | 160.323 |
| **9** Malcolm Campbell (UK), Bluebird K4, Coniston Water, UK, 19 Aug 1939 | 228.108 | 141.740 |
| **10** Malcolm Campbell, Bluebird K3, Hallwiler See, Switzerland, 17 Aug 1938 | 210.679 | 130.910 |

\* USA unless otherwise stated

All these record-holders were propeller-driven craft, taking the average of two runs over a measured kilometre or mile course.

*Fastest hydroplane*
Miss Budweiser *set a new record for propeller-driven craft, hitting 369 km/h (229 mph) on the return leg of its two runs.*

# In the Air

*Transatlantic cruiser*
One of three Douglas World Cruisers that embarked on a round-the-world journey in 1924, two of them successfully crossing the Atlantic.

## THE 10 FIRST TRANSATLANTIC FLIGHTS

| FLIGHT DETAILS / AIRCRAFT | DATE* |
|---|---|
| **1 Trepassy Harbor, Newfoundland, to Lisbon, Portugal** US Navy Curtiss flying boat *NC-4* | 16–27 May 1919 |

Lt-Cdr Albert Cushing Read and a crew of five crossed the Atlantic in a series of hops, refuelling at sea.

**2 St John's, Newfoundland, to Galway, Ireland**
Twin Rolls-Royce-engined
converted Vickers Vimy bomber　　　　14–15 Jun 1919
British pilot Capt John Alcock and navigator Lt Arthur Whitten Brown achieved the first non-stop flight, ditching in Derrygimla bog after their epic 16 hr 28 min journey.

**3 East Fortune, Scotland to Roosevelt Field, New York**
British *R-34* airship　　　　　　　　　　2–6 Jul 1919
Major George Herbert Scott and a crew of 30 made the first east–west crossing, the first airship to do so.

**4 Lisbon, Portugal to Recife, Brazil –**
Fairey IIID seaplane *Santa Cruz*　　30 Mar–5 Jun 1922
Portuguese pilots Admiral Gago Coutinho and Commander Sacadura Cabral were the first to fly the South Atlantic in stages.

**5 Orkneys, Scotland to Labrador, Canada**
Two Douglas seaplanes, *Chicago*
and *New Orleans*　　　　　　　　　　2–31 Aug 1924
Lt Lowell H. Smith and Leslie P. Arnold in one biplane and Erik Nelson and John Harding in another set out and crossed the North Atlantic in a series of hops via Iceland and Greenland.

**6 Friedrichshafen, Germany to Lakehurst, New Jersey**
*Los Angeles*, a renamed German-built
*ZR 3* airship　　　　　　　　　　　12–15 Oct 1924
Piloted by Dr Hugo Eckener, with 31 passengers and crew.

**7 Huelva, Spain to Recife, Brazil**
*Plus Ultra*, a Dornier Wal
twin-engined flying boat　　　　22 Jan–10 Feb 1926
A crew of three Spaniards including General Franco's brother Ramón plus a photographer crossed the South Atlantic in stages.

**8 Cagliari, Sardinia to Recife, Brazil**　　8–24 Feb 1927
*Santa Maria*, a Savoia-Marchetti S.55 flying boat
Francesco Marquis de Pinedo, Capt Carlo del Prete and Lt Vitale Zacchetti crossed in stages as part of a goodwill trip.

**9 Lisbon, Portugal to Natal, Brazil**
Dornier Wal flying boat　　　　　　16–17 Mar 1927
Portuguese flyers Sarmento de Beires and Jorge de Castilho took the route via Casablanca.

**10 Genoa, Italy to Natal, Brazil**
Savoia-Marchetti flying boat　　28 Apr–14 May 1927
A Brazilian crew set out on 17 October 1926, flying in stages via the Canaries and Cape Verde Islands.

\* All dates refer to the Atlantic legs of the journeys; some started earlier and ended beyond their first transatlantic landfalls

## TOP 10 LONGEST AIRCRAFT

| | | LENGTH | |
|---|---|---|---|
| AIRCRAFT | M | FT | IN |
| **1** Ekranoplan KM Caspian Sea Monster | 106.1 | 348 | 0 |
| **2** Antonov An-225 Cossack | 84.0 | 275 | 7 |
| **3** Lockheed C-5 Galaxy | 75.5 | 247 | 10 |
| **4** Airbus A340-600 | 75.3 | 246 | 11 |
| **5** Boeing 777 | 73.9 | 242 | 4 |
| **6** Lun Ekranoplan | 73.2 | 240 | 0 |
| **7** Airbus A380-800 | 73.0 | 239 | 6 |
| **8** Boeing 747 | 70.7 | 231 | 10 |
| **9** Antonov An-124 Condor | 69.1 | 226 | 9 |
| **10** H-4 Hercules ('Spruce Goose') | 66.6 | 218 | 6 |

## THE 10 FIRST ROCKET AND JET AIRCRAFT

| AIRCRAFT | COUNTRY | FIRST FLIGHT |
|---|---|---|
| **1** Heinkel He 176* | Germany | 20 Jun 1939 |
| **2** Heinkel He 178 | Germany | 27 Aug 1939 |
| **3** DFS 194* | Germany | Aug 1940# |
| **4** Caproni-Campini N-1 | Italy | 28 Aug 1940 |
| **5** Heinkel He 280V-1 | Germany | 2 Apr 1941 |
| **6** Gloster E.28/39 | UK | 15 May 1941 |
| **7** Messerschmitt Me 163 Komet* | Germany | 13 Aug 1941 |
| **8** Messerschmitt Me 262V-3 | Germany | 18 Jul 1942 |
| **9** Bell XP-59A Airacomet | USA | 2 Oct 1942 |
| **10** Gloster Meteor F Mk 1 | UK | 5 Mar 1943 |

\* Rocket-powered
# Precise date unknown

*Fastest jet*
*In 1976 the Lockheed SR-71A 'Blackbird' set a jet record of Mach 3.3 that still stands over 30 years later.*

# THE 10 **LATEST AIR SPEED RECORDS HELD BY JETS**\*

| | PILOT | COUNTRY | LOCATION | AIRCRAFT | SPEED KM/H | SPEED MPH | DATE |
|---|---|---|---|---|---|---|---|
| **1** | Eldon W. Joersz/ George T. Morgan Jr | USA | Beale AFB, California, USA | Lockheed SR-71A | 3,529.560 | 2,193.167 | 28 Jul 1976 |
| **2** | Adolphus Bledsoe/ John T. Fuller | USA | Beale AFB, USA | Lockheed SR-71A | 3,367.221 | 2,092.294 | 27 Jul 1976 |
| **3** | Robert L. Stephens/ Daniel Andre | USA | Edwards AFB, California, USA | Lockheed YF-12A | 3,331.507 | 2,070.102 | 1 May 1965 |
| **4** | Georgi Mossolov | USSR | Podmoskownoe, USSR | Mikoyan E-166 | 2,681.000 | 1,665.896 | 7 Jul 1962 |
| **5** | Robert B. Robinson | USA | Edwards AFB, USA | McDonnell F4H-1F Phantom II | 2,585.425 | 1,606.509 | 22 Nov 1961 |
| **6** | Joseph W. Rogers | USA | Edwards AFB, USA | Convair F-106A Delta Dart | 2,455.736 | 1,525.924 | 15 Dec 1959 |
| **7** | Georgi Mossolov | USSR | Jukowski-Petrowskol, USSR | Mikoyan E-66 | 2,388.000 | 1,483.834 | 31 Oct 1959 |
| **8** | Walter W. Irwin | USA | Edwards AFB, USA | Lockheed YF-104A Starfighter | 2,259.538 | 1,404.012 | 16 May 1958 |
| **9** | Adrian E. Drew | USA | Edwards AFB, USA | McDonnell F-101A Voodoo | 1,943.500 | 1,207.635 | 12 Dec 1957 |
| **10** | Peter Twiss | UK | Chichester, UK | Fairey Delta Two | 1,822.000 | 1,132.138 | 10 Mar 1956 |

\* Ground-launched only, hence excluding X-15 records

The speed of 1,323.312 km/h (822.268 mph) achieved on 20 August 1955 by Horace A. Hanes (USA) at Palmdale, USA, in a North American F-100C Super Sabre, was the first official supersonic record-holder. The next holder, that of Peter Twiss, was the greatest-ever incremental increase in the air speed record – 498.688 km/h (309.870 mph). It should be noted that although air records are customarily expressed to three decimal places, few flights have ever been recorded to such a level of accuracy.

# Transport Disasters

*Train tragedy*
*Burned-out carriages at Reqa al-Gharbiya, Egypt. Overcrowded with travellers during the religious holiday of Eid al-Adha, the train caught fire after a cooking stove exploded. Some of the 373 victims jumped to their deaths, while many were trapped on board in the country's worst-ever rail disaster.*

## THE 10 **WORST RAIL DISASTERS**

LOCATION / DATE / INCIDENT     NO. KILLED

**1 Telwatta**, Sri Lanka, 26 Dec 2004    up to 2,000
The *Queen of the Sea* train was struck by the Indian Ocean tsunami. It was impossible to determine the precise number of casualties in the devastation.

**2 Bagmati River**, India, 6 Jun 1981    c. 800
The carriages of a train plunged off a bridge over the river Bagmati near Mansi when the driver braked, apparently to avoid hitting a sacred cow.

**3 Chelyabinsk**, Russia, 3 Jun 1989    up to 800
Two passenger trains, laden with holidaymakers, were destroyed when liquid gas from a nearby pipeline exploded.

**4 Guadalajara**, Mexico, 18 Jan 1915    >600
A train derailed on a steep incline, but political strife in the country meant that full details of the disaster were suppressed.

**5 Modane**, France, 12 Dec 1917    573
A troop-carrying train ran out of control and it has been claimed that it was overloaded and that as many as 1,000 may have died.

**6 Balvano**, Italy, 2 Mar 1944    521
A heavily laden train stalled in the Armi Tunnel, and many passengers were asphyxiated.

**7 Torre**, Spain, 3 Jan 1944    >500
A double collision and fire in a tunnel resulted in many deaths.

**8 Awash**, Ethiopia, 13 Jan 1985    428
A derailment hurled a train into a ravine.

**9 Cireau**, Romania, 7 Jan 1917    374
An overcrowded passenger train crashed into a military train and was derailed.

**10 Reqa al-Gharbiya**, Egypt, 20 Feb 2002    373
A fire on the Cairo-Luxor train engulfed the carriages. Passengers were burned or leaped from the train to their deaths.

## THE 10 **WORST MARINE DISASTERS**

LOCATION / DATE / INCIDENT     NO. KILLED

**1 Off Gdansk**, Poland, 30 Jan 1945    up to 7,800
The German liner *Wilhelm Gustloff*, laden with refugees, was torpedoed by a Soviet submarine, S-13. The precise death toll remains uncertain, but recent research suggests a total of 10,582 on board.

**2 Off Cape Rixhöft (Rozeewie)**, Poland, 16 Apr 1945    6,800
German ship *Goya*, carrying evacuees from Gdansk, was torpedoed in the Baltic.

**3 Off Yingkow**, China, 3 Dec 1948    >6,000
The boilers of an unidentified Chinese troopship carrying soldiers from Manchuria exploded, detonating ammunition.

**4 Off Sumatra**, 18 Sep 1944    5,620
The Japanese ship *Junyo Maru*, carrying Dutch, British, American and Australian prisoners of war and Javanese slave labourers, was torpedoed by British submarine HMS *Tradewind*.

**5 En route for Okinawa**, 29 Jun 1944    5,400
Japanese troop transport *Toyama Maru* was torpedoed by American submarine USS *Sturgeon*.

**6 Lübeck**, Germany, 3 May 1945    5,000
The German ship *Cap Arcona*, carrying concentration-camp survivors, was bombed and sunk by British fighter-bombers.

**7 Off British coast**, Aug to Oct 1588    4,000
Military conflict and storms combined to destroy the Spanish Armada.

**8 Off Stolpmünde (Ustka)**, Poland, 10 Feb 1945    3,500
German war-wounded and refugees were lost when the *General Steuben* was torpedoed by the same Russian submarine that had sunk the *Wilhelm Gustloff* 10 days earlier.

**9 Off St Nazaire**, France, 17 Jun 1940    >3,000
The British ship *Lancastria*, carrying troops and French refugees, sank after a dive-bombing attack by Luftwaffe aircraft.

**10 Tabias Strait**, Philippines, 21 Dec 1987    up to 3,000
The ferry *Doña Paz* was struck by oil tanker *MV Vector*. The *Doña Paz* was so overcrowded that a death toll of 4,341 claimed by some sources may be possible.

Recent reassessments of the death tolls in some of the World War II marine disasters means that the most famous marine disaster of all, the *Titanic*, which sank on 15 April 1912 with the loss of 1,517 lives, no longer ranks in the Top 10. However, the *Titanic* tragedy remains one of the worst peacetime disasters, along with such incidents as the *General Slocum*, a steamboat that caught fire off New York on 15 June 1904 with the loss of 1,021.

# THE 10 **WORST AIR DISASTERS**

LOCATION / DATE / INCIDENT                                    NO. KILLED

**1** **New York**, USA, 11 Sep 2001     *c.* 1,622
Following a hijacking by terrorists, an American Airlines Boeing 767 was deliberately flown into the North Tower of the World Trade Center, killing all 81 passengers (including five hijackers), 11 crew on board and an estimated 1,530 on the ground, both as a direct result of the crash and the subsequent fire and collapse of the building, which also killed 479 rescue workers.

**2** **New York**, USA, 11 Sep 2001     *c.* 677
As part of the coordinated attack, hijackers commandeered a second Boeing 747 and crashed it into the South Tower of the World Trade Center, killing all 56 passengers and 9 crew on board, and approximately 612 on the ground.

**3** **Tenerife**, Canary Islands, 27 Mar 1977     583
Two Boeing 747s (PanAm and KLM, carrying 380 passengers and 16 crew, and 234 passengers and 14 crew respectively) collided and caught fire on the runway of Los Rodeos airport after the pilots received incorrect control-tower instructions. A total of 61 escaped.

**4** **Mt Ogura**, Japan, 12 Aug 1985     520
A JAL Boeing 747 on an internal flight from Tokyo to Osaka crashed, killing all but four of the 509 passengers and all 15 crew on board.

**5** **Charkhi Dadri**, India, 12 Nov 1996     349
Soon after taking off from New Delhi's Indira Gandhi International Airport, a Saudi Arabian Airlines Boeing 747 collided with a Kazakh Airlines Ilyushin IL76 cargo aircraft on its descent and exploded, killing all 312 (289 passengers and 23 crew) on the Boeing and all 37 (27 passengers and 10 crew) on the Ilyushin in the world's worst mid-air crash.

LOCATION / DATE / INCIDENT                                    NO. KILLED

**6** **Paris**, France, 3 Mar 1974     346
Immediately after take-off for London, a Turkish Airlines DC-10 suffered an explosive decompression when a door burst open, and crashed at Ermenonville, north of Paris, killing all 335 passengers, including many England rugby supporters, and its crew of 11.

**7** **Off the Irish coast**, 23 Jun 1985     329
An Air India Boeing 747 on a flight from Vancouver to Delhi exploded in mid-air, probably as a result of a terrorist bomb, killing all 307 passengers and 22 crew.

**8** **Riyadh**, Saudi Arabia, 19 Aug 1980     301
Following an emergency landing a Saudia (Saudi Arabian) Airlines Lockheed TriStar caught fire. The crew were unable to open the doors and all 287 passengers and 14 crew died from smoke inhalation.

**9** **Off the Iranian coast**, 3 Jul 1988     290
An Iran Air A300 airbus was shot down in error by a missile fired by the USS *Vincennes*, which mistook the airliner for an Iranian fighter aircraft, resulting in the deaths of all 274 passengers and 16 crew. In 1996 the USA paid $61.8 million in compensation to the families of the victims.

**10** **Sirach Mountain**, Iran, 19 Feb 2003     275
An Ilyushin 76 on a flight from Zahedan to Kerman crashed into the mountain in poor weather. It was carrying 257 Revolutionary Guards and a crew of 18, none of whom survived.

*No survivors*
*The aftermath of the Charkhi Dadri disaster, the world's worst involving a mid-air collision.*

# World Tourism

## TOP 10 **TOURIST DESTINATIONS**

| COUNTRY | INTERNATIONAL VISITORS (2005) |
|---|---|
| 1 France | 76,000,000 |
| 2 Spain | 55,600,000 |
| 3 USA | 49,400,000 |
| 4 China | 46,800,000 |
| 5 Italy | 36,500,000 |
| 6 UK | 30,000,000 |
| 7 Mexico | 21,900,000 |
| 8 Germany | 21,500,000 |
| 9 Turkey | 20,300,000 |
| 10 Austria | 20,000,000 |
| *World total* | *806,000,000* |

Source: World Tourism Organization

## TOP 10 **TOURIST DESTINATIONS OF UK RESIDENTS**

| COUNTRY | VISITORS (2005) |
|---|---|
| 1 Spain | 13,837,000 |
| 2 France | 11,094,000 |
| 3 USA | 4,241,000 |
| 4 Ireland | 4,221,000 |
| 5 Italy | 3,374,000 |
| 6 Germany | 2,493,000 |
| 7 Greece | 2,435,000 |
| 8 Netherlands | 2,174,000 |
| 9 Portugal | 1,855,000 |
| 10 Belgium | 1,733,000 |
| *Total (all countries)* | *66,441,000* |

Source: National Statistics

## TOP 10 **COUNTRIES WITH THE BIGGEST INCREASE IN TOURISM**

| COUNTRY | VISITORS INCREASE 2004–05 (%) |
|---|---|
| 1 Swaziland | 82.8 |
| 2 Laos | 65.1 |
| 3 Venezuela | 45.2 |
| 4 Cambodia | 34.7 |
| 5 Honduras | 25.9 |
| 6 Turkey | 20.5 |
| 7 El Salvador | 19.5 |
| 8 Vietnam | 18.4 |
| 9 Colombia | 18.0 |
| 10 Algeria | 16.9 |
| *UK* | *8.0* |

Source: World Tourism Organization

*French leave*
*The tranquility of rural France combines with its urban attractions and culinary delights to make it the world's foremost tourist destination.*

**Fall and rise**
The appeal of such features as Venezuela's Angel Falls have prompted a substantial rise in its tourist numbers.

## TOP 10 **TOURIST EARNING COUNTRIES**

| COUNTRY | INTERNATIONAL TOURISM RECEIPTS, 2005 ($) |
|---|---|
| 1 USA | 81,680,000,000 |
| 2 Spain | 47,891,000,000 |
| 3 France | 42,276,000,000 |
| 4 Italy | 35,398,000,000 |
| 5 UK | 30,669,000,000 |
| 6 China | 29,296,000,000 |
| 7 Germany | 29,204,000,000 |
| 8 Turkey | 18,152,000,000 |
| 9 Austria | 15,467,000,000 |
| 10 Australia | 14,952,000,000 |
| *World total* | *680,000,000,000* |

Source: World Tourism Organization

## TOP 10 **TOURISM SPENDING COUNTRIES**

| COUNTRY | INTERNATIONAL TOURISM EXPENDITURE, 2005 ($) |
|---|---|
| 1 Germany | 71,000,000,000 |
| 2 USA | 69,200,000,000 |
| 3 UK | 59,600,000,000 |
| 4 Japan | 37,500,000,000 |
| 5 France | 31,200,000,000 |
| 6 Italy | 22,400,000,000 |
| 7 China | 21,800,000,000 |
| 8 Canada | 18,400,000,000 |
| 9 Russia | 17,800,000,000 |
| 10 Netherlands | 16,200,000,000 |
| *World total* | *680,000,000,000* |

Source: World Tourism Organization

**La Serenissima**
A magnet for tourists since the days of the Grand Tour, Venice remains of one of Italy's most popular cities.

**Gambling capital**
Almost 40 million people a year visit Las Vegas, placing it among the USA's principal tourist venues.

# Tourist Attractions

## TOP 10 **SPENDING VISITORS TO THE UK***

| | COUNTRY | PER VISIT AVERAGE (£) | SPENDING TOTAL |
|---|---|---|---|
| 1 | USA | 691 | 2,384,000,000 |
| 2 | Germany | 303 | 998,000,000 |
| 3 | Ireland | 315 | 895,000,000 |
| 4 | France | 239 | 796,000,000 |
| 5 | Spain | 389 | 697,000,000 |
| 6 | Australia | 702 | 647,000,000 |
| 7 | Italy | 472 | 561,000,000 |
| 8 | Netherlands | 263 | 453,000,000 |
| 9 | Canada | 547 | 438,000,000 |
| 10 | Poland | 372 | 389,000,000 |
| | *World total* | *471* | *14,248,000,000* |

* 2005, by country of residence

Source: National Statistics

## TOP 10 **COUNTRIES OF ORIGIN OF OVERSEAS VISITORS TO THE UK**

| | COUNTRY | OVERSEAS VISITORS (2005) |
|---|---|---|
| 1 | USA | 3,438,000 |
| 2 | France | 3,324,000 |
| 3 | Germany | 3,294,000 |
| 4 | Ireland | 2,806,000 |
| 5 | Spain | 1,786,000 |
| 6 | Netherlands | 1,720,000 |
| 7 | Italy | 1,186,000 |
| 8 | Belgium | 1,112,000 |
| 9 | Poland | 1,041,000 |
| 10 | Australia | 919,000 |
| | *Total (all countries)* | *29,970,000* |

Source: National Statistics

Festival Pier

## TOP 10 OLDEST AMUSEMENT PARKS IN THE UK

| PARK / LOCATION | YEAR FOUNDED |
|---|---|
| **1 Blackgang Chine Cliff Top Theme Park,** Ventnor, Isle of Wight | 1843 |
| **2 Grand Pier,** Teignmouth | 1865 |
| **3 Blackpool Central Pier,** Blackpool | 1868 |
| **4 Clacton Pier,** Clacton | 1871 |
| **5 Skegness Pier,** Skegness | 1881 |
| **6 New Walton Pier,** Walton-on-the-Naze | 1895 |
| **7 Blackpool Pleasure Beach,** Blackpool | 1896 |
| **8 Mumbles Pier,** Mumbles | 1898 |
| **9 Brighton Palace Pier,** Brighton | 1901 |
| **10 Britannia Pier,** Great Yarmouth | 1902 |

Source: National Amusement Park Historical Association

Blackgang Chine was founded by Alexander Dabell (1808–98). The first of the site's attractions displayed the skeleton of a whale. As the Isle of Wight became a popular seaside resort, further exhibits were added, including Adventureland in 1970 and Dinosaurland in 1972. The park continues to operate under the same family's ownership.

*Capital city*
*Almost half of all visitors to the UK spend at least part of their trip in London.*

## TOP 10 AREAS FOR OVERSEAS VISITORS TO THE UK*

| AREA | TOTAL SPENDING (£) | TOTAL VISITORS |
|---|---|---|
| **1 London** | 6,859,000,000 | 13,893,000 |
| **2 Lothian** (Edinburgh, etc.) | 421,000,000 | 1,199,000 |
| **3 Manchester** | 405,000,000 | 1,079,000 |
| **4 West Midlands** | 299,000,000 | 1,007,000 |
| **5 Kent** | 191,000,000 | 792,000 |
| **6 Greater Glasgow** | 228,000,000 | 775,000 |
| **7 Surrey** | 202,000,000 | 691,000 |
| **8 East Sussex** | 217,000,000 | 577,000 |
| **9 Cambridgeshire** | 216,000,000 | 573,000 |
| **10 Oxfordshire** | 220,000,000 | 557,000 |
| *England* | *12,302,000,000* | *25,323,000* |
| *Scotland* | *1,208,000,000* | *2,392,000* |
| *Wales* | *311,000,000* | *973,000* |
| *Northern Ireland* | *131,000,000* | *292,000* |
| *UK total* | *14,248,000,000* | *29,970,000* |

\* 2005

Source: National Statistics

# 10

# SPORT & LEISURE

# Winter Sports

## TOP 10 MEDAL-WINNING COUNTRIES AT THE WINTER OLYMPICS*

| | COUNTRY | G | S | B | TOTAL |
|---|---|---|---|---|---|
| 1 | USSR/Unified Team/Russia | 121 | 87 | 86 | 294 |
| 2 | Norway | 98 | 100 | 85 | 280 |
| 3 | USA | 78 | 81 | 59 | 218 |
| 4 | Germany/West Germany | 71 | 73 | 52 | 196 |
| 5 | Austria | 51 | 64 | 70 | 185 |
| 6 | Finland | 42 | 58 | 52 | 152 |
| 7 | Sweden | 46 | 33 | 45 | 124 |
| 8 | Canada | 39 | 38 | 43 | 120 |
| 9 | Switzerland | 38 | 37 | 43 | 118 |
| 10 | East Germany | 40 | 38 | 37 | 115 |

\* Up to and including the 2006 Turin Games, and also includes medals won at figure skating and ice hockey included in the Summer games prior to the launch of the Winter Olympics in 1924

G – Gold; S – Silver; B – Bronze

*Speed skater*
*American speed skater Shani Davis took gold in the 1,000 metres and silver in the 1,500 metres at Turin 2006.*

## TOP 10 LONGEST BOBSLEIGH AND TOBOGGAN TRACKS*

| | LOCATION / COUNTRY | CURVES | LENGTH M | LENGTH FT |
|---|---|---|---|---|
| 1 | Nagano, Japan | 13 | 1,762 | 5,780 |
| 2 | St Moritz, Switzerland | 13 | 1,722 | 5,649 |
| 3 | La Plagne, France | 19 | 1,507 | 4,944 |
| 4 | Calgary, Canada | 14 | 1,475 | 4,839 |
| 5 | Lake Placid, USA | 20 | 1,455 | 4,773 |
| 6 | Cesana, Italy | 19 | 1,435 | 4,708 |
| 7 | Altenberg, Germany | 17 | 1,413 | 4,635 |
| 8 | Lillehammer, Norway | 16 | 1,365 | 4,478 |
| 9 | Cortina d'Ampezzo, Italy | 11 | 1,350 | 4,429 |
| 10 | Salt Lake City, USA | 15 | 1,340 | 4,396 |

The most famous of all bobsleigh and toboggan tracks is the Cresta Run at St Moritz. Toboggan racing has taken place there since the first Grand National in 1885, which attracted 20 entrants.

\* Top-level competition tracks

## TOP 10 MOST SKIING WORLD CUP RACE WINS IN A CAREER (MEN)*

| | NAME / COUNTRY | FIRST SEASON | LAST SEASON | WINS |
|---|---|---|---|---|
| 1 | Ingemar Stenmark, Sweden | 1974–75 | 1988–89 | 86 |
| 2 | Hermann Maier, Austria | 1996–97 | 2005–06 | 53 |
| 3 | Alberto Tomba, Italy | 1987–88 | 1997–98 | 50 |
| 4 | Marc Girardelli, Luxembourg | 1982–83 | 1995–96 | 46 |
| 5 | Pirmin Zurbriggen, Switzerland | 1981–82 | 1989–90 | 40 |
| 6 = | Stephan Eberharter, Austria | 1997–98 | 2003–04 | 29 |
| = | Benjamin Raich, Austria | 1998–99 | 2006–07 | 29 |
| 8 | Phil Mahre, USA | 1976–77 | 1982–83 | 27 |
| 9 | Franz Klammer, Austria | 1973–74 | 1983–84 | 26 |
| 10 | Bode Miller, USA | 2000–01 | 2006–07 | 25 |

* Up to and including the 2006–07 season

## TOP 10 MOST WORLD FIGURE SKATING TITLES*

| | NAME / COUNTRY | MEN | WOMEN | PAIRS | DANCE | TOTAL |
|---|---|---|---|---|---|---|
| 1 = | Sonja Henie, Norway | 0 | 10 | 0 | 0 | 10 |
| = | Irina Rodnina, USSR | 0 | 0 | 10 | 0 | 10 |
| = | Ulrich Salchow, Sweden | 10 | 0 | 0 | 0 | 10 |
| 4 = | Herma Planck (née Szabo), Austria | 0 | 5 | 2 | 0 | 7 |
| = | Karl Schafer, Austria | 7 | 0 | 0 | 0 | 7 |
| 6 = | Aleksandr Gorshkov, USSR | 0 | 0 | 6 | 0 | 6 |
| = | Lyudmila Pakhomova, USSR | 0 | 0 | 0 | 6 | 6 |
| = | Aleksandr Zaitsev, USSR | 0 | 0 | 6 | 0 | 6 |
| 9 | Dick Button, USA | 5 | 0 | 0 | 0 | 5 |
| = | Lawrence Demmy, GB | 0 | 0 | 0 | 5 | 5 |
| = | Carol Heiss, USA | 0 | 5 | 0 | 0 | 5 |
| = | Jean Westwood, UK | 0 | 0 | 0 | 5 | 5 |

* Up to and including 2007

## TOP 10 MOST ALPINE SKIING OLYMPIC MEDALS*

| | NAME / COUNTRY | M/F | YEARS | G | S | B | TOTAL |
|---|---|---|---|---|---|---|---|
| 1 | Kjetil André Aamodt, Norway | M | 1992–2006 | 4 | 2 | 2 | 8 |
| 2 | Janica Kostelic, Croatia | F | 2002–2006 | 4 | 2 | 0 | 6 |
| 3 = | Vreni Schneider, Switzerland | F | 1988–94 | 3 | 1 | 1 | 5 |
| = | Alberto Tomba, Italy | M | 1988–94 | 3 | 2 | 0 | 5 |
| = | Katja Seizinger, Germany | F | 1992–98 | 3 | 0 | 2 | 5 |
| = | Lasse Kjus, Norway | M | 1994–2002 | 1 | 3 | 1 | 5 |
| = | Anja Paerson, Sweden | F | 2002–06 | 1 | 1 | 3 | 5 |
| 8 = | Hanni Wenzel, Liechtenstein | F | 1976–80 | 2 | 1 | 1 | 4 |
| = | Deborah Compagnoni, Italy | F | 1992–98 | 3 | 1 | 0 | 4 |
| = | Stephan Eberharter, Austria | M | 1998–2002 | 1 | 2 | 1 | 4 |
| = | Hermann Maier, Austria | M | 1998–2006 | 2 | 1 | 1 | 4 |

* Up to and including the 2006 Olympics

M/F – Male/Female; G – Gold; S – Silver; B – Bronze

*Downhill racer*
*Croatia's Janica Kostelic won gold in the Alpine Combined event and silver in the Super-G at Turin in 2006. This took her medal tally to six, making her the second most successful Olympic Alpine skier.*

# Summer Olympics

## TOP 10 **SUMMER OLYMPIC GOLD-MEDAL WINNERS (MEN)***

| | NAME / COUNTRY | SPORT | YEARS | GOLD MEDALS |
|---|---|---|---|---|
| **1** | = Paavo Nurmi, Finland | Athletics | 1920–28 | 9 |
| | = Mark Spitz, USA | Swimming | 1968–72 | 9 |
| | = Carl Lewis, USA | Athletics | 1984–96 | 9 |
| **4** | = Sawao Kato, Japan | Gymnastics | 1968–76 | 8 |
| | = Matt Biondi, USA | Swimming | 1984–92 | 8 |
| | = Ray Ewry, USA | Athletics | 1900–08 | 8 |
| **7** | = Nikolay Andrianov, USSR | Gymnastics | 1972–80 | 7 |
| | = Boris Shakhlin, USSR | Gymnastics | 1956–64 | 7 |
| | = Viktor Chukarin, USSR | Gymnastics | 1952–56 | 7 |
| | = Aladàr Gerevich, Hungary | Fencing | 1932–60 | 7 |

* Up to and including 2004

If his total from the 1906 Intercalated Games – the results from which are not recognized by the IOC – were included, Ray Ewry would have won a record 10 gold medals.

## TOP 10 **SUMMER OLYMPIC GOLD-MEDAL WINNERS (WOMEN)***

| | NAME / COUNTRY | SPORT | YEARS | GOLD MEDALS |
|---|---|---|---|---|
| **1** | Larissa Latynina, USSR | Gymnastics | 1956–64 | 9 |
| **2** | = Birgit Fischer (née Schmidt) East Germany/Germany | Canoeing | 1980–2004 | 8 |
| | = Jenny Thompson, USA | Swimming | 1992–2000 | 8 |
| **4** | Vera Casalavska, Czechoslovakia | Gymnastics | 1964–68 | 7 |
| **5** | = Kristin Otto, Germany | Swimming | 1988 | 6 |
| | = Amy van Dyken, USA | Swimming | 1996–2000 | 6 |
| **7** | = Agnes Keleti, Hungary | Gymnastics | 1952–56 | 5 |
| | = Nadia Comaneci, Romania | Gymnastics | 1976–80 | 5 |
| | = Polina Astakhova, USSR | Gymnastics | 1956–64 | 5 |
| | = Elisabeta Oleniuc–Lipa, Romania | Rowing | 1984–2004 | 5 |
| | = Krisztina Egerszegi, Hungary | Swimming | 1988–96 | 5 |
| | = Nelli Kim, USSR | Gymnastics | 1976–80 | 5 |

* Up to and including 2004

Larissa Latynina holds the record for winning the most Olympic medals (18), and also for the most individual medals (15). She is also one of four athletes to win nine Olympic golds, and one of only three women to win the same individual event (floor exercises) at three consecutive Olympics. She coached the Soviet team from 1967 to 1977.

## RAY EWRY

Born in Lafayette, Indiana in 1873, Ray Ewry contracted polio as a child and was confined to a wheelchair. He overcame his disabilities to win golds in the now-discontinued 'standing' jumps: high jump, long jump and triple jump, in which competitors had to jump without a run-up.

First held at the 1900 Paris Games, Ewry won all three gold medals on the same day, successfully defending his titles at St Louis in 1904.

In London in 1908 he won both the high jump and long jump and at Athens in 1906 the high jump and long jump. The standing events were discontinued after the 1912 Olympics, and Ewry's world record of 3.476 metres for the standing long jump, set in 1904, was still standing at the time of his death in 1937.

## TOP 10 **MEDAL-WINNING COUNTRIES AT THE SUMMER OLYMPICS, 1896–2004**

| | COUNTRY | GOLD | SILVER | BRONZE | TOTAL |
|---|---|---|---|---|---|
| **1** | USA | 907 | 697 | 615 | 2,219 |
| **2** | USSR/Unified Team/Russia | 525 | 436 | 409 | 1,370 |
| **3** | Germany/West Germany | 229 | 258 | 298 | 785 |
| **4** | UK | 189 | 242 | 237 | 668 |
| **5** | France | 199 | 202 | 230 | 631 |
| **6** | Italy | 189 | 154 | 168 | 511 |
| **7** | Sweden | 140 | 157 | 179 | 476 |
| **8** | Hungary | 158 | 141 | 161 | 460 |
| **9** | East Germany | 159 | 150 | 136 | 445 |
| **10** | Australia | 119 | 126 | 154 | 399 |

## THE 10 **NEWEST SUMMER OLYMPIC SPORTS**\*

| | SPORT | FIRST CONTESTED |
|---|---|---|
| **1** | = Taekwondo | 2000 |
| | = Triathlon | 2000 |
| **3** | Softball | 1996 |
| **4** | = Badminton | 1992 |
| | = Baseball | 1992 |
| **6** | Table tennis | 1988 |
| **7** | = Judo | 1964 |
| | = Volleyball | 1964 |
| **9** | = Canoeing | 1936 |
| | = Handball | 1936 |

\* By date they first became official Olympic sports

Beach volleyball was introduced at the 1996 Olympics, but the IOC recognizes it as volleyball rather than a separate sport.

*Against the odds*
*Germany's Wojtek Czyz (born Poland) won the 100-metres gold in the T42 (leg amputees) class at the 2004 Athens Olympics. Czyz lost his lower left leg in a footballing accident in 2001. He has held world records at 100 metres, 200 metres and long jump.*

## TOP 10 **MEDAL-WINNING COUNTRIES AT THE SUMMER PARALYMPICS**

The first international games for the disabled took place at Stoke Mandeville, UK, in 1952, when 130 athletes from the UK and the Netherlands competed. The first Paralympics to take place at the same venue as the Olympic Games was in Rome in 1960, since when they have been held every four years and, since Seoul in 1988, at the same venue as the Summer Olympics. Some 400 athletes from 23 countries took part in 1960, while at Athens in 2004 a total of 3,806 athletes from 136 nations competed. The USA won a record 131 gold medals in 1984.

| | COUNTRY | GOLD | SILVER | BRONZE | TOTAL |
|---|---|---|---|---|---|
| **1** | USA | 665 | 579 | 607 | 1,851 |
| **2** | UK | 470 | 468 | 454 | 1,392 |
| **3** | Germany/West Germany | 437 | 431 | 413 | 1,281 |
| **4** | Canada | 445 | 275 | 294 | 1,014 |
| **5** | France | 326 | 300 | 283 | 909 |
| **6** | Australia | 292 | 306 | 272 | 870 |
| **7** | Holland | 238 | 200 | 169 | 607 |
| **8** | Poland | 204 | 209 | 167 | 580 |
| **9** | Sweden | 206 | 203 | 145 | 554 |
| **10** | Spain | 176 | 166 | 182 | 524 |

# Athletics

## MARATHON CENTENARY

According to legend, Greek soldier Pheidippides ran from Marathon to Athens – a distance of approximately 40.8 km (25 miles) – to announce the defeat of the Persians in the Battle of Marathon – and promptly fell dead. The Marathon was included in the first Modern Olympics at Athens in 1896, with a distance of 40 km (24 miles 1,496 yd). It was slightly longer, at 40.26 km (25 miles 35 yd) in 1900, reverting to 40 km in 1904, and at the 1906 Intercalated Games revised to 41.86 km (26 miles). The Marathon at the 1908 London Olympics, starting at Windsor Castle and ending in the Olympic Stadium at Shepherd's Bush, was also scheduled for 41.86 km (26 miles). However, as the finishing line did not end in front of the Royal Box, it was moved forward by 385 yards so the royal party could get a good view. The next two Olympics saw the race run over 40.2 km (24 miles 1,725 yd) and 42.75 km (26 miles 986 yd), but in 1921 it was standardized by the International Amateur Athletic Federation (IAAF) at the 1908 London distance, and has remained so internationally ever since.

*Dorando Pietri won the 1908 Olympic Marathon, but was disqualified.*

## TOP 10 ATHLETES WITH THE MOST OLYMPIC TRACK AND FIELD GOLD MEDALS*

| | ATHLETE / COUNTRY | YEARS | GOLD MEDALS |
|---|---|---|---|
| 1 | = Paavo Nurmi, Finland | 1920–28 | 9 |
| | = Carl Lewis, USA | 1984–96 | 9 |
| 3 | Ray Ewry#, USA | 1900–08 | 8 |
| 4 | = Vilho Ritola, Finland | 1924–28 | 5 |
| | = Michael Johnson, USA | 1992–2000 | 5 |
| 6 | = Alvin Kraenzlein, USA | 1900 | 4 |
| | = Melvin Sheppard, USA | 1908–12 | 4 |
| | = Hannes Kolehmainen, Finland | 1912–20 | 4 |
| | = Jesse Owens, USA | 1936 | 4 |
| | = Fanny Blankers-Koen, Netherlands | 1948 | 4 |
| | = Harrison Dillard, USA | 1948–52 | 4 |
| | = Emil Zátopek, Czechoslovakia | 1948–52 | 4 |
| | = Betty Cuthbert, Australia | 1956–64 | 4 |
| | = Al Oerter, USA | 1956–68 | 4 |
| | = Lasse Viren, Finland | 1972–76 | 4 |
| | = Bärbel Wöckel (née Eckert), East Germany | 1976–80 | 4 |
| | = Evelyn Ashford, USA | 1984–92 | 4 |
| | = Robert Korzeniowski, Poland | 1996–2004 | 4 |

* Men 1896–2004, women 1928–2004
# Ewry also won two gold medals at the 1906 Intercalated Games

## TOP 10 FASTEST WINNING TIMES FOR THE LONDON MARATHON

| | RUNNER / COUNTRY | YEAR | TIME HR:MIN:SEC |
|---|---|---|---|
| 1 | Khalid Khannouchi, USA | 2002 | 2:05:38 |
| 2 | Antonio Pinto, Portugal | 2000 | 2:06:11 |
| 3 | Evans Rutto, Kenya | 2004 | 2:06:18 |
| 4 | Felix Lemo, Kenya | 2006 | 2:06:39 |
| 5 | Abdelkader El Mouaziz, Morocco | 2001 | 2:07:09 |
| 6 | Martin Lel, Kenya | 2005 | 2:07:35 |
| 7 | Antonio Pinto, Portugal | 1997 | 2:07:55 |
| 8 | Gezahegne Abera, Ethiopia | 2003 | 2:07:56 |
| 9 | = Abel Anton, Spain | 1998 | 2:07:57 |
| | = Abdelkader El Mouaziz, Morocco | 1999 | 2:07:57 |

The first London Marathon was run in March 1981, the idea of former Olympic steeplechaser Chris Brasher after he had competed in the 1979 New York City Marathon. The women's record was set in 2003 when Paula Radcliffe (UK) won in 2 hours 15 minutes and 25 seconds.

# TOP 10 **MOST IAAF WORLD CHAMPIONSHIP MEDALS (MEN)**

| | ATHLETE / COUNTRY | YEARS | GOLD | MEDALS SILVER | BRONZE | TOTAL |
|---|---|---|---|---|---|---|
| **1** | Carl Lewis, USA | 1983–93 | 8 | 1 | 1 | 10 |
| **2** | Michael Johnson, USA | 1991–99 | 9 | 0 | 0 | 9 |
| **3** | Haile Gebrselassie, Ethiopia | 1993–2003 | 4 | 2 | 1 | 7 |
| **4** | =Sergey Bubka, USSR/Ukraine | 1983–97 | 6 | 0 | 0 | 6 |
| | =Butch Reynolds, USA | 1987–95 | 3 | 2 | 1 | 6 |
| | =Lars Riedel, Germany | 1991–2001 | 5 | 0 | 1 | 6 |
| **7** | =Colin Jackson, UK | 1987–99 | 2 | 2 | 1 | 5 |
| | =Jan Zelezny, Czechoslovakia/ Czech Republic | 1987–2001 | 3 | 0 | 2 | 5 |
| | =Dennis Mitchell, USA | 1991–2001 | 3 | 0 | 2 | 5 |
| | =Antonio Pettigrew, USA | 1991–2001 | 4 | 1 | 0 | 5 |
| | =Jonathan Edwards, UK | 1993–2001 | 2 | 1 | 2 | 5 |
| | =Bruny Surin, Canada | 1995–99 | 2 | 2 | 1 | 5 |
| | =Allen Johnson, USA | 1995–2003 | 4 | 0 | 1 | 5 |
| | =Maurice Greene, USA | 1997–2001 | 5 | 0 | 0 | 5 |
| | =Hicham El Guerrouj, Morocco | 1997–2003 | 4 | 1 | 0 | 5 |

First held at Helsinki in 1983, the IAAF (International Amateur Athletics Federation) World Championships in Athletics were originally held every four years, but since 1993 have been held every two years. Helsinki hosted the 10th anniversary championships in 2005. A record 1,882 athletes competed at Athens in 1997.

# TOP 10 **MOST IAAF WORLD CHAMPIONSHIP MEDALS (WOMEN)**

| | ATHLETE / COUNTRY | YEARS | GOLD | MEDALS SILVER | BRONZE | TOTAL |
|---|---|---|---|---|---|---|
| **1** | Merlene Ottey, Jamaica | 1983–95 | 3 | 4 | 7 | 14 |
| **2** | Jearl Miles-Clark, USA | 1991–2003 | 4 | 3 | 2 | 9 |
| **3** | =Gwen Torrence, USA | 1991–95 | 3 | 4 | 1 | 8 |
| | =Gail Devers, USA | 1993–2001 | 5 | 3 | 0 | 8 |
| **5** | Marion Jones, USA | 1997–2001 | 5 | 1 | 1 | 7 |
| **6** | =Heike Daute (née Dreschler), GDR/Germany | 1983–93 | 2 | 2 | 2 | 6 |
| | =Yuliya Pechonkina Nosova, Russia | 2001–05 | 2 | 2 | 2 | 6 |
| **8** | =Maria Lourdes Mutola, Mozambique | 1993–2003 | 3 | 1 | 1 | 5 |
| | =Inger Miller, USA | 1997–2003 | 3 | 2 | 0 | 5 |
| | =Eunice Barber, France | 1999–2005 | 2 | 2 | 1 | 5 |

*Age no barrier*
*In winning the 200 metres at the 1995 World Championships, Merlene Ottey became the oldest gold medallist at 35 years 92 days.*

# Boxing

## TOP 10 **CURRENT WORLD CHAMPIONS WITH THE LONGEST CONTINUOUS REIGN***

| BOXER / COUNTRY / WEIGHT | DATE TITLE WON |
|---|---|
| **1 Joe Calzaghe**, UK<br>WBO Super-middleweight | 11 Oct 1997 |
| **2 Pongsaklek Wonjongkam**, Thailand<br>WBC Flyweight | 2 Mar 2001 |
| **3 Antonio Margarito**, Mexico<br>WBO Welterweight | 16 Mar 2002 |
| **4 Omar Andrés Narváez**, Argentina<br>WBO Flyweight | 13 Jul 2002 |
| **5 Rafael Márquez**, Mexico<br>IBF Bantamweight | 15 Feb 2003 |
| **6 Ivan Calderón**, Puerto Rico<br>WBO Strawweight | 3 May 2003 |
| **7 Lorenzo Parra**, Venezuela<br>WBA Flyweight | 6 Dec 2003 |
| **8 Zsolt Erdei**, Hungary<br>WBO Light-heavyweight | 17 Jan 2004 |
| **9 Yutaka Niida**, Japan<br>WBA Strawweight | 3 Jul 2004 |
| **10 Juan Díaz**, USA<br>WBA Lightweight | 17 Jul 2004 |

* As at 1 January 2007

## THE 10 **LATEST WBA HEAVYWEIGHT CHAMPIONS***

| | | REIGN(S) | |
|---|---|---|---|
| BOXER / COUNTRY | | FROM | TO |
| **1 Nikolay Valuev**, Russia | | 17 Dec 2005 | Present |
| **2 John Ruiz**, Puerto Rico | | 24 Feb 2004<br>2 Mar 2001 | 17 Dec 2005<br>1 Mar 2003 |
| **3 Roy Jones Jr**, USA | | 1 Mar 2003 | 20 Feb 2004 |
| **4 Evander Holyfield**, USA | | 12 Aug 2000<br>9 Nov 1996<br>6 Nov 1993<br>25 Oct 1990 | 2 Mar 2001<br>13 Nov 1999<br>22 Apr 1994<br>13 Nov 1992 |
| **5 Lennox Lewis**, UK | | 13 Nov 1999 | 29 Apr 2000 |
| **6 Mike Tyson**, USA | | 7 Sep 1996<br>7 Mar 1987 | 9 Nov 1996<br>11 Feb 1990 |
| **7 Bruce Seldon**, USA | | 8 Apr 1995 | 7 Sep 1996 |
| **8 George Foreman**, USA | | 5 Nov 1994<br>22 Jan 1973 | 4 Mar 1995<br>30 Oct 1974 |
| **9 Michael Moorer**, USA | | 22 Apr 1994 | 5 Nov 1994 |
| **10 Riddick Bowe**, USA | | 13 Nov 1992 | 6 Nov 1993 |

* Last 10 different men to hold the WBA title, as at 1 January 2007

The WBA (World Boxing Association) started life in 1921 as the NBA (National Boxing Association). It changed its name in 1962.

*Long-reigning champ*
*Joe Calzaghe won all 42 of his professional fights up to 2007.*

## THE 10 **LATEST WBC HEAVYWEIGHT CHAMPIONS***

| | | REIGN(S) | |
|---|---|---|---|
| BOXER / COUNTRY | | FROM | TO |
| **1 Oleg Maskaev**, Kazakhstan | | 12 Aug 2006 | Present |
| **2 Hasim Rahman**, USA | | 9 Nov 2005<br>22 Apr 2001 | 12 Aug 2006<br>17 Nov 2001 |
| **3 Vitali Klitschko**, Ukraine | | 24 Apr 2004 | 9 Nov 2005 |
| **4 Lennox Lewis**, UK | | 17 Nov 2001<br>7 Feb 1997<br>14 Dec 1992 | 6 Feb 2004<br>22 Apr 2001<br>24 Sep 1994 |
| **5 Mike Tyson**, USA | | 16 Mar 1996<br>22 Nov 1986 | 24 Sep 1996<br>11 Feb 1990 |
| **6 Frank Bruno**, UK | | 2 Sep 1995 | 16 Mar 1996 |
| **7 Oliver McCall**, USA | | 24 Sep 1994 | 2 Sep 1995 |
| **8 Riddick Bowe**, USA | | 13 Nov 1992 | 14 Dec 1992 |
| **9 Evander Holyfield**, USA | | 25 Oct 1990 | 13 Nov 1992 |
| **10 James 'Buster' Douglas**, USA | | 11 Feb 1990 | 25 Oct 1990 |

* Last 10 different men to hold the WBC title, as at 1 January 2007

The WBC (World Boxing Council) was formed in Mexico on 14 February 1963 in response to opposition from many bodies, including the British Boxing Board of Control, to the WBA's assuming 'world' control of boxing.

## TOP 10 **LONGEST WORLD CHAMPIONSHIP FIGHTS**

| | BOXERS (WINNERS FIRST) | WEIGHT | DATE | ROUNDS |
|---|---|---|---|---|
| **1** | Ike Weir v. Frank Murphy | Featherweight | 31 Mar 1889 | 80 |
| **2** | Jack McAuliffe v. Jem Carney | Lightweight | 16 Nov 1887 | 74 |
| **3** | Paddy Duffy v. Tom Meadows | Welterweight | 29 Mar 1889 | 45 |
| **4** | Joe Gans v. Battling Nelson | Lightweight | 3 Sep 1906 | 42 |
| **5** | = George Dixon v. Johnny Murphy | Bantamweight | 23 Oct 1890 | 40 |
| | = Ad Wolgast v. Battling Nelson | Lightweight | 22 Feb 1910 | 40 |
| **7** | = George LaBlanche v. Jack Dempsey | Middleweight | 27 Aug 1889 | 32 |
| | = Stanley Ketchel v. Joe Thomas | Middleweight | 2 Sep 1907 | 32 |
| **9** | Jack Dempsey v. Billy McCarthy | Middleweight | 18 Feb 1890 | 28 |
| **10** | Jack Dempsey v. Jack Fogarty | Middleweight | 3 Feb 1886 | 27 |

All these were World Championship contests under the Marquess of Queensberry Rules (published in 1866), which stipulate the length of a round at three minutes. Prior to the Rules, a round ended when a fighter was knocked down, and consequently a great number of fights in the bare-knuckle days consisted of many rounds, the longest being the 276-round contest between Jack Jones and Patsy Tunney in Cheshire in 1825. The fight lasted 4 hours 30 minutes. The longest heavyweight contest under Queensberry Rules was the Jess Willard v. Jack Johnson contest on 5 April 1915, which lasted 26 rounds.

*Joe Louis*
*Joe Louis held the world heavyweight title from 22 June 1937, after beating James J. Braddock, until his retirement in 1949.*

### 100 Years Ago: Jack Johnson

On 26 December 1908, Jack Johnson became the heavyweight champion of the world, and the first black fighter to hold the title, gaining it from reigning champion Tommy Burns (Canada). A series of 'Great White Hopes' challenged Johnson, but he held his title until 1915, when he was defeated by Jess Willard.

## TOP 10 **MOST WINS IN WORLD HEAVYWEIGHT TITLE FIGHTS**\*

| | BOXER / COUNTRY# | BOUTS | WINS |
|---|---|---|---|
| **1** | Joe Louis | 27 | 26 |
| **2** | Muhammad Ali/ Cassius Clay | 25 | 22 |
| **3** | Larry Holmes | 25 | 21 |
| **4** | Lennox Lewis, UK | 22 | 17 |
| **5** | = Tommy Burns, Canada | 13 | 12 |
| | = Mike Tyson | 16 | 12 |
| **7** | = Joe Frazier | 11 | 10 |
| | = Evander Holyfield | 16 | 10 |
| | = Jack Johnson | 11 | 10 |
| **10** | Ezzard Charles | 13 | 9 |

\* As at 1 January 2007
# USA unless otherwise stated

This list also represents the Top 10 most World Heavyweight title bouts, with the exception of Floyd Patterson (USA), who would be in 9th place with 12 fights. James J. Jeffries, with eight wins from eight fights, represents the best record of boxers undefeated in World Heavyweight Championship fights.

# Basketball

## TOP 10 **BEST POINTS AVERAGES PER GAME IN THE NBA***

| | PLAYER | YEARS | GAMES | POINTS | AVERAGE |
|---|---|---|---|---|---|
| 1 = | Michael Jordan | 1984–2003 | 1,072 | 32,292 | 30.1 |
| = | Wilt Chamberlain | 1959–73 | 1,045 | 31,419 | 30.1 |
| 3 | Allen Iverson | 1996–2006 | 682 | 19,115 | 28.0 |
| 4 | Elgin Baylor | 1958–72 | 846 | 23,149 | 27.4 |
| 5 | Jerry West | 1960–74 | 932 | 25,192 | 27.0 |
| 6 | Bob Pettit | 1954–65 | 792 | 20,880 | 26.4 |
| 7 | Shaquille O'Neal | 1992–2006 | 941 | 24,764 | 26.3 |
| 8 | George Gervin | 1976–86 | 791 | 20,708 | 26.2 |
| 9 | Oscar Robertson | 1960–74 | 1,040 | 26,710 | 25.7 |
| 10 | Karl Malone | 1985–2004 | 1,476 | 36,928 | 25.0 |

* As at the end of the 2005–06 season

Source: NBA

## TOP 10 **ALL-TIME CAREER SCORING LEADERS IN THE NBA***

| | PLAYER | YEARS | GAMES | POINTS |
|---|---|---|---|---|
| 1 | Kareem Abdul-Jabbar[#] | 1969–89 | 1,560 | 38,387 |
| 2 | Karl Malone | 1985–2004 | 1,476 | 36,928 |
| 3 | Michael Jordan | 1984–2003 | 1,072 | 32,292 |
| 4 | Wilt Chamberlain | 1959–73 | 1,045 | 31,419 |
| 5 | Moses Malone | 1976–95 | 1,329 | 27,409 |
| 6 | Elvin Hayes | 1968–84 | 1,303 | 27,313 |
| 7 | Hakeem Olajuwon | 1984–2002 | 1,238 | 26,946 |
| 8 | Oscar Robertson | 1960–74 | 1,040 | 26,710 |
| 9 | Dominique Wilkins | 1982–99 | 1,074 | 26,668 |
| 10 | John Havlicek | 1962–78 | 1,270 | 26,395 |

* As at the end of the 2005–06 season
# Lew Alcindor in 1971

Source: NBA

## TOP 10 **PLAYERS MOST FREQUENTLY LEADING THE ANNUAL SCORING LIST***

| | PLAYERS / TEAM(S) | YEARS | FREQUENCY |
|---|---|---|---|
| 1 | Michael Jordan, Chicago Bulls | 1987–98 | 10 |
| 2 | Wilt Chamberlain, San Francisco Warriors/Philadelphia Warriors | 1960–66 | 7 |
| 3 = | George Gervin, San Antonio Spurs | 1978–82 | 4 |
| = | Allen Iverson, Philadelphia 76ers | 1999–2005 | 4 |
| 5 = | George Mikan, Minneapolis Lakers | 1949–51 | 3 |
| = | Neil Johnston, Philadelphia Warriors | 1953–55 | 3 |
| = | Bob McAdoo, Buffalo Braves | 1974–76 | 3 |
| 8 = | Paul Arizin, Philadelphia Warriors | 1952–57 | 2 |
| = | Bob Pettit, St Louis Hawks | 1956–59 | 2 |
| = | Kareem Abdul-Jabbar[#], Milwaukee Bucks | 1971–72 | 2 |
| = | Adrian Dantley, Utah Jazz | 1981–84 | 2 |
| = | Shaquille O'Neal, Orlando Magic/ Los Angeles Lakers | 1995–2000 | 2 |
| = | Tracy McGrady, Orlando Magic | 2003–04 | 2 |

* As at the end of the 2005–06 season
# Lew Alcindor in 1971

Up to the 1969–70 season the scoring leader was based on the player scoring the most points, but since then it has been based on points average per game.

*Michael Jordan*
Considered one of the greatest basketball players of all time, he won five NBA titles with the Chicago Bulls.

*Charlotte Bobcats*
*The Charlotte Bobcats joined the NBA in 2004, two years after Charlotte's other team, the Hornets, relocated to New Orleans. One of the Bobcats' co-owners is former player Michael Jordan.*

# THE 10 TEAMS WITH THE LONGEST DROUGHT SINCE THEIR LAST APPEARANCE IN THE NBA FINAL*

| | TEAM | LAST APPEARANCE IN NBA FINAL |
|---|---|---|
| 1 | Sacramento Kings | 1951 |
| 2 | Atlanta Hawks | 1961 |
| 3 | = Cleveland Cavaliers | 1971# |
| | = Los Angeles Clippers | 1971# |
| 5 | Milwaukee Bucks | 1974 |
| 6 | Golden State Warriors | 1975 |
| 7 | Denver Nuggets | 1977# |
| 8 | Washington Wizards | 1979 |
| 9 | Boston Celtics | 1987 |
| 10 | New Orleans Hornets | 1989# |

* Up to and including the 2006 Final
# Team has never appeared in the Final – year shows the season they joined the NBA and hence eligible for Final

# THE 10 NEWEST CURRENT NBA TEAMS

| | TEAM | FIRST SEASON IN THE NBA |
|---|---|---|
| 1 | Charlotte Bobcats | 2004–05 |
| 2 | = Memphis Grizzlies | 1995–96 |
| | = Toronto Raptors | 1995–96 |
| 4 | = Minnesota Timberwolves | 1989–90 |
| | = Orlando Magic | 1989–90 |
| 6 | = Miami Heat | 1988–89 |
| | = New Orleans/Oklahoma City Hornets | 1988–89 |
| 8 | Dallas Mavericks | 1980–81 |
| 9 | Utah Jazz | 1974–75 |
| 10 | = Cleveland Cavaliers | 1970–71 |
| | = Los Angeles Clippers | 1970–71 |
| | = Portland Trail Blazers | 1970–71 |

The Oklahoma City Hornets entered the League as the Charlotte Hornets in 1988 and moved to New Orleans in 2002. Because of Hurricane Katrina, they moved to Oklahoma City for the remainder of the 2005–06 season and also for the 2006–07 season, becoming known as the New Orleans/Oklahoma City Hornets.

# TOP 10 MEDAL-WINNING COUNTRIES IN THE BASKETBALL WORLD CHAMPIONSHIPS*

| | COUNTRY | GOLD | SILVER | BRONZE | TOTAL |
|---|---|---|---|---|---|
| 1 | = USA | 3 | 3 | 4 | 10 |
| | = Yugoslavia | 5 | 3 | 2 | 10 |
| 3 | USSR/Russia | 3 | 5 | 1 | 9 |
| 4 | Brazil | 2 | 2 | 1 | 5 |
| 5 | = Argentina | 1 | 1 | 0 | 2 |
| | = Chile | 0 | 0 | 2 | 2 |
| 7 | = Croatia | 0 | 0 | 1 | 1 |
| | = Germany | 0 | 0 | 1 | 1 |
| | = Greece | 0 | 1 | 0 | 1 |
| | = Philippines | 0 | 0 | 1 | 1 |
| | = Spain | 1 | 0 | 0 | 1 |

* Up to and including the 2006 Championships

Correctly known as the FIBA World Championship, the first Basketball World Championship was held at Buenos Aires, Argentina, in 1950. It is now held every four years and since 1967 the winning nation has received the Naismith Trophy. The Women's World Championship was first held at Santiago, Chile, in 1953.

# American Football

## TOP 10 MOST POINTS IN AN NFL CAREER*

| | PLAYER | YEARS | POINTS |
|---|---|---|---|
| 1 | Morten Andersen | 1982–2006 | 2,445 |
| 2 | Gary Anderson | 1982–2004 | 2,434 |
| 3 | George Blanda | 1949–75 | 2,002 |
| 4 | John Carney | 1988–2006 | 1,749 |
| 5 | Norm Johnson | 1982–99 | 1,736 |
| 6 | Matt Stover | 1991–2006 | 1,715 |
| 7 | Nick Lowery | 1980–96 | 1,711 |
| 8 | Jan Stenerud | 1967–85 | 1,699 |
| 9 | Jason Elam | 1993–2006 | 1,672 |
| 10 | Eddie Murray | 1980–2000 | 1,594 |

* To the end of the 2006 regular season

## TOP 10 MOST PASSING YARDS IN THE NFL*

| | PLAYER | YEARS | YARDS |
|---|---|---|---|
| 1 | Dan Marino | 1983–99 | 61,361 |
| 2 | Brett Favre | 1991–2006 | 57,500 |
| 3 | John Elway | 1983–98 | 51,475 |
| 4 | Warren Moon | 1984–2000 | 49,325 |
| 5 | Fran Tarkenton | 1961–78 | 47,003 |
| 6 | Vinny Testaverde | 1987–2006 | 45,281 |
| 7 | Drew Bledsoe | 1993–2006 | 44,611 |
| 8 | Dan Fouts | 1973–87 | 43,040 |
| 9 | Joe Montana | 1979–94 | 40,551 |
| 10 | Johnny Unitas | 1956–73 | 40,239 |

* To the end of the 2006 regular season

## TOP 10 MOST POINTS IN A SUPER BOWL CAREER

| | PLAYER / TEAM | GAMES | TD* | FG* | PAT* | POINTS |
|---|---|---|---|---|---|---|
| 1 | Jerry Rice, San Francisco 49ers/Oakland Raiders | 4 | 8 | 0 | 0 | 48 |
| 2 | Adam Vinatieri, New England Patriots, Indianapolis Colts | 5 | 0 | 7 | 11 | 32 |
| 3 | Emmitt Smith, Dallas Cowboys | 3 | 5 | 0 | 0 | 30 |
| 4 = | Roger Craig, San Francisco 49ers | 3 | 4 | 0 | 0 | 24 |
| = | John Elway, Denver Broncos | 5 | 4 | 0 | 0 | 24 |
| = | Franco Harris, Pittsburgh Steelers | 4 | 4 | 0 | 0 | 24 |
| = | Thurman Thomas, Buffalo Bills | 4 | 4 | 0 | 0 | 24 |
| 8 | Ray Wersching, San Francisco 49ers | 2 | 0 | 5 | 7 | 22 |
| 9 | Don Chandler, Green Bay Packers | 2 | 0 | 4 | 8 | 20 |
| 10 = | Cliff Branch, Los Angeles Raiders | 3 | 3 | 0 | 0 | 18 |
| = | Terrell Davis, Denver Broncos | 2 | 3 | 0 | 0 | 18 |
| = | Antonio Freeman, Green Bay Packers | 2 | 3 | 0 | 0 | 18 |
| = | John Stallworth, Pittsburgh Steelers | 4 | 3 | 0 | 0 | 18 |
| = | Lynn Swann, Pittsburgh Steelers | 4 | 3 | 0 | 0 | 18 |
| = | Ricky Watters, San Francisco 49ers | 1 | 3 | 0 | 0 | 18 |

* TD – Touchdowns; FG – Field Goals; PAT – Point after touchdown

## TOP 10 MOST CONFERENCE CHAMPIONSHIPS*

| | TEAM | CURRENT CONFERENCE | FIRST WIN | LAST WIN | TOTAL |
|---|---|---|---|---|---|
| 1 | Green Bay Packers | NFC | 1936 | 1997 | 10 |
| 2 = | Chicago Bears | NFC | 1933 | 2006 | 8 |
| = | Dallas Cowboys | NFC | 1970 | 1995 | 8 |
| 4 | Washington Redskins | NFC | 1937 | 1991 | 7 |
| 5 = | Buffalo Bills | AFC | 1964 | 1994 | 6 |
| = | Denver Broncos | AFC | 1977 | 1998 | 6 |
| = | New York Giants | NFC | 1934 | 2000 | 6 |
| = | Pittsburgh Steelers | AFC | 1974 | 2005 | 6 |
| 9 = | Miami Dolphins | AFC | 1971 | 1984 | 5 |
| = | San Francisco 49ers | NFC | 1981 | 1994 | 5 |
| = | Cleveland/LA/ St Louis Rams | NFC | 1945 | 2001 | 5 |
| = | Oakland/LA Raiders | AFC | 1967 | 2002 | 5 |
| = | Philadelphia Eagles | NFC | 1948 | 2004 | 5 |
| = | New England Patriots | AFC | 1985 | 2004 | 5 |

* Up to and including the 2006 season

Championship games were introduced in 1933, when the National Football League (NFL) divided the teams into Eastern and Western Divisions. The Bears beat the Giants 23–21 in the first Championship game. The AFL (American Football League) was formed in 1960 and following the merger of the NFL and AFL in 1969, the two present Conferences, NFC (National Football Conference) and AFC (American Football Conference), were created. Each Conference is currently divided into four divisions – North, South, East and West – each containing four teams. Unlike the National Hockey League, National Basketball Association and Major League Baseball, there are no teams based in Canada.

## TOP 10 LONGEST DROUGHTS SINCE A SUPER BOWL APPEARANCE*

| | TEAM | LAST APPEARANCE |
|---|---|---|
| 1 | New York Jets | 1969 |
| 2 | Kansas City Chiefs | 1970 |
| 3 | Minnesota Vikings | 1977 |
| 4 | Miami Dolphins | 1985 |
| 5 | Cincinnati Bengals | 1989 |
| 6 | Washington Redskins | 1992 |
| 7 | Buffalo Bills | 1994 |
| 8 = | San Diego Chargers | 1995 |
| = | San Francisco 49ers | 1995 |
| 10 | Dallas Cowboys | 1996 |

* Of all current NFL teams who have appeared in the Super Bowl

Of current NFL teams, Arizona Cardinals, Cleveland Browns, Detroit Lions, Houston Texans, Jacksonville Jaguars and New Orleans Saints have never appeared in the Super Bowl.

## TOP 10 MOST SUPER BOWL APPEARANCES

| | TEAM | WON | LOST | APPEARANCES |
|---|---|---|---|---|
| 1 | Dallas Cowboys | 5 | 3 | 8 |
| 2 = | Denver Broncos | 2 | 4 | 6 |
| = | Pittsburgh Steelers | 5 | 1 | 6 |
| 4 = | Miami Dolphins | 2 | 3 | 5 |
| = | New England Patriots | 3 | 2 | 5 |
| = | Oakland/LA Raiders | 3 | 2 | 5 |
| = | San Francisco 49ers | 5 | 0 | 5 |
| = | Washington Redskins | 3 | 2 | 5 |
| 9 = | Buffalo Bills | 0 | 4 | 4 |
| = | Green Bay Packers | 3 | 1 | 4 |
| = | Minnesota Vikings | 0 | 4 | 4 |

Dallas Cowboys, with 221, have also scored more points in the Super Bowl than any other team. Denver Broncos have conceded the most – 206.

*Special rice*
*Jerry Rice won three Super Bowl rings with the 49ers, and in winning the Super Bowl MVP in 1988 became only the third wide receiver to win the award.*

# International Soccer

## TOP 10 GOALSCORERS IN THE UEFA EUROPEAN CHAMPIONSHIP*

| | PLAYER / COUNTRY | YEARS | GOALS |
|---|---|---|---|
| 1 | Michel Platini, France | 1984 | 9 |
| 2 | Alan Shearer, England | 1996–2000 | 7 |
| 3 | Patrick Kluivert, Netherlands | 1996–2000 | 6 |
| 4 | = Marco van Basten, Netherlands | 1988 | 5 |
| | = Jürgen Klinsmann, West Germany/Germany | 1988–96 | 5 |
| | = Savo Milosevic, Yugoslavia | 2000 | 5 |
| | = Nuno Gomes, Portugal | 2000–04 | 5 |
| | = Thierry Henry, France | 2000–04 | 5 |
| | = Zinedine Zidane, France | 2000–04 | 5 |
| | = Milan Baros, Czech Republic | 2004 | 5 |

\* In the final stages, 1960–2004

*Italian victory*
*Fabio Cannavaro holds aloft the World Cup after Italy's 2006 defeat of France on penalties.*

## TOP 10 WORLD CUP GOALSCORERS*

| | PLAYER / COUNTRY | YEARS | GOALS |
|---|---|---|---|
| 1 | Ronaldo, Brazil | 1998–2006 | 15 |
| 2 | Gerd Müller, West Germany | 1970–74 | 14 |
| 3 | Just Fontaine, France | 1958 | 13 |
| 4 | Pelé, Brazil | 1958–70 | 12 |
| 5 | = Sándor Kocsis, Hungary | 1954 | 11 |
| | = Jürgen Klinsmann, Germany | 1990–98 | 11 |
| 7 | = Helmut Rahn, West Germany | 1954–58 | 10 |
| | = Teófilio Cubillas, Peru | 1970–78 | 10 |
| | = Grzegorz Lato, Poland | 1974–82 | 10 |
| | = Gary Lineker, England | 1986–90 | 10 |
| | = Gabriel Batistuta, Argentina | 1994–2002 | 10 |
| | = Miroslav Klose, Germany | 2002–2006 | 10 |

\* In the final stages, 1930–2006

Fontaine's 13 goals in the 1958 finals is a record for one tournament.

## TOP 10 INTERNATIONAL GOALSCORERS*

| | PLAYER / COUNTRY | YEARS | MATCHES | GOALS |
|---|---|---|---|---|
| 1 | Ali Daei, Iran | 1993–2006 | 149 | 109 |
| 2 | Ferenc Puskás, Hungary/Spain | 1945–56 | 89 | 84 |
| 3 | Pelé, Brazil | 1957–71 | 92 | 77 |
| 4 | Sándor Kocsis, Hungary | 1948–56 | 68 | 75 |
| 5 | Bashar Abdullah, Kuwait | 1996–2005 | 132 | 74 |
| 6 | Hossam Hassan, Egypt | 1985–2006 | 170 | 69 |
| 7 | Gerd Müller, West Germany | 1966–74 | 62 | 68 |
| 8 | = Majed Abdullah, Saudi Arabia | 1978–94 | 139 | 67 |
| | = Stern John, Trinidad & Tobago | 1995–2006 | 100 | 67 |
| 10 | Kiatisuk Senamuang, Thailand | 1993–2006 | 121 | 65 |

* As at 1 January 2007

The most by a British Isles player is 49, Bobby Charlton (England) 1958–70. Vivian Woodward of England scored 73 goals in 53 matches between 1903 and 1914. However, 44 of them were in Amateur Internationals, which are not recognized as full international goals.

## TOP 10 COUNTRIES IN THE FIFA WORLD CUP*

| | COUNTRY | 1ST | 2ND | 3RD | 4TH | POINTS |
|---|---|---|---|---|---|---|
| 1 | = Brazil | 5 | 2 | 2 | 1 | 31 |
| | = West Germany/Germany | 3 | 4 | 3 | 1 | 31 |
| 3 | Italy | 4 | 2 | 1 | 1 | 25 |
| 4 | Argentina | 2 | 2 | 0 | 0 | 14 |
| 5 | France | 1 | 1 | 2 | 1 | 12 |
| 6 | Uruguay | 2 | 0 | 0 | 2 | 10 |
| 7 | Sweden | 0 | 1 | 2 | 1 | 8 |
| 8 | Netherlands | 0 | 2 | 0 | 1 | 7 |
| 9 | = Czechoslovakia | 0 | 2 | 0 | 0 | 6 |
| | = Hungary | 0 | 2 | 0 | 0 | 6 |

* In the FIFA World Cup 1930–2006, based on 4 points for winning the trophy, 3 points for finishing as runners-up, 2 points for finishing 3rd and 1 point for finishing 4th

Source: FIFA

Up to the end of the 2006 tournament, a total of 708 matches had been played and 2,063 goals scored at an average of 2.91 per game. A total of 76 different teams have competed and 30,930,108 spectators have watched World Cup matches at an average of 43,687 per game. The best-placed UK team is England, with 5 points from 1 win and a 4th place.

## TOP 10 COUNTRIES IN THE UEFA EUROPEAN CHAMPIONSHIP*

| | COUNTRY | WINS | RUNNER-UP | SEMI-FINAL | POINTS |
|---|---|---|---|---|---|
| 1 | West Germany/Germany | 3 | 2 | 1 | 14 |
| 2 | Soviet Union | 1 | 3 | 1 | 10 |
| 3 | = France | 2 | 0 | 2 | 8 |
| | = Czechoslovakia/Czech Republic | 1 | 1 | 3 | 8 |
| 5 | = Italy | 1 | 1 | 2 | 7 |
| | = Netherlands | 1 | 0 | 4 | 7 |
| 7 | = Denmark | 1 | 0 | 2 | 5 |
| | = Spain | 1 | 1 | 0 | 5 |
| | = Yugoslavia | 0 | 2 | 1 | 5 |
| 10 | Portugal | 0 | 1 | 2 | 4 |

* Based on 3 points for winning the tournament, 2 points for being the runner–up, and 1 point for being a losing semi-finalist, 1960–2004

The leading UK country is England, with two points from two semi-final appearances. The European Championship, then the European Nations' Cup, was inaugurated in 1958, with the first final being played two years later, when the Soviet Union beat Yugoslavia 2-1 after extra time in Paris.

## TOP 10 INTERNATIONAL APPEARANCES*

| | PLAYER/COUNTRY | YEARS | APPEARANCES |
|---|---|---|---|
| 1 | Mohamed Al-Deayea, Saudi Arabia | 1990–2006 | 181 |
| 2 | Claudio Suárez, Mexico | 1992–2006 | 178 |
| 3 | Hossam Hassan, Egypt | 1985–2006 | 170 |
| 4 | = Adnan Kh. Al-Talyani, UAE | 1984–97 | 164 |
| | = Cobi Jones, US | 1992–2004 | 164 |
| 6 | Sami Al-Jaber, Saudi Arabia | 1992–2006 | 163 |
| 7 | Lothar Matthäus, West Germany/Germany | 1980–2000 | 150 |
| 8 | Ali Daei, Iran | 1993–2006 | 149 |
| 9 | Martin Reim, Estonia | 1992–2006 | 148 |
| 10 | = Thomas Ravelli, Sweden | 1981–97 | 143 |
| | = Mohammed Al-Khilaiwi, Saudi Arabia | 1990–2001 | 143 |
| | = Marko Kristal, Estonia | 1992–2005 | 143 |

* As at 1 January 2007

Mohamed Al-Deayea made his international debut in 1990 and in 1996 helped his country win the Asian Cup. He played in the 1994, 1998 and 2002 World Cups and was a squad member in 2006. The record for a British Isles player is 125, Peter Shilton (England) 1970–90.

# Football

## THE 10 MOST FA CUP FINAL APPEARANCES*

| | TEAM | YEAR OF FIRST FINAL | YEAR OF LAST FINAL | TOTAL |
|---|---|---|---|---|
| 1 | = Arsenal | 1927 | 2005 | 17 |
| | = Manchester United | 1909 | 2005 | 17 |
| 3 | = Liverpool | 1914 | 2006 | 13 |
| | = Newcastle United | 1905 | 1999 | 13 |
| 5 | Everton | 1893 | 1995 | 12 |
| 6 | = Aston Villa | 1887 | 2000 | 10 |
| | = West Bromwich Albion | 1886 | 1968 | 10 |
| 8 | Tottenham Hotspur | 1901 | 1991 | 9 |
| 9 | = Blackburn Rovers | 1882 | 1960 | 8 |
| | = Manchester City | 1904 | 1981 | 8 |
| | = Wolverhampton Wanderers | 1889 | 1960 | 8 |

\* FA Cup Finals 1872–2006

## THE MUNICH AIR CRASH

One of the blackest days in British sporting history was 6 February 1958. Having won two consecutive League titles, Manchester United were heading for their third consecutive title and chasing the dream of manager Matt Busby to become the 'Kings of Europe'. Returning from a match in Belgrade, the BEA Elizabethan carrying the United team, officials and members of the press, crashed on take-off after refuelling at Munich airport, killing 28 passengers, including eight players. Captain Roger Byrne along with Geoff Bent, Eddie Colman, Mark Jones, David Pegg, Bill Whelan and Tommy Taylor all died, while Duncan Edwards died two weeks later.

*Albert Scanlon and Dennis Viollet recover after the Munich disaster.*

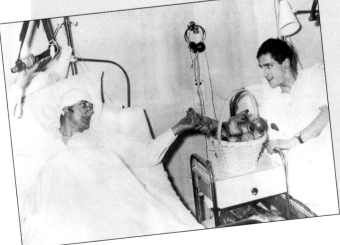

*Arsenal's top scorer*
*On 17 October 2005 Thierry Henry broke Ian Wright's career record of 185 goals for Arsenal when he scored two against Sparta Prague.*

## TOP 10 GOALSCORERS FOR UK INTERNATIONAL TEAMS

| | PLAYER / COUNTRY | YEARS | GOALS |
|---|---|---|---|
| 1 | Bobby Charlton, England | 1958–70 | 49 |
| 2 | Gary Lineker, England | 1984–92 | 48 |
| 3 | Jimmy Greaves, England | 1959–67 | 44 |
| 4 | Michael Owen, England | 1997–2006 | 36 |
| 5 | = Tom Finney, England | 1946–58 | 30 |
| | = Nat Lofthouse, England | 1950–58 | 30 |
| | = Denis Law, Scotland | 1959–74 | 30 |
| | = Kenny Dalglish, Scotland | 1972–87 | 30 |
| | = Alan Shearer, England | 1992–2000 | 30 |
| 10 | Vivian Woodward, England | 1903–11 | 29 |
| | *Wales: Ian Rush* | *1980–96* | *28* |
| | *Northern Ireland: David Healy* | *2000–06* | *24* |

\* As at 1 January 2007

## TOP 10 FA PREMIERSHIP GOALSCORERS*

| | PLAYERS | CLUB(S) | GOALS |
|---|---|---|---|
| **1** | Alan Shearer | Blackburn Rovers, Newcastle United | 260 |
| **2** | Andy Cole | Newcastle United, Manchester United, Blackburn Rovers, Fulham, Manchester City, Portsmouth | 188 |
| **3** | Thierry Henry | Arsenal | 171 |
| **4** | Robbie Fowler | Liverpool, Leeds United, Manchester City | 161 |
| **5** | Les Ferdinand | Queens Park Rangers, Newcastle United, Tottenham Hotspur, West Ham United, Leicester City, Bolton Wanderers | 149 |
| **6** | Teddy Sheringham | Nottingham Forest, Tottenham Hotspur, Manchester United, Portsmouth, West Ham United | 146 |
| **7** | Jimmy Floyd Hasselbaink | Leeds United, Chelsea, Middlesbrough, Charlton Athletic | 126 |
| **8** | Michael Owen | Liverpool, Newcastle United | 125 |
| **9** | Dwight Yorke | Aston Villa, Manchester United, Blackburn Rovers, Birmingham City | 122 |
| **10** | Ian Wright | Arsenal, West Ham United | 113 |

\* As at 1 January 2007

Alan Shearer hit the headlines on 9 April 1988 when he scored three goals on his full debut for Southampton against Arsenal, and at the age of 17 years 240 days became the youngest ever scorer of a hat-trick in the first division of English soccer. In a career spanning 17 years with Southampton, Blackburn Rovers and Newcastle United, he went on to score 341 goals in 559 appearances. He also scored 30 goals for England.

## TOP 10 BRITISH TEAMS IN EUROPE*

| | TEAM | CL W | CL RU | UEFA W | UEFA RU | CWC W | CWC RU | SC W | SC RU | TOTAL W | TOTAL RU | POINTS |
|---|---|---|---|---|---|---|---|---|---|---|---|---|
| **1** | Liverpool | 5 | 1 | 3 | 0 | 0 | 1 | 3 | 2 | 11 | 4 | 26 |
| **2** | = Arsenal | 0 | 1 | 1 | 1 | 1 | 2 | 0 | 1 | 2 | 5 | 9 |
| | = Manchester United | 2 | 0 | 0 | 0 | 1 | 0 | 1 | 1 | 4 | 1 | 9 |
| **4** | = Leeds United | 0 | 1 | 2 | 1 | 0 | 1 | 0 | 0 | 2 | 3 | 7 |
| | = Nottingham Forest | 2 | 0 | 0 | 0 | 0 | 0 | 1 | 1 | 3 | 1 | 7 |
| | = Tottenham Hotspur | 0 | 0 | 2 | 1 | 1 | 0 | 0 | 0 | 3 | 1 | 7 |
| **7** | Chelsea | 0 | 0 | 0 | 0 | 2 | 0 | 1 | 0 | 3 | 0 | 6 |
| **8** | Glasgow Rangers | 0 | 0 | 0 | 0 | 1 | 2 | 0 | 1 | 1 | 3 | 5 |
| **9** | = Aberdeen | 0 | 0 | 0 | 0 | 1 | 0 | 1 | 0 | 2 | 0 | 4 |
| | = Aston Villa | 1 | 0 | 0 | 0 | 0 | 0 | 1 | 0 | 2 | 0 | 4 |
| | = Glasgow Celtic | 1 | 1 | 0 | 1 | 0 | 0 | 0 | 0 | 1 | 2 | 4 |

\* All competitions up to and including the 2005–06 season, based on two points for winning the four main competitions and one point for being runners-up. The four main competitions are: Champions League (CL) formerly Champions' Cup, UEFA Cup (UEFA) formerly Fairs Cup, Cup-winners' Cup (CWC) and Super Cup (SC).

The first British team to win a European competition was Tottenham Hotspur in 1963, when they beat Atletico Madrid 5-1 in Rotterdam to win the Cup-winners' Cup.

## TOP 10 CURRENT FA PREMIERSHIP TEAMS WITH THE LONGEST CONTINUOUS SPELL IN THE TOP DIVISION

| | TEAM | SEASON LAST PROMOTED |
|---|---|---|
| **1** | Arsenal | 1919–20 |
| **2** | Everton | 1954–55 |
| **3** | Liverpool | 1962–63 |
| **4** | Manchester United | 1975–76 |
| **5** | Tottenham Hotspur | 1978–79 |
| **6** | Aston Villa | 1988–89 |
| **7** | Chelsea | 1989–90 |
| **8** | Newcastle United | 1993–94 |
| **9** | Middlesbrough | 1998–99 |
| **10** | Charlton Athletic | 2000–01 |

Arsenal were promoted to the old Division One in the first season after World War I, when League soccer returned – despite finishing 5th in the last season before the start of hostilities. After the war, the First Division was extended by two teams to 22. Two teams were promoted from Division Two and the bottom two clubs in Division One, Chelsea and Tottenham also expected to stay up. Chelsea did so, but Tottenham, along with Arsenal and five other teams, went to a vote to decide which went into the Top Division. Arsenal won and have never been out of the top flight to this day, despite not winning promotion.

# Rugby

## TOP 10 BIGGEST WINS IN THE SIX NATIONS CHAMPIONSHIP*

| | WINNER / LOSER | YEAR | VENUE | SCORE |
|---|---|---|---|---|
| 1 | England v. Italy | 2001 | Twickenham | 80–23 |
| 2 | Ireland v. Italy | 2000 | Lansdowne Road | 60–13 |
| 3 | England v. Italy | 2000 | Rome | 59–12 |
| 4 | France v. Italy | 2005 | Rome | 56–13 |
| 5 | Ireland v. Wales | 2002 | Lansdowne Road | 54–10 |
| 6 | France v. Italy | 2003 | Rome | 53–27 |
| 7 | Ireland v. Italy | 2007 | Rome | 51–24 |
| 8 | =England v. Ireland | 2000 | Twickenham | 50–18 |
| | =England v. Wales | 2002 | Twickenham | 50–10 |
| | =England v. Italy | 2004 | Rome | 50–9 |

* Since 2000 when Italy joined the competition; up to and including the 2007 Championship; ranked by score of winning team

## TOP 10 BIGGEST WINS IN THE WOMEN'S RUGBY WORLD CUP*

| | WINNERS / LOSER | YEAR | VENUE | SCORE |
|---|---|---|---|---|
| 1 | New Zealand v. Germany | 1998 | Amsterdam | 134–6 |
| 2 | USA v. Japan | 1994 | Edinburgh | 121–0 |
| 3 | New Zealand v. Germany | 2002 | Barcelona | 117–0 |
| 4 | USA v. Sweden | 1994 | Edinburgh | 111–0 |
| 5 | France v. Japan | 1994 | Edinburgh | 99–0 |
| 6 | USA v. Netherlands | 2002 | Barcelona | 87–0 |
| 7 | USA v. Russia | 1998 | Amsterdam | 84–0 |
| 8 | Wales v. Russia | 1998 | Amsterdam | 83–7 |
| 9 | Canada v. Spain | 2006 | Edmonton | 79–0 |
| 10 | France v. Scottish Students | 1994 | Edinburgh | 77–0 |

* Based on score of winning team; up to and including the 2006 World Cup

The first Women's World Cup was in Cardiff in 1991, but was an unofficial event. The first official World Cup was held in Amsterdam in 1998, since when there have been two more: Barcelona, Spain, in 2002 and Edmonton, Canada, in 2006. The USA beat England 19–6 in the first final, with England gaining revenge in 1994. New Zealand have won all three subsequent finals.

## TOP 10 MOST POINTS IN A WORLD CUP CAREER*

| | PLAYER | COUNTRY | YEARS | POINTS |
|---|---|---|---|---|
| 1 | Gavin Hastings | Scotland | 1987–95 | 227 |
| 2 | Michael Lynagh | Australia | 1987–95 | 195 |
| 3 | Jonny Wilkinson | England | 1999–2003 | 182 |
| 4 | Grant Fox | New Zealand | 1987–91 | 170 |
| 5 | Andrew Mehrtens | New Zealand | 1995–99 | 163 |
| 6 | Gonzalo Quesada | Argentina | 1995––99 | 135 |
| 7 | Matt Burke | Australia | 1995–99 | 125 |
| 8 | Thierry Lacroix | France | 1991–95 | 124 |
| 9 | Gareth Rees | Canada | 1987–99 | 120 |
| 10 | Frederic Michalak | France | 2003 | 103 |

* Up to and including the 2003 tournament

The only other man to score 100 points is Elton Flatley of Australia. Grant Fox scored 126 points in 1995, which represents the biggest haul in a single tournament.

## TOP 10 MOST RUGBY UNION TEST MATCHES AS CAPTAIN*

| | PLAYER / COUNTRY | YEARS | NO. OF TIMES CAPTAIN |
|---|---|---|---|
| 1 | Will Carling, England | 1988–96 | 59 |
| 2 | George Gregan, Australia | 2001–06 | 58 |
| 3 | John Eales, Australia | 1996–2001 | 55 |
| 4 | =Sean Fitzpatrick, New Zealand | 1992–97 | 51 |
| | =Martin Johnson, England/Lions | 1997–2003 | 51 |
| 6 | Hugo Porta, Argentina/Jaguars | 1971–90 | 46 |
| 7 | Fabien Pelous, France | 1995–2006 | 40 |
| 8 | John Smit, South Africa | 2003–06 | 38 |
| 9 | =Nick Farr-Jones, Australia | 1988–92 | 36 |
| | =Gary Teichmann, South Africa | 1996–99 | 36 |

* As at 1 January 2007

Johnson's total includes six appearances as British Lions' captain. Hugo Porta's includes eight appearances as captain of the South American Jaguars, formed in the 1980s to play South Africa.

## TOP 10 **MOST TRIES IN ONE WORLD CUP***

| | PLAYER / COUNTRY | YEAR | TRIES |
|---|---|---|---|
| **1** | Jonah Lomu, New Zealand | 1999 | 8 |
| **2** | = Mark Ellis, New Zealand | 1995 | 7 |
| | = Jonah Lomu, New Zealand | 1995 | 7 |
| | = Doug Howlett, New Zealand | 2003 | 7 |
| | = Mils Muliaina, New Zealand | 2003 | 7 |
| **6** | = Craig Green, New Zealand | 1987 | 6 |
| | = John Kirwan, New Zealand | 1987 | 6 |
| | = David Campese, Australia | 1991 | 6 |
| | = Jean-Baptiste Lafond, France | 1991 | 6 |
| | = Jeff Wilson, New Zealand | 1999 | 6 |
| | = Joe Rokocoko, New Zealand | 2003 | 6 |

* Up to and including 2003

**Jonah Lomu**
*New Zealand's Johan Lomu has scored a record 15 tries in the World Cup, four more than England's Rory Underwood.*

## TOP 10 **BIGGEST WINS IN THE RUGBY WORLD CUP***

| | WINNERS / OPPONENTS | YEAR | VENUE | SCORE |
|---|---|---|---|---|
| **1** | New Zealand v. Japan | 1995 | Free State Stadium, Bloemfontein, South Africa | 145–17 |
| **2** | Australia v. Namibia | 2003 | Adelaide Oval, Australia | 142–0 |
| **3** | England v. Uruguay | 2003 | Suncorp Metway Stadium, Brisbane, Australia | 111–13 |
| **4** | = England v. Tonga | 1999 | Twickenham, England | 101–10 |
| | = New Zealand v. Italy | 1999 | McAlpine Stadium, Huddersfield, England | 101–3 |
| **6** | New Zealand v. Tonga | 2003 | Suncorp Metway Stadium, Brisbane, Australia | 91–7 |
| **7** | Australia v. Romania | 2003 | Suncorp Metway Stadium, Brisbane, Australia | 90–8 |
| **8** | Scotland v. Ivory Coast | 1995 | Olympia Park, Rustenburg, South Africa | 89–0 |
| **9** | England v. Georgia | 2003 | Subiaco Oval, Perth, Australia | 84–6 |
| **10** | New Zealand v. Fiji | 1987 | Lancaster Park, Christchurch, New Zealand | 74–13 |

* Ranked by score of the winning team in final stages of the competition

# Cricket

## TOP 10 **MOST RUNS IN ONE-DAY INTERNATIONALS***

| PLAYER / COUNTRY | YEARS | MATCHES | INNINGS | RUNS |
|---|---|---|---|---|
| **1** Sachin Tendulkar, India | 1989–2006 | 374 | 365 | 14,537 |
| **2** Inzamam-ul-Haq, Pakistan | 1991–2006 | 370 | 342 | 11,591 |
| **3** Sanath Jayasuriya, Sri Lanka | 1989–2006 | 373 | 363 | 11,372 |
| **4** Sourav Ganguly, India | 1992–2005 | 279 | 270 | 10,123 |
| **5** Brian Lara, West Indies | 1990–2006 | 287 | 278 | 10,019 |
| **6** Rahul Dravid, India | 1996–2006 | 302 | 281 | 9,762 |
| **7** Ricky Ponting, Australia | 1995–2006 | 261 | 255 | 9,411 |
| **8** Mohammad Azharuddin, India | 1985–2000 | 334 | 308 | 9,378 |
| **9** Aravinda de Silva, Sri Lanka | 1984–2003 | 308 | 296 | 9,284 |
| **10** Saeed Anwar, Pakistan | 1989–2003 | 247 | 244 | 8,823 |

* As at 1 February 2007

## TOP 10 **MOST RUNS IN TEST CRICKET**

| BATSMAN / COUNTRY | YEARS | MATCHES | INNINGS | RUNS |
|---|---|---|---|---|
| **1** Brian Lara, West Indies | 1990–2006 | 131 | 232 | 11,953 |
| **2** Allan Border, Australia | 1978–94 | 156 | 265 | 11,174 |
| **3** Steve Waugh, Australia | 1985–2004 | 168 | 260 | 10,927 |
| **4** Sachin Tendulkar, India | 1989–2006 | 134 | 215 | 10,590 |
| **5** Sunil Gavaskar, India | 1971–87 | 125 | 214 | 10,122 |
| **6** Ricky Ponting, Australia | 1995–2006 | 110 | 183 | 9,368 |
| **7** Rahul Dravid, India | 1996–2006 | 106 | 180 | 9,098 |
| **8** Graham Gooch, England | 1975–95 | 118 | 215 | 8,900 |
| **9** Javed Miandad, Pakistan | 1976–93 | 124 | 189 | 8,832 |
| **10** Inzaman–ul–Haq, Pakistan | 1992–2006 | 116 | 192 | 8,615 |

* As at 1 February 2007

## TOP 10 **MOST RUNS IN THE ICC WORLD CUP**

| BATSMAN / COUNTRY | YEARS | MATCHES | INNINGS | RUNS |
|---|---|---|---|---|
| **1** Sachin Tendulkar, India | 1992–2003 | 33 | 32 | 1,732 |
| **2** Javed Miandad, Pakistan | 1979–92 | 33 | 30 | 1,083 |
| **3** Aravinda de Silva, Sri Lanka | 1987–2003 | 35 | 32 | 1,064 |
| **4** Viv Richards, West Indies | 1975–87 | 23 | 21 | 1,013 |
| **5** Mark Waugh, Australia | 1992–99 | 22 | 22 | 1,004 |
| **6** Ricky Ponting, Australia | 1996–2003 | 28 | 27 | 998 |
| **7** Steve Waugh, Australia | 1987–2003 | 33 | 30 | 978 |
| **8** Arjuna Ranatunga, Sri Lanka | 1983–99 | 30 | 29 | 969 |
| **9** Brian Lara, West Indies | 1992–2003 | 25 | 25 | 956 |
| **10** Saeed Anwar, Pakistan | 1996–2003 | 21 | 21 | 915 |

Of all the players on the above list, Viv Richards had the best average, with 63.31 runs per innings.

## TOP 10 **MOST WICKETS IN TEST CRICKET**

| BOWLER / COUNTRY | YEARS | MATCHES | WICKETS |
|---|---|---|---|
| **1** Shane Warne, Australia | 1992–2006 | 145 | 708 |
| **2** Muttiah Muralitharan, Sri Lanka | 1992–2006 | 110 | 674 |
| **3** Glenn McGrath, Australia | 1993–2006 | 124 | 563 |
| **4** Anil Kumble, India | 1990–2006 | 112 | 542 |
| **5** Courtney Walsh, West Indies | 1984–2001 | 132 | 519 |
| **6** Kapil Dev, India | 1978–94 | 131 | 434 |
| **7** Richard Hadlee, New Zealand | 1973–90 | 86 | 431 |
| **8** Wasim Akram, Pakistan | 1985–2002 | 104 | 414 |
| **9** Curtly Ambrose, West Indies | 1988–2000 | 98 | 405 |
| **10** Shaun Pollock, South Africa | 1995–2006 | 104 | 403 |

* As at 1 February 2007

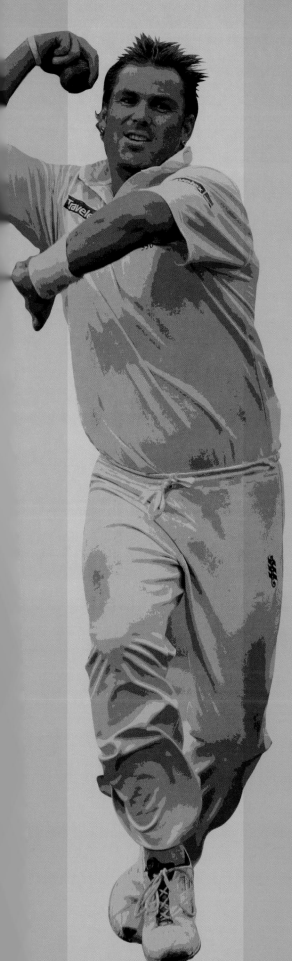

## TOP 10 **HIGHEST TEAM TOTALS IN ONE-DAY INTERNATIONALS**\*

| | MATCH | VENUE | SEASON | TOTAL# |
|---|---|---|---|---|
| 1 | Sri Lanka v. Netherlands | Amstelveen, Netherlands | 2006 | (50) 443-9 |
| 2 | South Africa v. Australia | Johannesburg, South Africa | 2005–06 | (49.5) 438-9 |
| 3 | Australia v. South Africa | Johannesburg | 2005–06 | (50) 434-4 |
| 4 | South Africa v. Zimbabwe | Potchefstroom, South Africa | 2006–07 | (50) 418-5 |
| 5 | Sri Lanka v. Kenya | Kandy, Sri Lanka | 1995–96 | (50) 398-5 |
| 6 | New Zealand v. Zimbabwe | Bulawayo, Zimbabwe | 2005–06 | (44) 397-5 |
| 7 | England v. Bangladesh | Nottingham, UK | 2005 | (50) 391-4 |
| 8 | India v. New Zealand | Hyderabad, India | 1999–2000 | (50) 376-2 |
| 9 | India v. Sri Lanka | Taunton, UK | 1999 | (50) 373-6 |
| 10 | Pakistan v. Sri Lanka | Nairobi, Kenya | 1996–97 | (50) 371-9 |

\* As at 1 January 2007
# Figures in brackets indicate number of overs

Australia and South Africa's totals at Nos. 2 and 3 were in the same match, with the aggregate runs, 872 for the loss of just 13 wickets, a One Day International record. Ricky Ponting was Australia's top scorer with 164 while South Africa's was Herschelle Gibbs with 175. No other match has produced as many as 700 runs; the next best, and former record, was the 693 runs scored by India and Pakistan at Karachi in 2003–04.

## TOP 10 **MOST SUCCESSFUL COUNTRIES IN THE ICC WORLD CUP**\*

| | COUNTRY | TOURNAMENTS | YEARS | PLAYED | WON | PERCENTAGE |
|---|---|---|---|---|---|---|
| 1 | Australia | 8 | 1975–2003 | 58 | 40 | 68.97 |
| 2 | West Indies | 8 | 1975–2003 | 48 | 31 | 64.58 |
| 3 | England | 8 | 1975–2003 | 50 | 31 | 62.00 |
| 4 | South Africa | 4 | 1992–2003 | 30 | 19 | 59.38 |
| 5 | India | 8 | 1975–2003 | 55 | 31 | 56.36 |
| 6 | Pakistan | 8 | 1975–2003 | 53 | 29 | 54.72 |
| 7 | New Zealand | 8 | 1975–2003 | 52 | 28 | 53.85 |
| 8 | Sri Lanka | 8 | 1975–2003 | 46 | 17 | 36.96 |
| 9 | Kenya | 3 | 1996–2003 | 20 | 5 | 25.00 |
| 10 | United Arab Emirates | 1 | 1996 | 5 | 1 | 20.00 |

\* Based on percentage wins to matches played in all tournaments 1975–2003

The first ICC World Cup was held in England in 1975, when the six traditional Test-playing nations at that time – Australia, England, India, New Zealand, Pakistan and the West Indies – were joined by Sri Lanka and East Africa. The West Indies beat Australia by 17 runs in the first final at Lord's. Australia has won the trophy a record three times – in 1987, 1999 and 2003.

# Tennis

**Top rank**
*Steffi Graf first topped the rankings on 17 August 1987. The following year she completed the Grand Slam and also won the women's singles title at the Olympic Games.*

## TOP 10 **MOST WEEKS AT NO. 1 ON THE WTA RANKINGS***

| PLAYER / COUNTRY | YEARS | WEEKS | |
|---|---|---|---|
| Steffi Graf, Germany | 1987–97 | 377 | 1 |
| Martina Navratilova, Czechoslovakia/USA | 1978–87 | 331 | 2 |
| Chris Evert, USA | 1975–85 | 262 | 3 |
| Martina Hingis, Switzerland | 1997–2001 | 209 | 4 |
| Monica Seles, Yugoslavia/USA | 1991–96 | 178 | 5 |
| Lindsay Davenport, USA | 1998–2006 | 98 | 6 |
| Serena Williams, USA | 2002–03 | 57 | 7 |
| Justine Henin-Hardenne, Belgium | 2003–06 | 46 | 8 |
| Amélie Mauresmo, France | 2004–06 | 39 | 9 |
| Tracy Austin, USA | 1980 | 22 | 10 |

\* To 1 January 2007

Source: WTA (Women's Tennis Association)

## TOP 10 **MOST GRAND SLAM SINGLES TITLES***

| | PLAYER / COUNTRY | YEARS | A | F | W | US | TOTAL |
|---|---|---|---|---|---|---|---|
| 1 | Margaret Court (née Smith), Australia | 1960–73 | 11 | 5 | 3 | 5 | 24 |
| 2 | Steffi Graf, Germany | 1987–99 | 4 | 6 | 7 | 5 | 22 |
| 3 | Helen Wills-Moody, USA | 1923–38 | 0 | 4 | 8 | 7 | 19 |
| 4 = | Chris Evert-Lloyd, USA | 1974–86 | 2 | 7 | 3 | 6 | 18 |
| = | Martina Navratilova, Czechoslovakia/USA | 1978–90 | 3 | 2 | 9 | 4 | 18 |
| 6 | Pete Sampras, USA | 1990–2002 | 2 | 0 | 7 | 5 | 14 |
| 7 = | Roy Emerson, Australia | 1961–67 | 6 | 2 | 2 | 2 | 12 |
| = | Billie Jean King, USA | 1966–75 | 1 | 1 | 6 | 4 | 12 |
| 9 = | Björn Borg, Sweden | 1974–81 | 0 | 6 | 5 | 0 | 11 |
| = | Rod Laver, Australia | 1960–69 | 3 | 2 | 4 | 2 | 11 |

\* Up to and including 2006

A – Australian Open; F – French Open; W – Wimbledon; US – US Open

## TOP 10 **MOST WINS IN THE DAVIS CUP***

| | COUNTRY | YEARS | WINS |
|---|---|---|---|
| 1 = | Sweden | 1975, 1984–85, 1987, 1994, 1997–98 | 7 |
| = | USA | 1978–79, 1981–82, 1990, 1992, 1995 | 7 |
| 3 | Australia | 1973, 1977, 1983, 1986, 1999, 2003 | 6 |
| 4 = | Germany | 1988–89, 1993 | 3 |
| = | France | 1991, 1996, 2001 | 3 |
| 6 | Spain | 2000, 2004 | 2 |
| = | Russia | 2002, 2006 | 2 |
| 8 = | South Africa | 1974 | 1 |
| = | Italy | 1976 | 1 |
| = | Czechoslovakia | 1980 | 1 |
| = | Croatia | 2005 | 1 |

\* Since the abolition of the Challenge system in 1972

## TOP 10 **MOST WEEKS AT NO. 1 ON THE ATP RANKINGS***

| | PLAYER / COUNTRY | YEARS | WEEKS |
|---|---|---|---|
| 1 | Pete Sampras, USA | 1993–2000 | 286 |
| 2 | Ivan Lendl, Czechoslovakia/USA | 1983–90 | 270 |
| 3 | Jimmy Connors, USA | 1974–83 | 268 |
| 4 | John McEnroe, USA | 1980–85 | 170 |
| 5 | Roger Federer, Switzerland | 2004–06 | 152 |
| 6 | Björn Borg, Sweden | 1977–81 | 109 |
| 7 | Andre Agassi, USA | 1995–2003 | 101 |
| 8 | Lleyton Hewitt, Australia | 2001–03 | 80 |
| 9 | Stefan Edberg, Sweden | 1990–92 | 72 |
| 10 | Jim Courier, USA | 1992–93 | 58 |

\* To 1 January 2007

Source: ATP (Association of Tennis Professionals)

Top of the first ATP rankings on 23 August 1973 was Ille Nastase (Romania). The most consecutive weeks at No. 1 is 160 by Jimmy Connors between 29 July 1974 and 22 August 1977.

### Martina's Victories

Martina Navratilova won her last mixed doubles title at Flushing Meadow in 2006 – at the remarkable age of 46. She had won her first Grand Slam title at the 1974 French Open, partnering Ivan Molina of Colombia. The first of her 30 women's doubles titles – 21 of them with Pam Shriver – was with Chris Evert at the 1975 French Open. The first of her Wimbledon singles triumphs, over Chris Evert, was in 1978, and the last in 1990 when she beat Zina Garrison. She won 167 singles titles in her career, stretching from Orlando in 1974 to the Paris indoor title in 1994.

**Grand master**
*Roger Federer came close to a fourth Grand Slam victory in 2006, losing out to Spain's Rafael Nadal in the French Open.*

## THE 10 **LAST MEN TO WIN THREE OR MORE GRAND SLAM TITLES IN ONE YEAR**

| | PLAYER / COUNTRY | EVENTS WON | YEAR |
|---|---|---|---|
| 1 | Roger Federer, Switzerland | A, W, US | 2006 |
| 2 | Roger Federer, Switzerland | A, W, US | 2004 |
| 3 | Mats Wilander, Sweden | A, F, US | 1988 |
| 4 | Jimmy Connors, USA | A, W, US | 1974 |
| 5 | Rod Laver, Australia | A, F, W, US | 1969 |
| 6 | Roy Emerson, Australia | A, F, W | 1964 |
| 7 | Rod Laver, Australia | A, F, W, US | 1962 |
| 8 | Ashley Cooper, Australia | A, W, US | 1958 |
| 9 | Lew Hoad, Australia | A, F, W | 1956 |
| 10 | Tony Trabert, USA | F, W, US | 1955 |

A – Australian Open; F – French Open; W – Wimbledon; US – US Open

The only other men to win three or more Grand Slam singles titles in the same year are Jack Crawford (Australia, 1933), Fred Perry (UK, 1934) and Donald Budge (USA, 1938) – who won all four titles.

# Golf

## TOP 10 MOST APPEARANCES FOR THE EUROPEAN TEAM IN THE RYDER CUP*

| | PLAYER / COUNTRY | FIRST YEAR | LAST YEAR | APPEARANCES |
|---|---|---|---|---|
| 1 | Nick Faldo, England | 1977 | 1997 | 11 |
| 2 = | Christy O'Connor Snr, Ireland | 1955 | 1973 | 10 |
| = | Bernhard Langer, Germany | 1981 | 2002 | 10 |
| 4 | Dai Rees, Wales | 1937 | 1961 | 9 |
| 5 = | Peter Alliss, England | 1953 | 1969 | 8 |
| = | Bernard Hunt, England | 1953 | 1969 | 8 |
| = | Neil Coles, England | 1961 | 1977 | 8 |
| = | Bernard Gallacher, Scotland | 1969 | 1983 | 8 |
| = | Severiano Ballesteros, Spain | 1979 | 1995 | 8 |
| = | Sam Torrance, Scotland | 1981 | 1995 | 8 |
| = | Ian Woosnam, Wales | 1983 | 1997 | 8 |
| = | Colin Montgomerie, Scotland | 1991 | 2006 | 8 |

* Great Britain – 1921 to 1971; Great Britain & Ireland – 1973 to 1977; Europe – 1979 to 2006; up to and including 2006

Nick Faldo, with 25, has gained the most points for the Great Britain and Ireland/European teams.

## TOP 10 MOST APPEARANCES FOR THE US TEAM IN THE RYDER CUP*

| | PLAYER | FIRST YEAR | LAST YEAR | APPEARANCES |
|---|---|---|---|---|
| 1 = | Billy Casper | 1961 | 1975 | 8 |
| = | Raymond Floyd | 1969 | 1983 | 8 |
| = | Lanny Wadkins | 1977 | 1993 | 8 |
| 4 = | Sam Snead | 1937 | 1959 | 7 |
| = | Gene Littler | 1961 | 1975 | 7 |
| = | Tom Kite | 1979 | 1993 | 7 |
| 7 = | Gene Sarazen | 1927 | 1937 | 6 |
| = | Arnold Palmer | 1961 | 1973 | 6 |
| = | Jack Nicklaus | 1969 | 1981 | 6 |
| = | Lee Trevino | 1969 | 1981 | 6 |
| = | Davis Love III | 1993 | 2004 | 6 |
| = | Phil Mickelson | 1995 | 2006 | 6 |

* Up to and including 2006

Billy Casper holds the record for winning the most points for the USA – 23.5, which is half a point more than Arnold Palmer. Casper also holds the record for appearing in the most matches, 37, and jointly holds the record for the most points won in singles, fourballs and foursomes matches.

## TOP 10 MOST WINS ON THE PGA EUROPEAN TOUR*

| | PLAYER / COUNTRY | YEARS | WINS |
|---|---|---|---|
| 1 | Severiano Ballesteros, Spain | 1976–95 | 49 |
| 2 | Bernhard Langer, Germany | 1980–2002 | 40 |
| 3 | Colin Montgomerie, Scotland | 1989–2005# | 30 |
| 4 | Ian Woosnam, Wales | 1982–97 | 28 |
| 5 | Nick Faldo, England | 1977–94 | 27 |
| 6 = | José Maria Olazábal, Spain | 1986–2005 | 22 |
| = | Ernie Els, South Africa | 1994–2006 | 22 |
| 8 | Sam Torrance, Scotland | 1976–98 | 21 |
| 9 | Mark James, England | 1978–97 | 18 |
| 10 | Sandy Lyle, Scotland | 1979–92 | 17 |

* As at 1 January 2007
# Montgomerie won the Hong Kong Open in 2005, although it was part of the 2006 European PGA Tour of 2006

Ballesteros first enjoyed success in the 1976 Dutch Open. He went on to win five Majors in his career, his 49th and last European Tour success in the 1995 Peugeot Spanish Open at San Roque Golf Club, Andalucia.

## TOP 10 MOST MEN'S MAJORS IN A CAREER*

| | PLAYER / COUNTRY# | YEARS | MASTERS | US OPEN | BRITISH OPEN | PGA | TOTAL |
|---|---|---|---|---|---|---|---|
| 1 | Jack Nicklaus | 1962–86 | 6 | 4 | 3 | 5 | 18 |
| 2 | Tiger Woods | 1997–2006 | 4 | 2 | 3 | 3 | 12 |
| 3 | Walter Hagen | 1914–29 | 0 | 2 | 4 | 5 | 11 |
| 4 = | Ben Hogan | 1946–53 | 2 | 4 | 1 | 2 | 9 |
| = | Gary Player (South Africa) | 1959–78 | 3 | 1 | 3 | 2 | 9 |
| 6 | Tom Watson | 1975–83 | 2 | 1 | 5 | 0 | 8 |
| 7 = | Harry Vardon (England) | 1896–1914 | 0 | 1 | 6 | 0 | 7 |
| = | Gene Sarazen | 1922–35 | 1 | 2 | 1 | 3 | 7 |
| = | Bobby Jones | 1923–30 | 0 | 4 | 3 | 0 | 7 |
| = | Sam Snead | 1942–54 | 3 | 0 | 1 | 3 | 7 |
| = | Arnold Palmer | 1958–64 | 4 | 1 | 2 | 0 | 7 |

* Professional Majors only, up to and including 2006
# All from the USA unless otherwise stated

In 1930, Bobby Jones achieved an unprecedented Grand Slam when he won the US and British Open titles as well as both Amateur titles. Nicklaus, Woods, Hogan, Player and Sarazen are the only golfers to have won all four Majors at least once. Tiger Woods is the only player to hold all four Majors at the same time.

## TOP 10 **MONEY WINNERS ON THE LPGA TOUR**\*

| | PLAYER / COUNTRY# | WINNINGS ($) |
|---|---|---|
| **1** | Annika Sörenstam, Sweden | 20,304,562 |
| **2** | Karrie Webb, Australia | 12,826,995 |
| **3** | Juli Inkster | 11,255,669 |
| **4** | Se Ri Pak, South Korea | 8,966,948 |
| **5** | Meg Mallon | 8,818,462 |
| **6** | Beth Daniel | 8,755,733 |
| **7** | Rosie Jones | 8,355,068 |
| **8** | Laura Davies, England | 7,716,726 |
| **9** | Betsy King | 7,637,621 |
| **10** | Dottie Pepper | 6,827,284 |

\* As at 1 January 2007
# All from the USA unless otherwise stated

Kathy Whitworth (USA) holds the record for the most wins – 88 – on the LPGA Tour. Like her male counterpart, Sam Snead, she never won the US Open.

## TOP 10 **MONEY WINNERS ON THE PGA CHAMPIONS TOUR**\*

| | PLAYER# | WINNINGS ($) |
|---|---|---|
| **1** | Hale Irwin | 23,384,705 |
| **2** | Gil Morgan | 17,208,472 |
| **3** | Bruce Fleisher | 13,260,442 |
| **4** | Dana Quigley | 13,166,725 |
| **5** | Larry Nelson | 12,893,736 |
| **6** | Allen Doyle | 12,118,228 |
| **7** | Jim Colbert | 11,575,162 |
| **8** | Jim Thorpe | 11,429,823 |
| **9** | Dave Stockton | 10,840,231 |
| **10** | Tom Jenkins | 10,624,407 |

\* As at 1 January 2007
# All players from the USA

The Champions Tour was founded in 1980 as the Senior PGA Tour, and changed its name in 2002. Run by the PGA Tour it is for professional golfers who have reached the age of 50 and many ex-stars of the regular Tour compete on the Champions Tour.

*The 'Golden Bear'*
*Jack Nicklaus is widely regarded as one of the greatest of all golfers.*

# Water Sports

## TOP 10 OLYMPIC CANOEING COUNTRIES*

| | COUNTRY | GOLD | SILVER | BRONZE | TOTAL |
|---|---|---|---|---|---|
| 1 | Germany/West Germany | 29 | 23 | 20 | 72 |
| 2 | Hungary | 17 | 26 | 25 | 68 |
| 3 | USSR/Unified Team/Russia | 30 | 16 | 12 | 58 |
| 4 | Romania | 10 | 11 | 14 | 35 |
| 5 | East Germany | 14 | 7 | 9 | 30 |
| 6 | =France | 6 | 6 | 17 | 29 |
| | =Sweden | 15 | 11 | 3 | 29 |
| 8 | Czechoslovakia/Czech Republic | 10 | 8 | 3 | 21 |
| 9 | Canada | 4 | 8 | 7 | 19 |
| 10 | Bulgaria | 4 | 5 | 8 | 17 |

* Up to and including the 2004 Olympics

A Kayak singles race was contested at the 1906 Intercalated Games in Athens, but it was not until 1936 that canoeing became a regular Olympic sport. Women first contested canoeing events at the 1948 London Olympics.

## TOP 10 MOST GOLD MEDALS AT THE WORLD AQUATIC CHAMPIONSHIPS*

| | SWIMMER / COUNTRY | YEARS | GOLD MEDALS |
|---|---|---|---|
| 1 | Grant Hackett, Australia | 1998–2005 | 7 |
| 2 | =Ian Thorpe, Australia | 1998–2003 | 6 |
| | =Michael Phelps, USA | 2001–05 | 6 |
| 4 | =Aleksandr Popov, Russia | 1994–2003 | 5 |
| | =Hannah Stockbauer, Germany | 2001–03 | 5 |
| | =Inge de Bruijn, Netherlands | 2001–03 | 5 |
| | =Aaron Peirsol, USA | 2001–05 | 5 |
| 8 | =Kornelia Ender, East Germany | 1973–75 | 4 |
| | =Vladimir Salnikov, USSR | 1978–82 | 4 |
| | =Michael Gross, West Germany | 1982–86 | 4 |
| | =Tamas Darnyi, Hungary | 1986–91 | 4 |
| | =Yana Klochkova, Ukraine | 2001–03 | 4 |
| | =Xuejuan Luo, China | 2001–03 | 4 |

* Individual medals at the FINA World Long Course Championships, 1973–2005

*Wish granted*
*Grant Hackett celebrates winning a record seven golds at the World Aquatic Championships.*

## TOP 10 WATERSKIERS WITH THE MOST WORLD CUP WINS*

| | SKIER / COUNTRY | M/F# | SLALOM | JUMP | TOTAL |
|---|---|---|---|---|---|
| 1 | Andy Mapple, UK | M | 31 | – | 31 |
| 2 | = Emma Sheers, Australia | F | 2 | 16 | 18 |
| | = Jaret Llewellyn, Canada | M | – | 18 | 18 |
| 4 | = Toni Neville, Australia | F | 3 | 10 | 13 |
| | = Kristi Johnson (née Overton), USA | F | 13 | – | 13 |
| 6 | Freddy Krueger, USA | M | – | 12 | 12 |
| 7 | Wade Cox, USA | M | 10 | – | 10 |
| 8 | Bruce Neville, Australia | M | – | 9 | 9 |
| 9 | Scot Ellis, USA | M | – | 7 | 7 |
| 10 | = Susi Graham, Canada | F | 6 | – | 6 |
| | = Carl Roberge, USA | M | 1 | 5 | 6 |

* Up to and including 2006
# Male/female

Waterskiing was invented in 1922 by 18-year-old Ralph W. Samuelson of Lake City, Minnesota, USA, using two 2.4-m (8-ft) planks and 30 m (100 ft) of sash cord. It grew in popularity, and the first international governing body, the World Water Ski Union, was established in 1946 in Geneva, Switzerland. Its successor, the International Water Ski Federation, organized the Water Ski World Cup, which started in 1996. It ceased after the 2000 event but was revived in 2004.

### Record-Breaking Spitz

Having won two golds, a silver and a bronze medal at the Mexico City Olympics in 1968, at the 1972 Munich Games Mark Spitz (USA) not only won a record seven gold medals, but all, including the 100 and 200 metres freestyle and butterfly, were achieved in new world-record times.

## THE 10 MOST OLYMPIC SWIMMING MEDALS BY A FEMALE SWIMMER*

| | SWIMMER / NATIONALITY | YEARS | GOLD | SILVER | BRONZE | TOTAL |
|---|---|---|---|---|---|---|
| 1 | Jenny Thompson, USA | 1992–2004 | 7 | 3 | 1 | 11 |
| 2 | Franziska van Almsick, Germany | 1992–2004 | 0 | 4 | 6 | 10 |
| 3 | = Inge de Bruin, Netherlands | 2000–04 | 4 | 2 | 2 | 8 |
| | = Shirley Babashoff, USA | 1972–76 | 2 | 6 | 0 | 8 |
| | = Kornelia Ender, East Germany | 1972–76 | 4 | 4 | 0 | 8 |
| | = Dawn Fraser, Australia | 1956–64 | 4 | 4 | 0 | 8 |
| | = Dagmar Hase, Germany | 1992–96 | 2 | 5 | 1 | 8 |
| | = Susie O'Neill, Australia | 1996–2000 | 2 | 4 | 2 | 8 |
| | = Dara Torres, USA | 1984–2000 | 4 | 0 | 4 | 8 |
| 10 | = Krisztina Egerszegi, Hungary | 1988–96 | 5 | 1 | 1 | 7 |
| | = Amanda Beard, USA | 1996–2004 | 2 | 4 | 1 | 7 |

* Up to and including the 2004 Olympics

## TOP 10 OLYMPIC COUNTRIES ON AND IN WATER*

| | COUNTRY | SWIMMING# | SAILING | ROWING | CANOEING | MOTOR BOATING† | TOTAL |
|---|---|---|---|---|---|---|---|
| 1 | USA | 260 | 17 | 30 | 5 | 0 | 312 |
| 2 | East Germany | 40 | 2 | 33 | 14 | 0 | 89 |
| 3 | Germany/West Germany | 22 | 6 | 27 | 28 | 0 | 83 |
| 4 | USSR/Unified Team/Russia | 32 | 4 | 13 | 30 | 0 | 79 |
| 5 | Australia | 54 | 5 | 8 | 1 | 0 | 68 |
| 6 | UK | 18 | 24 | 22 | 0 | 2 | 66 |
| 7 | Hungary | 32 | 0 | 0 | 17 | 0 | 49 |
| 8 | Sweden | 12 | 9 | 0 | 15 | 0 | 36 |
| 9 | Italy | 10 | 3 | 14 | 5 | 0 | 32 |
| 10 | Romania | 3 | 0 | 18 | 10 | 0 | 31 |

* Gold medals won at all games 1896 to 2004, including the Intercalated Games of 1906 and discontinued events
# Including water polo and diving but excluding triathlon
† Motor boating was part of the Olympic programme only in 1908

# Motor Sports

## TOP 10 FASTEST WINNING SPEEDS OF THE INDIANAPOLIS 500*

| | DRIVER / COUNTRY# | CAR | YEAR | KM/H | MPH |
|---|---|---|---|---|---|
| 1 | Arie Luyendyk, Netherlands | Lola-Chevrolet | 1990 | 299.307 | 185.981 |
| 2 | Rick Mears | Chevrolet-Lumina | 1991 | 283.980 | 176.457 |
| 3 | Bobby Rahal | March-Cosworth | 1986 | 274.750 | 170.722 |
| 4 | Juan Montoya, Colombia | G Force–Aurora | 2000 | 269.730 | 167.607 |
| 5 | Emerson Fittipaldi, Brazil | Penske-Chevrolet | 1989 | 269.695 | 167.581 |
| 6 | Helio Castroneves, Brazil | Dallara–Chevrolet | 2002 | 267.954 | 166.499 |
| 7 | Rick Mears | March-Cosworth | 1984 | 263.308 | 163.612 |
| 8 | Mark Donohue | McLaren-Offenhauser | 1972 | 262.619 | 162.962 |
| 9 | Al Unser | March-Cosworth | 1987 | 260.995 | 162.175 |
| 10 | Tom Sneva | March-Cosworth | 1983 | 260.902 | 162.117 |

* Up to and including the 2006 race
# All from USA unless otherwise stated

## TOP 10 MOST CAREER WINS IN CHAMP CAR RACES*

| | DRIVER# | CAREER | WINS |
|---|---|---|---|
| 1 | A. J. Foyt | 1960–81 | 67 |
| 2 | Mario Andretti | 1965–93 | 52 |
| 3 | Michael Andretti | 1986–2003 | 42 |
| 4 | Al Unser | 1967–87 | 39 |
| 5 | Bobby Unser | 1966–81 | 38 |
| 6 | Al Unser, Jr | 1984–95 | 31 |
| 7 | Paul Tracy, Canada | 1993–2006 | 30 |
| 8 | Rick Mears | 1978–91 | 29 |
| 9 | Johnny Rutherford | 1965–86 | 27 |
| 10 | Rodger Ward | 1953–66 | 26 |

* Formerly CART (Championship Auto Racing Teams), Champ Car since 2004; as at the end of 2006 season
# All from USA unless otherwise stated

## TOP 10 MOST RACE WINS IN A FORMULA ONE CAREER BY A DRIVER*

| | DRIVER / COUNTRY | YEARS | WINS |
|---|---|---|---|
| 1 | Michael Schumacher, Germany | 1992–2006 | 91 |
| 2 | Alain Prost, France | 1981–93 | 51 |
| 3 | Ayrton Senna, Brazil | 1985–93 | 41 |
| 4 | Nigel Mansell, UK | 1985–94 | 31 |
| 5 | Jackie Stewart, UK | 1965–73 | 27 |
| 6 | =Jim Clark, UK | 1962–68 | 25 |
| | =Niki Lauda, Austria | 1974–85 | 25 |
| 8 | Juan-Manuel Fangio, Argentina | 1950–57 | 24 |
| 9 | Nelson Piquet, Brazil | 1980–91 | 23 |
| 10 | Damon Hill, UK | 1993–98 | 22 |

* Up to and including 2006 season

Michael Schumacher's first Grand Prix was the Belgian GP in 1991 and his first win was in the same race the following year, driving a Benetton. He switched to Ferrari in 1996 and stayed with them until his retirement in 2006. His final win was in the 2006 Chinese GP.

## TOP 10 MOST NEXTEL CUP WINS IN A SEASON*

| | DRIVER# | CAR | YEAR | STARTS | WINS |
|---|---|---|---|---|---|
| 1 | Richard Petty | Plymouth Satellite | 1967 | 48 | 27 |
| 2 | Richard Petty | Plymouth Satellite | 1971 | 46 | 21 |
| 3 | Tim Flock | Chrysler 300 | 1955 | 39 | 18 |
| 4 | David Pearson | Ford Torino | 1968 | 48 | 16 |
| 5 | David Pearson | Dodge Charger | 1966 | 42 | 15 |
| 6 | Buck Baker | Chrysler 300-B | 1956 | 48 | 14 |
| 7 | =Ned Jarrett | Ford Galaxie | 1965 | 54 | 13 |
| | =Richard Petty | Dodge Charger | 1975 | 30 | 13 |
| | =Jeff Gordon | Chevrolet Monte Carlo | 1998 | 33 | 13 |
| 10 | =Herb Thomas | Hudson Hornet | 1953 | 37 | 12 |
| | =Darrell Waltrip | Buick Regal | 1981 | 31 | 12 |
| | =Darrell Waltrip | Buick Regal | 1982 | 30 | 12 |

* By the champion driver; up to and including 2006 season
# All drivers from the USA

The premier series in the NASCAR calendar, it was known as the Grand National from 1950 to 1971 and the Winston Cup 1973–2002.

# TOP 10 **DISTANCES COVERED IN THE LE MANS 24-HOUR RACE**\*

| | DRIVERS / NATIONALITY | CAR | YEAR | KM | DISTANCE MILES |
|---|---|---|---|---|---|
| 1 | Helmut Marko (Austria), Gijs van Lennep (Holland) | Porsche 917K | 1971 | 5,335.31 | 3,315.20 |
| 2 | Jan Lammers (Holland), Johnny Dumfries (UK), Andy Wallace (UK) | Jaguar XJR-9LM | 1988 | 5,332.79 | 3,313.64 |
| 3 | Jochen Mass (West Germany), Manuel Reuter (West Germany), Stanley Dickens (Sweden) | Sauber Mercedes C9 | 1989 | 5,265.12 | 3,271.59 |
| 4 | Dan Gurney (USA), A.J. Foyt (USA) | Ford GT40 Mk IV | 1967 | 5,232.90 | 3,251.57 |
| 5 | Frank Biela (Germany), Emanuele Pirro (Italy), Marco Werner (Germany) | Audi R10 | 2006 | 5,187.00 | 3,223.05 |
| 6 | Seiji Ara (Japan), Tom Kristensen (Denmark), Rinaldo Capello (Italy) | Audi R8 | 2004 | 5,169.97 | 3,212.46 |
| 7 | Tom Kristensen (Denmark), Rinaldo Capello (Italy), Guy Smith (UK) | Bentley Speed 8 | 2003 | 5,143.93 | 3,196.28 |
| 8 | Frank Biela (Germany), Tom Kristensen (Denmark), Emanuele Pirro (Italy) | Audi R8 | 2002 | 5,118.75 | 3,180.64 |
| 9 | Gary Brabham (Australia), Christophe Bouchut (France), Eric Hélary (France) | Peugeot 905B | 1993 | 5,100.00 | 3,168.99 |
| 10 | Klaus Ludwig (West Germany), Paolo Barilla (Italy), 'John Winter' (Louis Krages) (West Germany) | Porsche 956 | 1985 | 5,088.51 | 3,161.85 |

\* Up to and including the 2006 race

*Sebastian Loeb*
*Sebastian Loeb had the first of his victories in the Rally of Germany in 2002 in a Citroën Xsara.*

# TOP 10 **MOST WINS IN WORLD RALLY CHAMPIONSHIP RACES**\*

| | DRIVER / COUNTRY | WINS |
|---|---|---|
| 1 | Sébastien Loeb, France | 28 |
| 2 | Carlos Sainz, Spain | 26 |
| 3 | = Marcus Grönholm, Finland | 25 |
| | = Colin McRae, UK | 25 |
| 5 | Tommi Mäkinen, Finland | 24 |
| 6 | Juha Kankkunen, Finland | 23 |
| 7 | = Markku Alén, Finland | 20 |
| | = Didier Auriol, France | 20 |
| 9 | Hannu Mikkola, Finland | 18 |
| 10 | Massimo Biasion, Italy | 17 |

\* Up to and including 2006 season

# Motorcycling

## TOP 10 MOST CONSECUTIVE WORLD MOTORCYCLING TITLES*

| | RIDER / COUNTRY | YEARS | CLASS | WINS |
|---|---|---|---|---|
| 1 = | Giacomo Agostini, Italy | 1966–72 | 500cc | 7 |
| = | Giacomo Agostini, Italy | 1968–74 | 350cc | 7 |
| 3 = | Michael Doohan, Australia | 1994–98 | 500cc | 5 |
| = | Valentino Rossi, Italy | 2001–05 | Moto GP | 5 |
| 5 = | Mike Hailwood, UK | 1962–65 | 500cc | 4 |
| = | Jim Redman, Southern Rhodesia | 1962–65 | 350cc | 4 |
| = | Angel Nieto, Spain | 1981–84 | 125cc | 4 |
| = | Stefan Dörflinger, Switzerland | 1982–85 | 50/80cc# | 4 |
| = | Massimiliano 'Max' Biaggi, Italy | 1994–97 | 250cc | 4 |
| 10 = | Carlo Ubbiali, Italy | 1958–60 | 125cc | 3 |
| = | Hans Anscheidt, West Germany | 1966–68 | 50cc | 3 |
| = | Walter Villa, Italy | 1974–76 | 250cc | 3 |
| = | Angel Nieto, Spain | 1975–77 | 50cc | 3 |
| = | Jorge Aspar, Spain | 1986–88 | 80cc | 3 |

* In the same class; as at the end of the 2006 season
# The 50cc class was abandoned at the end of the 1983 season and replaced by 80cc in 1984

## TOP 10 RIDERS WITH THE MOST WORLD ROAD RACE CHAMPIONSHIP WINS*

| | RIDER / COUNTRY | YEARS | WINS |
|---|---|---|---|
| 1 | Giacomo Agostini, Italy | 1965–76 | 122 |
| 2 | Angel Nieto, Spain | 1969–85 | 90 |
| 3 | Valentino Rossi, Italy | 1996–2006 | 84 |
| 4 | Mike Hailwood, UK | 1959–67 | 76 |
| 5 | Mick Doohan, Australia | 1990–98 | 54 |
| 6 | Phil Read, UK | 1961–75 | 52 |
| 7 | Jim Redman, Southern Rhodesia | 1961–66 | 45 |
| 8 = | Anton Mang, West Germany | 1976–88 | 42 |
| = | Massimiliano 'Max' Biaggi, Italy | 1992–2004 | 42 |
| 10 | Carlo Ubbiali, Italy | 1950–60 | 39 |

* Solo classes only; as at end of 2006 season

*Valentino Rossi*
*Italy's Valentino Rossi won seven world motorcycling titles between 1997 and 2005 and narrowly missed out on number eight in 2006.*

## TOP 10 **RIDERS WITH THE MOST SPEEDWAY WORLD TITLES**\*

| | RIDER | NATIONALITY | YEARS | TITLES |
|---|---|---|---|---|
| **1** | Ivan Mauger | New Zealand | 1968–79 | 6 |
| = | Tony Rickardsson | Sweden | 1994–2005 | 6 |
| **3** | Ove Fundin | Sweden | 1956–67 | 5 |
| **4** = | Barry Briggs | New Zealand | 1957–66 | 4 |
| = | Hans Nielsen | Denmark | 1986–95 | 4 |
| **6** = | Ole Olsen | Denmark | 1971–78 | 3 |
| = | Erik Gundersen | Denmark | 1984–88 | 3 |
| **8** = | Jack Young | Australia | 1951–52 | 2 |
| = | Fred Williams | UK | 1950–53 | 2 |
| = | Ronnie Moore | New Zealand | 1954–59 | 2 |
| = | Peter Craven | UK | 1955–62 | 2 |
| = | Bruce Penhall | USA | 1981–82 | 2 |
| = | Greg Hancock | USA | 1992–97 | 2 |
| = | Jason Crump | Australia | 2004–06 | 2 |

\* Individual titles; up to and including 2006

Up to 1995 the world title was decided by a series of qualifying heats with the final a single-night event. Since that year it has been a season-long series of Grand Prix events, with points tallied up ultimately to decide the champion.

*Leader of the pack*
*AMA Motorcycle Hall of Famer Jeremy McGrath leading the field into the turn.*

## TOP 10 **RIDERS WITH THE MOST AMA SUPERCROSS RACE WINS**\*

| | RIDER | 250CC | 125CC | TOTAL WINS |
|---|---|---|---|---|
| **1** | Jeremy McGrath | 72 | 13 | 85 |
| **2** | Ricky Carmichael | 40 | 11 | 51 |
| **3** | Chad Reed | 24 | 6 | 30 |
| **4** | James Stewart Jr | 11 | 18 | 29 |
| **5** | Ricky Johnson | 28 | – | 28 |
| **6** | Bob Hannah | 27 | – | 27 |
| **7** | Damon Bradshaw | 19 | 6 | 25 |
| **8** | Kevin Windham | 12 | 11 | 23 |
| **9** | Jeff Ward | 20 | – | 20 |
| **10** | Ezra Lusk | 12 | 7 | 19 |

\* 1974–2006; all riders from USA

Supercross racing was introduced in 1972, with the American Motorcyclist Association (AMA) staging its first championship in 1974, in which Pierre Karsmakers won the 250cc class and Gary Semics the 500cc class.

## TOP 10 **MANUFACTURERS WITH THE MOST WORLD ROAD-RACE CHAMPIONSHIP WINS**\*

| | MANUFACTURER / COUNTRY | YEAR OF FIRST WIN | TOTAL WINS |
|---|---|---|---|
| **1** | Honda (Japan) | 1961 | 616 |
| **2** | Yamaha (Japan) | 1963 | 426 |
| **3** | MV Agusta (Italy) | 1952 | 275 |
| **4** | Aprilia (Italy) | 1987 | 209 |
| **5** | Suzuki (Japan) | 1962 | 154 |
| **6** = | Kawasaki (Japan) | 1969 | 85 |
| = | Derbi (Spain) | 1968 | 85 |
| **8** | Kreidler (Germany) | 1962 | 65 |
| **9** | Garelli (Italy) | 1982 | 51 |
| **10** | Gilera (Italy) | 1949 | 47 |

\* Solo classes only; as at the end of 2006 season

Honda's first World Championship win was at Montjuich, Barcelona on 23 April 1961, when Australia's Tom Phillis won the 125cc class. He was also Honda's first World Champion.

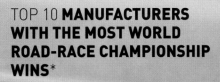

**Two Wheels and Four**
John Surtees from the UK remains the only man ever to win world titles on both two wheels and four wheels. He achieved seven world motor cycling titles between 1956 and 1960 before switching to driving cars in 1960. In 1964 he took the Formula One world title, driving a Ferrari.

# Cycling

## TOP 10 MOST WINS IN THE THREE MAJOR TOURS*

| | CYCLIST / COUNTRY | YEARS | TOUR | GIRO | VUELTA | TOTAL |
|---|---|---|---|---|---|---|
| 1 | Eddy Merckx, Belgium | 1968–74 | 5 | 5 | 1 | 11 |
| 2 | Bernard Hinault, France | 1978–85 | 5 | 3 | 2 | 10 |
| 3 | Jacques Anquetil, France | 1957–64 | 5 | 2 | 1 | 8 |
| 4 | =Fausto Coppi, Italy | 1940–53 | 2 | 5 | 0 | 7 |
| | =Miguel Induráin, Spain | 1991–95 | 5 | 2 | 0 | 7 |
| | =Lance Armstrong, USA | 1999–2005 | 7 | 0 | 0 | 7 |
| 7 | =Alfredo Binda, Italy | 1925–33 | 0 | 5 | 0 | 5 |
| | =Gino Bartali, Italy | 1938–48 | 2 | 3 | 0 | 5 |
| | =Felice Gimondi, Italy | 1965–76 | 1 | 3 | 1 | 5 |
| 10 | =Toni Rominger, Switzerland | 1992–95 | 0 | 1 | 3 | 4 |
| | =Roberto Heras, Spain | 2000–05 | 0 | 0 | 4 | 4 |

\* Up to and including 2006

The three major tours are the Tour de France, launched in 1903 and first won by Maurice Garin of France, the Tour of Italy (Giro d'Italia), first contested in 1909 and won by Luigi Ganna of Italy, and the Tour of Spain (Vuelta de España), first held in 1935 and won by Gustave Deloor of Belgium.

## TOP 10 MOST DAYS SPENT WEARING THE YELLOW JERSEY IN THE TOUR DE FRANCE*

| | CYCLIST / COUNTRY | YEARS | TOTAL DAYS |
|---|---|---|---|
| 1 | Eddy Merckx, Belgium | 1969–74 | 111 |
| 2 | Lance Armstrong, USA | 1999–2005 | 81 |
| 3 | Bernard Hinault, France | 1978–85 | 79 |
| 4 | Miguel Induráin, Spain | 1991–95 | 60 |
| 5 | Jacques Anquetil, France | 1957–64 | 52 |
| 6 | Sylvère Maes, Belgium | 1936–39 | 41 |
| 7 | Antonin Magne, France | 1931–34 | 39 |
| 8 | Nicolas Frantz, Switzerland | 1927–28 | 37 |
| 9 | Louison Bobet, France | 1953–55 | 36 |
| 10 | André Leducq, France | 1930–32 | 34 |

\* Up to and including 2006

The leader of the Tour de France has been wearing the coveted yellow jersey since 19 July 1919, when Eugène Christophe (France) became the first rider to do so on the stage from Grenoble to Geneva. Journalists covering the race had asked the organizers if they could arrange for the race leader to wear a distinctively coloured jersey so they could easily identify him. As the Tour director was Henri Desgrange, and the pages of his newspaper, L'Auto, were printed on yellow paper, he chose yellow.

## PETIT-BRETON CENTENARY

Lucien Petit-Breton (1882–1917) holds the unique distinction of being the first man to win the Tour de France in consecutive years, 1907 and 1908. He moved to Argentina when he was six and started cycling as a child. His real name was Lucien Mazan; he was nicknamed Lucien Breton after his Brittany birthplace, but because there was another cyclist of that name, he changed it to Lucien Petit-Breton. He returned to France in 1902 and started competitive road racing in 1905, also setting a new one-hour distance record prior to his double Tour de France victories.

This achievement was later equalled by Guy Thys (Belgium) and others, but it took until 1955 for a rider – Louison Bobet (France) – to win three consecutive Tours. Jacques Anquetil (France) won his fourth consecutive Tour in 1961, a feat equalled by Eddy Merckx (Belgium). Miguel Induráin (Spain) won six years in a row (1991–95) and Lance Armstrong (USA) a remarkable seven in succession between 1999 and 2005.

# TOP 10 **OLDEST CYCLING CLASSIC RACES AND TOURS**

| | RACE | FIRST HELD |
|---|---|---|
| 1 | Liège–Bastogne–Liège | 1892 |
| 2 | Paris–Brussels | 1893 |
| 3 | Paris–Roubaix | 1896 |
| 4 | Paris–Tours | 1896 |
| 5 | Tour de France | 1903 |
| 6 | Tour of Lombardy | 1905 |
| 7 | Milan–San Remo | 1907 |
| 8 | Tour of Italy | 1909 |
| 9 | Tour of Flanders | 1913 |
| 10 | Championship of Zurich | 1914 |

The Bordeaux–Paris race was the first major cycling race and was, until its demise in 1988, the oldest Classic. The race lasted for around 16 hours, starting in darkness in the early hours of the morning. The first race in 1891 was won by Britain's George Pilkington Mills.

*Oldest race*
*Raced since 1892 in the Ardennes region of Belgium, the Liège–Bastogne–Liège takes place every April and is one of the races on professional cycling's UCI Pro Tour.*

# TOP 10 **COUNTRIES WITH THE MOST OLYMPIC CYCLING MEDALS**\*

| | COUNTRY | GOLD | SILVER | BRONZE | TOTAL |
|---|---|---|---|---|---|
| 1 | France | 39 | 15 | 26 | 80 |
| 2 | Italy | 36 | 13 | 7 | 56 |
| 3 | Germany/West Germany | 16 | 18 | 21 | 55 |
| 4 | UK | 12 | 23 | 19 | 54 |
| 5 | Australia | 13 | 14 | 13 | 40 |
| 6 | USA | 13 | 9 | 17 | 39 |
| 7 | Netherlands | 14 | 14 | 9 | 37 |
| 8 | USSR/Russia | 15 | 8 | 12 | 35 |
| 9 | Belgium | 6 | 7 | 11 | 24 |
| 10 | Denmark | 6 | 4 | 7 | 17 |

\* All events (men and women) up to and including the 2004 Athens Games, including discontinued events and the 1906 Intercalated Games in Greece

# TOP 10 **FASTEST TOURS DE FRANCE**\*

| | YEAR | WINNER / COUNTRY | DISTANCE | | AVERAGE SPEED | |
|---|---|---|---|---|---|---|
| | | | KM | MILES | KM/H | MPH |
| 1 | 2005 | Lance Armstrong, USA | 3,596.5 | 2,234.8 | 41.689 | 25.904 |
| 2 | 2003 | Lance Armstrong, USA | 3,427.5 | 2,129.7 | 40.956 | 25.449 |
| 3 | 2006 | Floyd Landis, USA# | 3,657.1 | 2.272.4 | 40.784 | 25.341 |
| 4 | 2004 | Lance Armstrong, USA | 3,391.1 | 2,107.1 | 40.563 | 25.205 |
| 5 | 1999 | Lance Armstrong, USA | 3,686.8 | 2,290.9 | 40.276 | 25.026 |
| 6 | 2001 | Lance Armstrong, USA | 3,456.2 | 2,147.6 | 40.053 | 24.888 |
| 7 | 1998 | Marco Pantani, Italy | 3,712.1 | 2,306.6 | 39.988 | 24.847 |
| 8 | 2002 | Lance Armstrong, USA | 3,277.5 | 2.036.5 | 39.927 | 24.809 |
| 9 | 2000 | Lance Armstrong, USA | 3,662.5 | 2,275.8 | 39.572 | 24.589 |
| 10 | 1992 | Miguel Induráin, Spain | 3,983.0 | 2,474.9 | 39.504 | 24.547 |

\* Based on average time of Tour winner
# At the time of going to print the outcome of the appeal against Floyd Landis' win in 2006 was still undecided

# Horse Sports

## TOP 10 OLYMPIC EQUESTRIAN COUNTRIES*

| | COUNTRY | GOLD | SILVER | BRONZE | TOTAL |
|---|---|---|---|---|---|
| 1 | Germany/West Germany | 35 | 19 | 21 | 75 |
| 2 | USA | 9 | 19 | 18 | 46 |
| 3 | Sweden | 17 | 8 | 14 | 39 |
| 4 | France | 12 | 12 | 11 | 35 |
| 5 | UK | 6 | 9 | 10 | 25 |
| 6 | Italy | 7 | 9 | 7 | 23 |
| 7 | Switzerland | 4 | 10 | 7 | 21 |
| 8 | Netherlands | 9 | 9 | 2 | 20 |
| 9 | USSR/Unified Team/Russia | 6 | 5 | 4 | 15 |
| 10 | Belgium | 4 | 2 | 5 | 11 |

* Up to and including the 2004 Olympics

These figures include the medal totals for both individual and team disciplines: Show Jumping, Three-Day Event and Dressage.

*Jumping to victory*
*Peter Wylde of the gold medal-winning show jumping US team on Fein Cera at the 2004 Olympic Games.*

## TOP 10 FLAT-RACE JOCKEYS WITH THE MOST WINS IN A CAREER IN THE UK*

| | JOCKEY | YEARS | WINS |
|---|---|---|---|
| 1 | Gordon Richards | 1921—54 | 4,870 |
| 2 | Pat Eddery | 1969—2003 | 4,585 |
| 3 | Lester Piggott | 1948—95 | 4,493 |
| 4 | Willie Carson | 1962—96 | 3,828 |
| 5 | Doug Smith | 1931—67 | 3,111 |
| 6 | Joe Mercer | 1950—85 | 2,810 |
| 7 | Fred Archer | 1870—86 | 2,748 |
| 8 | Edward Hide | 1951—85 | 2,591 |
| 9 | George Fordham | 1850—84 | 2,587 |
| 10 | George Duffield | 1967–2005 | 2,418 |

* As at 1 January 2007

## TOP 10 FASTEST WINNING TIMES OF THE EPSOM DERBY*

| | HORSE | YEAR | TIME MINS:SECS |
|---|---|---|---|
| 1 | Lammtarra | 1995 | 2:32.31 |
| 2 | Galileo | 2001 | 2:33.27 |
| 3 | Kris Kin | 2003 | 2:33.35 |
| 4 | Royal Palace | 1967 | 2:33.36 |
| 5 | Northern Light | 2004 | 2:33.72 |
| 6 | Mahmoud | 1936 | 2:33.80 |
| 7 | Kahyasi | 1988 | 2:33.84 |
| 8 | High-Rise | 1998 | 2:33.88 |
| 9 | Reference Point | 1987 | 2:33.90 |
| 10 =| Hyperion | 1933 | 2:34.00 |
| =| Windsor Lad | 1934 | 2:34.00 |
| =| Generous | 1991 | 2:34.00 |

* Up to and including 2006, excluding wartime races run at Newmarket 1915–18 and 1940–45

Lammtarra also won the prestigious King George VI & Queen Elizabeth Diamond Stakes and the Prix de l'Arc de Triomphe in 1995.

## TOP 10 FASTEST WINNING TIMES OF THE KENTUCKY DERBY*

| | HORSE | YEAR | TIME MINS:SECS |
|---|---|---|---|
| 1 | Secretariat | 1973 | 1:59.40 |
| 2 | Monarchos | 2001 | 1:59.97 |
| 3 | Northern Dancer | 1964 | 2:00.00 |
| 4 | Spend A Buck | 1985 | 2:00.20 |
| 5 | Decidedly | 1962 | 2:00.40 |
| 6 | Proud Clarion | 1967 | 2:00.60 |
| 7 =| Grindstone | 1996 | 2:01.00 |
| =| Fusaichi Pegasus | 2000 | 2:01.00 |
| 9 | War Emblem | 2002 | 2:01.13 |
| 10 | Funny Cide | 2003 | 2:01.19 |

* Up to and including 2006

The Kentucky Derby – which provided the name of the hat once popularly worn at the event – is held on the first Saturday in May at Churchill Downs, Louisville, Kentucky. It was first raced in 1875 over a distance of 1 mile 4 furlongs, but after 1896 was reduced to 1 mile 2 furlongs.

*Galileo triumph*
*Ridden by Mick Kinane in his second Epsom Derby win, favourite Galileo romps home.*

## TOP 10 OLYMPIC EQUESTRIAN MEDALLISTS*

| | RIDER / COUNTRY | YEARS | GOLD | SILVER | BRONZE | TOTAL |
|---|---|---|---|---|---|---|
| 1 | Reiner Klimke, West Germany | 1964–88 | 6 | 0 | 2 | 8 |
| 2 | Hans-Günther Winkler, West Germany | 1956–76 | 5 | 1 | 1 | 7 |
| 3 =| Piero d'Inzeo, Italy | 1956–72 | 0 | 2 | 4 | 6 |
| =| Raimondo d'Inzeo, Italy | 1956–72 | 1 | 2 | 3 | 6 |
| =| Josef Neckerman, West Germany | 1960–72 | 2 | 2 | 2 | 6 |
| =| Michael Plumb, USA | 1964–84 | 2 | 4 | 0 | 6 |
| =| Isabell Werth, Germany | 1992–2000 | 4 | 2 | 0 | 6 |
| =| Anky van Grunsven, Netherlands | 1992–2004 | 2 | 4 | 0 | 6 |
| 9 =| Earl Thomson, USA | 1932–48 | 2 | 3 | 0 | 5 |
| =| André Jousseaumé, France | 1932–52 | 2 | 2 | 1 | 5 |
| =| Henri Chammartin, Switzerland | 1952–68 | 1 | 2 | 2 | 5 |
| =| Gustav Fischer, Switzerland | 1952–68 | 0 | 3 | 2 | 5 |
| =| Liselott Linsenhoff, West Germany | 1956–72 | 2 | 2 | 1 | 5 |
| =| Christine Stückelberger, Switzerland | 1976–88 | 1 | 3 | 1 | 5 |
| =| Mark Todd, New Zealand | 1984–2000 | 2 | 1 | 2 | 5 |

* Up to and including 2004 Olympics

Born in Münster in 1936, Reiner Klimke's record haul of Olympic medals all came in the dressage event. He was a member of the German team that won five team golds.

# Sports Miscellany

*Bundesliga*
*As at the start of the 2006–07 season, SV Hamburg was the only team to play in every season of the Bundesliga.*

## TOP 10 **LARGEST SPORTS STADIUMS**\*

| | STADIUM / LOCATION / YEAR OPENED | CAPACITY |
|---|---|---|
| **1** | **Rungnado May Day Stadium** Pyöngyang, South Korea, 1989 | 150,000 |
| **2** | **Saltlake Stadium** Calcutta, India, 1984 | 120,000 |
| **3** | **Estadio Azteca** Mexico City, Mexico, 1966 | 114,465 |
| **4** | **Michigan Stadium** Ann Arbor, USA, 1927 | 107,501 |
| **5** | **Beaver Stadium** Penn State, USA, 1960 | 107,282 |
| **6** | **Neyland Stadium** Knoxville, Tennessee, USA,1921 | 104,079 |
| **7** | **Jornalista Mário Filho#** Rio de Janeiro, Brazil, 1950 | 103,045 |
| **8** | **Ohio Stadium** Colombus, USA, 1922 | 101,568 |
| **9** | **National Stadium Bukit Jalil** Kuala Lumpur, Malaysia, 1998 | 100,200 |
| **10 =** | **Melbourne Cricket Ground** Melbourne, Australia, 1853 | 100,000 |
| **=** | **Bung Karno Stadium** Jakarta, Indonesia, 1962 | 100,000 |
| **=** | **Azadi Stadium** Tehran, Iran, 1971 | 100,000 |
| **=** | **Jawaharlal Stadium** New Delhi, India, 1982 | 100,000 |

\* Based on official capacity 2006; excludes motor-racing and horse-racing tracks
# Formerly Maracanã Stadium

## TOP 10 **MOST-WATCHED SPORTS LEAGUES**\*

| | LEAGUE | SPORT | COUNTRY | AVERAGE ATTENDANCE |
|---|---|---|---|---|
| **1** | National Football League (NFL) | American football | USA | 67,738 |
| **2** | Bundesliga | Soccer | Germany | 40,775 |
| **3** | Australian Football League (AFL) | Australian football | Australia | 35,250 |
| **4** | FA Premier League | Soccer | England | 33,875 |
| **5** | Major League Baseball (MLB) | Baseball | USA | 31,423 |
| **6** | Canadian Football League (CFL) | Canadian football | Canada | 29,943 |
| **7** | La Liga | Soccer | Spain | 29,029 |
| **8** | Mexican Football League | Soccer | Mexico | 24,970 |
| **9** | Nippon Professional Baseball (NPB) | Baseball | Japan | 23,552 |
| **10** | Serie A | Soccer | Italy | 21,968 |

\* Based on average attendance of last completed season, as at 1 February 2007

## THE 10 **LATEST WINNERS OF THE BBC SPORTS PERSONALITY OF THE YEAR AWARD**

YEAR   WINNER / SPORT

**2006** Zara Phillips, eventing
**2005** Andrew Flintoff, cricket
**2004** Kelly Holmes, athletics
**2003** Jonny Wilkinson, rugby
**2002** Paula Radcliffe, athletics

**2001** David Beckham, football
**2000** Steve Redgrave, rowing
**1999** Lennox Lewis, boxing
**1998** Michael Owen, football
**1997** Greg Rusedski, tennis

First presented in 1954, when it was won by athlete Chris Chataway, the annual award is based on a poll of BBC viewers. At the end of the 20th century, Muhammed Ali was voted the Sports Personality of the Century. Athletes have won the award on a record 17 occasions.

## THE 10 WORST DISASTERS AT SPORTS VENUES

| | LOCATION / DISASTER | DATE | NO. KILLED |
|---|---|---|---|
| 1 | **Hong Kong Jockey Club** – Stand collapse and fire | 26 Feb 1918 | 604 |
| 2 | **Lenin Stadium**, Moscow – Crush in football stadium | 20 Oct 1982 | 340 |
| 3 | **Lima**, Peru – Football stadium riot | 24 May 1964 | 320 |
| 4 | **Sinceljo**, Colombia – Bullring stand collapse | 20 Jan 1980 | 222 |
| 5 | **Accra**, Ghana – Riot and stampede in football stadium | 9 May 2001 | 127 |
| 6 | **Hillsborough**, Sheffield, UK – Crush in football stadium | 15 Apr 1989 | 96 |
| 7 | **Mateo Flores National Stadium**, Guatemala City, Guatemala – Stampede during World Cup soccer qualifying match, Guatemala v Costa Rica, with 147 injured | 16 Oct 1996 | 84 |
| 8 | **Le Mans**, France – Racing-car crash | 11 Jun 1955 | 82 |
| 9 | **Katmandu**, Nepal – Stampede in football stadium | 12 Mar 1988 | 80 |
| 10 = | **Buenos Aires**, Argentina – Riot in football stadium | 23 May 1968 | 74 |
| = | **PhilSports Arena**, Manila, Philippines – Stampede (related to TV show, not sporting event) | 4 Feb 2006 | 74 |

## TOP 10 HIGHEST-EARNING SPORTSMEN

| | SPORTSMAN / COUNTRY* | SPORT | EARNINGS $# |
|---|---|---|---|
| 1 | **Tiger Woods** | Golf | 90,000,000 |
| 2 | **Michael Schumacher** (Germany) | Motor racing | 58,000,000 |
| 3 | **Muhammad Ali** | Boxing | 55,000,000 |
| 4 | **Phil Mickelson** | Golf | 47,000,000 |
| 5 | **Michael Jordan** | Basketball | 32,000,000 |
| 6 | **Kobe Bryant** | Basketball | 31,000,000 |
| 7 = | **Shaquille O'Neal** | Basketball | 30,000,000 |
| = | **Valentino Rossi** (Italy) | Motorcycling | 30,000,000 |
| 9 = | **Tom Brady** | American football | 29,000,000 |
| = | **Alex Rodriguez** | Baseball | 29,000,000 |

\* USA unless otherwise stated
# Estimated June 2005–June 2006

Source: Forbes

Footballer David Beckham's $27 million makes him the highest-earning British sportsman, while Russian tennis player Maria Sharapova's $19 million establishes her at the top of the earnings league among sportswomen.

***Tiger Woods***
*The world's greatest golfer, Tiger Woods is now fast approaching Jack Nicklaus' all-time record of 18 wins in professional Majors.*

# Leisure Activities

## TOP 10 SPORTS, GAMES AND PHYSICAL ACTIVITES IN GREAT BRITAIN

| | ACTIVITY | PERCENTAGE* |
|---|---|---|
| 1 | Walking | 35 |
| 2 | Swimming | 14 |
| 3 | Keep fit/yoga | 12 |
| 4 = | Cycling | 9 |
| = | Snooker/pool/billiards | 9 |
| 6 | Weight training | 6 |
| 7 = | Football | 5 |
| = | Golf | 5 |
| = | Running, jogging, etc. | 5 |
| 10 | Tenpin bowls/skittles | 3 |

* Of those aged over 16 who had engaged in activity during previous 4 weeks

Source: *General Household Survey*/Office for National Statistics

## TOP 10 FORMS OF GAMBLING IN THE UK*

| | FORM | £ (2003–04) |
|---|---|---|
| 1 | Off-course betting | 32,265,000,000 |
| 2 | Lotto | 3,225,000,000 |
| 3 | Bingo clubs | 1,381,000,000 |
| 4 | Instants | 641,000,000 |
| 5 | Thunderball | 351,000,000 |
| 6 | HotPicks | 244,000,000 |
| 7 | Lotteries (excluding National) | 127,000,000 |
| 8 | Football pools | 112,000,000 |
| 9 | Lottery extra | 78,000,000 |
| 10 | Daily Play | 45,000,000 |

* Excluding online gambling

Source: *Annual Abstract of Statistics*/National Lottery Commission/Gaming Board for Great Britain/Department for Culture, Media and Sport/Totesport

This official survey presents a picture of the prevalence of gambling in the UK a decade after the introduction of the National Lottery in 1994. In the period covered, a total of £4.6 billion was spent the National Lottery, with 5.3 per cent of the adult population of the UK participating regularly.

## TOP 10 TRADITIONAL TOY AND GAME-BUYING COUNTRIES

COUNTRY / TRADITIONAL TOY AND GAME SALES 2008 (£)*

**1** USA 18,437,530,000

**2** China 4,593,210,000

**3** Japan 4,498,450,000

**4** UK 4,400,810,000

**5** France 3,131,960,000

**6** Germany 2,368,900,000

**7** Mexico 2,021,660,000

**8** Italy 1,916,780,000

**9** Spain 1,517,540,000

**10** South Korea 1,455,990,000

Traditional toys encompass toys other than video games. The category leader is pre-school toys but also includes model vehicles, construction toys, dolls and action figures, soft toys and teddy bears.

* Forecast

Source: Euromonitor

## TOP 10 **VIDEO GAME-BUYING COUNTRIES**

COUNTRY / VIDEO GAME SALES PER CAPITA 2008 (£)*

UK  36.95

Australia  31.03

South Korea  26.41

USA  23.33

France  21.42

Netherlands  20.04

Spain  17.23

Canada  16.20

Belgium  15.17

Japan  14.43

* Forecast

Source: Euromonitor

## TOP 10 **BRITISH LEISURE AND CULTURAL ACTIVITIES**

| | ACTIVITY | PERCENTAGE ATTENDING* | | |
|---|---|---|---|---|
| | | MEN | WOMEN | TOTAL |
| **1** | **Sports** (watching) | 76 | 60 | 68 |
| **2** | **Cinema** | 65 | 65 | 65 |
| **3** | **Sports** (participation) | 54 | 42 | 48 |
| **4** | = Plays | 22 | 27 | 25 |
| | = Pop/rock concerts | 26 | 24 | 25 |
| **6** | Art galleries/exhibitions | 24 | 25 | 24 |
| **7** | Classical music | 12 | 14 | 13 |
| **8** | Ballet | 5 | 10 | 8 |
| **9** | Opera | 7 | 8 | 7 |
| **10** | Contemporary dance | 4 | 7 | 6 |

* Aged 15 and over, 2004–05; selected activities

Source: *Annual Abstract of Statistics*/Target Group Index, BRMB International

# Further Information

## THE UNIVERSE & THE EARTH

**Astronautics**
http://www.astronautix.com/
Spaceflight news and reference

**Caves**
http://www.caverbob.com/home.htm
List of long and deep caves

**Comets**
http://www.cometography.com/
Comet catalogue and descriptions

**Islands**
http://islands.unep.ch/isldir.htm
Information on the world's islands

**Mountains**
http://peaklist.org/
Lists of the world's tallest mountains

**NASA**
http://www.nasa.gov/home/index.html
The main website for the US space
programme

**Oceans**
http://www.oceansatlas.org/index.jsp
The UN's resource on oceanographic issues

**Planets**
http://www.nineplanets.org/
A multimedia tour of the Solar System

**Space**
http://www.space.com/
Reports on events in space exploration

**Waterfalls**
http://www.world-waterfalls.com/
Data on the world's tallest and largest
waterfalls

## LIFE ON EARTH

**Animals**
http://animaldiversity.ummz.umich.edu/site/
index.html
A wealth of animal data

**Birds**
http://www.bsc-eoc.org/avibase/avibase.jsp
A database on the world's birds

**Conservation**
http://iucn.org/
The leading nature conservation site

**Endangered**
http://www.cites.org/
Lists of endangered species of flora and
fauna

**Environment**
http://www.unep.ch/
The UN's Earthwatch and other programmes

**Fish**
http://www.fishbase.org/
Global information on fishes

**Food and Agriculture Organization**
http://www.fao.org/
Statistics from the UN's FAO website

**Forests**
http://www.forestry.gov.uk/
The website of the Forestry Commission

**Insects**
http://ufbir.ifas.ufl.edu/
The University of Florida Book of Insect
Records

**Trees**
http://www.tree-register.org/
A guide to Britain's and Ireland's most
notable trees

## THE HUMAN WORLD

**Crime, international**
http://www.interpol.int/
Interpol's crime statistics

**Crime, UK**
http://www.homeoffice.gov.uk/
Home Office crime and prison population
figures

**Leaders**
http://www.terra.es/personal2/monolith/
home.htm
Facts about world leaders since 1945

**Military**
http://www.globalfirepower.com/
World military statistics and rankings

**Population and names**
http://www.statistics.gov.uk/
The UK in figures and naming trends for the
UK population

**Religions**
http://www.worldchristiandatabase.org/wcd/
World religion data

**Royalty**
http://www.royal.gov.uk/
The official site of the British monarchy, with
histories

**Rulers**
http://rulers.org/
A database of the world's rulers and political
leaders

**US Presidents**
http://www.whitehouse.gov/history/presidents/
Biographies, facts and figures from the White
House

**World Health Organization**
http://www.who.int/en/
World health information and advice

## TOWN & COUNTRY

**Bridges and tunnels**
http://en.structurae.de/
Facts and figures on the world's buildings,
tunnels and other structures

**Countries**
http://www.theodora.com/wfb/
Country data, rankings, etc.

**Country and city populations**
http://www.citypopulation.de/cities.html
A searchable guide to the world's countries
and major cities

**Country data**
https://www.cia.gov/cia/publications/
factbook/index.html
The CIA World Factbook

**Country populations**
http://www.un.org/esa/population/unpop.htm
The UN's worldwide data on population
issues

**Development**
http://www.worldbank.org/
Development and other statistics from
around the world

**Population**
http://www.census.gov/ipc/www/
International population statistics

**Population issues**
http://www.un.org/esa/population/unpop.htm
The UN's Population Division

**Skyscrapers**
http://www.emporis.com/en/bu/sk/
The Emporis database of high-rise buildings

**Tunnels**
http://home.no.net/lotsberg/
A database of the longest rail, road and
canal tunnels

## CULTURE

*The Art Newspaper*
http://www.theartnewspaper.com/
News and views on the art world

*The Bookseller*
http://www.thebookseller.com/
The organ of the British book trade

**The British Library**
http://www.bl.uk/
The route to the catalogues and exhibitions
in the national library

**Education**
http://www.dfes.gov.uk/statistics/
Official statistics relating to education in the
UK

**Languages of the world**
http://www.ethnologue.com/
Online reference work on the world's 6,912
living languages

**Library loans**
http://www.plr.uk.com/
Public Lending Right's lists of the UK's most-
borrowed books

**The Man Booker Prize**
http://www.themanbookerprize.com/
Britain's most prestigious literary prize

**Museums & galleries**
http://www.24hourmuseum.org.uk/
A guide to exhibitions and events at the UK

**UNESCO**
http://www.unesco.org/
Comparative international statistics on
education and culture

**World Heritage sites**
http://whc.unesco.org/
A searchable database of the sites on
UNESCO's World Heritage list

## MUSIC

**All Music Guide**
http://www.allmusic.com/
A comprehensive guide to all genres of music

**Billboard**
http://www.billboard.com/
US music news and charts data

**The BRIT Awards**
http://www.brits.co.uk/
The official website for the popular music awards

**The British Phonographic Industry Ltd**
http://www.bpi.co.uk/
Searchable database of gold discs and other certified awards

**Grammy Awards**
http://www.naras.org/
The official site for the famous US music awards

**Launch**
http://uk.launch.yahoo.com/index.html
UK music charts and news from Yahoo

**MTV**
http://www.mtv.co.uk/
The online site for the MTV UK music channel

*New Musical Express*
http://www.nme.com/
The online version of the popular music magazine

**The Official UK Charts Company**
http://www.theofficialcharts.com/
Weekly and historical music charts

**VH1**
http://www.vh1.com/
Online UK music news

## STAGE & SCREEN

**Academy Awards**
http://www.oscars.org/
The official 'Oscars' website

**BAFTAs**
http://www.bafta.org
The home of the BAFTA Awards

**BBC**
http://www.bbc.co.uk/
Gateway to BBC TV and radio, with a powerful Internet search engine

**Film Distributors' Association**
http://www.launchingfilms.com/
Trade site for UK film releases and statistics

**Golden Globe Awards**
http://www.hfpa.org/
Hollywood Foreign Press Association's Golden Globes site

**Internet Movie Database**
http://www.imdb.com/
The best of the publicly accessible film websites; IMDbPro is available to subscribers

**London Theatre Guide**
http://www.londontheatre.co.uk/
A comprehensive guide to West End theatre productions

**Screen Daily**
http://www.screendaily.com/
Daily news from the film world at the website of UK weekly Screen International

**Variety**
http://www.variety.com/
Extensive entertainment information (extra features available to subscribers)

**Yahoo! Movies**
http://uk.movies.yahoo.com/
Charts plus features, trailers and links to the latest film UK releases

## THE COMMERCIAL WORLD

*The Economist*
http://www.economist.com/
Global economic and political news

**Energy**
http://www.bp.com/
The BP Statistical Review of World Energy

**Environmental Sustainability Index**
http://sedac.ciesin.columbia.edu/es/esi/
Data on the planet's future

**Gold**
http://www.gold.org/
The website of the World Gold Council

**Internet**
http://www.internetworldstats.com/
Internet World Stats

**Organisation for Economic Co-operation and Development**
http://www.oecd.org/home/
World economic and social statistics

**Rich lists**
http://www.forbes.com/
*Forbes* magazine's celebrated lists of the world's wealthiest people

**Telecommunications**
http://www.itu.int
Worldwide telecommunications statistics

**United Nations Development Programme**
http://www.undp.org/
Country GDPs and other development data

**The World Bank**
http://www.worldbank.org/
World development, trade and labour statistics

## TRANSPORT & TOURISM

**Air disasters**
http://www.airdisaster.com/
Reports on aviation disasters

**Air speed records**
http://www.fai.org/records
The website of the official air speed record governing body

**Amusement parks**
http://napha.org/nnn/
Historical facts and links to amusement parks, roller coasters, etc

**Association of Leading Visitor Attractions**
http://www.alva.org.uk/
Information and visitor statistics on the UK's top tourist attractions

**Car manufacture**
http://www.oica.net/
The International Organization of Motor Vehicle Manufacturers' website

**Railways**
http://www.railwaygazette.com/
The world's railway business in depth from *Railway Gazette International*

**Shipwrecks**
http://www.shipwreckregistry.com/
A huge database of the world's wrecked and lost ships

**Tourism UK**
http://www.staruk.org.uk/
UK tourism facts and statistics

**Tourism Offices Worldwide Directory**
http://www.towd.com/
Contact details for tourism offices around the world

**World Tourism Organisation**
http://www.world-tourism.org/
The world's principal travel and tourism organization

## SPORT

**Athletics**
http://www.iaaf.org/
The world governing body of athletics

**Cricket**
http://www.cricinfo.com/
Cricinfo, launched in 1993, since merged with the online version of *Wisden*

**Cycling**
http://www.uci.ch/
The Union Cycliste Internationale, the competitive cycling governing body

**FIFA**
http://www.fifa.com
The official website of FIFA, the world governing body of soccer

**Football**
www.football-league.co.uk
The official site of the Football League

**Formula One**
http://www.formula1.com/
The official F1 website

**Olympics**
www.olympic.org/uk/games/index_uk.asp
The official Olympics website

**Premier League**
http://www.premierleague.com
The official web site of soccer's Premier League

**Rugby**
http://www.itsrugby.co.uk/
Comprehensive rugby site

**Skiing**
http://www.fis-ski.com/
Fédèration Internationale de Ski, the world governing body of skiing and snowboarding

# Index

# Acknowledgements

**Special research:** Ian Morrison (sport);
Dafydd Rees (music)

Roland Bert
Peter Bond
Richard Braddish
Thomas Brinkhoff
Philip Eden
Christopher Forbes
Russell E. Gough
Robert Grant
Angela Hayes
Larry Kilman
Benjamin Lucas
Aylla Macphail
Chris Mead
Sylvia Morris
Roberto Ortiz de Zarate
Robert Senior
Lucy T. Verma

Academy of Motion Picture Arts and Sciences
– Oscar® statuette is the registered
trademark and copyrighted property of the
Academy of Motion Picture Arts and Sciences
*Advertising Age*
American Film Institute
American Society for Aesthetic Plastic Surgery
Animated Film Society (Annie Awards)
*The Art Newspaper*
Association of Leading Visitor Attractions
Association of Tennis Professionals
Audit Bureau of Circulations Ltd
BBC
*Billboard*
Box Office Mojo
*BP Statistical Review of World Energy 2006*
British Academy of Film and Television Awards
The BRIT Awards
British Comedy Awards
British Council
British Film Institute
British Library
British National Corpus
British Phonographic Industry
British Video Association
*BusinessWeek*
Cameron Mackintosh Ltd
Central Institute of Indian Languages
Central Intelligence Agency
Channel 4
Charities Direct
*Checkout*
*China Statistical Yearbook 2006*
Christie's
Computer Industry Almanac
*CRC Handbook of Chemistry and Physics*
*Criminal Statistics England & Wales*
Department for Environment, Food and Rural
Affairs
Department of Trade and Industry
*Diamond Facts*

Earth Impact Database
EarthTrends
*The Economist*
EM-DAT, CRED, University of Louvain
Emporis
Energy Information Administration
*Essential Science Indicators*
Ethnologue
Euromonitor
Europa
*Evening Standard* Awards
Federal Bureau of Investigation
Fédération Internationale de Football
Association
Fédération Internationale de Motorcyclisme
Fédération Internationale de Ski
Food and Agriculture Organization of the
United Nations
*Forbes*
*Global Education Digest* (UNESCO)
GlobalFirePower.com
*Global Forest Resources Assessment* (FAO)
Golden Raspberry Awards
Gold Fields Mineral Services
HM Treasury
Hollywood Foreign Press Association (Golden
Globe Awards)
Home Office
*Human Development Report* (United Nations)
Imperial War Museum
Interbrand
International Association of Athletics
Federations
International Centre for Prison Studies
International Commission on Large Dams
International Federation of Audit Bureaux of
Circulations
International Federation of Robotics
The International Institute for Strategic
Studies, *The Military Balance 2006–2007*
International Intellectual Property Alliance
International Iron & Steel Institute
International Obesity Task Force
International Olympic Committee
International Organization of Motor Vehicle
Manufacturers
International Telecommunication Union
International Union for Conservation of
Nature and Natural Resources
Internet Movie Database
Internet World Stats
Interpol
Ladies Professional Golf Association
Lipmann Walton
Lloyds Register-Fairplay Ltd
London Marathon
Meteorological Office
MRIB
Music Information Database
National Academy of Recording Arts and
Sciences (Grammy Awards)

National Aeronautics and Space
Administration (NASA)
National Amusement Park Historical
Association
National Basketball Association
National Football League
National Statistics
National Trust
Niagara Falls Museum
AC Nielsen
Nobel Foundation
Northwest Territories
Office for Health Economics
The Official UK Charts Company
Organisation for Economic Co-operation and
Development
Organisation Internationale des Constructeurs
d'Automobiles
Periodical Publishers Association
Pilot 2006 Environmental Performance Index
Point Topic
Population Reference Bureau
Professional Golfers' Association
*Railway Gazette International*
River Systems of the World
Royal Astronomical Society
Royal Opera House, Covent Garden
*Screen Digest*
*Screen International*
Shakespeare Centre
The Silver Institute, *World Silver Survey 2006*
Society of London Theatre (Laurence Olivier
Awards)
Sotheby's
*Stores*
The Tree Register of the British Isles
Transparency International
*Uniform Crime Reports* (FBI)
United Nations
United Nations Educational, Scientific and
Cultural Organization
United Nations Environment Programme
United Nations Population Division
US Census Bureau International Data Base
US Geological Survey
*Ward's Motor Vehicle Facts & Figures 2006*
World Association of Girl Guides and Girl
Scouts
World Association of Newspapers
World Conservation Monitoring Centre
*World Development Indicators* (World Bank)
World Gold Council
*World Health Report* (World Health
Organization)
World Intellectual Property Organization
*World of Learning*
World Organization of the Scout Movement
World Tennis Association
World Tourism Organization

# Picture Credits

The publisher would like to thank the following sources for their kind permission to reproduce the photographs and illustrations in this book.

(Abbreviations key: t = top, b = bottom, r = right, l = left, c = centre)

**Big Blu Picture Library:** 34-35 Jonathan Bonnick

**Christie's Images Ltd:** 118

**Corbis:** 10b Charles & Josette Lenars, 16-17 Digital Art, 17 STScI/NASA, 19 Layne Kennedy, 20 Alison Wright, 20-21, 23 Sharna Balfour/Gallo Images, 25 Lawson Wood, 26 Dean Conger, 28-29, 32 Visuals Unlimited, 33 Stapleton Collection, 34tr Frank Krahmer, 35tr DLILLC, 36b Jeff Vanuga, 37b Royalty Free, 38b Joe McDonald, 39 Kennan Ward, 42t Volkmar Brockhaus/zefa, 43r Anthony Bannister/Gallo, 44t Flavio Pagani/Sygma, 47 Michel Setboun, 48 Keren Su, 50 Ricky Rogers/Reuters, 51 Catherine Karnow, 55 Bettmann, 58 Norbert Schaefer, 59 Christophe Boisvieux, 60tl Uli Wiesmeier/zefa, 60r Ann Johansson, 61 Amet Jean Pierre/Sygma, 64 Farahnaz Karimy/epa, 66 Kim Ludbrook/epa, 67r Nevada Wier, 68b David Pollack, 69r Thierry Roge/Reuters, 70t Archivo Iconografico, SA, 71 Webistan, 73l&r Bettmann, 77t Eric Preau/Sygma, 78 John-Francis Bourke/zefa, 79r Paul A. Souders, 81r Sygma, 82t, 83r Nik Wheeler, 83b Hulton-Deutsch, 85 Philip Wallick, 88 Bob Krist, 89 Frank Lukasseck/zefa, 90 Peter Adams/zefa, 90-91 Michael Hagedorn/zefa, 92 Paul Thompson/Eye Ubiquitous, 93 David Churchill/Arcaid, 95 Christophe Boisvieux, 96-97 Remi Benali, 99 Jose Fuste Raga, 100, 101 Macduff Everton, 102 Murat Taner/zefa, 106-107 Ladislav Janicek/zefa, 108t Earl & Nazima Kowall, 110 Randy Faris, 111 Leonard de Selva, 112 Rune Hellestad, 114-115 Tom Grill, 116-117 & 117 Archivo Iconografico, SA, 119 Hulton-Deutsch, 122r & 123t Bettmann, 124l Reuters, 125t Denis O'Regan, 126 Jacqueline Sallow, 127t, 128t Cardinale Stephane/Sygma, 129 Reuters, 131 Steffen Schmidt/epa, 135 Suzanne Tenner/20th Century Fox/Bureau L.A. Collection, 138 Robbie Jack, 139 Seth Wenig/Reuters, 141 Reuters, 143t Arko Datta/Reuters, 144 Bureau L.A. Collection, 146 Bettmann, 150 Blue Sky Studios/20th Century Fox/Bureau L.A. Collection, 151 DreamWorks Animation/Zuma, 155t Melissa Moseley/Sony Pictures/ Bureau L.A. Collection, 156l Bettmann, 158t Sunset Boulevard, 160 John Springer Collection, 165 DreamWorks SKG/Zuma, 166 Sergei Ilnitsky/epa, 171 Frank May/dpa, 173t Kevin P. Casey, 174b Michael S. Yamashita, 177 Adam Woolfitt, 180l Shepard Sherbell, 182-183 Lester Lefkowitz, 185 H. Sung Hyok/Sygma, 187 Oliver Berg/dpa, 188-189 Yang Liu, 192l Toyota Motor Corp/Handout/Reuters, 195b Bryan F. Peterson, 196l The Mariners' Museum, 197b Neil Rabinowitz, 198l Museum of Flight, 199 George Hall, 200 Reuters, 201 Kapoor Balder/Sygma, 203l Pablo Corral V, 203b Jon Hicks, 204-205 Paul Hardy, 208t Troy Wayrynen/NewSport, 209b Karl-Josef Hildenbrand/epa, 211t Alexandros Vlachos/epa, 212b Hulton-Deutsch Collection, 213r Dimitri Lundt/TempSport, 212-213 Robert Ghement/epa, 215 Bettmann, 216b Duomo, 217 Bob Leverone/TSN/Zuma, 219 Reuters, 220-221 Alan Schein Photography, 220b Kay Nietfeld/epa, 222r Hugo Philpott/epa, 225 Reuters, 227 Ian Hodgson/Reuters, 228l Le Segretain/Sygma, 229r Christian Liewig/Liewig Media Sports, 231r Tony Roberts, 232b Jim Young/Reuters, 235b Nikos Mitsouras/epa, 236-237 Tolga Bozoglu/epa, 237r Rick Rickman/NewSport, 239r Gero Breloer/DPA/epa, 240b Mike Finn-Kelcey/Reuters, 241 Michael Crabtree/Reuters, 242t Kay Nietfeld/epa, 243 Charles W Luzier/Reuters, 245 Ken Kaminesky/Take 2 Productions.

**Getty Images:** 28, 41 National Geographic, 46 Don Farrall, 76, 132, 175r, 193r, 194t&b, 210r, 214t, 222bl, 238r Roger Viollet.

**Ivan Hissey:** 21r, 32-33, 37t, 44r, 45r, 49l&r, 56r, 66-67b, 72b, 98, 111l, 157b, 158-159, 176t, 181t&c, 208b, 210b.

**iStockphoto:** 18, 22, 24, 24-25, 26t&b, 27t&r, 34-35, 35tr, 36t, 38t, 40, 42b, 43t&l, 45l&b, 49t&l, 50b, 54t, 56t&b, 57r, 58t, 64-65, 65l&r, 67l, 68t, 69l, 72t, 75r&b, 77b, 79t&b, 80 all, 81, 82b, 84t&b, 88b, 94t&b, 96t, 100-101, 103, 106l, 107r, 108b, 109r&b, 110t, 112-113, 113b, 119t&b, 122b, 123b, 125l&b, 127b, 128b, 130, 133t&b, 134-135, 138-139t&b, 140, 141b, 143b, 147b, 155b, 163l, 167, 170, 173b, 175t&b, 176b, 178, 179, 180t, 181b, 183r, 184t&b, 186, 192t, 192t&b, 193t&b, 195t, 196-197, 198t, 202 all, 203t, 209t, 210t, 211b, 214b, 216t, 223, 226, 228t,r&b, 229l, 230-231, 232-233, 234, 235t, 238t, 240-241, 242b, 243t, 244r&b, 247.

**Kobal Collection:** 134 20th Century Fox, 142 Warner Bros/DC Comics, 145 Lucas Film/20th Century Fox, 147t Universal, 148 20th Century Fox, 149t MGM/United Artists/Sony/Maidment, Jay, 152 Walt Disney, 153 20th Century Fox, 154 Miramax/James, David, 156r Universal, 157t Warner Bros., 159t Fox Searchlight, 161 Miramax/Sparham, Laurie, 162 Oil Flick/UK Film Council/16 Films/Element/Barratt, Joss, 163t Sony/Buitendijk, Jaap, 164 New Line/Saw Zaentz/Wing Nut/Vinet, Pierre, 172 Universal/Amblin/James, David.

**Mary Evans Picture Library:** 29, 74, 77c, 114.

**NASA:** 10-11, 11l, 12tr, 13 Jet Propulsion Laboratory, 14, 15, 15r Kennedy Space Center, 15l Johnson Space Center, 15br Marshall Space Flight Center, 37t.

**Science Photo Library:** 12tl David Nunuk, 54r John Daugherty, 57 Adam Gault.

**Publisher's Acknowledgements**
Cover design: Ron Callow

**Packager's Acknowledgements**
Palazzo Editions would like to thank Richard Constable and Robert Walster for their design contributions.